The Modern Amazons

The Modern Amazons
Warrior Women On-Screen

Dominique Mainon
and
James Ursini

Limelight Editions

Published in 2006 by Limelight Editions (an imprint of Amadeus Press, LLC)
512 Newark Pompton Turnpike, Pompton Plains, New Jersey 07444, USA
Website: www.limelighteditions.com

Book design by Clare Cerullo

Printed in Canada

Library of Congress Cataloging-in-Publication Data is available upon request.

ISBN 0-87910-327-2

To

Liam

aka "Chickenwing"

&

Justice

aka "Thunderfoot"

Contents

Acknowledgments

Thanks to David Chierichetti, Timothy Otto, and Lee Sanders for photos from their personal archives. Thanks also to Alain Silver for advice and technical assistance and to Whoosh.org for assistance. Filmographic research was done at the Academy of Motion Pictures Arts and Sciences Library in Beverly Hills, California, and online at Internet Movie Database (imdb.com).

Movie and television photos and posters are reproduced courtesy of MGM, United Artists, Anchor Bay, Miramax, Paramount, RKO, 20th Century Fox, Warner Bros., Universal, Galatea, Columbia, Spelling Productions, De Laurentis Films, ABC-TV, Lions Gate, BBC, AIP, Lakeshore, Oliane Productions, Russ Meyer Films, MTV, TNT, HBO, USA Cable, Navarron Films, Allied Artists, Buena Vista, Touchstone, Shaw Films, Golden Harvest, Zhang Yimou Studios, IFC, Hollywood Pictures, Disney, Cartoon Network, New Line, Gaumont, Marvel Comics, Creation Books, and White Wolf Publishing. Much appreciation also to contributing author David Koenigsberg.

Dominique Mainon would like to give special thanks to Elizabeth Bohroquez, Nina Ruchirat, Lena Kartzov, Rose Day, Jodeen Vance, Artemis Michael, Doug of Hypnox Photography, Miss Eva Von Slut, the PT Group, and Hiyoko for invaluable assistance. Thank you to Daniel McNeeley for ongoing martial arts research and consultation, and deepest appreciation to Cassandra Taylor-Collins.

Introduction

———

Amazon women cut off their right breast in order to better aim their arrows.

———

I read the above line in Barbara Delinsky's *Uplift: Secrets from the Sisterhood of Breast Cancer Survivors* in April of 2004 while I was recovering from surgery for breast cancer. The quote about Amazons appeared in a chapter aimed at encouraging a feeling of empowerment to patients who have experienced mastectomies. I found it interesting that the book referenced the mythical Amazons as a symbol of strength to apply to a modern-day situation.

I recalled that according to ancient Greek myth Amazon women were rumored to be one-breasted. The very name Amazon is allegedly derived from the Greek prefix *a*, meaning "without," and *mazos*, a derivative of *mastos*, meaning "breast." This sort of etymology, perpetuated by historical figures such as Hellanicus of Lesbos, has spurred numerous representations of Amazon women sacrificing a breast, usually for purposes of warfare or religious rites.

Regardless of the myth, the image of single-breasted female warriors running around seemed peculiar to me. I was raised in an environment that conditioned me to think of the legendary Amazon women as tall, large-breasted, muscular women wearing skimpy leather outfits, like the characters in *Heavy Metal* magazine. Perhaps something more akin to the women in the plethora of soft-core videos that came out during the eighties. You know the story—the male hero stumbles across a secret tribe of beautiful, scantily clad women in the jungle. The blond goddesses take him prisoner, and then one by one become seduced by his irresistible masculinity, resulting in numerous erotic catfights amongst them.

I can guarantee none of *them* would be missing a breast. Most of us tend to share this programmed fantasy interpretation of the Amazon archetype based on exposure to media. We have been replaying this fantasy over and over for years. From Homer's female warriors in *The Iliad* to *Xena: Warrior Princess*, the lust

Lucy Lawless in *Xena: Warrior Princess.*

for Amazon imagery in modern popular culture is developing at a feverish pace.

During spring of 2004, I also attended the highly anticipated second installment of the *Kill Bill* series. This second cinematic journey into Quentin Tarantino's universe struck me with the realization of just how far women had come in action films. In her quest for vengeance, Uma Thurman's character, the Bride, single-handedly kills, maims, and decapitates so many people that it isn't possible to keep count. And it is presented as perfectly natural that most of the killers in the story are women with skills easily equal to or greater than most men's. Ang Lee's *Crouching Tiger, Hidden Dragon,* with Michelle Yeoh, Zhang Ziyi, and Pei-Pei Chang, also had a predominantly female cast. Women were no longer mere sidekicks in action films. They were taking the lead roles and becoming the stars of the show.

The audience's obsession with the cliché "butt-kicking babes" is gaining momentum so rapidly that movie studios can't seem

Uma Thurman and Lucy Liu in *Kill Bill*.

to pump out the action flicks fast enough. The concept of independent female warriors crops up in countless hybrid forms and genres, from vampiric warriors, to genetically enhanced science fiction characters, to spandex-clad remakes of classic comic book characters. In many cases, traditional gender roles are reversed, and the women end up saving the men. Or viciously killing them.

Kill Bill Volume 2 was soon followed by *King Arthur*, with Keira Knightley stripped down to a few strategically placed leather straps and war paint, playing the most ferocious Guinevere portrayed to date. Milla Jovovich resumed zombie-killing in *Resident Evil: Apocalypse*. Zhang Ziyi and the female-led group of Flying Daggers waged war against a corrupt male-run empire. The list goes on and on, especially in popular TV shows like *Dark Angel*, *Buffy the Vampire Slayer*, and *Alias*, to name just a few.

What does this ever growing trend of powerful women on-screen mean? Is this a reflection of society's attitude toward

Keira Knightley as Guinevere in *King Arthur.*

women? Under what conditions did this trend begin and develop? Women, commonly portrayed as screaming victims in past, now take on the role of vicious avengers and warriors. Why are these women depicted with increasingly superhuman abilities? Is this a feminist victory? Could these portrayals actually be more of a double-edged sword, showing women as independent and powerful, yet fetishized for this display of phallic power, reduced by the male gaze to a live version of a one-sided video game character?

Today's superheroines often rely on their considerable physical attributes and sex appeal to lure and confuse men in order to achieve their aims. There is a distinct feeling that many of these characters are "packaged" for maximum commercial consumption.

In *Dark Angel*, Jessica Alba's character is shown gaining entrance into a crowded club despite the long queue of impatient women waiting outside. The camera focuses in slowly and sensuously over her body as she strides down a dark alley, peeling off her long-sleeved shirt to reveal a skimpy, low-cut tank top (the scene is

Milla Jovovich in *Resident Evil: Apocalypse.*

rapidly replayed several times to intensify the effect). The camera then takes a back view, settling on the rhythm of her swaying hips as she turns up the manipulative charm. Background music pipes up with a pulsating beat, "Boy, I'm gonna make you want me . . ." The large, imposing male bouncer at the door is suddenly made docile by her appearance, and unable to stop her from walking right past him and into the club with a seductive smile.

Alba herself expresses her thoughts on this matter in an interview with *Entertainment Weekly*: "Guys are visually stimulated. They're easy to manipulate. All you have to do is dress up in a sexy outfit . . . Guys are sort of stupid that way." And, sadly, men are being portrayed as stupid, incapable, wishy-washy, or just plain weak. Not that we don't have enough Rambos out there on TV already. But the point is, to make some of these uber-third-wave slayer chicks look even more impressive and powerful, it is effective to surround them with incapable men to stress who is wearing the pants in the generally dysfunctional family.

Zhang Ziyi in *House of Flying Daggers*.

Emma Peel, played by Uma Thurman in *The Avengers* movie remake, has a similar scene that shows her character confidently walk straight past the front desk of an exclusive private men's club. She jaunts right into the sauna room, where Mr. Steed is discovered nude, reading a newspaper. The porter protests, as she strides up the stairs in her classic boots, that no woman has been permitted inside the establishment since 1922.

"Congratulations," Mr. Steed tells her, "you've penetrated a bastion of male privilege."

In the much hyped film *Mr. and Mrs. Smith*, former Oscar-winner Angelina Jolie gains entrance to her target's hotel room with the same self-assured swagger. She then fulfills the fantasies of a large percentage of the audience when she sheds her trench coat to reveal the shiny black, fitted outfit of a dominatrix. She is later shown to be the leader of an all-female organization of assassins, all of whom are dressed in an assortment of short dresses, thigh-high stockings, and high-heeled boots.

Despite their powers, sexual and otherwise, female action characters tend to be internally fractured in some way. Either they must become masculine, maybe even symbolically or physically disguise themselves as a man in order to gain status and have the same opportunities as their male counterparts, or they go in the opposite direction and become a sex goddess—a sultry, purring kitten with a whip.

These issues that face women all the time in career and social situations, issues of duality in sexual roles and repression, are played out in many a fictional comic book character. When passions grip them, women literally turn into a different being (often feline) and prowl around rooftops. Or as in the case of Jessica Alba's character in *Fantastic Four*, she turns invisible when emotional, as if being switched off from communicating her deeper needs. Managing the balance of femininity versus masculinity, and passion versus repression, becomes the primary challenge of many a female action character.

Jessica Alba as Invisible Woman in *Fantastic Four*.

Angelina Jolie in *Mr. and Mrs. Smith.*

It cannot be denied that some of the most prolific female action stars of recent years are not only icons of beauty and sexual allure (Milla Jovovich, Jennifer Garner, Angelina Jolie, Uma Thurman, Jessica Alba, Kate Beckinsale, to name a few), but also seasoned wire-fighters by now. The modern-day celebrity herself must be in top condition, superpowered and ready to perform many difficult stunts, though few approach the hard-earned but lesser-seen expertise of some of Hong Kong's female action superstars and real-life champion fighters like Kathy Long, Moon Lee, and Cynthia Rothrock.

Female vengeance themes seem to have taken on an increasingly raw and vicious physical quality in recent years. Female action characters are now constantly hunting down the rapists, abusers, and molesters who wronged them, and making them pay harshly. Many films feature a group of women who gang up together and participate in the punishment of the offender (*Sin City, Foxfire, Tank Girl,* etc.).

Is society playing out some of its fears on-screen? Or are women and men alike indulging in repressed fantasies? The unforgettable divas and femme fatales of the past appeared to spend most of their time lounging around in evening gowns and furs, smoking cigarettes on long holders. When violence was committed, it was often motivated by money or jealousy, their main weapon manipulation. They simply used the male himself as a gun to do their dirty work, maybe delivering the occasional blow to men through a witty put-down or quick slap in the face with a manicured hand.

These glamazons of the past have somehow evolved over time into highly acrobatic, cat-suited, and corset-wearing heroines who leap tall buildings in a single bound (and generally don't smudge their makeup doing so.) And don't forget they also put in hours on their politically correct day jobs as scientists, brain surgeons, and MIG pilots. They are soccer moms on steroids.

Yet like almost all superheroes, despite fantastic abilities that

Kate Beckinsale in *Underworld: Evolution.*

Brittany Murphy as Shellie in *Sin City*.

we all envy, they also have ongoing issues of emotional isolation and being different. They have issues with their fathers or issues of past abuse, which they tend to work out in a very physical manner. Their downfall almost inevitably comes from falling for the opposite sex, which makes them more vulnerable, more sacrificial, and in some cases even completely de-powered. Struggling between the tides of feminine and masculine qualities, some of them learn to find themselves in the end. Those who don't might turn to the dark side, and die later in a spectacular impalement scene.

In any case, the audience's fascination with this genre speaks for itself through the popularity of these movies and TV shows. I became determined to explore this trend and invited renowned expert and commentator on the femme fatale James Ursini to join in my mission. James has co-authored more than eleven books with Alain Silver, including the well-acclaimed *Film Noir Reader* series, *The Noir Style*, *Horror Film Reader*, and *The Vampire Film*. David Koenigsberg also helps us analyze the phenomenon of anime, concentrating on the popular series *Sailormoon*.

Criteria for the choices of women and films featured in this book are discussed in the upcoming chapters. However, we must admit that this edition really only covers the tip of the iceberg in a sense. It would take at least two volumes to cover most of the films and TV series in existence as of this date, and more are being released every week. We sincerely regret leaving out any characters deserving mention, but hope you will enjoy the vast array of information and pictures that we present to you.

Our main goal in writing this book is to document and explore some of the many interesting action roles played by women actors over the years and note some of the trends and patterns, including the folkloric origins of many characters. Some of the characters covered in this book have changed our lives since the early seventies, becoming our cultural icons and influencing our choices on many levels, from consumer to political. Cinema is a contemporary form of church in many senses, with TV in second place. We place the television set, like an altar, as the centerpiece of a room. Furniture is arranged so that we can all gather around at certain hours of the day and gaze upon it in meditation. Whether we intend it or not, the media we absorb forms an important part of our collective memory. The characters act as a virtual reality simulation, carefully testing the social waters in the midst of changes and spurring our acceptance or decline of new concepts.

For women the roles are complex. The warrior woman theme has developed with great momentum, depicting women less often as merely "castrated" in the Freudian sense but more often in the symbolic role of the "castrator." The phallusized heroine is not only an object of fascination because she is depicted waging war against a patriarchal enemy; she is often battling a *monstrous femme* version of herself also.

Either way, as a society we seem to be exhilarated by the cinematic portrayals of powerful women, and it will be fascinating to observe the further development of this new breed of heroine. We invite you to join us in the exploration and celebration of the many captivating faces of the modern Amazons of cinema.

—Dominique Mainon

Chapter 1
The Warrior Woman Archetype in Popular Culture

"I named this island Paradise for an excellent reason. There are no men on it. Thus, it is free from their wars, their greed, their hostility, their . . . barbaric . . . masculine . . . behavior."

—Queen Hippolyte, *The New Original Wonder Woman*

Throughout the ages the classic Amazon, the emblem of the warrior woman, has provided a multifaceted symbol of womanhood combining archaic and modern elements. She has developed continuously, representing her creator's state of mind, environment, politics, and motivations. And while we do not have definitive evidence of the existence of a separate tribe of Amazon women, there is no doubt from ancient artifacts, paintings, pottery, statues, as well as significant literary references, that the mythos of these female warriors has been alive and thriving for a very long time. The idea of a past in which women lived on their own terms and served as capable warriors is a captivating idea and inspires search for proof to reclaim this fascinating legend as history.

Excavations in recent years have produced a good deal of compelling evidence that some of the legends may well be based in fact. In *Warrior Women: An Archaeologist's Search for History's Hidden Heroines,* Jeannine Davis-Kimball and Mona Behan document the discovery of numerous burial sites for what are believed to be warrior women of the Scythian and Sauro-Sarmatian peoples of Southern Russia. In addition, there is evidence that these women may have traveled as far east as China and as far west as the British Isles. Many historians believe that the mythical Amazons were linked to these Scythian and Sauro-Sarmatian

Miranda Otto in *Lord of the Rings: The Return of the King*.

warriors. They may well have been the warlike females the Greek historian Herotodus (circa 500 B.C.) wrote about.

However, the intent of this book is not to speculate about the possible existence of Amazon women in past, but rather to document the proliferation of the warrior woman archetype in popular culture, in film and television in particular. By doing so, it is easier to study the larger sociological picture that then comes into view, examining the trends and themes that become more readily apparent.

Although perhaps we focus most often on cinematic derivatives of the ancient Greek Amazon myth, we do also take into consideration the significant influences of many other historical and mythical representations of warrior women, such as the Valkyries of Norse mythology (from which Robert E. Howard borrowed extensively in his *Conan the Barbarian,* as did J. R. R. Tolkien in *The Lord of the Rings),* Roman gladiatrices, African and Eastern warriors, and many others.

Regardless of origin, we use the term Amazon loosely and interchangeably with general references to "warrior women." Popular culture appropriates the term Amazons to describe female-run societies in general, or simply to label women who attempt fight the system or appear strong-spirited or rebellious. These are the traits that we have set out to investigate within female action characters. "The Modern Amazons" is a term we have assigned to women who have incorporated and adapted the warrior woman archetype, reclaiming it in a variety of new hybrid forms.

Butt-Kicking Babes or Bad-Ass Bitches?

Considering the vast array of manifestations that the Amazon archetype presents in media, it makes sense to examine the different motivations that inspire the creation of these works. In Batya Weinbaum's comprehensive and encyclopedic book *Islands of Women and Amazons: Representations and Realities* (1999), she suggests organizing material incorporating the Amazon archetype in popular culture into categories of "reclamation," "revitalization," and "reaction," based upon Northrop Frye's methods of critical analysis. Reclamation occurs when the Amazon motif is appropriated in its classic form, usually as a symbol of female empowerment. Revitalization is the adaptation of the original form, applying a new element or interpretation that generally bolsters the positive characteristics. In opposition, the reactionary stance is a negative or otherwise disempowering interpretation.

The spirit of reclamation is revealed in many films and TV series that attempt to portray the warrior woman in her primary historical form. It is, however, somewhat rare to see any truly unadulterated accounts of warrior women on-screen. This is to be expected in a commercially driven society that is inclined to add love stories to every historical event (consider *Pearl Harbor* and *Titanic,* for instance) in order to maximize popularity. But the fact is also that we lack hard evidence about warrior women, so plots may be more inclined toward distortion, regardless.

Hammer Studios, for example, took on the story of Queen Boudicca in *The Viking Queen* (1967). Boudicca (also called Boadicea) was the ancient British warrior queen of the Iceni, who pushed the Romans out of London and kept them at bay, temporarily at least. Her legend is widespread in Britain, and there is even a bronze statue of her leading her chariot into battle on the banks of the Thames in London. Hammer, however, with its eye on commercial exploitation, decided to "jazz up" the historical queen by somewhat inexplicably making her a descendant of a Viking mother, hence the title of the movie, and by renaming her Salina.

The other significant variance from historical truth is her love affair with the Roman governor Justinian. This is, of course, more easily understood, as Hammer, which could be cutting edge in its portrayal of violence and nudity in the sixties, as well as predictably traditional in its plot structures, could not conceive of a movie about a woman without a love story. In 2003 director Andrew Davies made a more historically accurate stab at the legend of Boudica in *Boudica, Warrior Queen*. In this version the queen, played by Alex Kingston, was a warrior from beginning to end.

The myth and history of the mystic warrior Joan of Arc was also a subject for several film adaptations in the first decades of the cinema: Carl Dreyer's *The Passion of Joan of Arc* (1928), Hollywood's prestigious *Joan of Arc* (1948) with Ingrid Bergman, and an adaptation of George Bernard Shaw's iconoclastic *Saint Joan* in 1957. But what is notable about all these versions of the "Joan myth," especially when compared with the two versions made in 1999 (*Messenger* with Milla Jovovich and *Joan of Arc* with Lee Lee Sobieski), is, with the exception of Shaw's work, their emphasis on her virginal and saintly qualities. She has been largely neutered as far as her status as a warrior. In fact there are very few battle scenes in these films as a whole. Instead, she seems generally submissive to the patriarchal system, which she in fact outwitted and outfought until her final betrayal.

Overall, reclamation of the warrior woman without bias is rare, and much more often we see a tendency toward revitalizing or reactionary interpretations that inevitably reflect the interests and motives of their creators, as well as societal values of the time.

Female artists might be inclined to apply their own social concerns to the concept of warrior women in history, enhancing it with the power of sisterhood and the sociopolitical organization of matriarchal societies. Female-inspired literature often departs from traditional Greek myth and veers toward a feminist utopian dream—a culture devoid of victimization and subservience to a male-dominated society. Female heroes fight or overcome a patriarchal system against all odds. We note the creation of alter-universes in science fiction tales, where gynocentric social and political systems are the norm.

Feminist visionary Charlotte Perkins Gilman used a fictional matriarchal society of Amazons to illustrate several points in her novel *Herland* (1915). Applying the Amazon theme to her current active culture, she tells the tale of three male explorers who stumble across an all-female society isolated somewhere in South

America, and how they react to the notion of women running their own lives in complete independence.

"They've no modesty," snapped Terry. "No patience, no submissiveness, none of that natural yielding which is woman's greatest charm."

Contemporary authors such as Hillary Raphael use the Amazon archetype to create a group of modern-day warrior women who use a different set of weapons to ultimately achieve their goals. In her transgressive novel *I (heart) Lord Buddha* (2004), Raphael recounts a faux history of the Neo-Geisha Organization of the late nineties, a sex-and-death cult comprised of the beautiful women of the adult industry in Tokyo. Mixing shades of *manga*, pro-hedonism, and Eastern philosophy, the book outlines their ruthless yet organized quest under their outspoken leader, Hiyoko, as they strive to correct the imbalance of karmic energy caused by the overly consumerist male attitude toward women and sex.

We also see contemporary expression of warrior women in films such as *Tank Girl* (1995), with actor Lori Petty as the post-apocalyptic feminist hero. She exhibits not only a very aggressive attitude, but also a tendency toward sisterhood, inspiring other women to organize and fight back against a common enemy. She shows no shame at being openly sexually aggressive, often taking the traditional "man's" role, but still enjoys dressing in her own personal style (she wears eighteen different outfits in the course of the movie), painting her nails and wearing makeup.

In every situation when she is expected to finally be broken and made subservient by her male captors, she rebels, usually with an emasculating or raunchy quip showing that even when bound, she is still her own person. When tied up and left in a freezer for hours to suffer, her only complaint to her captor is "I can't play with myself in this straightjacket."

Other films and literature about warrior women may depart from traditional myth in an entirely different direction. Many writers and filmmakers are torn between erotic fascination with the idea of powerful female warriors who don't depend on men and the threat of such a concept to a patriarchal society. We often see the warrior woman portrayed in a sexually objectified

Lori Petty in *Tank Girl*.

manner, as a seductive and dangerous temptress. Animal-like and mysterious, she is reduced to an almost subhuman status in this way, which is always one of the first steps toward oppression and discrimination. This treatment also illustrates some of the traditional fear related to the association of the female and the "unknown."

We see numerous more "comfortable" depictions of Amazon women on film as being wildly beautiful but with rather child-like mentalities. Encountering men for the first time, they are inevitably awakened (sexually) and fascinated (by the phallus) and suddenly in need of leadership. They revert to subservience and a male savior to get them out of a jam, as opposed to being intelligently organized, fierce, and ruthless. (Also note: If they are blond-haired, they are "good" and will cooperate. If they are dark-haired, they are "bad.")

Authors such as D. H. Lawrence who were against the women's suffrage movement (though fully in favor of women *naturally* having power over men) wrote in reactionary style about rebellious women. Batya Weinbaum discusses this in detail in *Islands of Women and Amazons: Representations and Realities*:

> D. H. Lawrence depicted Clara, the Amazon character in *Sons and Lovers*, as quick to anger. Clara also favors women fighting for themselves. A socialist and a speaker for suffrage, she lives with her mother, not with her brutish husband.
>
> Lawrence's narrator first refers to Clara as the Amazon because she is strong and can run. Yet in the course of the novel, Lawrence puts her back into the diminished, conquered place belonging to women. He showed her as helpless, in need of the powers of the character Paul to get her a job in the factory. Once employed, Clara obviously becomes Paul's favorite, and the other factory women, jealous, resent her. She develops no friendship ties with other women (odd conduct, to say the least, for an Amazon). Clara is self-educated, most certainly a sign of the modern Amazon who wants to prepare herself to fight in a time when survival of the fittest no longer means strength in physical terms but rather in intellectual terms.

Yet in true reactionary manner, Lawrence portrayed her as wanting to submit, especially sexually, and as wanting to please men. By the end of the novel, the author reduced the so-called Amazon to begging the main male character to marry her.

This pattern is repeated in several of Lawrence's books. He uses references to Amazons not only in *Sons and Lovers*, but also in *Women in Love*, *The Lost Girl*, and *Lady Chatterley's Lover*. At one point in *Women in Love*, male characters Birkin and Gerald discuss what they consider to be an irrational act committed by Gudrun, who had slapped Gerald in the face when he implied that she was fearful.

"But how do you account for her having such an impulse? I'd done her no harm."

Birkin shook his head.

"The Amazon suddenly came up in her, I suppose."

Another famous artist, Federico Fellini, was notoriously in awe of the natural sexual power of women over men. However, despite his obvious submissive posturing toward the female figure, his dreamy masochistic exploits in the film *City of Women* (1980) paints a picture of the feminist movement as silly and absurd. His ambivalence about feminism and general fear of women plays out with heavy-handed Freudian symbolism as the film begins, with a train entering a tunnel.

The male character played by Marcello Mastroianni unwittingly steps into a feminist rally soon after, where crowds of women are singing songs with lyrics that make no sense, and conducting a dizzy three-ring circus of female bonding and sisterhood that includes gym classes where they viciously attack a hanging dummy dressed in men's clothing. One young woman Marcello is attracted to announces gleefully, "I got first prize for best kick in the testicles!"

In reactionary literature and films we often see women's power acknowledged; however, it is both tightly bound and defined in the accoutrements of male fantasy. Countless films (which we will cover in more detail later in this book) depict strong women as threatening. When women are complex, difficult to figure out,

Kristanna Loken in *Terminator 3: Rise of the Machines.*

unpredictable, they may be portrayed as part-animal, part-alien, mutated, or genetically engineered. These half-breed or otherwise nonhuman women can be expected to be exceptionally alluring and aesthetically perfect. Extremely attractive women in real life tend to be perceived as impenetrable "ice queens." On-screen they are revealed as androids, incapable of human emotion and true kindness. Supermodels-turned-actors do well in these sorts of roles. Think, for instance, of Natasha Henstridge in *Species*, Jeri Ryan as Seven of Nine in *Voyager*, Kristanna Loken as a killing machine in *T3*, or Daryl Hannah in *Blade Runner*.

Whether reactionary or empowering, many of the female action films and TV series produced over the years give fascinating insight into society's process of absorbing new concepts or resisting them. From the first experimental steps of television series like *The Avengers*, *Wonder Woman*, and the "three little girls" of *Charlie's Angels*, we see an interesting journey take place as the warrior woman takes grasp of our collective imagination and begins to challenge stereotypes, transcending decades into the new millennium.

Chapter 2
Amazons in Hollywood

Amazon women were destined for an unfair battle in Hollywood from the start. Their entrance into world literature had already defined them within the confines of the dominant culture. Batya Weinbaum sums up the transition well:

> Into this rather richly detailed textual tapestry enters the somewhat opaque Amazon, fighting, yet relatively unadorned. She readies herself for the history of world literature, which then arms, dresses, characterizes, marries, cloaks, kills and buries her.

Weinbaum also outlines this pattern of appropriation of the Amazon motif by dominant cultures. In one instance she assigned students in a class studying sex role reversals in utopian literature to compare the Amazons as expressed by García Rodríguez Montalvo in *Sergas de Esplandian* (1510) and Christine de Pizan in *The Book of the City of Ladies* (1405). The biases were obvious, as she explains their results:

> Montalvo's Amazons were silly, vain, overdressed, erotic, helpless, cruel, and inept. Pizan's Amazons were intelligent, resourceful, cooperative, nurturing, strong, brave, courageous, practically dressed, and creative.
>
> Pizan depicted Amazons in a state of strength; her Amazons could overcome any hurdle they approached. However, Montalvo depicted the Amazons as evil giants attracted to male dominance. His Amazons wanted to participate in the domain of men even though they had

their own separated island sphere with its own cultural rules. Pizan focused on intellect, prowess, and ingenuity. These were all internal attributes which dictated how they *acted* on the outside world.

Montalvo focuses on looks, stature, and costume, or how the Amazons appeared to the outside world of the men they attracted. Montalvo's Amazons killed their male children, while Pizan's gave their male children back to the fathers. The Amazons created by Montalvo were motivated by glory; Pizan's, by self defense.

Moving forward to present times, we see many different expressions of the Amazon in modern media, from *Wonder Woman* to Clarice Starling of *The Silence of the Lambs*. Early Hollywood, in particular, favored displaying the physical assets of warrior women. These tamed versions of Amazons could be as scantily clad as any Victoria's Secret model, yet appear completely and innocently unaware of the stimulating effect this might have on the men around them.

The fantasy of the warrior woman developed in many directions. Science fiction is a particularly fertile breeding ground for the virtual creation of female-run societies and planets, playing so well into the "lost civilization" theme. And comic books are responsible in a large way for bringing the Amazon from page to screen.

But before we move forward, let's take a look at the criteria we have used for the purpose of this book in deciding which characters, films, and TV series to feature. As mentioned previously, we do tend to be more inclusive than exclusive in the selections covered. Some characters obviously fit the warrior woman archetype. Others appear to have developed in different directions, yet their roots are still similar.

In Susan Isaac's book *Brave Dames and Wimpettes: What Women Are Really Doing on Page and Screen*, she includes a "Brave Dame Philosophy" consisting of seven articles of criteria to qualify as a brave dame. They include such concepts as "A brave dame is passionate about something besides passion" and "A brave dame stands up to injustice."

We subjected the warrior women considered for this book

to a similar criteria system. The necessary traits of the selected women, chosen from hundreds of relevant action movies and TV shows, have been broken down as follows:

Warrior Woman Checklist

(At least two or three of these traits must be present in some form.)

1. She fights in an aggressive and physical manner when required.

Although we include many women who use intelligence and/or even charm and sex appeal to attain their goals, the main point is that she does not behave in a passive-aggressive manner. At some point she does end up in a physical fighting situation. She faces things head on—at least by the end of the story. Many stories illustrate the transformation of a naïve victim-type into a full-blown fighter. The character may not always be the protagonist or female lead. We cover many "evil" characters that also fit some of the criteria outlined.

2. She is not merely a sidekick to a man.

If she is a sidekick, then it must be at least implied that she has superior skills in spite of her allotted status, often reversing the roles and saving the man. For instance, Emma Peel of *The Avengers* TV series (Diana Rigg) clearly ran the show, though she was partnered up with John Steed (Patrick Macnee).

3. She is part of a female-run organization or culture.

The all-female organization pops up in many places. Even in the recent film *Mr. and Mrs. Smith* (2005), Angelina Jolie's character seems to head up an exclusively female organization (a fact that is never really explained). Girl gangs abound in movies, together for bad and good purposes. *Charlie's Angels* is the type of series where it gets a little cloudy. On one hand, three extremely capable women are at the center of the story and perform all of the action. However, they are subordinate to a central male figure. We frequently see this sort of a "daddy" character in pop culture. At the end of the day, the male psyche can rest easy that the women will switch back to the traditional gender role and try to cook them din-

Diana Rigg in *The Avengers*.

Angelina Jolie (on right) leads a female organization in *Mr. and Mrs. Smith*.

ner—even if it does get burned a little in the process. After all, the normal-girl persona is part of their cover.

4. She displays some level of kinship and sisterhood with her own gender.

The issue of sisterhood can be tricky. We see a lot of loners out there: the stereotypical emotionally damaged female heroine seeking revenge, isolated or unable to connect with others. However, in many of these situations we can see that past sisterhood is implied. In some senses, even when a woman is fighting another woman (or female monster), we do recognize a latent sense of gender kinship. Sigourney Weaver almost foreshadows her character Ripley's later dark bond with the Alien Queen when she threatens the creature with the memorable line "Get away from her, you bitch." There is a very clear female-to-female element in the interaction.

In the *Kill Bill* films, the Bride (Uma Thurman) seems to be completely on her own and most definitely not very sym-

pathetic to the women she's killing off one by one. However, there is definite past sisterhood implied in many scenes, such as when she encounters O-Ren (Lucy Liu) in the House of Blue Leaves. O-Ren speaks the words "Silly rabbit . . ." to which the Bride automatically replies, "Trix are for . . ." O-Ren joins in with ". . . kids," as if this was perhaps a familiar phrase between them from when they were together as part of the Deadly Viper Assassination Squad (DiVAS). There is also an interesting scene where the Bride seems to share a bonding moment with another assassin sent to kill her. She talks the assassin Karen (Helen Kim) into backing down by explaining that she just found out she was pregnant. Karen leaves her alone, at great risk to herself, even saying "Congratulations" as she departs with a knife still sticking straight out of one arm. We see numerous situations like these where the character is implied to have a kinship to other females, even if in the past.

From left to right: Dylan (Drew Barrymore), Natalie (Cameron Diaz), and Alex (Lucy Liu) set to enter an extreme motocross event in the movie *Charlie's Angels: Full Throttle*.

5. She uses classic warrior woman weapons and tools.
Probably the most archetypical weapon is the bow and arrow, which we see used by far more women than men in action films. Even in futuristic science fiction films, we see interesting modifications of the traditional bow and arrow. A number of other weapons also seem to be preferred by women. We shall discuss these in subsequent chapters.

She may also embody the Amazon archetype by her choice of transportation. Instead of a horse, she may ride a motorcycle, which not only replaces the horse, but acts as a form of phallic symbolism. Jessica Alba's character Max rides a motorcycle in the *Dark Angel* TV series. *Charlie's Angels Full Throttle* has an extensive dirt-bike race scene. If female action characters use cars, they don't tend to be "girly" cars. They are usually muscle cars or extremely fast cars.

6. She dresses and adorns herself in warrior garments.
This could be anything from your classic Xena/Gladiator-type

Xena (Lucy Lawless) wears warrior attire in *Xena: Warrior Princess.*

apparel to the immensely popular catsuit, which serves to allow a wide range of movement. Black leather goes almost hand in hand with female action leads, as well as boots and bondage-style gear containing a variety of holsters to hold weapons. Amazon jewelry is often incorporated, with significant symbols, spirals, or medallions.

7. She is independent and doesn't need a man to save her.

This trait needs no explanation. However, even though many female heroines do not *need* a man to save them, inevitably many plotlines have their assigned love interest save them at some point, regardless. This also may be a tool to allow the female protagonist to "trust" him, to show motivation for letting down her guard and allowing intimacy.

8. She lives or comes from a "lost civilization."

Traditionally this might be an island, upon which the male lead will wash up one day, to find himself in the midst of an exclusive society of women. In Fellini's *City of Women,*

Lesbian tendencies are hinted at between Xena and Gabrielle.

it was a surreal town accessed via a strange train stop and a walk through a forest. Jungles are largely featured, of course, echoing the abundant theories of Amazons living in South America. However, with notable frequency, the fantasy of matriarchal societies occurs in space, upon female-dominated planets, as created by science fiction writer Leslie F. Stone in the thirties and the creator of *Star Trek*, Gene Roddenberry, in the sixties, although the Amazons in Outer Space theme is usually more spoof or satire than serious depiction.

9. She may be homosexual, bisexual, or simply not desire men.

Rarely has this aspect been fully explored outside of exploitation films. We see most aggressive women depicted as emotionally isolated and dysfunctional in relationships, maybe engaging only in casual flings. Or they are far too angry and bitter to even desire a man and appear to be asexual. It's interesting that women who are so courageous display such fear of intimacy. But this is a hallmark of the popular rape-revenge theme also. Lesbian tendencies may well be implied or hinted at, but not absolutely confirmed. Case in point: Xena and Gabrielle.

And so, these are the basic criteria for the women included in this book. We will further break down these characters into genre categories, such as fantasy and folklore, science fiction, Gothic heroines, comic-book-inspired characters, and many more. Within those categories you'll see a variety of roles played, from the vengeful female to the politically correct token feminist, to bad-girl gangs.

Chapter 3
Fur Bikinis and Jungle Love

———

One of the maidens was squatting beside me, holding a small gourd that had been scooped out and turned into a drinking cup. She put one hand under my head, lifted me gently, and brought the gourd to my lips. The water was sweet and fresh, almost cool. But I hardly noticed. Her young breasts were just inches away from my eyes, pointing tenderly into my brain as a reminder that it has been weeks since . . .

ADVERTISEMENT: *Free!!! Powerful Muscles Fast! Results Guaranteed.*

(cont.) What a hell of a time to be thinking about *that*, I told myself. I tried not to look and sipped the water. There wasn't time and this wasn't the place. I had to get out of here and get in touch with Brazilian officials of some sort. Most of all, I had to run, even if it meant leaving those twin cones of delicate, tender and inviting . . . *Dammit*, I said, *cut it out.*

ADVERTISEMENT: *Starting to get bald? Take HOPE. New system. Guaranteed.*

(cont.) "Can you understand me?" I asked her. She looked puzzled and frowned. She couldn't have been more than sixteen. No wonder they dragged her back to this hole in the jungle wall. I would have done the same . . .

—David Keddin, "War of the Women,"
For Men Only magazine

———

Opposite: Raquel Welch assumes an assertive pose in her fur bikini from *One Million Years B.C.*

During the sixties, amidst advertisements for male girdles and artist renderings of Frederick's of Hollywood lingerie, readers could be exhilarated by manly adventure stories such as the one above. That particular male hero, by the way, had to kill no less than a dozen ferocious animals with this .357 Magnum Smith & Wesson revolver and "turn a 20-foot alligator into a well-ventilated suitcase hide" before encountering those two young breasts that "pointed tenderly" into his brain.

Early visual images of warrior women on-screen probably caused a good deal of similar brain intrusions. Filmmakers set their heroines in an exotic or prehistoric landscape, a "land before time" (and before the existence of clothing in most cases). In this Garden of Eden, lines were very clearly drawn. Almost inevitably the female protagonist was blond and most definitely white. The word *white* is often used in taglines, such as "White Goddess of the dark jungle." The exotic, dark-haired Raquel Welch was portrayed as blond in *One Million Years B.C.* (1966) and her all-blond tribe was depicted as clearly superior to the dark-haired people.

Though some of the mythos regarding Amazons does seem to point to fair hair being a physical trait on a historical level (most notably in the writings of the ancient historian Herodotus), it also seems obvious that the positioning of "light" against "dark" demonstrated racial themes of the fifties and sixties. However, the "white = good, black = bad" theme is still a constant motif in films, especially those that have graduated from the pages of famous works written by authors of earlier times. The *Lord of the Rings* trilogy portrays the blond tribes of Rohan (aka "the Whiteskins") as good and the ominous, dark-skinned, dark-haired wild men of the hills as working on behalf of evil.

The female heroines of some of these productions are unforgettable though, mainly for their entrancing images, which are still reproduced to this day. Though many of the films tend to be a bit silly or absurd, they are in keeping with the many of the perceptions of women of the time period. They also may have been responsible for opening the door to future warrior women on-screen by the strength of their physical magnetism, as seen through the male gaze.

One Million Years B.C. — The Birth of an Icon

"Travel back through time and space to the edge of man's beginnings . . . discover a savage world whose only law was lust!"

It is hard to accept the fact that Raquel Welch stands only five-feet-five inches from the ground. Throughout her career she has been able to exude such a powerful physical allure that she literally dominates the screen.

Hammer Films' prehistoric adventure fantasy *One Million Years B.C.* (1966) remains the film that elevated Raquel Welch to international sex-symbol status. The pseudo-primitive image of Welch in her fur-lined pushup bra and loincloth, legs and arms outstretched in warrior-like stance, is as unforgettable as Farrah Fawcett's record-breaking swimsuit poster.

A remake of the original 1940 version of *One Million Years B.C.* starring Carole Landis and Victor Mature, which actually earned an Oscar nomination for special effects, the 1966 version also relies heavily upon the charms of its leading lady over plot. The primitive setting, shot in the Canary Islands, and adventure storyline act as framework, allowing Welch to be lusciously portrayed in her anachronistic bikini for the entire length of the film. The studio makes the most of her stunning physical qualities with gratuitous scenes of her character, Loana, emerging from a swim, dripping wet, and in a heated fight scene with another striking cavewoman that borders on the edge of erotic frottage. At the climax of the fight, spurred on by a crowd of eager cavemen, Loana throws her competitor to the ground and straddles her. She is handed a horn (phallic symbol, of course) to finish the job by impalement. She does not carry out the act, however, and scenes of female bonding follow. Unfortunately there were problems with the DVD release of the movie from 20th Century Fox Home Video. Some of the original footage is missing, including a portion where Martine Beswick's cavegirl character performs a sexy tribal dance.

Loana (Raquel Welch) battles cave-woman Nupondi (Martine Beswick) in *One Million Years B.C.:* light vs. dark in a classic confrontation.

Falling into the category of warrior women films that express their heroines as essentially "good" and rather childlike in their guileless, barbaric ways, Welch's character, Loana, takes a physically aggressive but sacrificial role in rescuing the male protagonist (Tumak—John Richardson) from a giant sea turtle and attempting to rescue tribal children from various creatures. As mentioned earlier, racial lines are drawn, with the "good" people (the shell tribe of the coast) portrayed as fair-skinned, attractive blonds with a more refined culture. The "bad" ones (the rock people) are savage and carnivorous dark-haired cave dwellers. At one point we see the former tribe tenderly bury one of their dead

One Million Years B.C.

with a respectful ceremony, while the latter leave an injured old man to suffer and die in a ditch.

Inevitably Loana falls in love with the wounded Tumak. When he is forced to leave the tribe to return home, Loana sacrifices her peaceful home and tribal family ties and decides to go with him on his trek across the dangerous desert. She faces the dangers as an equal, fighting dinosaurs, as well as members of the rock tribe, but she does not alienate the male audience with her nontraditional warrior ways, because she is still a nurturing, civilizing influence, a more traditional and accepted role for women in literature and film.

Irish McCalla: fifties blond pinup meets Amazon warrior as *Sheena, Queen of the Jungle.*

Sheena, Queen of the Jungle (TV: 1955–1957)

The low-angle shot of Sheena (as played by the six-foot-one-inch ex-model Irish McCalla), dressed in leopard skins and blowing her buffalo horn, haunted the dreams of many a male child growing up in the stultifying fifties. David Broad, in his article "Sheena, Queen of the Jungle: White Goddess of the Dumont Era" (in *Studies in Popular Culture*, 1997), in fact compares this exact image of Sheena to the depictions of ancient fertility goddesses:

> This pose is strikingly similar to that of the Venus of Laussel, a Paleolithic goddess carving unearthed in France and attributed to some 20,000 years ago. The figure depicts a fertile-looking female holding in one hand a crescent-shaped bison horn, symbolic of the moon, with thirteen notches carved on it. Her other hand is on her abdomen.

Sheena was a product, like many of the early warrior women in television, including Wonder Woman and Batgirl, of the comic book. She was a brainchild of comic genius Will Eisner and his then-partner S. M. Iger, who created her as a female rival to Tarzan. They based her name and some of her goddess-like characteristics on H. Rider Haggard's immortal character *She.* Like her male counterpart Tarzan, Sheena also was abandoned in the jungle and raised there, developing in the process the mental and physical strength of a native. And, like Tarzan, she displayed a flawless, powerful body, as well as an innate sense of right and wrong.

However, by the mid-fifties Sheena's popularity was beginning to wane. She, like so many other strong female characters, fell victim to the repressive atmosphere of the Eisenhower-McCarthy era. With the social emphasis on creating a nuclear family and pushing women out of the workforce that had previously welcomed them during the Second World War, the media no longer sought strong independent women as lead characters. Joan Crawford and Bette Davis's characters were replaced by supportive housewives like those seen on sitcoms such as *Leave*

It to Beaver and *Father Knows Best* or blonde "bombshells" like those played by Marilyn Monroe in films such as *Gentlemen Prefer Blondes* or Jayne Mansfield in classics such as *Will Success Spoil Rock Hunter?* It was surprising when in 1956 the networks picked up the independently produced, low-budget TV series called *Sheena, Queen of the Jungle*, based on the Eisner-Iger comic book character.

One can surmise that a large part of the show's appeal to network brass was the presence of Irish McCalla, whose pinup-style appearance corresponded roughly with the Monroe-Mansfield model. She did not, however, project the standard helpless blonde starlet stereotype. TV's Sheena was innocent yet resourceful and strong-willed (her favorite line was "You stay here!!!") like her comic book predecessor. She fought and defeated the men who tried to plunder her jungle. At the same time she demonstrated the nurturing, maternal spirit expected of most female characters, even jungle girls. Acting as mother to her animals, she cradled her chimp in her arms like a child. And she often rescued her somewhat incompetent "boyfriend" Bob, the hunter (his relationship to Sheena is never made clear in either the comic incarnation or the TV show) whose heroics often went awry.

Elissa Landi (Antiope) gazes into the eyes of her lover (David Manners) from *The Warrior's Husband*.

The Warrior's Husband, Amazon Myth in Pre-Code Hollywood

In 1933 Fox released an odd film called *The Warrior's Husband*. It was based on a successful play that starred Katharine Hepburn as the lead Amazon Antiope. As is commonly done in Hollywood, the stage star was dumped to be replaced by a film star they thought was more photogenic, in this case, Elissa Landi. David Manners, of *Dracula* and *Mummy* fame, played Theseus. The film drew on the Greek myth of the hero arriving in the land of the Amazons in order to find a wife. There he encounters Antiope. Theseus marries her, and she becomes queen of Athens, ruling alongside her husband. The movie itself is largely a satire, poking fun at gender roles in a period before Hollywood caved into pressure and enacted the stifling Production Code that, among other things, put a damper on overt references to "deviant" sexuality.

Jungle Girl, "Mistress of an Empire of Savages and Beasts"

Above: "Jungle girl" Frances Gifford from the Republic serial of the same name.

Below: Another blond warrior: Lana (Catherine Schell) from *Lana, Queen of the Amazons.*

Jungle Girl (1941) is a fifteen-part serial from the king of serial makers Republic Studios. Based on the novel by Tarzan creator Edgar Rice Burroughs, it tells the story of Nyoka (Frances Gifford) who has been raised in the jungle by her father, a doctor. He has gained the trust of the natives through his good works and benevolence. With the assistance of natives, Nyoka becomes adept at survival skills and is shown in the series wrestling various animals, as well as defeating villains set on stealing her father's cache of diamonds.

As with all serials, each episode ends with a cliff-hanger, such as the plane running out of gasoline or Nyoka facing sure death at the hands of the villain. Like her literary brother Tarzan, Nyoka swings through the trees and befriends animals and natives alike. Her conflicts are fairly black-and-white, and she spends a great deal of time unraveling the plans of her father's evil twin.

The Saga of the Viking Women and Their Voyage to the Waters of the Great Sea Serpent

"The raw courage of women without men lost in a fantastic Hell on Earth."

Roger Corman's *Saga of the Viking Women and their Voyage to the Waters of the Great Sea Serpent* (1957) pits several Amazon women of Viking stock against each other, as well as against the villainous King of the Grimolts (Richard Devon), who holds their men in captivity. The women risk shipwreck in the monster-infested seas and death at the hands of the Grimolts as they pursue their quest.

Traditional roles are reversed here, as the men are kept in bondage while the women plot to rescue them. Desir (Abby Dalton) is the classic long-legged Nordic blonde, while her antagonist, the more petite, dark-haired, and pouty Enger (Susan

Cabot—also the star of Corman's *The Wasp Woman*), steals the show with her double-dealing and clever dialogue. In the end, however, Enger sees the error of her ways and dies to help free the Vikings from their servitude.

Queen of the Amazons

This 1947 film *Queen of the Amazons* hardly lived up to its tagline: "White Goddess of the dark jungle. She offered ecstasy and death." Instead it is a Z-budget Hollywood production that is at times incomprehensible. It incorporates stock footage into its story, which only further muddles the plot and characterization. There is an Amazon tribe of white women, apparently castaways, and a queen named Zita (Amira Moustafa), but the "ecstasy" and "death" she offers is in very small doses.

Lana, Queen of the Amazons (aka *Lana, Königin der Amazonen*)

Another white queen paired with dark natives. The German movie *Lana, Queen of the Amazons* (1964) is in the long tradition of blond goddesses ruling dark natives. In this entry Lana wears the traditional fur bikini and rules the Brazilian Amazon, assisted by her tribe of female warriors. Her weak spot is the very masculine explorer Peter (Christian Wolff). Commentary about the film in a 1965 Portuguese newspaper probably sums it up:

> Vulgar adventure movie, with a number of characters in the nude; its public showing would be against prevalent moral standards. Banned. National Board of Film Censorship.

Love Slaves of the Amazons

———

> "This the lost tribe of white women savages. Each a beauty . . . each a deadly trap for the men they make their love slaves."

———

Poster from Roger Corman's *The Saga of the Viking Women and the Sea Serpent* (one of its many titles).

Poster from *Love Slaves of the Amazons,* advertising "fantastic orgies" and "man-killing rituals."

Oh, the horror of being captured by women and used as a living "sperm bank"! What torture! Curt Siodmak, horror expert (*I Walked with a Zombie, The Beast with Five Fingers,* etc.), directed and wrote the 1957 *Love Slaves of the Amazon* for Universal. It was an extremely low-budget production that fed upon the male audience's erotic fantasies.

Kilma, Queen of the Amazons

"Her power was more than any man could handle."

Kilma, Queen of the Amazons (1975) is a Spanish production starring the European "sex star" Blanca Estrada (aka Eva Miller) in the title role. As in so many of these low-budget Amazon "epics," a wandering male washes up on the shore of an Amazon island. There scantily clad women both delight and torture him, depending on their mood. This castaway seems to get more torture than loving as he is whipped while bound to a rock and then spread-eagled for more sadistic sport.

Colossus and the Amazon Queen

Sword, sandal, musclemen, and Amazons. Italians created what came to be called the "sword and sandal" epic. Beginning with the international success of *Hercules* starring muscleman Steve Reeves in 1958, the Italian movie industry churned out these low-budget epics year after year. They usually mixed myth with history, distorting both, and always featured "beefcake" for the women and gay men in the audience (most of these films have become favorites in the gay community over the years).

Colossus and the Amazon Queen (1960) takes the "sword and sandal" formula and pokes fun at it. Two Greek heroes—Pirro (Rod Taylor) and Glauco (Ed Fury)—sail to the mythical island of the Amazons and there meet Antiope (Dorian Gray)

and her Queen (Gianna Maria Canale). There are wonderfully funny touches like the Amazons dancing to sixties mambo
music and Glauco flexing his body for the entertainment of
the women. The happy ending is expected, although somewhat
unusual.

Amazons from *Kilma, Queen of the Amazons.*

Chapter 4
Fantasy, Myth, and Folklore

Fantasy is probably the most traditional genre for warrior women. The female characters of the fantasy genre often have origins rooted in history, some more solidly than others. Many beckon back to a pre-patriarchal time when women leading troops into battle or even ruling was not the exception. However, others still require warrior women to don a male disguise in order to have the opportunity to fight. Either way, this genre allows far more action in the area of aggressive physical combat on film and TV, which has not been a customary role for women in the media.

Joan of Arc

The figure of Jeanne d'Arc is so shrouded in myth it is difficult for historians to find the real teenage warrior among all the volumes of words that have been written about her since her death in 1431. One fact is sure, however, Joan of Lorraine was the first *true* woman warrior to be dealt with by the cinema and the only one to be so honored for the first sixty years of movie history.

Why is that so? Why is Joan an exception? The answer is deceptively simple. Joan was a saint, canonized by the Catholic Church more than five hundred years after that same Church burned her at the stake as a heretic. And so she was safe. Yes, she dressed in men's clothes, fought as a soldier to push the English out of her beloved France, and even argued effectively against her learned prosecutors at her trial. But she was also neatly sanitized by religion as its own martyr, and, of course, she was punished for her transgressions by being burned alive.

The first important film to deal with Joan was *La Passion de*

Jeanne d'Arc (1928), directed by the prestigious Danish director Carl Dreyer. The film deals almost exclusively with the trial, suffering, and punishment of Joan. Dreyer's purpose in making the film, as is obvious by the title, was to raise "the maid" up to the level of Christ, to compare her passion and execution to that of the Christian Messiah. In order to accomplish this the director concentrates on close-ups of Joan as she is questioned by the Inquisition, as she is tortured by her captors, as she burns at the stake. These close-ups are haunting and powerful but ultimately give only a partial picture of Joan, portraying her as victim and transcendent being rather than as a warrior who pushed the English back from Orleans to the gates of Paris.

With *Joan of Arc* (1948) RKO, under industrialist Howard Hughes, tried to create an epic on the cheap. They adapted a Broadway play by Maxwell Anderson called *Joan of Lorraine* and imported its lead, Ingrid Bergman, already a star in Hollywood, to tell the story of Joan on a grand scale, battles included. As opposed to the Dreyer film, the filmmakers here *do* show Joan in battle in full armor, on a white horse, carrying her white banner. They do show her courage in demanding an audience with the dauphin so that she might lead him to be crowned king of France. And they do demonstrate her bravery at the battle for Orleans as she prods the disorganized and initially hostile generals to take Orleans and its surrounding forts. They also foreground the hostility of the males around her, not only because of her commanding ways, but also because she dons men's clothes and cuts her hair short, not so incidentally a major charge during her trial.

The filmmakers are, however, careful to overcome whatever objections a male audience of the time might have to this "butch-looking" teenager by emphasizing her saintly character, her submission to God and to the Dauphin, even though he is a weak and feebleminded ruler. The camera dwells on her ecstatic face in prayer. Angelic music accompanies many of the key moments of the movie, reinforcing her supernatural quality and removing her from the ranks of ordinary women. She is again made safe by neutering her and delivering up a character more angel than warrior.

The first movie to break with tradition and attempt to portray Joan in a more realistic manner was director Otto Preminger's

Opposite: Jean Seberg, in full armor, brings to the screen George Bernard Shaw's interpretation of Saint Joan, chaste and determined.

Milla Jovovich prepares for battle as Joan of Arc in *The Messenger*.

adaptation of George Bernard Shaw's *Saint Joan* (1957), written by famed novelist Graham Greene. Shaw's view of Joan is decidedly nonconformist, as might be expected from this iconoclastic writer. Shaw sees Joan as a historical agent, a revolutionary saint who helped bring about an end to feudalism and the power of the Catholic Church by means of her victories on the field, as well as through her death. Her execution by the English in conjunction with the Burgundians led the French to adopt her as a symbol of national spirit.

Shaw was in many ways a feminist in his philosophy regarding women. He believed that they carried the "life force" and were on some levels superior to men (for reference see his play *Man and Superman*). Consequently, in *Saint Joan* it is this teenage girl who must inspire war-weary commanders and a childlike monarch to defend their nation and act. She calls the captains "batheads" and tells them to attack Orleans and not to fear. They do and succeed. When she wants to continue on to Paris, the

Milla Jovovich enters battle as Joan of Arc in *The Messenger.*

Dauphin demurs, opting for negotiations with the English. But she goes ahead without him, with insufficient funds and forces but a strength of will that inspires her soldiers.

The Messenger (1999) is the most modern and unconventional look at Joan to date. The director Luc Besson (*La Femme Nikita, The Fifth Element*) plays fast and loose with both the history and myth of the maid of Orleans in creating a Joan for the ironic postmodern age. First of all, he casts the Amazonish star of his *Fifth Element*, Milla Jovovich, in the title part. She is in physical dimensions and in sexual intensity far removed from any of the Joans before her. There is little evidence of submission in her personality, even though she does fall to her knees on occasion (most notably when she embraces the overwhelmed dauphin, almost knocking him off his feet) and does claim loyalty to both God and country. But it is obvious from the first sequences of the film that this Joan is more self-actualized and inner-directed than any of the others before her.

The audience first sees her as a child running through the fields of her native Lorraine. In fact Joan never seems to walk anywhere, whether it is to her confessor to unburden her soul on a daily basis or bursting in on her family to announce a new vision from heaven. She even at one point, after witnessing the rape and murder of her sister by the English invaders (a scene that has little historical basis), becomes dissatisfied with the response of the Church to her feelings of guilt, and so she decides to co-opt the male prerogative of transubstantiation (turning the bread and wine into the body and blood of Christ) and performs Mass herself.

Jovovich's Joan, like her historical ancestor, continues her largely unconscious attack on the patriarchy when she goes to Chinon to coerce and persuade the Dauphin (John Malkovich) to give her an army, over the objections of his advisors, generals, and captains. The Dauphin, of course, finds he has neither the will nor the courage to stand up to this tall, blond force of nature who chides him while caressing his face in a disturbingly sensual manner.

Joan's attitude toward her generals in the field evidences the same nervous, almost frenetic impatience. She cannot stand still and gives these grizzled veterans no quarter, screaming at them, "All you have to do is do what you are told!" During battle she is far more active than any of her cinematic sisters before her. She climbs the ramparts of the fortress, where she is shot and then miraculously healed by morning. She enters Orleans covered in blood and swinging her sword, her body twitching with emotion. As her commanders begin to love and respect this strange, visionary "ball of fire," they also begin to believe that she is possibly insane. But they and their soldiers follow her anyway, drawn by her courage and her sensual appeal: "Let all those who love me follow me."

The film's take on Joan's trial by the Church is also decidedly postmodern. The audience sees little of the actual trial (the transcripts of which have been used in all the Joan films before). Instead the filmmakers concentrate on the internal rather than the external struggle. Visions once again plague this visionary. This time they are not of Jesus or swords falling from the heavens but of a figure in black who reifies her own doubts and fears. The Vision (Dustin Hoffman) torments Joan in the pain and isolation her cell. He forces her to remember the death and destruction she has left in her wake and the arrogance she has demonstrated every step of the way. In this manner the filmmakers allow Joan to prosecute herself on several charges far more serious than the ones the Church has trumped up in order to get rid of this pesky female warrior who dresses like a man and defies her male "superiors."

Through this process of self-examination Joan comes to realize the horror of violence, as well as her great sin of hubris. She even reaches a state of peace, where she is physically calm for the first time in the movie. She asks for forgiveness, and the Vision, in reality her own conscience, absolves her. The film then cuts briefly to Joan burning at the stake. The filmmakers spend very little time on this event because it is now anticlimactic. Joan has already suffered and found her salvation, alone and without the aid of the world around her. Joan has died much as she lived, an outsider.

The history and legend of Joan of Arc continues to march on. In the same year *The Messenger* was released, TV produced a miniseries on Joan's life, *Joan of Arc*, starring Lee Lee Sobieski. And most recently CBS produced a series called *Joan of Arcadia* (2003). In this version Joan is a suburban teenager who is filled with the normal amount of teenage angst and confusion but is also subject to visitations by God in various incarnations. This modern Joan, however, fights with her visions and God's directions and only does his will after much complaining and skeptical questioning.

The Warrior Women of *Conan the Barbarian*

The three *Conan* movies, inspired by the writings of Robert E. Howard, did more than secure the fame of the muscleman/actor/politician Arnold Schwarzenegger. They also brought together several elements in the depiction of warrior women that had been in gestation in the seventies.

First of all, there was the influence of TV shows like *Wonder Woman* and *The Bionic Woman*, which featured, respectively, a comic book mythical Amazon and a modern cybernetic warrior woman. There was also the voluptuous yet almost hypertrophic warrior women of the popular French comic book *Metal Hurlant* and its English sister *Heavy Metal*. Finally, there was the phenomenon of sword and sorcery role-playing games such as *Dungeons*

Poster for the *Heavy Metal* movie made in 2000, a female warrior typical of the style begun with the magazine *Metal Hurlant*.

and Dragons, which has to this day a massive following, as well as the popularity of many other fantasy video games, which were rapidly improving in technology at the time. Bringing such characters in the flesh to the big screen was the source of much excitement and anticipation among fans of the genre. The first *Conan the Barbarian* fulfilled most people's wishes, although Robert E. Howard purists noted the many changes made from the original stories.

———

"Come on! Do you want to live forever?"

—Valeria, *Conan the Barbarian*

———

The first of the *Conan* women to integrate all three of the above influences was Valeria in *Conan the Barbarian* (1982). As played by dancer Sandahl Bergman, she epitomized the Viking ideal of power and beauty. She was tall, blond, muscular, and a match for Conan on every level. She was as good a thief as he was, helping him to enter the tower of the snake cult that she had penetrated before him. She was his equal in sexual prowess, as she dominated their lovemaking as often as the animalistic Conan did. And finally she ultimately wins his eternal devotion by sacrificing herself while rescuing Conan from the villain Thulsa Doom (James Earl Jones). It is interesting to note that Valeria dies from impalement with a snake arrow. In the final scenes a distraught Conan builds a funeral pyre for his beloved.

The sequel *Conan the Destroyer* (1984) finds Conan still mourning his lost Valeria at the site of her ashes. Queen Tamaris (Sarah Douglas) promises Conan that she will bring his love back to life if he does her bidding. The love-besotted and somewhat intellectually dim Conan agrees. He and his ragtag band are to accompany a pouty teen princess named Jehnna (Olivia D'Abo) to retrieve a sacred horn to revive the dreaming god Dagoth.

The women in this second *Conan* film are consistently strong-willed. The Queen is ruthless in her desire to awake the god Dagoth and rule with him. Jehnna is spoiled and demanding yet wise in trusting her instincts, as opposed to Conan's clouded intellect (not insignificantly the producer of the movie—Raffaela De Laurentiis—was a princess herself, in this case, of an Italian film empire). And most important, there is Zula.

Above: Sandahl Bergman as Valeria in *Conan the Barbarian.*

Opposite: Performance artist Grace Jones as the Amazon Zula in *Conan the Destroyer.*

Brigitte Nielsen as Red Sonja, based on the Conan stories of Robert E. Howard.

Zula, when first seen by Conan, is tied to a stake like an animal, almost nude. Her black, androgynous body gleams with sweat as she holds off the herd of men who captured her. Conan watches in admiration as she fends off the men, while Jehnna asks whimsically what kind of a woman Valeria was. Conan then directs her gaze to Zula. As played by Grace Jones, noted for pushing boundaries of gender stereotype and challenging primitive myths about the sexuality of people of color, she appears like one of Jones's performance-art incarnations—sleek, primal, and panther-like. She is direct and guttural like Conan but more developed in her sensibilities. When Jehnna, infatuated with Conan, asks her how to obtain a man, she replies with direct advice, "Grab him and take him!"

Red Sonja (1985) is the third film in the *Conan* series and arguably the weakest. Although originally it was anticipated that the *Conan* series would produce up to six films, similar to the James Bond series, *Sonja's* lack of financial and critical success put an end to further adaptations. Although the Conan character himself does not appear in the movie (and Schwarzenegger consents to play second fiddle to star Brigitte Nielsen in the part of Kalidor), the source material for the screenplay is once again from the *Conan* stories of Robert E. Howard. This time the central figure is a female warrior named Red Sonja, played by Nielsen. Sandahl Bergman also made an appearance in the film, playing the part of Queen Gedren.

Nielsen made an alluring fantasy warrior, with long, flowing red hair, though she didn't appear particularly muscular or athletic. She brought a definite level of interest to the film, but for many fans, even metal bikinis and fantasy apparel didn't make up for her limited acting skills or annoying attempts at comedic relief by the supporting characters. It can be more easily appreciated for its campy moments. There was also an atypical score by famed Italian composer Ennio Morricone, although it was no match for the dramatic scores in the first two films by Basil Poledouris. The sets and costumes were created by Fellini regular Danilo Donati, who modeled them after the brilliant comic book art of *Red Sonja*.

Besides the obvious Amazonian/Valkyrie motifs that appear in *Red Sonja,* the Amazon trait of "chastity" comes up on many occasions. Like the myth of Siegfried and Brunnhilde, she is too strong to be conquered. As with many female heroes, she is sexually and emotionally isolated from men because of her qualities of strength and self-sufficiency.

Red Sonja: No man may have me, unless he's beaten me in a fair fight.

Kalidor: So . . . the only man that can have you is one who's trying to kill you. That's logic.

Lord of the Rings: Eowyn, Shield Maiden to Warrior Queen

Eowyn (Miranda Otto) exposed as a woman disguised in male battle armor.

The orientation of J. R. R. Tolkien's epic fantasy *The Lord of the Rings* is predominantly male, like much of the genre. His "Middle-earth" is a land fought over and controlled by the male of the species—whether the species be hobbit, human, or elf. The human hero, Aragorn, the once and future king; the brave hobbit Frodo; and the wizard Gandalf—all push and pull the action of the novel by means of their heroic feats, as well as their psychological conflicts.

The only real exception to the male oriented fantasy universe is the "shield maiden" Eowyn—niece of King Theoden of Rohan. In the book she does take part in the Battle for Gondor, without the consent or knowledge of her uncle, who refuses to recognize her combat abilities because of her gender. She does defeat the Witch-King, although in destroying him she so depletes her resources that she is forced to retire from the field of battle.

Director-writer Peter Jackson, in his masterful adaptation of the fantasy classic, sets about to realign Tolkien's female characters, as few was they are, for a generation accustomed to females in roles of combat. In order to meet this pressing commercial and social need, Jackson has given the elf princess Arwen (Liv Tyler) several scenes in which she demonstrates her bravery and physical skill, most notably when she rescues the hobbit Frodo from the ringwraiths.

But the most important shift in characterization occurs with Eowyn herself (played by Mirando Otto). As interpreted

by Jackson and Otto, she is an aggressive warrior who demonstrates her expertise with arms in several early scenes. Although she is still repressed by her uncle, she pursues her desire for battle much more strenuously than her literary predecessor. In addition, Jackson changes the tone toward Theoden by underlining his sexism, particularly when he sends her back with the women and children before the Battle of Helm's Deep.

It is, however, in part three of the film, *The Return of the King*, that Eowyn comes into her own and strays radically from the Tolkien scenario. Jackson has returned Eowyn to her Celtic roots and restored her to warrior status in this final battle for Gondor. Before the battle Eowyn deceives her uncle and dresses like a male warrior, obviously echoing Joan of Arc. During the fight itself, she not only defeats the Witch-King, which none of the other heroes are able to do, but fights the monstrous oliphants, saving her uncle as well. Although Theoden ultimately dies from his wounds, it is Eowyn to whom he wills his kingdom. And so Eowyn becomes queen of Rohan and an equal to any of the other male members of the fellowship of the Ring.

Above: Eowyn (Miranda Otto) takes on the dreaded Nazgul in *The Lord of the Rings: Return of the King.*

Opposite: Liv Tyler as the powerful elf princess Arwen in *The Lord of the Rings.*

King Arthur, a New Guinevere

Keira Knightley incarnates in several movies the young warrior woman in the tradition of Joan of Arc. In *Princess of Thieves* (2001), she plays Gwyn, the daughter of legendary thief Robin Hood. Although Robin forbids her to fight and train, she nevertheless becomes a daunting archer and horsewoman without the knowledge of her restrictive father. When her father, who has been given a commission by the dying King Richard to aid his son Philip in ascending to the throne, fails in his mission and is captured by Prince John, Gwyn takes matters into her own hands. Dressed as a boy, she enthusiastically seizes her father's figurative mantel and becomes Philip's protector. Together Gwyn and Philip manage to free her father from prison. Reluctantly, Robin accepts his daughter's skills, as well as her iron-like determination. And so, side-by-side, both father and daughter defeat Prince John and restore the throne to King Richard's heir. In *Pirates of the Caribbean (2003)*, playing Elizabeth Swann, Knightley is as willful as ever as she transforms herself from helpless captive to an active agent in her own destiny.

In 2004 Knightley took on the role of Guinevere in a most modern version of the tale of Arthur and his knights, *King Arthur*. The filmmakers intended with this movie to restore some of the possible historical facts on which the myth of Arthur and Guinevere was based. Critics and some members of the audience didn't seem to enjoy this demystified view of King Arthur though, and the film was panned by some critics. Even this more realistic version of the story has much conjecture in it, as do the many past interpretations (most notably, the influential fifteenth-century epic *Le Morte d'Arthur*). Clive Owen portrays Arthur as a half-Roman, half-Briton who fights for Rome against the native peoples of the island, while Knightley shapes Guinevere into a savage Druidic tribal leader intent on converting Arthur to her cause, the overthrow of the imperialist Romans.

The first meeting of Arthur and Guinevere is at the fort of the Roman Marius, where she, as well as several of her countryman, are held captive in a cave-like torture chamber, persecuted for their Druidic religion, as well as their rebellious attitude. Arthur frees the emaciated girl, who treats him initially with suspicion.

Opposite: An atypical Guinevere (Keira Knightley) fights alongside the Knights of the Round Table.

Guinevere charges into battle.

She stares at him much like a wild animal, wounded but aggressive.

Guinevere tells Arthur early on that she knows who he is, that her father had told her heroic tales of him when she was a child. Even though he has legendary status in her eyes and superiority in age, she is not intimidated by this battle-worn warrior. She continually questions him as to his divided loyalties. Why does he not love the land of his mother? Why is he willing to serve an imperialistic power like Rome, which has subjugated the native peoples of her island? In this way Guinevere becomes as much a political warrior as physical one. It also gives her an excuse for not filling the traditional role of woman. She is made into a warrior because of a higher calling—the good of her people. However, many scenes do allow Guinevere to be seen as protective while looking after a little boy who was also saved from captivity. This standard display of the sacred maternal instinct serves to calm any psychological fear that she is not "normal" or too

unbalanced. (She might even make a good wife someday.)

Guinevere takes aim with her bow.

Her unexpected skill and bravery in battle gains everyone's attention. As with Peter Jackson's Eowyn, the filmmakers here have also modeled their Guinevere on the female Celtic warriors. She stands against marauding Saxons with bow in hand, as proficient as Lancelot, Arthur's first knight. When a jealous Lancelot (a detail taken from the original Arthurian legends) taunts Guinevere with intimations that she might be molested by the invading hordes, she answers sarcastically, "Don't worry, I won't let them rape you." Unlike previous Guineveres though, this one does not end up cuckolding Arthur with Lancelot.

Subsequent fight scenes feature Guinevere covered in war paint, breasts strapped down with a strip of leather. She is absolutely ferocious—once again reminiscent of an animal. Though she is backed up by other women, and the scenes are entertaining to watch, there is still some feeling that this is one of those "You go, girl!" moments that are embedded by filmmakers to show how progressive and pro-woman they are, yet at the same time play into the scopophiliac pleasures of the audience. The camera angle generally puts you at the viewpoint of her adversary, so she is viewed from the aggressor's angle. She taunts, smiling and snarling with blood coming out of her mouth. When things get too rough and she is overcome, once again she has to be saved by a man.

By the final scenes Arthur and his Sarmatian knights have defeated the Saxon army, with the aid of Guinevere and her troops, and thrown off the yoke of Rome. In a Druidic ceremony symbolizing his devotion to Britain, he marries Guinevere on a hilltop and is blessed by the high priest Merlin. Even though pains have been taken to portray Guinevere as a feminist hero, there is still a feeling that her transformation from a savage, self-sufficient warrior to a happily married queen wraps things up a little too neatly. You go forth with some idea that she will now be tamed and settle down into her regal position, eventually becoming the traditional Guinevere of legend that everyone is more accustomed to.

The Brothers Grimm

Terry Gilliam's vivid flight of imagination called *The Brothers Grimm* (2005) interlaces the historical reality of an occupied Germany (under Napoleonic rule) with the gruesome fairy tales collected by the brothers of the title. Following the popular "demystification" trend of *King Arthur* and *Batman Begins*, Gilliam's version shows us that the brothers are simply con men who try to convince townspeople that they have the skills and the knowledge to fight monsters and demons. They use elaborate props and devices to cause the very hauntings they offer to eradicate, for a fee, of course.

Eventually, however, they are captured and sent by the French occupying forces to a small town where inhabitants have actually mysteriously disappeared. There the brothers encounter "real" supernatural situations where their phony exorcisms are of little use. Luckily, they are aided by the huntress Angelika (Lena Headey). She is a nineteenth-century version of Artemis, replete with bow, arrow, and a sharp wit. Reminiscent of the character Anna in *Van Helsing*, Angelika has a relative who is a werewolf,

Monica Bellucci as the Mirror Queen in *The Brothers Grimm*.

and she does a majority of the fighting. She often berates the brothers for their cowardice and deceptions and saves their lives on several occasions. In archetypal fashion she is a loner, separate from the rest of the village, and doesn't get along with men. The brothers even make jokes about her. Though she is depicted as brave and capable, she ends up spending most of the second half of the movie in an enchanted sleep. There she waits passively in a coffin until the men are done saving the day and come to kiss her awake and lift the curse.

The main source of evil in the story is the Mirror Queen played by Monica Bellucci, who is far more interesting. As in *The Matrix* series, where she played Persephone, Bellucci embodies the role of an evil dominatrix who keeps slaves, driving metal spikes into their hearts as a sign of ownership and to control them. Her abject appearance as a shriveled corpse is gruesome, yet when her suitors gaze at her through the mirror (the male gaze) she is exquisite, illustrating the dual force of women as a symbol of grotesque ancient fear and erotic fascination. Her double phallic headdress further reinforces her mythic dimensions, as does her obvious link to the Evil Queen of the famous Grimm tale *Snow White*, a classic female icon for fetishists.

Lena Headey as Angelika in Terry Gilliam's *The Brothers Grimm*.

49

XENA
TM & © Studios I

Xena, Warrior Princess

Xena, Warrior Princess (1995–2000) is a watershed TV series not only in terms of the development of the warrior woman in media, but also in terms of the image of women in general. The show was designed by creators Sam Raimi and Robert Tapert (who would apply the same Amazon formula to the future in the television series *Cleopatra 2525* five years later). Originally it was thought of as a companion to their highly successful series *Hercules*, but very soon the show took on a life of its own, creating a massive fan base, largely female, which exceeded that of its brother series.

What is remarkable is how intimately fans connected with the series, showing that "Xenaverse" truly has no limits. Web sites such as Whoosh.org, the birthplace of the "International Association for Xena Studies," run by Kym Taborn, discuss and debate theories about each episode in insightful detail. *Xena* fans are not merely passive consumers, but interactive viewers who have actually shaped and steered the show with their influence. And, of course, *Xena* has also stimulated the frenzied creation of countless works of fan fiction and "slash" fiction, which bring up many issues on their own.

The Appeal of Lucy Lawless

———

Gabrielle: Another one's fallen for you.

Xena: Again? What is it?

Gabrielle: Oh, the blue eyes . . . the leather. Men love leather.

Xena: I think it's time for a wardrobe change.

Gabrielle: Yeah. You could try wearing chain mail.

Xena: Nah. That'd just attract a kinkier group.

———

A large part of the success of *Xena* lies in the charisma and physical presence of its star Lucy Lawless. The title sequence of the series speaks volumes in establishing the power and persona of Xena. It intercuts action footage with a montage of the warrior princess preparing for battle. The camera pans over Lawless's ath-

Opposite: Lucy Lawless, unrelenting as Xena in the midst of battle.

Lucy Lawless as Xena, fiercely intent.

letic body as she straps on her accoutrements of battle—sword, leggings, breastplate, etc., until she emerges as the warrior woman of the title.

Xena and Gabrielle

Another key element in the phenomenal success of the series is the strong relationship between the two female protagonists, Xena and her constant companion Gabrielle (Renee O'Connor). In the first episode of the series, "Sins of the Past," the creators unite the two almost immediately as Xena rescues Gabrielle for the first of many times (Gabrielle returns the favor later in the

Xena demonstrating her swordsman-ship.

episode). Through the series Gabrielle becomes Xena's primary love object, far above any man that she may have a dalliance with. Her ultimate allegiance is to Gabrielle. In many ways the two complement each other perfectly. Gabrielle is the more traditionally "feminine" of the two in both dress and attitude. She acts as Xena's conscience, as a counterweight to the warrior's violent instincts that have led her to commit so many depredations in the past, crimes that now haunt her. Gabrielle preaches a philosophy of forgiveness and compromise. While Xena has internalized the traditional "male" values of thoughtless violence and emotional anorexia, Gabrielle is always in touch with her instincts, as well as her spiritual side. It is this spiritual side that

Gabrielle (Renee O'Connor), Xena's
loyal companion.

eventually leads her to India, where she becomes, after a mighty
struggle, a tattooed spiritual healer and eventually queen of a
tribe of Amazons.

> *Xena:* Gabrielle, if I only had thirty seconds to live, this
> is how I'd want to live them—looking into your eyes.
> Always remember . . . I love you.

The power of the relationship between Gabrielle and Xena is that
they feed off each other throughout the show and grow as a result
of this symbiotic interchange. Their bond even defies the gods and
time in many episodes. Xena sacrifices herself for Gabrielle over
and over again. It then became almost inevitable that at some
point the couple would express their love in some physical form.

Xena and Gabrielle in a moment of companionship and joy.

That moment came in the episode called "The Quest." Xena, who had died in an earlier episode, enters the body of their old friend Autolycus (Bruce Campbell) and, transforming into herself briefly, tenderly kisses Gabrielle. The reaction the next day was earthshaking. Television talk show hosts childishly poked fun at the scene; fans on the Internet discussed the pros and cons of this first physical expression of love between the two heroines. But probably the best analysis came from *Xena* experts like Judy Fisher, who analyzed the scene in her article "The Quest Kiss and Its Aftermath" for Whoosh.org.

> By basic rules of drama, any *other* fictional couple—a couple that had romantically kissed, as had Xena and Gabrielle in "The Quest," and then been so disastrously divided as

in "The Rift"—would simply have been *required* to passionately embrace and kiss again, as part of a full reconciliation. However, in the culture in which *Xena: Warrior Princess* was produced (primarily North American, of the 1990s), *any physical intimacy of greater intensity* than *The Kiss* would mark out Xena and Gabrielle's relationship as *sexual*, and therefore, in this case, homosexual. This would make them *Lovers*, plain and simple. TPTB (The suits? The advertisers? The stations? Lawless? O'Connor? All of the above?) were simply *not ready for that*—not in season three, and, in terms of the series, really not *ever*.

As a result there was never a follow-up in any succeeding season to this brief physical exchange.

Callisto

———

Xena: Callisto, I didn't come here to fight!

Callisto: Well, then . . . you shouldn't have come at all.

———

Xena also features several female villains, which help balance the scales. Among the most memorable is Callisto. Again the creators play with traditional cultural images by casting in the role of Callisto a lithe, blond female (Hudson Leick) who looks like she just stepped off a California beach. The contrast to Xena is striking and purposeful, in both coloring and body type. Callisto, however, is no airhead. She is a maniacal woman warrior who resembles what Xena must have been like in the past, feeding off hate and violence. In addition, she is obsessed with Xena, even pretending to be her in one episode ("Callisto"). Not satisfied with just pretending to be Xena, the warrior in another episode ("Intimate Stranger") finally convinces Ares to allow her to enter Xena's body and live as her on Earth while Xena is forced into Callisto's body. This "freaky Friday" body swap has both sexual and psychological dimensions, as both characters begin to see the world through an enemy's eyes. Xena does regain her body, and with it an understanding of Callisto, which is part and parcel of the humanistic tone of the series.

Callisto (Hudson Leick) and Xena in one of their many struggles for dominance.

Xena Meets Julius Caesar

Hudson Leick as the evil Callisto, Xena's nemesis in the television series.

———

"Divide and conquer, my friend. You divide a woman's emotions from her sensibilities and you have her."

—Julius Caesar (in *Xena)*

———

Xena is also unique for the way it combines mythologies and histories from various cultures around the world, as witnessed by the series of episodes in countries like India and Japan. Although some critics have lambasted the show for being, at times, historically anachronistic and for twisting mythology to its own ends,

Xena remains consistent in its attempt to create a genuinely feminist mythology based on a creative use of both fact and myth.

An example of this interweaving of fact and myth is the series of episodes dealing with Julius Caesar. In these shows the filmmakers portray Caesar as a ruthless, imperialistic marauder, uninterested in the culture of the peoples he conquers, particularly the Amazons. Xena confronts him several times and battles him in defense of various indigenous peoples. Eventually Caesar, exasperated by the interference of this uppity woman warrior, crucifies Xena with her beloved Gabrielle by her side. They die on a cross. But a typical Xena-style resurrection is not far-off. In a particularly hallucinatory episode called "The Fallen Angel," the viewer experiences the afterlife with Xena and Gabrielle, as they become part of a war between the archangels of heaven and the fallen angels of hell. Although Xena has to again struggle with her dark side and the lure of the demon, she and Gabrielle ultimately come down on the side of compassion and forgiveness and so are reborn by means of a female angel who heals their bodies.

The Controversial Final Episode

———

When it first aired I was infuriated by how *Xena* ended with her trying to atone for her battered past . . .

—A loyal fan quoted on Amazon.com

———

Xena maintains its mission to the end. In the final episodes of the series, called "A Friend in Need, Parts I and II," the warrior princess travels to feudal Japan to defend a village against demonic samurai spirits. It is appropriate that the filmmakers pick feudal Japan as the site of the climax and resolution of the series. For traditionally Japan has remained one of the bastions of male dominance. In blatant defiance of this tradition, Xena dresses in samurai armor and wields a sword in defying the male legion of ghostly samurai, who fall before the weapons of a woman. Although she meets her end at the hands of one of the demons, Gabrielle is once again able to raise her from the dead. But this

time Xena decides to return to the land of the dead as an act of penitence for her many sins of the past, a constant theme in the show. And so Gabrielle leaves her companion for the last time, carrying with her the "spirit of Xena."

Many fans were displeased with Xena's death. Some wanted to see their two heroines "walk off arm and arm." And some just admitted to having a difficult time separating from a character who had become part of their lives. In the final analysis, it is a tribute to the power of the series that it inspired such intense emotions with its finale.

A scene from the final episode of *Xena: Warrior Princess*.

Weapons of Warrior Women

While most warrior women do carry a variety of exotic weapons in their arsenal, the choice of weapons between male and female characters tends split in different ways. It's pretty obvious that men like to blow things up in movies, whereas an affinity for explosives is rare in female characters. The following is a list of some of the classic weapons we see used in warrior woman films.

Above: Xena (Lucy Lawless) grasps her trademark chakram, one of several designs used throughout the series.

Opposite Top: Elektra (Jennifer Garner) transforms the traditional Amazonian weapon into a high-tech, compound-style bow.

Opposite Bottom: Abigail (Jessica Biel), in *Blade: Trinity*, with a modified compound bow that is suspiciously similar to the one used by Elektra in the image above.

Bow and Arrow

The most classic Amazon motif is undoubtedly the bow and arrow. Countless films feature women using a bow most effectively. However, it is remarkable to note how deeply rooted this symbol is for the woman warrior, as modified bows have been making appearances in many recent science fiction flicks like *Serenity* (2005). Considering that weapons of the future would be highly sophisticated, it wouldn't seem likely that an archaic bow might fit in. However, we see modified crossbows and elaborate compound bows used in movies like *Elektra* (2005) and *Blade: Trinity* (2004).

Throwing Weapons

Chakram The chakram seems to be originally an Indian weapon, hence its relation to the Sanskrit word *chakra*, meaning "circle of energy." The chakram is essentially an ideal decapitator, which is, according to Freud, also a symbol of castration. No, you don't see this one too often, but it's one of Xena's signature weapons.

Throwing Stars A mainstay of martial arts films, these are popping up more often in mainstream cinema. Prominently featured in *Sin City* was Miho's swastika-shaped throwing star. However, other weapons created by the prop department never made it to the screen due to time constraints, such as a fantastic three-blade throwing star, cast with sterling silver and a design of red flames. (You can see this weapon on page 81 of *Frank Miller's* Sin City: *The Making of the Movie* by Frank Miller and Robert Rodriguez, which is magnificently illustrated.)

Blades

A "penetrating analysis" shows us that women are partial to instruments of impalement. In *Crouching Tiger, Hidden Dragon,* Shu Lien (Michelle Yeoh) and Jen (Zhang Ziyi) go through a whole rack of different blades as they fight each other, woman to woman, over the Green Destiny, the famous sword stolen by Jen from Shu Lien's beloved man, Li Mu Bai (Chow Yun Fat).

Swords In feudal times samurais traditionally wore two swords (*daisho*): one short (*shoto-wakizashi*) and long (*daito-katana*).

They often named their swords and believed that in them resided the soul of their warriorship. In warrior women movies we first see female samurais wielding swords in such films as *Lady Snowblood* and *The Crimson Bat*, produced as part of a series in Japan in the seventies.

In recent years Western warrior women have begun to wield the weapon, most notably (and most destructively) in Quentin Tarantino's *Kill Bill* films. For the making of *Kill Bill*, 118 different fighting swords were commissioned from a martial arts facility in Siki City, Japan, at a cost of more than $65,000 dollars. Some were borrowed later for use in *Sin City*. The double-rig swords used by the character Miho are actually the same weapons used by the Crazy 88 in *Kill Bill Volume 1*.

The sword is symbolically male, a phallic weapon. The usage of swords by women in films is usually very interesting. It appears as a form of phallic empowerment, putting them on a "man's level." During *Kill Bill*, the unsheathing of swords, though no doubt a form of homage to other films also, takes on a very male ritualistic effect. The slow, sensuous unsheathing of the sword is a ceremony, a prelude to an act of life or death. The weapon is only slid out, partially at first, a tease and implied threat all at once as the combatants stare each other in the eyes.

It is revealing that at the end of *Kill Bill Volume 2*, Uma Thurman's character, Beatrix Kiddo, kills Bill by actually sheathing his sword and striking him in the heart with her bare hand. She no longer needs to enter the man's world symbolically or use a phallic instrument to win. She takes the control away from him by sheathing his weapon, rendering him momentarily vulnerable, and then kills him by literally "breaking" his heart.

Sai Originally a farm tool, it was used by farmers in Okinawa to fight marauding samurais and later adapted by karate practitioners as a weapon. It was featured prominently in the movie *Elektra*. It is interesting to note that Electra refers to it as an "offensive weapon," since these weapons were traditionally defensive, used to fend off or disarm a person of a sword. They still did double-duty as farm tools, sometimes sharpened to cut grass or cane, and Elektra might simply modify their usage to suit her needs.

Above: Eowyn (Miranda Otto) is highly accomplished with her sword, despite being banned from fighting on behalf of her people in *Lord of the Rings: Return of the King*.

Opposite Top: "Deadly little Miho" (Devon Aoki) aims her ominous swastika-shaped throwing star from Frank Miller's *Sin City*. Notice that her jewelry incorporates smaller throwing stars.

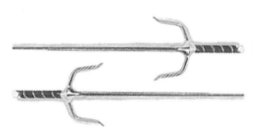

Guns

Warrior women like guns too, especially really big guns. Why? We can't say for sure. But the image of women in lingerie holding guns is very popular. Kate Nauta's character in *Transporter 2* (2005) walks around perpetually in lingerie wielding two guns. We see fallen angel Demi Moore doing the same in *Charlie's Angels Full Throttle* (2003).

There is also a lot to be said about how women are depicted holding weapons in comparison with men. Women wrap themselves around big guns in some cases. In the case of *Tank Girl*, she straddles a huge tank gun, positions it right in the face of her enemy as he is driving a truck, and asks, "Feeling a little inadequate?" Women are also often depicted holding guns up near their mouths, maybe even blowing on the tip.

Above: Lola (Kate Nauta) embodies the fantasy image of a gun-toting, lingerie-clad assassin in *Transporter 2*.

Opposite: Elektra (Jennifer Garner) assumes an offensive pose with a traditionally defensive weapon, the sai.

Poison

Poison is one weapon that in film is almost exclusively associated with women. The references to poison and women are many. There is an association between poison and snake venom, a type of poison—and snakes, of course, are signs of female sin. Poisoning someone is especially evil because it is deceitful, dishonorable. It's also sadistic, because there is usually significant suffering involved. But the whole point is that it is non-direct. It can be done anonymously. It catches one off-guard, often coming from a trusted source or confidante.

Poison and illness come into play in several female comic-book-inspired characters such as Typhoid, who appears in *Elektra* and comes closest to killing her with her deadly poisonous kiss. Even Rogue in *X-Men* seems to have a body that is a form of poison in itself. Many of these beautiful women who make people sick from touching them are a throwback from the fifties when scare tactics were utilized to discourage sexual contact between teenagers.

In her book *Aching for Beauty*, Wang Ping talks about the fascinating dual meanings of words in Chinese language and poetry. In the ancient erotic tale *The Golden Lotus,* the deadly female character Jinlian (so irresistibly alluring because of her perfectly bound feet) kills a man through sex. Ping speaks about the meaning of the word *Mei* (plum) as it is used in context with the erotic events of the story.

> *Mei* (plum) not only suggests the female genitals, femininity, and sex, but also poison, disease, and death. In fact the characters for syphilis in Chinese are *mei du*—literally, "plum poison."

Shortly after Budd (Michael Madsen) insults Elle Driver (Daryl Hannah) with a blond joke in *Kill Bill Volume 2*, he is struck in the face with a deadly black mamba snake, whose transference of venom is "gargantuan," as Elle sadistically points out to him. Budd dies in excruciating pain on the floor of his trailer, amidst a pile of pornography that he knocked over in his struggle.

Above: Typhoid (Natassia Maltha) incapacitates Elektra with her lethal, poisonous kiss.

Below: Lori Petty in *Tank Girl.*

Opposite: Jane Fonda as Barbarella illustrates adoration for a large weapon.

Novelty Weapons

If poison isn't a female enough weapon, there's always another stash of weapons that are particularly effective for a wide range of use. If you are Catwoman, that is. Imagine this arsenal:

Hair-Raising Bomb Destroys the hairdos of any women in the area.

Catamizer A specialized gun filled with catasonic acid that will "catalyze" the victim.

Cataphrenia Can be kept under the fingernails, so that when a person is scratched, they are infected with the drug. It reverses all of the victim's normal moral and ethical standards, turning them into the complete opposite of the person they used to be.

Cat-Radio Remote-control radio that sets off the school bell, so she can get out of class early (not exactly a weapon, but very useful).

Cat's Whiskers Thin ropes used to tie someone up; they contract when in contact with body heat.

Chapter 5
Haunted and Hunted Monster Killers

In her fascinating book *The Monstrous-Feminine*, Barbara Creed challenges the patriarchal view that women are conceptualized in horror films primarily as victims, stating instead that the prototype of all definitions of the monstrous is actually the female genitals and reproductive body. Contrary to classic Freudian theory that male anxiety stems from the perception of woman as castrated (and that he too shall be castrated like her, by the father), Creed offers evidence that fear is actually based on the idea of woman as *castrator*, the terrifying embodiment of *vagina dentata*. Even author Stephen King refers to such fears of female genitalia in *Bare Bones*:

> [My greatest sexual fear?] . . .The vagina dentata, the vagina with teeth. A story where you were making love to a woman and it just slammed shut and cut your penis off. That'd do it."

Particularly interesting are Creed's theories on the vampire and the witch, both of which have had far more representation in obvious female form. Witches are rarely ever presented as male. Creed outlines motifs that demonstrate that the vampire (even the male vampire) is essentially a "menstrual monster." And the witch takes on many different forms, for example, Stephen King's unforgettable blood-covered *Carrie*. By definition, several female *X-Men* characters qualify as witches also. Even ambiguous threats such as fog can be drawn back to female traits. The abject fear of the monstrous womb (presented in terrifying form in *Aliens*) and threat of reincorporation is a distinctly female threat.

RISE OF THE MACHINES

THE WAR BEGINS JULY 2

Above and Opposite: Three movie posters insinuating a dual monstrous nature of women as theme.

However, regardless of the implied sexual identity of the threatening creature/entity in horror films, the female still serves as the standard intended victim, in many cases the "final girl." It is this role that has changed much in nature over the years. As a matter of fact, many remakes of older films rewrite the female as far more strong and capable than in past versions. For instance, in George Romero's original *Night of the Living Dead* (1968), the female character Barbara sinks into a state of shock that renders her near catatonic through most of the movie. She takes action only near the end in order to save another woman, but she is attacked and taken by another zombie in the process.

This demonstration of passivity, emotional and physical weakness, the "wounded woman" syndrome, has been used extensively in film. Susan Isaacs talks about this phenomenon in her book *Brave Dames and Wimpettes,* documenting numerous films where the female protagonist is consistently portrayed lounging in bed, sleeping, comatose, ill, paralyzed, or confined to the home (her proper place). However, some filmmakers are rewriting these roles to inject more rebellion and aggression. In the 1990 version of *Night of the Living Dead,* also written by Romero, the formally passive character Barbara is remade into the only survivor, forceful and active. In *The Texas Chainsaw Massacre, Part 2,* the "final girl," Stretch, is vastly different than the screaming-squealing-running victim Sally from Part 1, who was terrorized nonstop until she conveniently had a last-minute male savior appear in a truck in the right place at the right time.

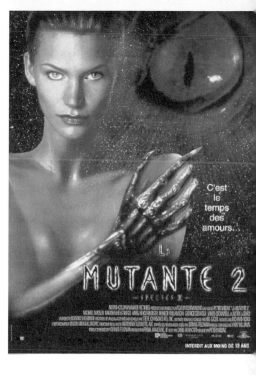

These days we see a theme of passive to aggressive transformation far more often. The Bride in *Kill Bill Volume 1* begins the film passively in a coma after being shot in the head by Bill. She is a helpless, paralyzed victim as the assassin Elle Driver, posing as a nurse, prepares to poison her, but is stopped from the act by a phone call. Later the prick of a mosquito sucking her blood suddenly wakes her from the coma. It doesn't take long to realize her plight, and regardless of the fact that her legs are too atrophied to walk, she cries out her grief and rage and begins her long and bloody revenge within minutes.

In yet another example of an "awakening" sequence, Alice, played by Milla Jovovich in *Resident Evil* (2002), awakens from a sleep with amnesia after having been rendered helpless from a nerve gas. She is incapacitated by trauma for some time, but when attacked by mutant creatures and zombies, she reacts automatically with instinctive power and acrobatic fighting techniques.

The classic Gothic heroines of the past, sensually portrayed in innocent victimhood, seem to have transformed from victim into savior—a new breed of female action hero. But taking into account Barbara Creed's ideology about the feminine nature of monsters, what does it mean when woman is fighting herself in a sense? The horror victim of the past screams and runs in fear, turning away from the horror. She fights only to protect herself or others. She does not go looking for trouble. Now, characters such as *Van Helsing's* Gothic heroine Anna (Kate Beckinsale) intentionally hunt down the monsters. In *Underworld,* Beckinsale did the same as a "death-dealer," pursuing the "lycan" (were-

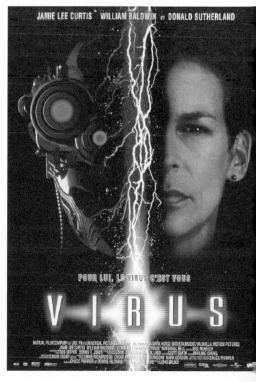

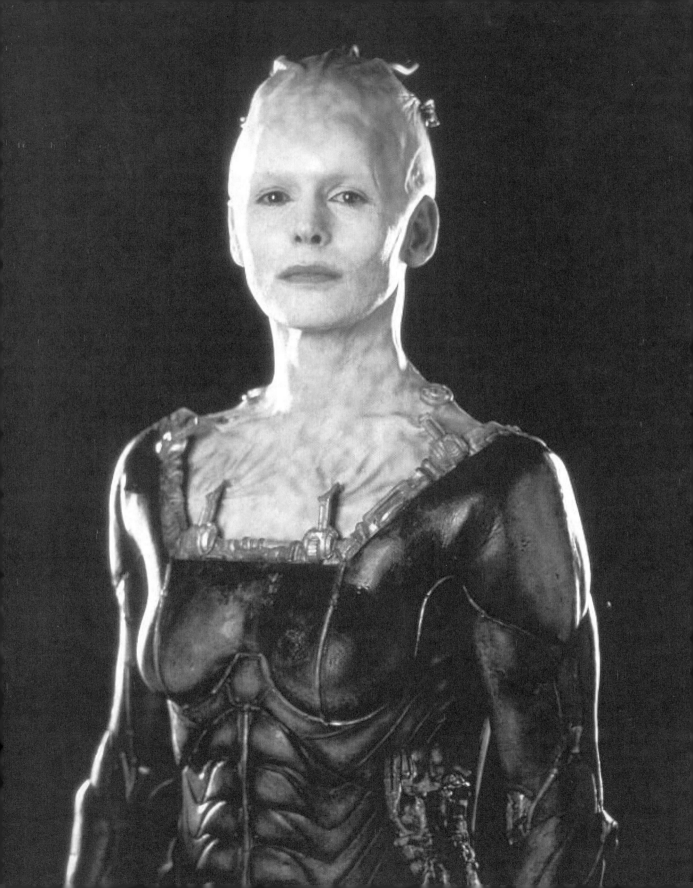

wolves). However, this time she was a monster herself also—a vampire who needs blood to survive.

The monster tends to manifest itself as the physical projection of our fears, the true nature on display, generally aggressive, highly sexual, or maybe abject, grotesque and all-engulfing. Does the female victim who avoids the monster and runs away in terror wish to escape or deny some "monstrous" part of her own nature? Does the heroine who hunts down the monster, to fight it and kill it, wish to contain and conquer the "dark" side of herself? Both the victim and female hero/savior are almost always presented as attractive and desirable. Whether they run away or fight, in both situations they *deny* reincorporation with the monstrous representation. Maybe then they are painted as "good" because they deny the alien, animal, or otherwise nonhuman side of their nature, rather than succumb to it or join with it, in which case they begin to look monstrous themselves. Consider all the horrifying depictions of women in possession movies, such as *The Exorcist* films.

We see numerous examples of female characters in science fiction or fantasy that are "half-breeds," genetically-altered, part human, or cyborgs in some cases. They might be like the character Selene in *Underworld*—a vampire, but a "good" vampire, because she has controlled her nature. She doesn't hunt mankind; she feeds off of blood, but in a non-messy, humane way via infusion or sipping from a fine crystal wine glass. Vampirism is explained as basically a virus that can spread and infect others if not controlled (much like propaganda, rebelliousness, immorality.)

Where there was previously clear-cut duality, today the lines seem to blur. The female monster killer, the new action hero, became that way because she was once the unwilling victim of the monster in most cases. She adapted to the situation and turned it around. Or maybe she was "infected." The part-Borg *Star Trek Voyager* character Seven of Nine was originally a victim as a little girl. She was a human who was caught and assimilated by the Borg, her body altered with implants that controlled her. At first after she was "rescued" and detached from the Borg Collective by Captain Janeway (another warrior woman), Seven of Nine was lost and confused. She tried to signal the Borg to come back and retrieve her. Over time she changed and even fought the

Opposite: The Borg Queen (Alice Krige) utilizes her female qualities to seduce and manipulate the android Data by activating his "emotion chip" in *Star Trek: First Contact*.

Hyperbolic gender imagery illustrated in the movie poster *The She-Creature* (1956).

Borg. But her allegiance was questionable on many occasions. Her slight deformities, the remaining Borg implants, express her as a form of half-breed, wavering on the border between two different natures.

Ridley Scott's *Blade Runner* featured a number of "skin-jobs," extremely lifelike artificially created beings, as characters. Bryant, commanding officer of the Blade Runner unit, gives Deckard the rundown on the replicants he needs to hunt down and "retire" (kill) in an early scene. "This is Zhora. She's trained for an off-world kick-murder squad. Talk about beauty and the beast, *she is both.*"

There are other female half-breeds in the science fiction horror arena that are similar, but with different leanings. *Species* (1995) presents yet another one of these genetically modified disasters. This time human DNA is spliced with alien DNA, creating a beautiful and deadly woman named Sil (Natasha Henstridge) with alien hormones raging out of control. She mates and kills. She can switch her stunning human form into a terrifying H. R. Giger–designed nightmare version of walking *vagina dentata*. She too was once a victim, kept in a cage by scientists as a little girl (albeit a dangerous little girl, with the ominous potential to reach adolescence and then unleash her full power). At the height of her power, her allegiance is to the engulfing alien side of her nature brought on by hormones. Hormones will also be blamed for causing Daryl Hannah's character growing into a giantess in the remake of *Attack of the 50 Foot Woman,* and causing the three witches of the *Charmed* TV series to turn into werewolves in one episode.

Author William Burroughs, who was very well-known to have fear of female power and genitalia, often referred to women in his writing as "not human," a different species altogether. In David Cronenberg's film interpretation of *Naked Lunch* (1991), the paranoid character Bill Lee hears voices from his typewriter (which he sees as a half-bug, half-machine). The "bug" asks him about his wife Joan Lee, "How do you know Joan Lee is even human?" His gender issues are brought vividly to life. "Women are a different species, Bill." Displacing the perceived flaws of weakness and inadequacy due to feeling overpowered or confounded by the mysterious nature of women, many writers and filmmakers project their own flaws directly onto the woman, painting her as "not human." By making her into an alien or creature incapable of having the same *human* emotions as the man, it becomes *her* fault, not his.

Even though the woman-as-victim theme has long been in effect in Gothic horror, perhaps the Amazon warrior has adapted in yet another direction and re-emerged in a slightly different form—as the prey that turns into the hunter. In the late nineteenth and early twentieth centuries, Gothic and decadent writers of the period like Edgar Allan Poe, Charles Baudelaire, J. Sheridan Le Fanu, Gustave Flaubert, H. Rider Haggard, Oscar Wilde, Hanns Heinz Ewers, Pierre Louys, and Octave Mirbeau resurrected another Amazon archetype in the form of the femme fatale.

She was a lesbian vampire in Le Fanu's *Carmilla* who formed an attachment to a shy country girl while wreaking havoc on the local population. The new femme fatale was a dancing Salome in Oscar Wilde's play of the same name, where she tormented the prophet John the Baptist and then had him beheaded (read: castrated). Haggard's lamia-like Queen Ayesha, "She Who Must Be Obeyed," ruled her hidden empire with ruthlessness as well as seductive cunning in *She*. Mirbeau in his decadent classic *Torture Garden* presented the mysterious Clara, who introduces the male protagonist to the religious ecstasies of sadomasochism in a surreal floral world she has designed. Mirbeau's brother in French decadence, Pierre Louys, in his novel *The Woman and the Puppet* (which was adapted into film several times, including Josef von Sternberg's *The Devil Is a Woman* in 1935 and Luis Bunuel's *Obscure Object of Desire* in 1977), developed the relationship between a Spanish femme fatale and a possessive older man whom she leads to destruction and ruin. German decadent Ewers in *Alraune* traced with great sympathy the depredations of a woman created artificially by a scientist in order to experiment on the male species.

"Goth" became a significant influence in warrior women films through the genres most suited to its mood, fashion, and philosophy: science fiction and horror. As early as 1927, Fritz Lang and Thea Von Harbou produced the classic science fiction film *Metropolis* with the seductive and evil cyborg (Maria—Brigitte Helm) who leads a revolt among the enslaved workers of a sleek and cold world of the future. We see the epitome of the virgin

The alien female in *Species*.

77

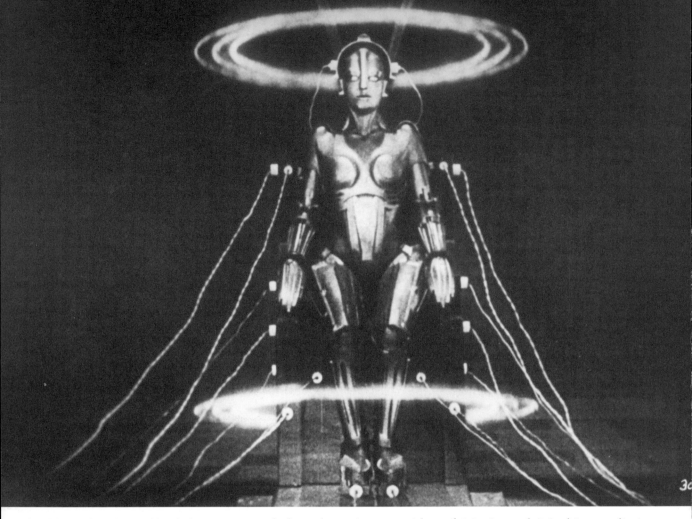

An ultimate female machine being created by the evil scientist in the silent film *Metropolis*.

and the whore in two sides of Maria and Machine, split into two separate entities. Even though the movie is silent, the images speak volumes. One particularly powerful scene actually shows a large-scale representation of *vagina dentata*. The male protagonist gazes at the giant machine that runs the city and perceives it as a hellish figure of a woman, complete with breasts and gaping mouth full of teeth. Male workers are shackled, stripped of their clothing, and forced up a flight of stairs by menacing guards with whips. They feed the monstrous machine by jumping into the great mouth full of mechanically chewing piston teeth. The scene incites not only severe castration anxiety, but also the terror of reincorporation with the great mother, loss of individuality and ego, engulfment within the woman-machine-monster, loss of all symbolic order.

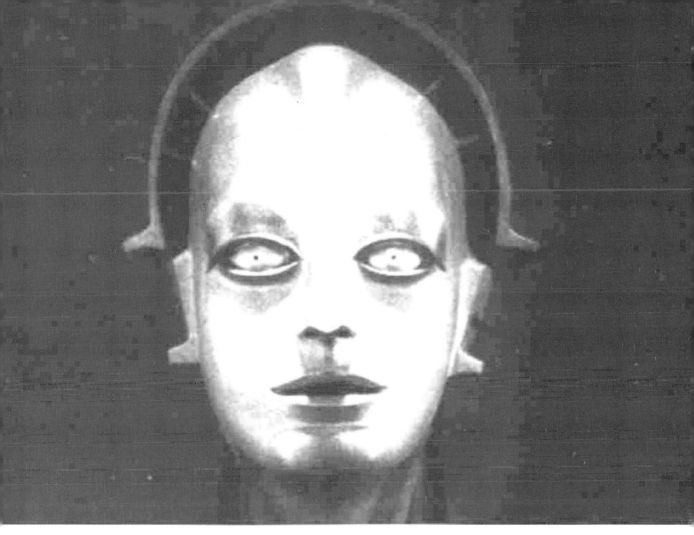

These days, sleek modern productions such as *The Matrix* series also inspire reincorporation fear, with graphic embryonic images of an adult figure plugged into a central system with a series of umbilical-like cords, floating in a pod of fluid. It's similar to the loss of identity implied in the embodiment of brainless zombies in countless horror movies, who are also quite similar to the frightening Borg Collective of *Star Trek*, all plugged into one female mind—the Borg Queen. In the case of the zombies of *Resident Evil*, there is a Red Queen, a female computer.

When female characters are the main heroes of such movies, they are usually juxtapositioned against an ineffectual male character to enhance the appearance of power. Almost inevitably the male is portrayed as less capable. But also the positioning of a "normal" woman against a feminine monstrosity, and having

A closeup of the ultimate female machine in *Metropolis*.

Sarah Michelle Gellar, with stake in hand, from the landmark television series *Buffy the Vampire Slayer*.

her conquer it in the end, reaffirms that normalcy and order can continue once the monster is conquered. She must be the one to take the lead and do it, because the ineffectual male character has failed, and she may have to save him too (from her own nature perhaps). She must temporarily take the place of the man in order to uphold the symbolic order in the end, fighting a force that she is already intimately familiar with as a woman.

In this chapter we will explore how the classic Gothic victim has changed, and how she has invaded the psyche of moviegoers, as well as saturating the world of television.

Buffy the Vampire Slayer

"Every girl who could have the power . . . will have the power . . . can stand up, will stand up. Slayers . . . every one of us. Make your choice. Are your ready to be strong?"

Joss Whedon's *Buffy the Vampire Slayer* (1997–2003), along with *Xena*, epitomizes what third-wave feminists like Irene Karras in her article "The Third Wave's Final Girl" call "girl power." Both series were aimed at young females of Generations X and Y who had rejected what they saw as the "victim feminism" of their mothers' generation for the "power feminism" of the nineties and the twenty-first century. *Buffy* (based on the 1992 movie of the same name) traces the seven-year growth of a teenage girl from perky, blond cheerleader to haunted slayer. The series attracted a huge and interactive fan base, and its appeal to fans is apparent if you look up the plethora of books published about the series, including *Buffy the Vampire Slayer and Philosophy* or *Fighting the Forces: What's at Stake in Buffy.*

The first season of the show takes up where the movie left off. Like its source, the series begins on a lighthearted note. Buffy (Sarah Michelle Gellar), who has been anointed by her last Watcher as the "slayer," flees her responsibilities for the comforts of a typical California suburb, where she plans to resume her life as a middle-class teenage girl: chasing "cute guys," cheerleading, and hanging out at the mall. Little does she know that Sunnydale High has been constructed on a "hellmouth" and that the school librarian (Giles, played by Anthony Head) is yet another Watcher in disguise. Her adventures in the first season mix horror with the comic hijinks endemic to teen comedies. She finds best friends: a shy, nerdy "schoolgirl," Willow (Alyson Hannigan), and an awkward, sex-obsessed loser, Xander (Nicholas Brendon). She meets the stereotypical "mean girl"—Cordelia (Charisma Carpenter). And she even falls for the dark "bad boy"—Angel (David Boreanaz), who just happens to be a vampire. It is a deft mix of teen misadventures, young love, and monster bashing—all given

The powerful Wicca Willow (Alyson Hannigan), foreground, with the shadowy vampire Spike (James Marsters), background.

an ironic tone by the insertion of classic lines like: "I've had it . . . You can attack me, you can send assassins after me. That's fine. But nobody messes with my boyfriend."

The Darkening Vision

The shift in tone from light to Gothic dark begins at the end of the first season when Buffy dies fighting the master vampire and is brought back to life through the intervention of Xander. This death and resurrection experience changes Buffy, who returns in the second season much moodier, more haunted. She is less breezy about her on-again, off-again relationship with Angel and even cruel to her friends, taunting Xander with her sexuality and turning a cold shoulder to Willow in the episode entitled "When She Was Bad." So unacceptable is her behavior that even Cordelia upbraids Buffy: "You're really campaigning for bitch-of-the-year, aren't you?"

Even though Buffy finds her way back to the "Scooby gang," her relationship with the brooding Angel remains tempestuous until in a moment of passion and weakness she makes love to him, releasing, unwittingly, the evil side of her lover. Buffy must then fight not only the punk vampire Spike (James Marsten) and his minions, but also Angel, who has rejoined his former associate. The season climaxes with Buffy killing her lover in order to save the world from yet another apocalypse (there are many in the series). Buffy, unable to return to normal life, leaves her friends and single mother and disappears into the city, seeking anonymity.

As the seasons progress, Buffy changes not only emotionally, becoming more introverted and self-protective, but also physically. By the third season she has become a more proficient fighter, adopting martial arts techniques. Her strength increases exponentially, surpassing that of any man in her life, including Angel and, later, the hunk soldier Riley (Marc Blucas). The creators of the show also begin to develop other women as warriors. Willow by the fourth season has become both a lesbian and a powerful Wicca who aids Buffy in her battles again the forces of evil and eventually becomes the leader when Buffy experiences a nervous breakdown in season five.

The creators also introduce the intriguing character of the dark slayer, Faith (Eliza Dushku), in season three. She is Buffy's complement physically and emotionally, externalizing all of the dark qualities in Buffy. She is openly sexual, treating men much like a traditional male treats women. She glories in battle, thriving on the adrenalin rush, and is willing to use whatever means necessary to achieve her ends, all qualities the viewer has seen in Buffy before but that the slayer has for the most part kept repressed.

Eliza Dushku as the dark slayer Faith.

In one particularly evocative episode called "Who Are You?" which crystallizes the deep connection between the two slayers, Faith and Buffy exchange bodies and experience what it is like to be the other. Faith ends the episode by saving a group of hostages, much as Buffy would have done, as she has gradually absorbed more of Buffy's positive energy. By the final season Faith has become Buffy's ally, and it is to her that Buffy entrusts the care of the young female slayers.

The Finale and a Spinoff

Every single night, the same arrangements.
I go out and fight the fight.
Still I always feel the strange estrangement.
Nothing here is real, nothing here is right.
I've been making shows of trading blows
Just hoping no one else knows
That I've been going through the motions
Walking through the part
Nothing seems to penetrate my heart.

—*Buffy the Vampire Slayer*, "Once More with Feeling"

The darkest season of the show is season six, where the Scooby gang, unable to accept Buffy's sacrifice at the end of season five, uses Willow's powers to raise an unwilling Buffy from the grave. As Buffy explains to them later in the season, in their refusal to accept her death they have dragged her from a form of "heaven" back to what for her is "hell," human life. She wanders through the season much like a zombie, unable to connect with anyone except Spike, whom she uses as a toy for sadomasochistic sexual interludes that give her a sense of being alive, at least for a moment. She gradually comes back to an acceptance of her friends and family, but the warrior is never the same.

Redemption is an important theme in *Buffy*. In fact Willow, with the aid of Buffy, is even able to restore Angel's soul, which allows him to start a new life and a new series. *Angel* (1999–2004) plops the vampire down in the midst of a *noir* landscape called Los Angeles. There he opens a detective agency, specializing in mysteries of the supernatural kind. This show also develops several female warriors during its run. Cordelia, the former "bitch goddess" of Sunnydale High, starts out as Angel's assistant, but by the end of the series has transformed herself into a an actual goddess with a deviously dark side. Fred (Amy Acker) starts the show as a geek whom Angel and his crew rescue from an alternate dimension, but by the end of the series she too has become a goddess whose powers cannot be contained or controlled.

Opposite: Sarah Michelle Gellar as Buffy.

Milla Jovovich: Alice in Apocalypticland

Of all the actresses who regularly play warrior women, Milla Jovovich delivers the most emotional and vulnerable performances while maintaining the strength and will necessary for the part. In *Resident Evil* (2002), based on the successful video game, Jovovich is a modern-day Alice in Wonderland (in a conscious reference, her name is Alice, and her nemesis is the artificial intelligence named the Red Queen). Like Alice she falls asleep, in this case because of a blast of nerve gas, and awakens to find her memory erased. She wanders through an eerie abandoned mansion, frightened by the emptiness, by the sound of a flock of birds taking flight, but most of all totally disoriented by this unfamiliar location. Just as suddenly as she was awakened, Alice is kidnapped by a group of commandos in full army gear.

The military team transports the perplexed Alice, along with a police officer, Matt (Eric Mabius), who also stumbles into the mansion, to the Beehive, the genetic laboratory of the insidious multinational Umbrella Corporation, which has been shut down by the artificial intelligence of the complex—the Red Queen—after the unit is infected by a powerful virus. Once there, they descend into a modern-day, high-tech rabbit hole and encounter riddle after riddle, all as complex as the ones in *Alice in Wonderland*, and find creatures far more frightening than those in Lewis Carroll's surreal masterpiece.

For the first part of the movie, Alice, like her namesake, is largely passive. She seems genuinely frightened and further debilitated by constant flashes of memory that are pieces to the puzzle of her identity. The military team tells her that she is a security operative who, with the man they pulled from the train, Chad (Martin Crewes), lived in the mansion aboveground. Her flashes of memory corroborate this as she remembers having sex with the man. But she also remembers meeting with a woman from Umbrella and planning to subvert the operations of the Beehive. Was she responsible for the death of thousands of employees in the complex? Or did she betray her collaborator and remain faithful to her boss? These questions haunt this modern-day Alice, wracking her with guilt and emotional upheaval that often interferes with her ability to stay in the fight and escape from the maze.

Opposite: Milla Jovovich as Alice in *Resident Evil*.

Alice (Milla Jovovich) returns to a post-apocalyptic world in *Resident Evil—Apocalypse.*

As the movie progresses the group is attacked, in video-game fashion, by various mutants who have been infected by the release of the "T-virus," including zombies, rabid dogs, and genetically altered "monsters." It is in the first battle with the zombies that Alice begins to sense her power and prowess as she dispatches the zombies with kicks, snaps their heads in her thigh locks, and performs gymnastic feats of wonder. After discovering her warrior persona, she begins to take a lead, demanding that they talk to the Red Queen in order to discover a way out of the complex, as well as an antidote for the virus, something she recalls seeing in one of her visions.

The Red Queen, like the one in *Alice,* is more devious than helpful. She is personified as a little girl bathed in red, connect-

ing her to Jovovich's Alice, who wears a red minidress through most of the movie. Alice manages to glean enough information to continue their way up the rabbit hole. Even though she is now in full warrior mode, she still registers emotions with intensity reminiscent of Jovovich's other peformances.

When the Latina commando Rain (Michelle Rodgriguez of *Girlfight*) becomes infected by a zombie and appears to die, Alice cries and then prepares to shoot her in order to save her from the fate of the undead. Rain wakes up suddenly and announces she is "not dead yet." Alice laughs happily, grabs her, and says lustfully, "I could kiss you, bitch," a line that crystallizes both sides of Alice, the traditional emotional "feminine" side and the harsher, blunter "male" side.

Rain (Michelle Rodriguez) takes aim in *Resident Evil.*

Above: Alice (Milla Jovovich) in pursuit in *Resident Evil: Apocalypse.*

The final scene of the movie finds Alice in a brightly lit laboratory room, hooked up to IV's and semi-naked on a gurney. She has escaped the underground only to be captured by the Umbrella Corporation's scientists. She screams as she rips out the tubes and pounds angrily on the window, tears flowing down her face. She does finally escape the facility, only to wander out into a city ravaged by plague and largely deserted. This final scene segues into *Resident Evil—Apocalypse* (2004), in which Alice must save the world from the virus and the mutants it has created.

In many ways *Resident Evil* is a Gothic horror movie rather than a science fiction film. It follows a number of the conventions of the Gothic movie. It begins in an abandoned mansion that the main character explores, frightened by every sound and shadow. It features horror archetypes like zombies and mad dogs. Its settings are for the most part dimly lit and shadowy. And finally the film employs black-metal music, a hybrid of heavy metal and Goth trance music, popularized by artists like Marilyn Manson, whose music is also used in this film.

Underworld, Dysfunction in the Vampire Family

With *Underworld* in 2003, *Van Helsing* in 2004, and *Underworld: Evolution* in 2006, Kate Beckinsale has entered the first rank of Goth warriors. The opening sequence of *Underworld* speaks volumes. Selene (Beckinsale) is crouched like a cat, evoking the classic image of the comic book world's Catwoman. She patiently examines the crowds below, safely ensconced on the ramparts of a Gothic structure in a city of constant rain and night. She narrates the opening, like a typical *noir* protagonist, relating the century-old battle between the vampires, her clan, and the werewolves (called lycans). She is dressed in a black vinyl coat, leather corset, and boots. Her long coat, à la *Matrix,* wafts in the wind as she examines the crowd for potential victims—*lycans* she must eliminate with her silver bullets. "I am a death-dealer . . . I live for it." Soon she spots a lycan and pounces on her victim's trail, following him to a subway where a violent shootout ensues.

After this unresolved battle where the lycans seem to be pursuing a human victim, a rare occurrence the audience is told, a perplexed Selene returns in her modern sports car to a Gothic mansion where others in her clan sit dressed in nineteenth-century corsets, gowns, and formal suits and enjoy the decadent lifestyle their obvious wealth affords them. Selene, however, ignores her sybaritic friends. She is intent on discovering the mystery behind this human named Corvin (Scott Speedman) and why the lycans have suddenly emerged in full force when they were defeated ages ago.

Selene is an intense, brooding vampire who rejects the advice and affection of her peers. Revenge motivates her, as it does so many women warriors. In her case, the anger is directed at the lycans, who were responsible for the murder of her family (another absentee father situation) when she was a child. Because of her single-mindedness, she finds herself in conflict with the new leader of her clan, Kraven (Shane Brolly), who has a secret agenda, one that includes an alliance with the lycan leader Lucian (Michael Sheen). Selene defies Kraven on every level, particularly in his desire to mate with her. In frustration she turns to her "foster father," Victor (Bill Nighy), the ancient vampire sleep-

Opposite: Selene (Kate Beckinsale), warrior and vampire in *Underworld: Evolution.*

93

Selene (Kate Bekinsale) with another crossbow-style weapon common to modern Amazons in *Underworld: Evolution*.

ing in a chamber below ground, and awakens him with her own blood.

The Oedipal dimensions of Selene's devotion to the vampire who saved her from the lycans, "turned her" into a vampire, and raised her as a daughter color the second half of the film as Selene defies Victor to save Corvin, whose DNA has the power to give lycans immortality. She escapes from the house arrest Victor has imposed on her and tracks Corvin to the lycan underground laboratories. There she learns from Lucian the truth about Victor, that he in fact killed her family, not the lycans. When Victor shows up to eliminate Lucian and destroy Corvin, Selene fights her surrogate father, slicing his head in two with her sword.

Selene's relationship with Corvin, the ostensible love interest, is worth mentioning because it expresses the dominant/submissive dimensions suggested by many of the female/male relationships in warrior women films, drawing much of its imagery and tone

Selene chooses yet another style of weapon from her arsenal.

from the world of fetish and kink (e.g., witness the scene where Selene takes great pleasure in handcuffing Corvin to a chair). It is obvious very early on that Selene is attracted to the handsome Corvin. She circles around him, smelling him, and touching his body in a very animal-like manner. But her interest seems far more sexual than romantic.

Selene's response to Corvin is visceral, not emotional. Her emotions are much more directed toward Victor, the only man to whom she is willing to bow, literally and figuratively. Corvin himself, at least until he turns into a vampire/lycan in the final scene, is a weak character who needs to be rescued by Selene several times, including during the final battle with Victor. This may be the reason the filmmakers chose to have no romantic reconciliation between the two as the film fades out. The final shot is of Selene walking away from the body of Victor, victorious but saddened.

Van Helsing, Vampires, Werewolves, and Frankenstein

In *Van Helsing* (2004), Beckinsale plays Princess Anna Valerious, the heir to a Transylvanian land that is overrun with vampires, werewolves, and even Frankenstein's creature. Apparently, all these different creatures just can't coexist in peace. When the audience first sees her she is, as in *Underworld*, fighting werewolves, this time to save her brother. The camera pans fetishistically up her boots and corset to reveal her in low angle wielding a sword. Her fighting abilities, like those of many of the screen's modern women warriors, are preternatural. She defies gravity, incorporates martial arts into her style, and is able to withstand the most horrendous punishment.

Anna's chief nemesis is Dracula, but more specifically the brides of Dracula, with whom she battles several times. The brides can fly as half-bat/half-female and lift humans from the ground. Their speed and ferociousness overpower most mortals, including at times Anna herself. Anna is willful and stubborn, however, even refusing, at least initially, the aid of the infamous demon slayer Van Helsing (Hugh Jackman). She suspects his motives, asking him if he is "a murderer or a holy man." But in order to save her brother, who has become a werewolf-slave of Dracula (Richard Roxburgh), and protect her people from the hordes of vampire children Dracula and his brides are procreating, she agrees to put aside her scruples and work with this mysterious man.

The look of *Van Helsing* is classic movie Gothic. It even opens with a black-and-white sequence modeled after the Universal horror films of the thirties and forties, a sequence that sets the ironic, postmodern tone of the whole movie. Anna lives in Dracula's ornate mansion, while the master himself hides out in Dr. Frankenstein's brooding castle. The battles are staged mostly at night or within the shadowy mansions and castles of Transylvania.

The climax of the movie begins once the brides capture Anna and deliver her to Dracula as another bride. The masquerade ball scene, where Dracula hopes to cement the "marriage" with Anna

Above: The brides of Dracula in *Van Helsing.*

Opposite: Anna (Kate Beckinsale) about to draw sword, from *Van Helsing.*

Anna (Kate Beckinsale) in corset, boots, and all, from *Van Helsing.*

while tricking Van Helsing into returning Frankenstein's creature to him, visually quotes one of the landmark Gothic vampire films of the sixties: Roman Polanski's black comedy *The Fearless Vampire Killers.* Vampires in high Gothic dress glide around the room in front of a huge mirror, in which, of course, they do not appear, as Dracula holds the still defiant Anna in his grasp through mesmerism.

Anna and Van Helsing take on Dracula, his brides, and his minions in the final sequence of the movie. As Anna stakes the brides Van Helsing, now part werewolf, battles Dracula and defeats him with a bite. Anna then rushes to Van Helsing, injecting him with an antidote and returning him to human form. But in the process Anna is mortally wounded.

The coda of the movie takes the viewer back to the Amazon films of *Conan,* most particularly the first one, *Conan the Barbarian.* Van Helsing stages a funeral for the heroic Anna. He builds a pyre for her and immolates her body in a Viking-style memorial. In this way the movie links Anna to her Amazon ancestors while deifying her as both princess and warrior.

Witchblade, Noir Meets the Warrior Woman

In *Witchblade* (2000–2002), based on the comic book of the same name, the filmmakers create a hybrid, much as Joss Whedon in *Angel* did, by grafting the supernatural onto a *film noir* story. Rather than a detective in Los Angeles like Angel, Sara Pezzini (Yancy Butler) is a New York cop who finds herself "chosen" as the inheritor of the powerful witchblade gauntlet, worn by such prestigious women warriors as Queen Boudicca and Joan of Arc. As a result, Sara synthesizes two archetypes, that of the warrior woman and that of the *film noir* protagonist (epitomized by such male characters as Jeff Bailey in *Out of the Past* and Steve Thompson in *Criss Cross).*

Sara is a mass of contradictions and dark conflicts. Her favorite saying is "Another day above ground is a special day," indicating her guarded and wary attitude toward life. She is haunted by a series of deaths: her model friend, her policeman father, her partner Lee (Danny Woo), and her Irish lover Conchabar (Kim de Lury), and spends much of the series attempting to investigate and avenge these various murders.

In the case of Lee, Sara is most successful in that she is able, at the beginning of the second season, to resurrect him through the power of the witchblade, which allows her to reverse time in that instance and create a different series of events. Ultimately, however, her often righteous anger and her sense of justice compel her to "do the right thing," but they also cause her to become a loner. She often hides out in her dark New York apartment, refusing to return phone calls, even from those who have her best interests at heart.

To add to her burden, Sara becomes the inheritor of the witchblade and subject to numerous attacks by the forces who wish to possess the powerful gauntlet. In "Periculum," she even undergoes a painful physical transformation that results in the witchblade being incorporated into her body. Her struggle with this burden is not only physical, but also psychological. Much like Buffy, she resists the mantle of "the chosen one" because she knows it will lead to suffering and sacrifice throughout her life, which it does. She loses Conchabar, the only man she is attracted to in the series, to a group of Irish militants who want to exchange him for a captive brother. And although she attempts to rescue him and almost succeeds, she is thrown again into despair and isolation after his murder by Fiona, one of the militants who momentarily takes control of the witchblade.

On a more "realistic," less supernatural level, Sara must fight the White Bulls, a group of vigilante cops who become a law unto themselves and may have been responsible for the death of her father. Her battle with them becomes even more complex when her partner Jake (David Chokachi) joins the organization out of his despair over being ignored by the distant Sara. With twists in the plot like this, the show continually moves from the territory of fantasy and the supernatural to the more mundane *noir* concerns of police corruption and loyalty between friends.

Sara (Yancy Butler), cop and warrior, displaying her witchblade weapon in *Witchblade*, the television series.

Tru Calling, Daddy Issues

In *Tru Calling* (2003–2005), Eliza Dushku (Faith from the *Buffy* series) plays a young woman who is haunted not only by the past, but also by a transcendental "calling" that invades every dark corner of her personal life. Tru Davies, while working as a morgue attendant, finds that she has the power to speak to the dead and then to relive the day over again in order to alter the chain of events that led to the death. Tru is a warrior battling not only potential killers and accidental chains of events, but also time.

Like many recent women warriors, including Buffy, Elektra, Lara Croft, and Sydney from *Alias,* Tru finds herself inextricably bound in the web of an Oedipal complex. Firstly, she has inherited this power to relive days from her mother, whose murder she witnessed as a small girl. It is an event she replays in her mind over and over and that she admits has heightened her fervor in saving others, as surrogates for the mother she could not save.

Secondly, Tru's relationship with her father (Cotter Smith) is troubled, to say the least. He deserted his three children after his wife's murder and married his mistress, a sin for which Tru is never able to forgive him. And although Tru does reconcile to some degree with him and his new wife, actually saving the wife from a brutal killer in the episode "Daddy's Girl," her feelings of resentment and distrust never fully disappear.

The absent father is a theme, as mentioned before, that runs through so many of the warrior women films of the last two decades, reflecting in fantasy form the statistical reality of the increase in single-mother families in American society. This hostility toward "the father" takes on a further ironic dimension in *Tru Calling* as the viewer learns by the end of the first season that Tru's father was responsible for the murder of her mother and that he is in fact her enemy, an agent of death who fights "to keep the dead *dead*." In fact he forms a conspiracy with Jack (Jason Priestley), a mysterious employee of the morgue who the audience later finds out is also an agent of death, to defeat his daughter in her resurrection activities. In "Two Weddings and a Funeral," Tru learns the truth about Jack and loses her lover in the process.

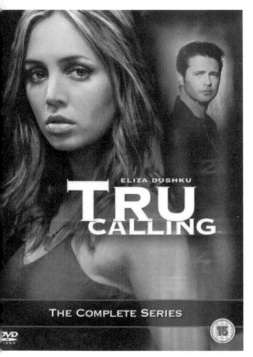

ELIZA DUSHKU

TRU CALLING.

THE COMPLETE SERIES

Charmed, the Sisterhood Is Powerful and Deadly

The Wiccan Trio from the long-running television series *Charmed.*

Paige: We're demons?

Piper: No, Paige, we are not demons.

Phoebe: We're monsters.

Paige: Okay, I knew we were a little testy this time of the month, but this is just crazy.

There are several reasons for the longevity of the WB series *Charmed* (1998–2006). One is, like *Buffy,* the show has an active fan base (in this case, largely female), which communicates with the producers and stars of the show through postings and chatrooms.

Secondly, the series is willing to deal openly with topics that some others would shy away from. For instance, in a seventh-season episode called "Once in a Blue Moon" the three Wiccan sisters suffer from PMS, and the rare "blue moon" that is rising makes it worse. The combination causes the sisters' normal PMS symptoms to implode and results in their transformations into werewolf-like creatures—very much a physical projection of the "menstrual monster."

The setting for the show is classic Gothic. It is a Victorian mansion set above the city of San Francisco. There the three attractive, single (at least initially, for later in the series Piper marries her spiritual protector, a "whitelighter") sisters who reside in a female form of the nuclear family (notice that warrior women are so often portrayed in trios). Prue (Shannen Doherty) is the dominant one. She has internalized much of the characteristics of the father figure she so despises for deserting his daughters at a young age. Piper (Holly Marie Combs) is the mediator, taking on the traditional mother role, eventually even marrying and giving birth to a "chosen one." Phoebe (Alyssa Milano) is the rebellious teen figure, highly sexual and stridently defiant.

Predictably the show presents the Wiccan powers these three have inherited as burdens as well as gifts. All of their relationships with others, including boyfriends, are stunted because of their need for secrecy and subterfuge in order to carry out their often metaphysical battles. (Again, the standard theme of powerful women being too "difficult" to be with men for long and emotionally isolated/punished because of their dominant powers.) Although they try to maintain somewhat normal everyday lives—Piper as an entrepreneur and mother, Phoebe as a writer, Prue as a photographer—their mission prevents such normality on a regular basis, throwing them into conflict with the world around them, as well as within their own tight circle. "The power of three" ultimately holds them together as sisters, but it is also responsible for the death of Prue and the dissolution of Piper's marriage. Like many of the women in these films, the sisters of *Charmed* often yearn for a life free of responsibility but by the final fade-out have come down on the side of duty and honor.

Peta Wilson as Mina Harker in *The League of Extraordinary Gentlemen.*

The League of Extraordinary Gentlemen, Mina Harker

Mina (Peta Wilson) battles the devious Dorian Gray (Stuart Townsend) in *The League of Extraordinary Gentlemen.*

"You're sweet . . . and you're young. Neither are traits that I hold in high regard."

—Mina to Tom Sawyer

In the 20th Century Fox adaptation of Alan Moore's inventive comic book series *The League of Extraordinary Gentlemen* (2003), Mina (played by Peta Wilson) is probably the most charismatic member, aside from perhaps her former lover Dorian Gray (Stuart Townsend). The part was originally designed for Monica Bellucci, but played with stylish charm by Peta Wilson. Alan Moore's Mina, however, was a far more complex and

MINA HARKER

shaded character than her cinematic sister. In creating the character, Moore picked up on the ambiguity at the end of Bram Stoker's novel *Dracula* as to whether or not Mina's vampiric infection could rear its ugly head again, even though her "sire" was dead. Moore's Mina *is* a vampire, but she does not, like the movie Mina, suck blood, wear leather corsets, or shapeshift.

In addition, in Moore's vision, Mina possesses qualities of leadership lacking in the movie Mina. While the filmmakers underlined her blood lust and sexuality (she even has a brief sexual interlude with Dorian Gray), Moore's Mina takes over direction of the League from the laudanum-addicted and aging Quatermain, as well as delivering the final blow to the archvillain M.

Peta Wilson's Mina may not show outer leadership, but she subtly steers the men and definitely holds her own ground. She uses wit as well as any weapon. In one initial scene at the end of a group scuffle, she is held captive momentarily, leading the men to think she is helpless. However, she simple turns and rips out her captor's throat and consumes his blood in a lustful frenzy, to the shock of those present. When finished, she elegantly dabs some blood off her lip with a handkerchief, murmuring, "Excuse me."

Also in the end, she does not show any emotional weakness toward her handsome former lover Dorian Gray (Stuart Townsend). They participate in a vigorous fight to the death (which is difficult, since they are both immortal), sparring with words in between blows.

Dorian Gray: Ah. The bedroom, Mina. Does it give you memories? Or ideas?

Mina Harker: Ideas.

[*Mina kicks him upward*]

Dorian Gray: If that had been permanent, I'd have been very upset.

Opposite: Peta Wilson as Mina in *The League of Extraordinary Gentlemen.*

Blade's Trinity, "A Knife of Sadness in My Heart"

In the third film of the *Blade* series, *Blade: Trinity* (2004), the half-human, half-vampire who has dedicated himself to eliminating his bloodsucking half-brothers as a species reluctantly takes on two partners as vampire slayers: the largely comic sidekick Hannibal (Ryan Reynolds) and the deadly and youthful slayer Abigail (Jessica Biel, who will reprise in 2005 her role as a woman warrior in *Stealth*). Abigail is the daughter of Blade's old friend and mentor Whistler (Kris Kristofferson), who is killed at the beginning of the film.

When the audience first sees Abigail, she is dressed up like a poor woman, carrying what looks like a baby. A group of skater vampires mark her as their prey. As they attack the seemingly helpless woman, the baby is thrown through the air, causing a sense of tension and panic. The vampire who catches it soon finds out that it is a deadly doll with the words "Fuck you" written on it. "Tell me if it hurts, chica," one of the vampires taunts her as he begins the attack.

With great skill, Abigail throws off her disguise and eliminates the vampires with a combination of blades and a classic Amazonian weapon: a bow with modified arrows. As she mounts the lead vampire, she turns his own words against him, "Tell me if it hurts, chica," thereby emasculating the vampire as she destroys him.

The world of Blade is, as he says to a small child, "not nice." It is a city almost always seen at night, with brightly lit neon skyscrapers towering over the streets and the violence below like disinterested mythic gods. It is a world constantly in a state of war, as the slayers battle not only vampires, but corrupt and ignorant city officials as well. Loss is a constant in Abigail's life: her father, her best friend. But still she fights on. Once again, we must assume that her warrior ways are motivated by loss, especially of a father, and desire for revenge. By having such a motivation, she is in essence given a pass to behave outside of her assigned gender role.

In the final confrontation the trio must face the iconic Gothic figure of Dracula (Dominic Purcell). While Hannibal is tortured

Jessica Biel, bow in hand, in *Blade: Trinity.*

by the sexually sadistic vampire Danica (Parker Posey, with a lot of eyeliner), who delights in thrusting her stiletto heel into his open wound, and Blade is otherwise occupied being pummeled by the king of vampires, it is Abigail who saves the day. She delivers, via her bow, the arrow tipped with a virus that can destroy not only Dracula, but his followers as well. Abigail saves the city of night once again and then disappears into the darkness, accompanied by her two fellow "nightstalkers."

Abigail (Jessica Biel) demonstrating her martial arts skills in *Blade· Trinity*.

Woman and the Serpent

Above: Poster from the surrealist movie *Possession* (1981) depicting the seductive side of Medusa imagery.

Throughout time women have been associated in myths with serpents in the form of snakes, dragons, and hydras. In Asian culture there are numerous stories about woman-snakes, who are often beneficial and willing to grant wishes to those who pamper them. In ancient Greek myths the Pythia, named after the Python that Apollo slew, were the oracle-priestesses of Delphi who delivered the prophecies from Apollo to pilgrims who sought their aid. In Minoan culture snake goddesses/priestesses led rituals in the sacred city of Knossos. Icons of them in mid-dance survive to this day.

It is only with the development of the Judaeo-Christian mythology over the last two millennia in the West and its obsession with repressing female power that snakes suddenly turned evil. The archetypal story is, of course, the Garden of Eden, where the snake, associated with Satan, inspires Eve, the first woman, to defy God's will and follow her own, leading to her punishment: "I will greatly multiply thy sorrow and thy conception; in sorrow thou shalt bring forth children; and thy desire shall be to thy husband, and he shall rule over thee."(Genesis 3:16)

The monstrous creature Medusa of early Greek mythology presents classic split representations of women, which are key elements to any assertive women presented on film. Athena transforms the beautiful young Medusa into a snake-haired monster as punishment for the "crime" of having been raped in her temple by Poseidon. From then on, her powerful female gaze turns men into stone. Medusa has been compared, by Freud and others, to the site of female genitalia, reproduction, life and death.

The serpent has been constantly placed in association with women throughout history, and frequently raises its head in me-

Opposite: Artist Lena Kartzov as Minoan Snake Goddess.
Photo by Nina Ruchirat.

Page 111: Diana Rigg as Mrs. Peel in a controversial episode from the television series *The Avengers*.

Above: Salma Hayek as Santanico Pandemonium in the Tarantino-Rodriguez horror film *From Dusk 'Til Dawn.*

Below: Poster for the Mario Bava horror classic *Black Sunday* (1960) depicts star Barbara Steele with Medusa-like tresses.

dia. The Western cinema took up the Christian equation of female = snake = evil and over its history has projected out into darkened theaters various images of evil women with serpent-like qualities, particularly in the genre of horror. In *Cult of the Cobra Woman* (1955), Faith Domergue plays the incarnation of an Asian snake goddess who takes revenge on a group of GI's who disrupt her cult of lamia worshippers. In 1961 British director Sidney Furie brought to the screen the story of a deadly serpent-woman named Atheris. Never to be outdone, Hammer Studios in 1964 made *The Gorgon,* which told of a visitation by the mythical Greek serpent-woman to the twentieth century, where she continues to turn offenders into stone. In 1971 Jack Hill, director of the Pam Grier warrior films *Coffy* and *Foxy Brown*, co-produced in Mexico *Isle of the Snake People* with Boris Karloff. In the film the exotic performer Tongolele dances with snakes in a ritual of the cursed. In *Blade Runner* (1982), Ridley Scott places his Amazon replicant Zhora (Joanna Cassidy) in a futuristic strip club, where she danced with snakes. And, of course, in 1996 we are introduced to Santanico Pandemonium (Salma Hayek), an exotic dancer/vampire/Aztec goddess who performs with a white python and in so doing not only invokes cheap horror films like Jack Hill's *Isle of the Snake People,* but links herself back to the Pythia of ancient Delphi.

In more specifically warrior women films, we see Roger Corman placing his valiant Viking women in peril as they battle a rather unconvincing-looking sea serpent in his *Saga of the Viking Women* (1957). In *Conan the Barbarian* (1982), the Amazon Valeria (Sandahl Bergman) is the only thief who has successfully entered the sanctuary of the snake cult, and for that infraction she is slain later in the film by a snake arrow that takes on symbolic overtones. Quentin Tarantino takes a more modern and feminist perspective in his *Kill Bill* films. He returns snakes to their mythical source by associating them with female power. His band of assassins is called the Deadly Viper Assassination Squad, and the members take on snake names as part of their ritual, for example, the Bride, aka Black Mamba; O-Ren, aka Cottonmouth; and Elle aka California Mountain Snake.

Chapter 6
Superheroes and Their Archenemies

Badly drawn, badly written, and badly printed—a strain on the young eyes and young nervous systems—the effect of these pulp-paper nightmares is that of a violent stimulant. Their crude blacks and reds spoil a child's natural sense of colour; their hypodermic injection of sex and murder make the child impatient with better, though quieter, stories. Unless we want a coming generation even more ferocious than the present one, parents and teachers throughout America must band together to break the "comic" magazine.

—Sterling North, *Chicago Daily News*, May 8, 1940

Frederic Wertham's condemning book *Seduction of the Innocent* warned parents about the subversive evil of comic books and nearly devastated the industry, spurring the introduction of the Comics Code Authority. Wertham points out

The only difference between surreptitious pornographic literature for adults and children's comic books is this: in one it is a question of attracting perverts, in the other of making them.

The appearance of warrior women on the pages of comics began slowly after the premiere of Wonder Woman and Catwoman in DC comics. In the seventies female superheroes spread throughout the comic world, including figures like Batgirl, Supergirl,

the women of Marvel's *X-Men*, and eventually to that offshoot of comics, video games like *Dungeons and Dragons, Mortal Kombat, Tomb Raider, Final Fantasy*, and *Everquest*, where female fantasy characters proliferated. Most of these games have been translated onto the big screen. *Mortal Kombat* is in production on its third sequel, *Mortal Kombat: Devastation*.

The representations of women in comics and games can be seen in several contexts. They can be action heroines, sex objects, icons, victims, or all of the above. This chapter explores some of the female characters that have made it to the screen and become household names, either as a superhero, a villain, or something in between.

Wonder Woman (1976–1979)

The figure of Wonder Woman has become a true cultural icon over the last several decades. Even characters in contemporary television shows like *Friends* and *The OC* have made references to fantasizing about having their girlfriends dress as Wonder Woman. Frank Miller's comic *Sin City* briefly depicted one the women of Old Town wearing a Wonder Woman outfit. The elevation of this classic Amazon warrior to pop-icon status began with her creation at DC Comics as a female counterpart to Superman. Appearing often with him in the Justice League series of the forties, Wonder Woman was designed, according to creator William Marston, to act as a role model for females: strong, independent, and intelligent. Consequently, his vision of Wonder Woman and her alter ego Diana Prince fit neatly into the second-wave feminist movement of the seventies and echoed deeply within young women of the period.

Lynda Carter was a struggling actor at the end of her savings, borrowing rent money, when the news finally came that she had won the role of Wonder Woman. Carter talks about what it was like for female actors back in the day when she was trying out for the part. "There just weren't any lead roles like this for women. If you wanted to work, you had to play a hooker, a secretary or a mother."

The role was a grueling one for her though. Waking up at 4:30 AM each morning, she spent the first couple of hours hav-

Opposite: The classic pose that influenced generations of artists and filmmakers: Lynda Carter as Wonder Woman.

ing her hair curled with the old-fashioned-style rods that sat in a small oven to warm up. The effect was so harsh that she says she had very little hair left after the end of the series. She also had trouble with her eyes, as she could hardly see at all without glasses. Sometimes in order to hit her marks (little marks made on the ground for actors to step on during scenes for purposes of lighting and camera focus) she had to have small sandbags placed on the ground. But regardless of the challenges, Lynda Carter enjoyed her time as Wonder Woman and was immensely successful with fans, especially women, who felt inspired by her character as a role model.

The legendary Wonder Woman costume first made its appearance back on Amazon Island when her mother had it made for her. Before that, the Amazon women of the island ran about in pastel-colored mini-togas. Wonder Woman's new patriotic stars-and-stripes apparel originally came with a matching wraparound skirt. However, the first time the skirt was removed in that episode, the audience took a collective breath at the sight of Carter's figure, and the skirt was never to be seen again.

Influenced by Batman's campy success, producers originally strove to make the episodes a bit on the corny side. But by the middle of the second season the producers began to sense a shift in the political and cultural wind, with the plethora of independent superwomen in series like *Charlie's Angels, Isis, Police Woman,* and *The Bionic Woman,* and they radically reduced the role of Trevor, her ostensible "boyfriend." In addition, they allowed Diana Prince's character to become more modern in her look, utilizing slacks in the office and various sleek bodysuits, such as her coordinated diving suit, when involved in operations. By the second season the producers had also abandoned the forties as their milieu and updated the stories to contemporary times.

Wonder Woman, the series, also introduced the character of Wonder Girl, aka Drusilla, Wonder Woman's sister, played by Debra Winger. Drusilla assisted Diana in a number of her espionage missions, notably in the two-part show "Feminum Mystique." In this long-form episode Nazis invade Paradise Island, the Amazon homeland, and try to harness the female power of the island for their own nefarious purposes. The sisters unite to defeat their enemies and once again save the world from evil.

Above: Wonder Woman (Lynda Carter) in a special operations wetsuit from the TV series.

Opposite: Wonder Woman (Lynda Carter), in disguise as a blonde on Amazon Island, deceives her mother, the Queen, in the pilot episode of the *Wonder Woman* TV series.

117

The Dynamic Duo's Deadly Divas

One of the first comic book warrior women to make the jump from page to screen, albeit the small screen, was DC's Catwoman. Her success paved the way for many others to come. In many ways Catwoman was the character most rooted in the world of fetish and sadomasochism, which is the way she has been played most recently in *Batman Returns* and *Catwoman*. The fact that *Batman's* comic author Bob Kane and his artists spent an inordinate amount of time creating and then designing her catsuit and whip testifies to her importance, at least to her creator, as an icon of fetish art. Frank Miller took all this yet another step by foregrounding the fetish elements of Catwoman's character in his *Batman: Year One* comic book series and turning her into a dominatrix.

The series *Batman* (1966–1968) remains a campy artifact of sixties television, which tried to corner the youth counterculture with shows like *Laugh-In* and *The Smothers Brothers*. As it turned out, the series was extremely successful in its first seasons. Emphasizing puns and witty quips, comic book–like bubbles, bright primary colors, it attracted famous guest stars like Milton Berle and Vincent Price, who took on roles as supervillains, and stars of other shows like Bruce Lee and Van Williams of *The Green Hornet,* who appeared in cameos.

The Original Catwoman

"When I flip that switch, the noise will be *excruciating*. [*She purrs.*] Shortly following that, your brains will be turned into . . . yech. And then you can be mine FOREVER, Batman! True, I'll have to sacrifice your intellect. Oh well, with a build like yours, who cares?"

—Catwoman, *Batman*

If anyone was meant to define the power of the infamous catsuit in no uncertain terms, it was the unforgettable Julie Newmar in the debut of the *Batman* TV series. Newmar assisted in the de-

Opposite: For many the most memorable Catwoman, Julie Newmar from the television series *Batman.*

119

Julie Newmar in her self-designed Lurex catsuit.

sign of the catsuit she wore, using a shiny, slinky material called Lurex to emphasize her dancer's body and accessorizing with a low-slung hip belt.

Julie had gained some notoriety previously for her part as Stupefyin' Jones, a six-foot-two-inch walking secret weapon who could turn men to stone by merely swinging her hips a certain way. Her part in the production of *Li'l Abner* (1959) was only ninety seconds long, but it seemed to stupefy even the reviewers, who raved over her performance, referring to Julie as a "stacked skyscraper."

Julie was intelligent, poised, and talented, an actor and dancer whose graceful feline movements made her ideal for the part of Catwoman, which her brother, Dr. John Newmeyer, encouraged her to accept. Even though she only ended up shooting a dozen episodes due to other commitments, she is so well remembered that she was even paid homage in the 1995 movie *To Wong Foo, Thanks For Everything, Julie Newmar*.

Possibly a part of her success in maintaining Catwoman's striking dominant persona (in addition to the stunning catsuit) is that the creators of the TV show decided to eliminate her alter ego—the mild-mannered Selina—for purposes of economy and to foreground her devious qualities as Batman's foil. This Catwoman projected, like she did in the comics, a distinct sexual quality. Yet her duality showed up in fleeting moments of apparent vulnerability toward Batman (Adam West), although it also appeared that she might be batting him around with her charms, as a cat to a mouse. It is interesting to note that Catwoman was often shot at an upward camera angle, so that she was generally gazing down at the viewer.

In the episode "Scat, Darn Catwoman" (1967), when cornered and caught, Catwoman gazes down at Batman from a rooftop.

Batman: I'll do everything I can to rehabilitate you.

Catwoman: Marry me.

Batman (looking distinctly uncomfortable): Anything but that!

Adam West chuckles when looking back at that episode in DVD commentary, reminiscing about his character Batman's reaction to Catwoman's marriage proposal. Offered a proposal by this incredible woman, Batman protests, "But what about Robin?"

Flipping back into bad-girl mode, Catwoman presents a solution to that dilemma:

"Robin??? Hmm . . . Oh, I've got it! We'll kill him."

Catwoman escapes capture, of course, to live on and torture Batman and Robin another day. She enjoyed taunting them with nicknames such as the "Dynamic Drips" or the "Turgid Twosome" and dismissing young Robin as "Boy Blunder" or the "Tenacious Teenager." She provided the sexual tension that the show desperately needed in contrast to Batman and Robin's squeaky-clean conservatism.

As unpredictable as a cat herself, Newmar left the show to pursue other opportunities, despite her great success in the part. The much coveted role was given next to former Miss America Lee Meriwether, who also starred in the feature film made to capitalize on the success of the series. Meriwether did not disappoint in the role and was also well-liked by fans.

Eartha Kitt enjoys herself as the new Catwoman in the television show *Batman.*

Eartha Kitt

"She may be evil, but she *is* attractive. You'll know more about that in a couple of years, Robin."

—Batman

Very memorable to many was Eartha Kitt's performance as Catwoman. According to articles of the period, producer Bill Dozier picked her because

She was a catwoman before we ever cast her as Catwoman. She had a catlike style. Her eyes were catlike and her singing was like a meow.

Eartha Kitt had a different, perhaps more commanding tone than her predecessors, and as Dozier noted, her voice was almost a true purr. She didn't seem to need men so much as she liked to simply collect them and taunt them. Her use of language was often unique. The following exchange takes place when Batman and Robin approach her for capture in one episode:

> *Batman:* Now are you going to come quietly, Catwoman? Or are we going to have to use force?
>
> *Catwoman (purring from her throne):* Your silver-tongued oratorical has convinced me, Batman. I hereby remit myself to your *muscular* custody.

"Life's a Bitch, and Now So Am I"

Batman Returns (1992), Tim Burton's sequel to his Gothic and heavily influential *Batman* (1989), concentrates more on the caped crusader's foes, namely the Penguin and Catwoman, than on the dark knight himself. Fans' excitement about the introduction of the beloved Catwoman on-screen was immense, and the role was aggressively sought after. Actor Sean Young (who had been slated to play Vicki Vale in the first *Batman* but had to withdraw due to an injury) is said to have gone as far as showing up at the Warner Bros. lot in a homemade Catwoman costume with an entourage of assistants carrying walkie-talkies to track down Tim Burton. According to Marion Dougherty, the casting director at the time, Burton hid in the bathroom.

Michelle Pfeiffer in a custom-formed catsuit from Tim Burton's *Batman Returns.*

Annette Bening was offered the role of Catwoman but chose pregnancy instead. Finally, the coveted role was taken by Michelle Pfeiffer. Selena, Catwoman's restored alter ego, first appears on-screen during an attack on Gotham city by Penguin's circus troupe of killers. Selena stumbles through the mayhem, dropping files and mumbling to herself, almost unaware of the turmoil around her. Her body language and mannerisms project "victim," and consequently she is attacked by one of Penguin's minions, who is almost immediately dispatched by the heroic Batman on his way to rescuing his beloved Gotham.

Director Burton further underlines Selena's submissiveness and low self-esteem when she returns to her lonely apartment with an ironic "Honey, I'm home." The apartment is bathed in pinks and "girly" pastels. It is filled with cutesy decorations and knickknacks, including a neon sign welcoming its only human companion with a "Hello There." At work Selena is a put-upon secretary (she tells others she is an "assistant"). Her boss, robber baron Max Schreck (Christopher Walken), exploits her willingness to please and her timidity. When she discovers a document exposing an illegal scheme, he pushes her out a high-rise window.

Selena's rebirth as Catwoman occurs as a result of this act of murder. While lying on the ground dead, she is revived by a pack of mystical cats. The second time the audience sees her return home she no longer is a whining, depressive victim. She immediately begins to destroy her apartment, smashing her decorations, spray-painting her pink walls and frumpy outfits. She finds a discarded vinyl coat and creates a new costume out of it, a tight-fitting catsuit. As she dons the uniform, she becomes a new person, a warrior reveling in her newfound freedom—"Life's a bitch, and now so am I."

Catwoman's relationship with Batman serves to crystallize the split in her personality, as well as the one in the dark knight's own psyche. The two alternate between romantic lovemaking (as Selena and Bruce Wayne—Batman's alter ego) and fighting as superpowered archenemies. As Batman tells Selena in their final confrontation, they are "both split down the center." In order to show his duality honestly, he unmasks himself for her, hoping his act will convince her of his honesty. But Catwoman cannot accept his offer. Her desire for revenge against the man who murdered her, Schreck, is too overwhelming. And so she electrifies herself and the true villain of the piece.

But, of course, cats have more than one life, as she repeatedly tells Schreck. And so in the final shot of the movie the audience sees Selena's figure peering up at Batman's symbol, which has been projected in the night sky above the city.

"The Halle Cat"

In *Catwoman* (2004), actor Halle Berry reconstructed the catsuit to reveal more sinuous muscle and skin than ever before, modifying it from the traditional one-piece outfit into a bustier top with crisscross, bondage-style straps, diamond-tipped claws, and, of course, the *de rigueur* whip designed to tap into the S&M aspects inherent in the part.

She transforms from meek and frumpy Patience (yes, they changed her name again), afraid to confront her partying neighbor who blasts music until the early morning, into Catwoman, who is able to knock down the neighbor's door and grab a piece of tubing to whip the offender into submission. As Patience she takes her employer's abuse quietly, but as Catwoman she performs a catlike dance and with whip in hand entraps one of her boss's henchman who had caused her death as Patience.

Veteran woman warrior Sharon Stone as Laurel taunts the newbie super-hero Halle Berry, Catwoman.

125

The archvillain in this piece is actor Sharon Stone. As Laurel she plays an ex-model whose skin has turned to marble as a result of a dangerous beauty product her company developed. (Yet another theme of bad women and beauty products gone wrong.) She is battling her partner/husband's attempts to retire her for a younger model (in both senses of the word). In response she murders her husband and attempts to blame it on Catwoman.

Though both Halle Berry and Sharon Stone are proven, talented actors, this version of *Catwoman* was notoriously clawed to shreds by critics and fans alike. As with *Elektra*, it was perceived that the studios were just casting "hot" women in the roles and not giving audiences a worthy plot or credible performances. Trying to capitalize on big-name sex appeal, the enormous popularity of the Catwoman character, and heavy merchandising (a multitude of slick commercials advertised the Catwoman video game released in conjunction with the movie), the studios failed to deliver the Catwoman that fans hoped for.

Although critics were harsh, Halle Berry accepted her punishment openly and with a good-natured attitude. Named "Worst Actress of 2004" by the Golden Raspberry Award Foundation for her role, she actually showed up at the ceremony the night before the Oscars, carrying the Oscar she won in 2002 for *Monster's Ball*. The crowd gave a standing ovation as she parodied her original Oscar acceptance speech, tears included.

"I want to thank Warner Bros. for casting me in this piece of shit," she said. Then dragging her agent onto the stage, she warned her, "Read the script first next time!" Catwoman also won worst film, director, and screenplay, and screenwriter John Rogers was there to collect his "Razzie." When asked why she attended, Halle answered, "My mother told me as a child that if you aren't able to be a good loser, you're not able to be a good winner."

Opposite: The "Halle Cat" (Halle Berry) poses in her customized catsuit in *Catwoman* (2004).

The Feline Woman

Historians trace the worship of the cat and its association with the feminine principle all the way back to ancient Egypt. The Egyptians deified the cat in the form of the mother goddess Bast, whose purview included love, fertility, birth, music, and dance. The Egyptians also were the first to domesticate cats.

Throughout the centuries following the Egyptian period, art and literature has elevated the status of cats to legitimate icons, still almost always associated with females. In the Middle Ages witches were depicted in art and story as keeping a black cat as a demonic familiar, thus reinforcing the negative Christian view of females and their sexuality. In the nineteenth century the Romantic-decadent writers like Edgar Allan Poe and Charles Baudelaire repeatedly linked their goddess-like femme fatales with cats. In the famous story by Poe "The Black Cat," the male protagonist murders his wife as well as a cat, hoping, somewhat unconsciously, to extinguish their combined threat in one stroke.

In relation to warrior women, we see comparisons of cats and women used very often. The cat seems to represent the mysterious and unpredictable nature of women. Whereas dogs are "man's best friend," women seem to be more in tune with cats as house pets, understanding their ways on a different level. In language, it is always defined as a feminine trait to be "catty" or to engage in a "catfight." Some women even carry the first name of "Kitty."

The cat also figures frequently into physical descriptions of women. Women may be admired for having sleek, feline bodies and graceful movements. A woman's eyes are often called cat-like, and that impression is often intensified by application of

Above: Patience (Halle Berry) from *Catwoman* about to be reborn.

Opposite Top: Poster for Val Lewton's classic *Cat People* with Simone Simon.

Opposite Bottom: Poster for Paul Schrader's remake of *Cat People* starring Nastassia Kinski.

eyeliner and other makeup. Numerous slang words, in relation to female genitalia in particular, are named after the cat, also demonstrating that the feline references are of sexual or passionate connotation. The cat is classic sign of duality. Even the most domesticated house cat could regress to a feral state under the right circumstances. Duality also can imply mood swings, mental illness, hysteria, traits still attributed more often to women than to men. Repressed aggression is a classic trait of many Hollywood versions of warrior women.

Popular media picked up the cat symbolism in the twentieth century and developed its sexual dimensions. Producer-writer Val Lewton made one of the most memorable movies on the subject in 1942—*Cat People*. In the film the main character, Irena (Simone Simon), has repressed her sexuality and turned frigid out of fear of triggering her "cat genes," which she inherited from ancestors who were said to have taken part in ancient satanic rituals. She even meets another woman like her, very attractive, with "catlike" eyes, according to a man's comments. The woman greets her in her own special language, calling her "sister."

Irena's ravenous sexual nature never could have been expressed directly on-screen during the forties. Instead it was projected as an untamed panther that lurked beneath her surface, ready to claw its way out when her emotions were aroused. "Don't ever make me angry or jealous," she begs her would-be husband. In a very telling moment in the movie, he brings home a house cat as a pet for her. But this works out disastrously. The cat only hisses at her and shies away, foreshadowing that she is too much a wild spirit to be contained in the marital domestic bondage that he is proposing to her. She will not be tamed. In the end she pays for her sins by sacrificing her life.

Also in the forties Batman creator Bob Kane and his artists introduced Catwoman to the world of comics. Like Irena, Selina, the alter ego of Catwoman, shed her more restrained persona for a much more powerful and sexual one when she put on her catsuit.

In 1982 director-writer Paul Schrader cast the exotic Nastassia Kinski in a remake of *Cat People*. By this time the movie production code had virtually disappeared, and Schrader was able to foreground the repressed sexuality of this modern-day Irena, as well as graphically portray her violent sexual outbursts. The film ends with this Irena in bondage as her lover commits essentially an act of bestiality in having sex with her as she changes over to her true nature. Punished for her sexual sins, of course, we see her next in her true leopard form, but sadly in captivity at the zoo, where he feeds her tidbits of a sandwich through the bars on his lunch break.

Even in stories where the theme does not directly revolve around cats, we see cats strategically placed. In the groundbreaking movie *Alien*, Sigourney Weaver's character Ripley survives the slaughter of her crewmates, yet has a strange affinity for a cat that resides on their spaceship. Considering how cautious and logical she was in the beginning of the movie, wishing to quarantine the man who was first attacked by the Alien, it is odd that she puts such risk into saving a common house cat.

In the pilot episode of *Dark Angel*, Jessica Alba's character Max uses her enhanced vision to spot a small statue of the cat-

headed goddess Bast in a building next door. She later dresses in a tight black suit (basically a catsuit) and leaps across to the other building to break in and steal the statue. Even the clever Hermione from *Harry Potter and the Sorcerer's Stone* (2001) turns herself into a half-human, half-cat hybrid creature by mistake temporarily when a spell goes wrong. She is embarrassed by the transformation, though, and hides out until it passes.

The cat was also depicted in far tamer form in *Josie and the Pussycats*, which premiered on television as a Hanna-Barbera cartoon and was made into a movie in 2001. While these characters had some Amazonian characteristics of sisterhood—they were an all-girl band, for example—they were still, largely, neutered cats. Interestingly, in one episode, the cartoon took on the classic Amazon tale of encountering Amazons in outer space.

Various movie posters depicting cats and women.

Batgirl

Batman: And you are?

Batgirl: Batgirl.

Batman: That's not very PC. What about "Batwoman," or "Batperson"?

—Batman and Robin

Above: Yvonne Craig, the original Batgirl from the *Batman* TV series.

Opposite: Alicia Silverstone as Batgirl in *Batman & Robin.*

The third film in the Warner Bros. *Batman* series, *Batman & Robin* (1997), is commonly considered the weakest of the trilogy, as it tries rather unsuccessfully to recapture the camp quality of the television series rather than concentrate on the dark dimensions of the characters. As one *Batman* fan succinctly put it, "It takes the concept of Dark Knight and turns it into Dork Knight."

It is notable, however, for introducing two female warriors to the big screen: Poison Ivy and Batgirl. Batgirl had various incarnations in the DC comic books, most often as a teen relative of Batman, similar to Supergirl (incarnated by Helen Slater in the 1984 movie of the same name), who was a cousin to Superman in fifties comics. Batgirl was introduced to the original *Batman* TV series when ratings had dropped off and it was decided that another female character in a formfitting suit might bring in some of the much needed sexual tension to match the earlier days of the show. The part of Batgirl was given to Yvonne Craig, who also happened to play the character Marta, one of the sexy green slave girls of Orion in *Star Trek*'s "Whom the Gods Destroy."

In the 1997 *Batman & Robin*, Alicia Silverstone as Batgirl is introduced as the niece of the faithful butler to the Waynes. She carries on the tradition of the dual life common to both comic book superheroes and villains. By day she is a refined private-school teen, dressed in tartan skirt and blazer. By night she wears leather, rides motorbikes, racing deadly hoods through the backstreets of Gotham. When she finally receives her anatomically correct rubber uniform (conveniently including nipples), designed lovingly by her uncle (in another perverse touch so common to

the world of comic books), she too is empowered and goes on to defeat Poison Ivy and save both of the Dynamic Duo.

Batgirl makes another appearance in a short-lived WB series called *Birds of Prey* (2002). In this Gothic-style series, Barbara Gordon (Dina Meyer), aka Batgirl, aka Oracle, now crippled after an attack by the Joker, joins forces with the daughter of Batman and Catwoman—the embittered Huntress (Ashley Scott)—to defend Gotham now that Batman has retired from the scene. Unfortunately the series did not enjoy the success of other WB comic book shows like *Smallville* and was canceled.

Poison Ivy

"I am Nature's arm. Her spirit. Her will. Hell, I am Mother Nature."

—Poison Ivy, *Batman & Robin*

The dynamic center of the 1997 *Batman & Robin* movie is the archenemy of Batman, Poison Ivy. Dr. Pamela Isley (played by Uma Thurman, soon to become an icon of warrior women films) is a bookish, frumpy eco-terrorist who during an explosion in an experimental facility re-emerges as a goddess-like half-plant, half-human warrior, bent on taking revenge on humanity for destroying the environment. Along with her hooded slave, she joins forces with Mr. Freeze (Arnold Schwarzenegger) to destroy humankind.

Ivy's transformation from demure female to pheromone-breathing, poison-lipped femme fatale exemplifies the pattern of change common to most female comic book villains. While most male characters like Superman and Batman simply become more powerful when they throw off their alter egos, female comic book warriors like Poison Ivy and Catwoman also become far more sexual and tempting, their dangerous powers acting as an aphrodisiac for men. This increased allure is a manifestation of power, illustrated by the reactions of those around them who are weakened by it.

Opposite: Uma Thurman as seductive eco-terrorist Poison Ivy in *Batman & Robin*.

Mr. Freeze (Arnold Schwarzenegger) and Poison Ivy (Uma Thurman) meet in *Batman & Robin*.

"A poison kiss? You have some real issues with women, you know that? You just couldn't stand it that she was going to kiss me and not you, wasn't it? You couldn't stand it that she wanted me and not you!"

—Robin to Batman

In the final scenes Ivy uses her sexuality to entrap the testosterone-driven adolescent Robin, and for this "dastardly" act the rubber-suited Batgirl tells her, "Chicks like you give women a bad name." In the fight that follows, Batgirl makes good her threat to defeat her and sends Ivy to Arkham Asylum to await yet another rebirth.

"Elektra is an assassin for hire," says Jennifer Garner. "Her body's for hire. She's a . . . whore. She's not a girl from West Virginia, that's for sure."

Elektra, "Before She Can Find Peace She Will Wage War"

The film *Elektra* (2005) is a spin-off from the adaptation of Marvel's *Daredevil* (2003) starring Ben Affleck as the superhero and Jennifer Garner as his love and fighting equal Elektra Natchios. The character of Elektra is based on Frank Miller's comic books, and so she is bathed in the same *noir* aura in which Miller surrounds his other creations, such as *Batman, the Dark Knight*, and *Sin City*.

The theme of Oedipal conflict (in its most comprehensive form, as defined by Freud) includes both men and women, although later psychologists separated the genders and applied the terms "Oedipal" to men and "Elektra complex" to women. Either way, the list of women warriors who are locked into a love-hate relationship with a parent, usually their father, is extensive and has been noted many times in this book. In the first movie, *Daredevil*, Elektra dotes on her father, and it is in fact his death that pushes her to the "dark side." In order to seek out his murderers, she gives up the love of Daredevil and confronts the villains, only to be killed during the final battle.

In the sequel, *Elektra*, the audience finds the superheroine resurrected and fully ensconced in darkness as a hired assassin à la Femme Nikita. Further, she has developed several psychological disorders in the process, including OCD (obsessive-compulsive disorder). After a "hit," in which she eliminates dozens of bodyguards as well as her target, her handler finds her compulsively scrubbing the floor to erase any evidence of her DNA. This resurrected Elektra is also haunted by nightmares in which she is drowning as her strict father forces her to learn to swim, and by repeated visions of her mother's murder by a group of assassins from the wicked Hand organization.

As her handler warns her, she needs a vacation or "to get laid." Otherwise she is on the edge of a nervous breakdown. But Elektra cannot rest, for she is also a workaholic, using her profession to push away emotions and other humans, except as victims. Her next mission sends her to a small island where she meets a mysterious man and his daughter, her next targets. Unfortunately or fortunately, depending on your perspective, Elektra forms a

Above: "The treasure" (Abby Miller) is a female prodigy in *Elektra*.

Opposite: Jennifer Garner as Elektra.

Jennifer Garner in her striking Elektra outfit.

bond with the daughter, Abby (Kirsten Prout), in whom she sees herself at that young age.

Soon she learns that Abby is in fact more like her than she originally imagined. She is "the treasure" the Hand seeks. She is a warrior woman in training, born with superhuman skills like Elektra herself. In protecting Abby and her father, Elektra opens up emotionally, if ever so slightly. In becoming a surrogate mother, much like Ripley in the *Alien* series, she begins to

Elektra displays her unique sai weapons.

work out her own Oedipal conflicts. Although she saves Abby from the clutches of Typhoid (Natassia Malthe), a Gothic warrior who infects her victims with disease, she does not stay with them. Like a true loner, in the tradition of Superman, she returns to her "fortress of solitude," but this time she has abandoned the dark side and rediscovered her original purpose as laid out to her by her sensei Stick (Terence Stamp) many years earlier.

Poster for *X-Men 2*.

Marvel's "X-Women"

X-Men, in the form of comic book, cartoon, or live-action movie, finds its moral center in the sixties. It is among the most politically radical of the comic book series. Growing out of the civil rights movement of that decade, the series is an allegory for the struggle for equal rights and freedom. The conflict between Professor X and Magneto is a classic battle between those who seek change through persuasion and those who see violent action as the only effective means to an end.

It is ironic that the Marvel comic book and the three filmic adaptations of that comic book, *X-Men* (2000), *X2* (2003), and *X-Men 3* (2006), bear the designation "X-Men." If anything, the

Jean Grey (Famke Janssen) and Storm (Halle Berry) in *X-Men 2*.

most powerful characters in the two movies are the female warriors, the "X-Women." Although Professor X (Patrick Stewart) and Magneto (Ian McKellen) each head a group of mutants who are seeking full rights from the ruling class of humans, it is the female mutants who constantly grab center stage and seize control of both the action and the emotional power of the films.

Jean Grey (Famke Janssen) is a doctor who researches the gene that has caused the DNA of certain humans to alter and endow the individual with preternatural powers. She is herself a mutant, possessing formidable psychic powers. In the first film she is the one who gains control of Cerebro, the mutant-finding computer, when Professor X fails. In the second film she sacrifices herself

to save the other mutants by holding back a flood while her colleagues escape via jet.

Mystique (Rebecca Romijn) is among the most powerful of the mutants. She is a shapeshifter who refuses to live in an acceptable human form and instead maintains her scaly blue skin in defiance of the ruling class. She is Magneto's right-hand woman, and in the second film she is the only one who can penetrate the underground experimental facility where Stryker (Brian Cox) experiments on both humans and mutants. Mystique is not above using her strong sexual drive as a weapon as well. In the second movie she seduces one of Stryker's guards in a public bathroom and later tries to seduce the recalcitrant Wolverine (Hugh Jackman).

Storm (Halle Berry) symbolizes the anger felt by most of the mutants toward their oppressors. Her power lies in her ability to alter weather (a traditionally feminine power, which witches used to be convicted of). Even filled with rage, she still manages to be among the most levelheaded of the mutants. She is also the most respected.

Rogue (Anna Paquin) is the most vulnerable and sympathetic of the group, largely due to her young age as well as the distress her power causes her. She learns of its properties as she is kissing her first boyfriend. Suddenly the boy begins to convulse from loss of energy, which has been siphoned off into Rogue. From then on, she wears gloves to protect others from her powers and becomes, understandably, fearful of forming close relationships. The violent and disgruntled Wolverine adopts her as a surrogate daughter, even though their first attempt at physical contact almost results in their deaths.

Deathstrike (Kelly Hu) appears only in the second film. She is another victim of Stryker's Nazi-like experimentation in his concentration camp underground (the thinly veiled allusions to Nazism are numerous in the film). Like Wolverine she has a skeletal system of steel and demonstrates an impressive knowledge of martial arts. The only one able to defeat her is her "brother-in-torture," Wolverine.

Above: Anna Paquin as Rogue.

Opposite: The rebellious Mystique (Rebecca Romijn) of *X-Men*.

Below: Deathstrike (Kelly Hu).

Lara Croft, Tomb Raider

In an article published in *Premiere* magazine, Angelina Jolie, the star of both *Lara Croft: Tomb Raider* (2001) and the sequel *Lara Croft Tomb Raider: The Cradle of Life* (2003), discussed why she found the part of Lara so empowering. "She is just so alive with purpose . . . She inspires adventure in people and a certain kind of pride in yourself. I suppose what people see in her is that she's a fighter."

Based on the hugely popular animated video game (which also inspired the television series *Relic Hunter*—1999–2002, starring Tia Carrere), the *Lara Croft* movies played into many a male gamer's fantasy. It was well publicized that Jolie wore a padded bra for the part, which she explains in *Premiere* magazine:

> I'm a 36C. Lara, she's a 36D. And in the game, she's a double D, so we took her down some. But we did give her a bit of padding there. For me, it was simply one size. So it was like having a padded bra. But no, I am not flat-chested anyway. So we still made it Lara Croft, but we didn't go to any extremes. And Lara doesn't apologize for herself for having that, you know, recognizable shape. So I'm not going to apologize for her either.

The popularity of Lara's "recognizable shape" is so widespread it even inspired the creation of a special "Nude Raider" game patch where Lara Croft does battle in the nude. Regardless of bra size, Jolie had such a resemblance to the character that she seemed the perfect choice to take on the cinematic portrayal. *Lara Croft* was not Jolie's first venture into the world of action heroes. In 1993 in the low-budget science fiction film *Cyborg 2*, she played a cybernetic female gone wrong who rebels against the corporation that created her and attempts to bring it down. She later went on to action roles in films like *Sky Captain and the World of Tomorrow* and *Mr. and Mrs. Smith*.

The *Lara Croft* films clearly establish Lara's fighting credentials, whether she is training with oversized and menacing robots, diving for treasure in the Mediterranean, or punching sharks. On a grand scale, she battles with the nefarious Illuminati or crosses

Lara (Angelina Jolie) in pursuit of Pandora's Box in *Lara Croft: The Cradle of Life*.

the globe to prevent the release of deadly viruses. No other important female characters are to be found in these movies. Lara is surrounded only by men, who fall into categories of wishing to worship her, or kill her, or both.

Jolie plays Lara Croft as constantly intense and often angry. Her only other expression is generally an aloof, sexy smirk. She is different when dealing with her father, though, who is deceased but seen in flashbacks in which she becomes soft and starry-eyed. She even puts on a feminine white dress and formal hat to commune with him in one scene. Viewers complained that they wanted to see *action* and could care less about the father figure. He certainly doesn't have anything to do with the game. Why is he there? To show that even the toughest heroine is still tempered by Daddy? (Ironically, her father is played by her real-life father, Jon Voight. They have long since been estranged from each other in a very public rift.)

Angelina Jolie as Lara in *Lara Croft: Tomb Raider.*

Her lovers in both films are men who have betrayed her and whom she never really trusted in the first place. In *Cradle of Life*, Sheridan (Gerard Butler), who accompanies her on her quest to find Pandora's Box (an artifact that releases evil in the form of viruses), confronts her about her inability to trust and let anyone into her life. As they begin to make love, he takes the missionary position that she cannot abide, and so she flips and mounts him. But her old fears of betrayal resurface. In response she takes out a pair of handcuffs and chains him to the bedpost, crouching near him like a wary animal. While lovers may betray the adult Lara, her memory of her dead father never disappoints.

And, of course, Lara's fears do prove to be accurate. Sheridan does betray her in the end, trying to steal Pandora's Box from this postmodern Pandora, who chooses not to open the "mythical" box, keeping the evil inside safely suppressed.

Charlize Theron from the live-action
Aeon Flux.

Aeon Flux, Surreal Anti-Heroine

Aeon Flux (1995), the animated experimental MTV series, has as its centerpiece an anti-hero very much in the tradition of Catwoman, *X-Men's* Mystique, or even La Femme Nikita. The title character is violent, predatory, and often sadistic. She dispatches her "hits" with cold delight and treats her lovers much the same way, with one exception. Trevor Goodchild (an ironic name if ever there was one) is the leader of the Breens and the person responsible for most of Aeon's freelance assignments. For this slippery macho man Aeon has a weakness, which sends her on an emotional roller-coaster ride of love and hate.

Although Aeon's sense of right and wrong in her surreal post-apocalyptic world is quite muted, she does have standards, no matter how ill-defined. Her actions are often whimsical and keyed to her own desires and instincts, but she does evidence a rudimentary moral sense, such as when she refuses to kill her friend Una, even though Una has tried to destroy her. Aeon also possesses the unique ability to resurrect herself from the dead, which she does several times in the series. This ability alone would mark her as a superheroine of the first order, but it is only one in an arsenal of powers that make Aeon a formidable warrior.

Director Karyn Kusama, of *Girlfight* fame, has directed a live-action version of the animated series starring Charlize Theron.

Frank Miller's *Sin City*

"Deadly little Miho. You won't feel a thing. Not unless she wants you to."

[*She twists the blade.*]

[*He feels it.*]

Devon Aoki as Miho from Frank Miller's *Sin City*.

Traveling into a far more sinister and adult realm of comic-inspired movies, *Sin City* (2005) is a brutal and breathtaking homage to the legendary graphic novelist Frank Miller, known to mainstream audiences as the man most responsible for "darkening" the image of Batman in comic books in the eighties. Director Robert Rodriguez, a longtime fan of Miller, had to hunt down the reluctant artist in a Hell's Kitchen saloon to convince him to check out the test footage he had prepared in advance.

"That's some powerful stuff, mister," Miller commented upon seeing what Rodriguez presented. The scenes were exact replicas of Miller's storyboards. Rodriguez didn't want to "adapt" the movie to the screen. He wanted to translate it as directly and faithfully as possible. With the help of Frank Miller and guest director Quentin Tarantino, the film interweaves three stories in a complex visual recreation of the *noir* world that Miller originally created as a reaction to being burnt out on Hollywood.

There are a number of feisty female characters throughout the story, although most of them are portrayed in the customary comic book formula—bound and tied for substantial amounts of time. It is appropriate perhaps that the character Nancy, memorably played by Jessica Alba, is an exotic dancer who twirls a rope

Dominatrix Gail (Rosario Dawson) deals with corrupt police invading Old Town in *Sin City*.

throughout her routine, considering she spends the most time bound up in ropes, innocent and vulnerable. Even the tough-as-nails dominatrix Gail (Rosario Dawson) ends up tied to a chair and tortured by the sadist Manute (Michael Clark). This bondage subtext, a standard of the genre, allows the male character to be the savior and avenger, and the reader/audience to enjoy the scopophiliac pleasure of being the sadist and savior all at once, a primary appeal of comics.

Granted, many male characters are also portrayed in bondage. But they tend to overcome the situation more often. Marv (Mickey Rourke), for instance, is tied to a chair and slapped around by Wendy (Jaime King). However, he just casually shakes off his ropes shortly afterward, to Gail's great surprise. He was never held unwillingly. He just allowed himself to appear incapacitated for his own reasons. Hartigan (Bruce Willis) is also bound and even hung from the neck by a rope in one scene. However, he is able to use his ingenuity to break free of the seemingly impossible situation, get away, and go save Nancy (for the second time). No woman in the film is able to break free from her bonds without male assistance.

One female character is clearly not a victim though. Deadly Little Miho. She is quite capable on her own, even saving the occasional man (on behalf of women who need him). Deadly little Miho is introduced to the audience in the story "Big Fat Kill." Superbly played by Devon Aoki, Miho guards the female-run Old Town, protecting its inhabitants. Frank Miller talks about Miho in *Sin City: The Making of the Movie*:

> I adored Miho from the moment I first started drawing her. She's a character of magic much more than any of the others are. I don't mean she can fly or anything, but close to it. And she is also a character of mystery. In *Sin City*, everybody talks a lot. Miho never says a word, and she is completely and literally lethal.

When corrupt cop Jackie-Boy (Benicio Del Toro) cruises into Old Town with his drunk friends looking to make trouble with one of the young sex workers, a gruesome bloodbath ensues. The pixie-like Miho disarms him from the roof of the building she is crouching on by slicing his gun hand clean off with a swastika-shaped throwing star. While Jackie-Boy crawls out of the car trying to retrieve his gun, Miho leaps down from the building, simultaneously unsheathing two samurai swords (which happen to be the same swords used by the Crazy 88 gang in Tarantino's *Kill Bill Volume 1*). Landing on the roof of the car, she plunges the swords right through the car's top and into the skulls of the two men in the backseat. When the remaining passenger tries to get out of the front seat, she neatly decapitates him. Jackie-Boy doesn't fare too well in the end either.

In the words of the narrator, Dwight,

"She doesn't quite chop his head off. She makes a PEZ dispenser out of him."

As in most *noir* films, a dark romanticism pervades not only this story, but all the stories in *Sin City*. Dwight is clearly obsessed with Gail, though he apparently has commitment issues. He calls her "my warrior woman, my Valkyrie." In the final scene he still hangs onto his object of desire as he tells the audience in somber voice-over (a staple of *film noir*) that their love will exist "always and . . . never."

The film was received with mixed reactions. Not many can deny that the digital film work is fantastic. Rodriguez brought black and white to a new level. The actors' scenes were all shot against a green screen and painstakingly custom edited to provide a unique effect of controlled lighting and backdrops. Color was added only to certain accented items and subtly shifted throughout, much in keeping with Miller's graphic novels, which are mostly stark black-and-white with occasional color, often red. The audience, though, was not prepared for the level of violence and brutality that was portrayed, however artfully executed. Rodriguez was aware that he made what he calls "the ultimate anti-movie," something that could never be made into a traditional movie; it could only exist in comics. But to those who love comics and graphic novels, this was probably about as close to Frank Miller's distinctive universe as ever could be achieved on-screen.

Jessica Alba as Nancy in *Sin City*.

Tank Girl, "In 2033 Justice Rides a Tank and Wears Lip Gloss"

"This comet came crashing into the Earth. BAM! Total devastation. No celebrities, no cable TV, *no water*! It hasn't rained in eleven years. Now, twenty people gotta squeeze into the same bathtub. So it ain't all bad."

Tank Girl (1995), a film adaptation of the British cult comic book of the same name, incorporates director Rachel Talalay's unique style with anti-establishment themes, quirky imagery, and punk culture. The film presents a surreal post-apocalyptic universe by mixing live-action images with drawings from the original comic books, inviting the audience into a desert world where water is the most valued commodity. The inhabitants of this world, the Rippers, are a mutant race of half men, half-kangaroos that spend their time battling for the "liquid gold" against an evil mega-corporation called Water and Power. Stray bands of rebellious survivors like Tank Girl wander the desert.

Tank Girl (Lori Petty) first appears dressed in one of the eighteen punk-style costumes she wears throughout the movie, a plethora of mismatched outfits usually altered with scissors and safety pins. She is riding a water buffalo creature; both are masked. In a later scene she is also shown wearing a bowler hat and distinctive makeup over one eye in homage to Malcolm McDowell's character Alex from Stanley Kubrick's own punk futuristic classic *A Clockwork Orange*. Malcolm McDowell himself plays Kesslee, the sinister head of Water and Power, in this film. Tank Girl's fashion sense works well with her cocky sense of humor. When she is beaten by the soldiers of Water and Power and then detained, she tells them, "Hey, what time is it? I don't want to miss *Baywatch*." When another soldier demands at gunpoint that she perform fellatio on him, she requests a pair of tweezers and a microscope in response.

Comic book adaptations are generally fertile ground for filmmakers to insert an abundance of gratuitous sexual objectification. However, Tank Girl stands out as being stridently feminist

Opposite: Tank Girl (Lori Petty) surveys the landscape.

Lori Petty, left, and Naomi Watts, right, in *Tank Girl*.

in theme, minus the cliché victim/avenger complex. Her character is likable, funny, sexy, and original. Her "sidekick" Jet Girl (Naomi Watts) is an intelligent and talented mechanic, who starts as a victim in a male-run prison colony but with the inspiration of Tank Girl learns to assert herself and break free.

The topic of the male gaze is humorously handled in a scene where Tank Girl and Jet Girl dress up as model and photographer and invade the site where workers are unloading shipments of guns, supposedly earmarked for the troops of Water and Power. But before the men can ogle them and make sexist comments, Tank Girl takes out a camera and turns the gaze on them. She commands the out-of shape truckers to start stripping off their shirts and posing for a supposed photo calendar. They readily agree and proceed to make fools of themselves.

In another scene the movie pokes fun at expected female stereotypes. Tank Girl infiltrates a bordello while trying to rescue a kidnapped girl and finds a female dressing room. She searches for an outfit to wear as a disguise. A computer training device in the middle of the room automatically comes on, speaking through a virtual model of a "perfect woman," instructing the listener as to how to present herself properly to men. "First of all, remove ALL conspicuous hair from your body," the voice tells her. It goes on to outline how to put on a blond wig, skimpy outfit, and makeup. "When done, you should look just like me," the voice says.

Tank Girl's main enemy is Kesslee, who spouts verse to her while wearing a minister's outfit (very patriarchal reference there). He tries to break her will repeatedly with various forms of torture but receives only defiance and derision in return. One of the most extreme forms of torture involves being dropped down a pipe that sends the victim downward to darkness until it is too narrow to pass. There a claustrophobic nightmare ensues as water slowly fills the pipe. Regardless of her distress, Tank Girl still manages to emasculate Kesslee with her witty comebacks every time he tries to hurt her.

> "Look, if you want to torture me, spank me, lick me, do it," she says, "but if this poetry shit continues, just shoot me now, please."

Tank Girl exacts her final revenge with the help of her friends when she returns in her stylishly decorated tank to destroy the headquarters of Water and Power. She sinks into Keslee's heart one of the suction devices he has designed to extract water from humans, effectively shrinking him down to just his android head.

Final Notes: Occupational Hazards of Superheroines

When Gail Simone realized one day that her favorite female comic characters often met "untimely and icky ends," she was prompted to do some investigation. Not wishing to place blame on any particular creator or character, she began compiling a list, which eventually appeared on the Web site titled Women in Refrigerators, aka WiF, (http://www.the-pantheon.net/wir/) and which ended up sparking a whirlwind of controversy. The site was named after a particular *Green Lantern* comic in which his long-term girlfriend is found stuffed into his fridge by the villain Major Disaster.

The WiF list was an alphabetical record of more than one hundred female characters who have suffered either death or extreme damage such as being raped, maimed, tortured, depowered, made infertile, sexually abused, paralyzed, enslaved, infected with HIV, having limbs amputated, and much more. Reading through the list in its entirety is rather shocking, even for comic books, when you realize just how common such horrific ends are for female characters, even popular ones. Are these superheroes or supervictims?

The publishing of the WiF list in 1999 sparked off many heated debates about why women in comics suffer such treatment, and how it compares to that of male characters. As a result, similar lists of men were brought up and discussed. Many famous comic creators kindly gave input in response, which also appeared on the Web site. Some found the list to be misleading or a distortion.

Firestar (powers were sterilizing her).

Tom Brevoort, a well-regarded Marvel editor, comments:

Well, I think, first off, that this isn't a problem that's only common to female characters. I'd hazard a guess that if you were to line up all of the black characters in comics, all of the Jewish characters in comics, or all of the left-handed characters in comics, you could put together a similar list of dire things that had happened to them.

And most of that is due to the fact that what we're writing is serialized fiction. In such a medium, contentment is boring. Stories occur when bad things happen to good people. And, given the monthly demand for new stories about these fictional characters—never mind those folks who are in series that carry more than one title—sooner or later everybody is going to be put through the ringer in some way.

Joan Hilty, an editor at DC Comics, remarks:

The response that "male characters get killed too" is completely disingenuous. You only need to have the faintest grasp of feminist or semiotic theory to know that it's not just how often it's done, it's HOW it's done and TO WHOM certain things are done. The sexually violent visual language of how these women get killed is remarkably consistent. Really, the larger reality is that American mainstream comics, built by guys for guys on the crumbling foundations of superhero fantasy, remain intensely hostile to women, consciously and subconsciously.

Nancy Collins, well-known for creating a variety of characters such as Sonja Blue, references the Amazons in a portion of her response:

Although Sonja Blue is raped and is transformed by it into a vampire, her rape isn't a way of receiving her "power" from a male force, but an attempt to mirror the Maimed Hero. In many fables and legends the hero is given a defect/maiming necessary to surmount to become the hero

(Oedipus, the Celtic guy with the silver hand I'm blanking on, King Arthur, Osiris). In some cases, the maiming is a sacrifice for knowledge (Odin), the badge of a warrior (the Amazons) or a means of disguising immense "inner" strength and ability (Papa Legba, Hephaestus, the Fisher King). However, you might notice few females in that list, except for the Amazons, who sacrificed a breast in order to be better archers. (Having caught a tit in a bow string, I can see why.) For women, a not-very-subtle symbolic form of maiming (i.e., loss of the self) is the rape. The rape is usually also symbolic in rendering the women sterile and, therefore, placing her outside the "natural" reproductive role of womanhood, enables her to pursue the more masculine role of avenging warrior. Many of the Greek and Roman goddesses of vengeance (Nemesis, Ate, the Furies) were represented as either virgins or hags—women who have yet to become part of the "bleeding sisterhood" or have passed beyond their fertile, nurturing years.

The rape-revenge syndrome is such a recurring theme in female action films that everyone knows it by heart. The emotional isolation, the inevitable flashbacks, the bitterness and distrust toward men as she seeks vengeance, if not for herself, then for every other woman who has or will possibly suffer the same fate. If anything, rape is trivialized by how commonly it is rather carelessly used in plots to provide motivation for the woman's sadistic and brutal actions.

One particularly insightful theory as to why we see such torture of powerful women in comics is brought up by D. Curtis Johnson, who has done considerable work for DC comics:

The urge that makes adolescent boys (and grown men, actually) feel good when the hero saves the damsel in distress is, scarily enough, the same urge that wants that damsel to be in distress in the first place, and the chivalrous desire to protect women from harm is inextricably tied to a secret thrill at the thought that those women are out there somewhere, being slapped around. Want to get

Japanese manga cover for the second volume of Sonja Blue's vampiric escapades, by Nancy Collins.

163

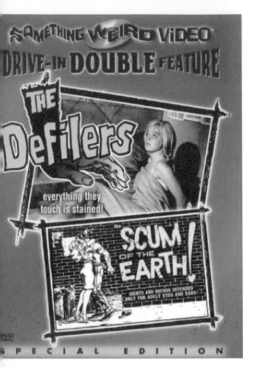

DVD cover of exploitation films *The Defilers* and *Scum of the Earth*.

a quick emotional flare out of an adolescent boy? Don't show him your hero saving Grandma from a train wreck, or pulling the little baby out of the burning house. Those are obviously heroic acts but your teenage reader won't identify with them, particularly—he doesn't understand old people or babies at all. But every teenage boy has at least one hot and sweaty crush going on at any given time, and if there's one thing he clearly knows and understands, it's wanting to rescue the love of his life from some horrible other guy who doesn't deserve her and is probably doing bad things to her . . . hopefully at the moment you actually bust in to save her, in fact, because then she's at her most vulnerable and needy and you're there to pick up the emotional slack.

Many comics are reminiscent of the classic "roughies" of sixties exploitation cinema, exemplified by filmmakers such as David Friedman, who produced such classics as *The Defilers* and *Scum of the Earth*. On one hand, watching the women get smacked around is shocking and disturbing. Yet projecting the blame onto the bad guys of the movie, and seeing the violence eroticized from the male point of view, with the dominant angle of the aggressor looking down at beautiful semi-nude women, the viewer can take secret pleasure in the acts of violence and perhaps in seeing women who would normally be unattainable "put in their place." The previous era of the harmless "nudie cutie" film just didn't cut it for most viewers for very long. Violence carried with it more emotional intensity and allowed for more plot. It wasn't long before slasher films took over, and they still rule the teenage horror market to a great degree.

Comic books wield an enormous amount of influence, which has migrated to the screen with some level of success. Hardcore comic fans tend to be fetishistic about their favorite series and characters. To please them on-screen, with all the bastardization that Hollywood tends to commit in adaptations, is challenging. Yet to duplicate the story and art more faithfully, as in Frank Miller's movie *Sin City*, tends to turn off mainstream audiences, who just "don't get it."

In regard to the substantial amount of abuse female comic

characters suffer, it really can't be denied that women get the short end of the stick, regardless of reason. Male heroes may suffer, but they generally come back stronger, their tragedy improving them in some other way. Women in comics don't get over their own rapes the way men get over watching their rapes take place. They might even be impregnated on top of it. No wonder they end up becoming psychotic, reverting to animal states or evil incarnations.

In the course of research for this book, a members-only adult pay Web site called Superheroines' Demise (www.sooperhero. com) was discovered. The following is an excerpt of its posted mission statement:

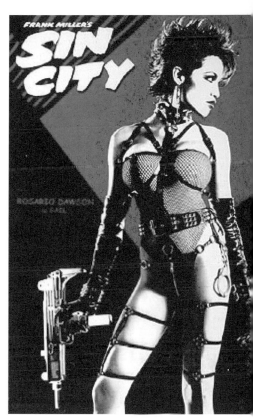

Movie poster from *Sin City*.

> The comic book industry has perpetually created beautiful costumed characters who have occupied our thoughts and imaginations for years. Although similarly based in fantasy, this site was made to bring intense and erotic fantasies to life. The image of supergirl or batgirl standing proud, hands on hips, ready to destroy their foes with just a flick of their powerful wrists is quite, quite sexy. Perhaps it's the tight costumes they wear, or perhaps it's their indescribable beauty matched with purity, power, and justice. But to us, nothing is more erotic than the photo images of these incredible costumed superheroines defeated and imperiled beyond your wildest dreams. Enter our site and see thousands of photos of professional models dressed as sexy superwomen and put through shockingly grueling adventures. See batwoman brutally defeated in hand to hand combat, and humiliatingly stripped, bound and photographed. See superwoman thrown through a wall and left sprawling on the ground in her shredded costume with plaster and debris all over her. These aren't fluff photos with weak stories like you see at other sites. These are the hard hitting, real live action photos and gut-wrenching storylines you've always lusted to see . . .
>
> —The Villain

And that's not all—if Hollywood hasn't brought female comic book characters to life on-screen to your satisfaction, you may order from this Web site your own custom movie to be made, choosing from a number of models who will dress up in the superhero costume of your choice and perform based on your own custom script. The following excerpt of a fan letter from a well-known comic book artist is also posted on the site:

> When I was the writer and artist for WONDER WOMAN years ago, these were the types of situations I would never have been allowed to do—but oh the images that swirled in my head. I'm looking forward to more *Sooperheroine* adventures and would just like to make a couple of suggestions, if I'm not being too presumptuous. A few more close-ups when the heroine is hit in the face might work from time to time as well as similar close-ups of her reacting to other attacks.
>
> Also, is there any possibility that the model could occasionally work barelegged rather than in the shimmery tights? Again, these are just suggestions based on my personal tastes. I see that in your FAQ section you receive quite a few of these (some very interesting indeed) and whatever you decide to do I just want to tell you that I'm here to enjoy the ride.
>
> Good Luck and Take Care,
>
> George Pérez

Chapter 7
Where No Man Has Gone Before

———

Space. The final frontier . . . for women warriors and feminist utopias.

———

The science fiction genre is the one place where almost anything goes, in terms of switched gender roles, edgy sexual situations, and definitely the exploration of lost civilizations of warrior women. Displaced myths from a variety of cultures eventually land in outer space. Fetishes are safely explored, many through cyborgs and postmodern romances. Even late sixties episodes of *Star Trek* feature some rather racy encounters with Amazon women. The classic "The Gamesters of Triskelion" episode of 1968 is one of the few *Star Trek* episodes that was written by a female—namely, Margaret Armen, a veteran of warrior women shows like *Wonder Woman* and *The Big Valley*.

The show opens with Kirk, Uhura, and Chekov attempting to beam down to one planet and instead being hijacked and taken to another named "Triskelion." There they are captured and fitted with obedience collars that shock them if they step out of line. Each is forced to participate in a sadistic game that involves gladiator-style tournaments, to the delight of an intergalactic audience. In order to prepare them, the trio is handed over to "drill thralls," experienced men and women who must train them for the next event.

Kirk's thrall is named Shahna (Angelique Pettyjohn). She dresses in traditional Amazon attire (except that it is made of metallic silver fabric). She is tall and blue-haired and deadly at the game. She is at first relentless with Captain Kirk, dominating him

Opposite: Seven of Nine (Jeri Ryan) rescued from the Borg collective.

Kirk (William Shatner), center, Uhura (Nichelle Nichols), right, and Chekov (Walter Koenig), left, suffering from a shock to their new obedience collars in the *Star Trek* episode "The Gamesters of Triskelion."

and setting up a harsh training schedule. However, she softens up as Kirk attempts to seduce her in order to gain an advantage and escape. But she too is controlled by the "providers" who bet on the games. And so his plan is thwarted, and he is shocked by his obedience collar, as well as whipped in the ring by the ferocious Kloog.

Uhura and Chekov are assigned their own drill instructors. Uhura's is a large, muscular man employed to assault her while Kirk and Chekov stand helpless in their cages, listening to the whimpering coming from her cell. But she seems to come out fine in the end. Chekov is assigned a large, rather manly woman who seems to take an uncomfortably intimate interest in him. Eventually Kirk, Uhura, and Chekov must meet their opponents in the ring. Although Shahna has become fond of her "student," she must face Kirk and do battle with him. Following the conventions of serial television, our hero, Kirk, wins, of course, and is allowed to return with Uhura and Chekov to *Enterprise*. But the show doesn't end without Kirk having his shirt ripped off and walking around bare-chested in a collar.

Another example of rather silly female domination occurred

much later on, in 1988, on *Star Trek: The Next Generation* in an episode titled "Angel One." In this one, Riker, who serves pretty much as an eighties version of ladies' man Captain Kirk, beams down to the planet Angel One with several of his crew to search for the crew of a freighter disabled years ago. They soon discover that the society running the planet is matriarchal in structure and that the crew of surviving men are fugitives hunted by the authorities as rebels, as they refuse to accept the rule of women.

Bowing to cultural protocol, Riker happily dresses in the objectifying garments that the males of the planet must wear: tights and a cutaway top to show his bare chest. The female leader of the planet takes a definite interest in Riker, who is much larger than the rather effeminate little men on their planet, who frolic about serving the women and sniffing perfume bottles. While Riker works on seducing the head female, to the jealousy of his female crew, his team discovers the rebel men have caused many of the women to break from tradition and seek a life where they don't have to be in charge anymore.

Riker does some fast-talking to stop the rebels from being executed. The leaders of the matriarchy are so impressed by his reason and compassion that they rethink their matriarchal leanings and open up to the idea of standard fifty-fifty equality between genders. The rebels and their families are exiled to a distant part of the planet to establish their own society, and Riker returns to *Enterprise* to regroup for his next mission.

Gene Roddenberry's Legacy: *Star Trek*'s Warrior Women in Space

Gene Roddenberry, creator of *Star Trek*, was, like his cohort Rod Serling (*Twilight Zone*), part of the progressive movement of the sixties that altered the conservative political bent of corporate-dominated television. Working under the cover of the science fiction genre, they were able to inject social themes into their shows that many mainstream series feared to tackle. Even though Roddenberry died in 1991, most of the spinoffs that followed his death in television or movie form were either inspired by his work or often based on outlines and scripts he had left behind.

Box cover from "Angel One," an episode of *Star Trek: The Next Generation* that features a female-ruled planet.

Nichelle Nichols—Uhura in *Star Trek,* wearing Amazon-inspired jewelry with snakes and spiral designs.

One of Roddenberry's most important innovations was including strong women as members of crew in all of his science fiction projects, beginning with *Star Trek* (1966–1969). He is also credited with showing the first interracial kiss on a TV series. Though, subsequently, the series has made significant steps in breaking down racial and gender barriers, many archaic biases and situations in the series haven't changed much since the sixties. The producers push the envelope on occasion with characters like Dax, whose gender is somewhat ambiguous, but never really go all the way.

However, a variety of women have taken on warrior roles on the series over the years. The following are a few of the many:

Nyota Uhura (Nichelle Nichols) began her career as chief communications officer aboard the starship *Enterprise* in the original *Star Trek* series. She was one of the few African-American characters on television who were not in subservient or comic roles. In the series of *Star Trek* movies made subsequent to the series, she was promoted to lieutenant commander.

Tasha Yar (Denise Crosby) was chief of security under Captain Picard on the starship *Enterprise* for the series *Star Trek: The Next Generation* (1987–1994). She was extremely professional and highly skilled in battle techniques, particularly martial arts. She died, after only a relatively short period in service, defending her comrades against an alien entity on a distant planet.

Kathryn Janeway (Kate Mulgrew) became captain of the starship *Voyager* on the series *Star Trek: Voyager* (1995–2001). She followed in the tradition of Kirk and Picard, combining tough leadership with empathetic compassion. She was always willing to trust her instincts about questionable subordinates, seen most definitely in the cases of the Borg Seven of Nine and the fiery half-Klingon B'Elanna Torres.

Kate Mulgrew as Captain Janeway in a publicity photo for *Voyager*.

B'Elanna Torres (Roxann Dawson) was the chief engineer aboard *Voyager*, entrusted with that position by Captain Janeway. Because of her Klingon heritage, she was combative and often antisocial, but as the series developed she found herself more in touch with her human side and even consented to marry a human and subsequently gave birth to a daughter. She was a fierce fighter, like all Klingons, and an important asset to Janeway in battle.

Seven of Nine (Jeri Ryan) was one of the most interesting of the warrior women of *Star Trek* because she was among the most conflicted. Janeway rescued her from the Borg collective mind by removing many of her implants. She had been kidnapped by the Borg as a child and raised by them as one of their drones. Even though she formed tentative attachments to various crew members, she still at times felt the call of the Borg collective and feared she would betray her comrades in arms.

Above: Roxann Dawson as the half-human, half-Klingon Torres on *Voyager*.

Below: *Battlestar Galactica* for a new generation: warrior women Katee Sackhoff, left, and Grace Park, right.

T'Pol (Jolene Blalock) was, in the series *Enterprise* (2001–2005), the female counterpart of the original *Star Trek's* Spock. As a Vulcan she maintained the superiority of reason over emotions. However, T'Pol's sexual drive, which was intense and at times overcame her reason, drove her to become almost predatory in search for release. She was placed on *Enterprise* by the Vulcans to monitor the captain—Archer, who was infamous for his rebellious actions. More often than not, however, she came down on the side of her captain, against the directives of her Vulcan superiors.

Hoshi Sato (Linda Park) was, in the series *Enterprise*, the linguist and communications expert. She initially had grave reservations about space travel and evidenced great trepidation. But as the series progressed she gradually conquered those fears and in an alternate dimension even became the conniving and seductive Empress of the Universe.

There have been several more series based on Roddenberry models, including *Earth: Final Conflict* (1997–2002) and *Andromeda* (2000–2005). Both feature women warriors, but *Andromeda* has the most unique one. Actress Lexa Doig plays Andromeda Ascendant, or Rommie, the artificial intelligence of the starship, which takes human form. She directs all the functions of the ship, as well as advising the captain on battle strategies. Because she has human form, she also begins to experience emotions and desires that cause the character to seem at times a bit schizophrenic.

Battlestar Galactica, Old and New, Gender Wars in Cyberspace

Glen Larson's short-lived but fondly remembered series *Battlestar Galactica* (1978) dealt with a group of humans wandering in space in search of the planet Earth, hoping to start a new life there. The show was chock-full of literary and biblical allusions. The commander was named Adama (read: Adam); the ship resembled Noah's Ark in its search for a safe homeland;

and one of the officers was named Starbuck after the first mate of the *Pequod* in *Moby Dick*, another story of a ship on a quest.

A very seventies cast picture from the television show *Battlestar Galactica*.

In 2003–2004 Ronald Moore revived the show in a mini-series and in doing so made some major alterations to reflect the changing tastes of audiences, particularly regarding the presence of warrior women. Larson's series had been the domain of males, utilizing in lead parts such forceful actors as Lorne Greene and Richard Hatch. Although Moore did leave the captain and commander male, he altered the gender of his two chief officers: Starbuck and Boomer. The storm of abuse from cyberspace was immediate. Moore was called a "she-male" for his decisions. The two women cast in the parts (Katee Sackhoff and Grace Park) were referred to condescendingly as "girls" and labeled "butch" simply because they took on male roles.

Whether the series proved successful or not, or even whether it was artistically of value, was no longer the issue. It was now a flash point for what Susan Faludi, in her perceptive book *Backlash,* has identified as a right-wing "male backlash" against feminism. Even though we were entering a new millennium, sexism seemed to still be an issue and once again pushed out any critical discussion of the merits of the show.

Serenity, "The Future Is Worth Fighting For"

Buffy the Vampire Slayer creator Joss Whedon set his sights on outer space in 2005 with a reworking of his ill-fated television series *Firefly.* With *Serenity,* Whedon brought his sense of irony to the story of a ragtag crew of mercenaries who lost their idealism when they lost the intergalactic war. Captain Reynolds (Nathan Fillion) is the captain, and his second in command is Zoe (Gina Torres).

Summer Glau, as the mystical River, uses her remarkable physical skills to escape capture in *Serenity.*

The plot involves the human cargo Reynolds has taken aboard, two fugitives from the oppressive Alliance that now controls the galaxy. One is a doctor, and the other his telepathic, mercurial sister (Summer Glau). In transporting these two, Reynolds and Zoe must reconnect with their moral center and defend them against the forces of the Alliance.

The character River, a pale, waifish, troubled girl, is first shown strapped to a chair, being brainwashed by a group of government men. There is a large hypodermic needle stuck in the middle of her forehead (major phallic symbol), and she suffers greatly as the brainwashing proceeds. She is saved though by her brother, who pulls out the needle and guides her to safety. Despite her slight appearance, she is a prodigy, a programmed warrior who can do incredible feats, fighting in a style that is as graceful as a dance.

Many strong women are portrayed in the crew, from the female engineer to the captain's second in command, Zoe. The character Inara (Morena Baccarin) even fights using an Amazonian-style bow.

Stargate SG-1, "Unlock the Universe"

The TV series *Stargate* (1997–2006) was inspired by the 1994 movie of the same name. In it scientists allied with the military unearth an ancient device that unlocks portals to other dimensions in time and space. The creators of the show made a few significant changes to the formula set by the movie, among them the introduction of a central female character—military operative Samantha Carter (Amanda Tapping).

The success of the *Stargate* series then inspired yet another spin-off—*Stargate Atlantis* (2004–2006). In this television show an international team launches an expedition through the stargate to the lost city of Atlantis. Among its cast is Teyla (Rachel Luttrell), a feisty alien who mixes compassion with impressive fighting skills.

Warrior woman Samantha Carter (Amanda Tapping) from the television series *Stargate SG-1*.

The Fifth Element, the Perfect Being

As we have seen, director-writer Luc Besson has spent a good part of his career creating warrior women of various shades. From *La Femme Nikita* to *The Messenger*, he has romanticized, glorified, and even criticized these half-mythical, half-human creatures. In *The Fifth Element* (1997), Besson introduces to the screen Leeloo (Milla Jovovich), a sort of futurist Pippi Longstocking, who is variously described as "perfect," "a supreme being," and "the salvation of humankind." As an irresistible evil in the form of a gaseous ball rushes toward Earth, scientists reconstitute Leeloo from DNA in the form of "the fifth element," a being who, with the other four elements (water, fire, earth, and air), can save the Earth and its inhabitants.

It is not accidental that in the early part of the movie the priests, who are involved in the ritual of salvation, and the scientists, who seek to reconstitute this being, all speak of the entity using masculine pronouns. They are unable to break out of the cultural box, which assumes that any *thing* with that power must be male. The scene where a machine reconstructs Leeloo underneath a plastic dome, using her perfect cells to replicate her body into its complete form, is visually reminiscent of the famous twenties silent science fiction film *Metropolis*, where Maria (Brigitte Helm) is encased under a similar dome while being transformed. She is even depicted wearing similar "thermal bandages."

In many ways the rebirth of Leeloo is a satire on *Barbarella*'s opening sequence where the astronautrix does a striptease in space. Here Leeloo is also nude, at least initially, and does radiate that same naïveté, having not yet absorbed the experiences of human life or even the language she needs to negotiate within her new environment. However, as the titillated general approaches, examining her body closely and talking to her as if she were a child (very much like the commander in *Barbarella*), Leeloo responds by pushing her fist through the supposedly impervious container and attacking the offending general. In contrast to Maria in *Metropolis,* who lies passively under the dome, Leeloo acts like a wild animal, breaking free and escaping.

An innocent abroad in this world of the future, Leeloo sets about to absorb as much information as possible, evidenced by

Leeloo (Milla Jovovich) takes aim in *The Fifth Element.*

her rapid scanning of human history in the form of video lessons designed by her servant priest (Ian Holm). When she finally comes to the realization of her mission, to find the four stones that represent the other four elements, she enlists the aid of an alienated, bitter ex-military man—Dallas (Bruce Willis), a character right out of *film noir*. He immediately falls for Leeloo and forms an obsession, which she rejects when he offends her by taking a kiss without her permission, as she tells him. She does, however, bend her rules a bit when Dallas proves himself by joining the quest for the stones.

In the battle to retrieve the stones, set in a luxury resort in

This scene from Fritz Lang's classic science fiction movie *Metropolis* bears a strong resemblance to a similar scene in *Fifth Element* where LeeLoo is regenerated underneath a clear dome.

outer space called Phloston, Leeloo is wounded after a Bruce Lee–style fight where she is outnumbered. Dallas and her priest retrieve her and transport her to Egypt, where the ritual must be performed. Leeloo, however, has become disillusioned with mankind and its penchant for violence and sees no purpose in completing the ritual. In a romantic ending, typical of Besson, Dallas places her at the center of the circle of stones and whispers to her that he loves her and that love is worth saving. And so she activates the stones and saves the world. The healing power of love, the theme in both *La Femme Nikita* and *The Professional*, is reaffirmed, and Dallas is permitted to kiss his "goddess."

Zhora (Joanna Cassidy) with Detective Deckard after her snake performance in *Blade Runner*.

Blade Runner, "More Human than Human"

One of the finest science fiction films ever produced on many levels, but particularly in regard to its unusual emotional depth for the genre, was Ridley Scott's cyberpunk classic, *Blade Runner* (1982), inspired by Philip K. Dick's 1968 book *Do Androids Dream of Electric Sheep?*

Blade Runner imagines a decaying universe where the poor and disenfranchised are relegated to Earth in overcrowded cities on which the sun rarely shines and the rain falls constantly. This world in fact resembles the nightmarish vision of *film noir* of the forties, filled with menacing shadows, slick wet streets, detectives in trench coats—Deckard (Harrison Ford)—and femme fatales with padded shoulders—Rachael (Sean Young). Scott even utilizes icons of the forties in his most important scenes: downtown Los Angeles, Chinatown, and the Bradbury Building.

The rampant and often nihilistic view of commercialism portrayed in the film is reminiscent of author Chuck Palahniuk's (*Fight Club*) alienated viewpoint of present-day society spinning out of control, reduced to a series of sound bites and hungry for artificially created drama. Blimps overhead advertise sponsors that are "helping America into a New World," laying bare an Illuminati-like occult system, reinforced by the pyramid structure that houses the Tyrell Corporation, the center of the ultimate commercialization—that of artificially created humans, known as "replicants." According to Tyrell, "Commerce is our goal. More human than human is our motto."

The replicants, however, have become rebellious against their maker's purpose. They've developed emotional reactions of their own and do not wish to fulfill their destined place in the new world order. Foreseeing that independent thought might become a problem, Tyrell set them with a failsafe mechanism to ensure their containment if necessary— their lifespan is only four years long. In addition, replicants can be weeded out from the human population by the Voight Kompf test, which measures emotional reactions.

Daryl Hannah as Pris, the deadly "pleasure model" in *Blade Runner*.

Deckard is the "Blade Runner" set to the task of "retiring" the replicants, referred to in slang as "skin-jobs." The fact that euphemism is employed in speaking about the extermination of the replicants is interesting. The power of words has long been a weapon used by dominant cultures and races to oppress minorities. Euphemism masks unpleasant or gruesome reality by substituting for the accurate word one that tells less than the truth, thereby reducing the tension or abhorrence associated with the true meaning of the word. Deckard "retires" replicants because they are a hazard. This euphemism, conceptually at least, removes some of the morally reprehensible implications of the action, as dehumanizing racial terms employed by the military in wars may make it easier to kill the enemy. But this latent moral confusion begins to build for Deckard, especially when the replicant Rachel asks him, "Have you ever killed a human by mistake, Mr. Deckard?"

The name Deckard is an interesting choice for the character. It is pronounced the same as (René) Descartes, the famous philosopher who originated the philosophical creed of rationalism— that human reason is the source of all knowledge, as opposed to the idea that at least some knowledge comes from what we perceive through our senses. This dilemma is very much splitting Deckard down the middle. On one side stands Tyrell Corporation and all patriarchal authorities; on the other, the woman/replicant Rachel, who is so convincingly human that the evidence of his senses begins to conflict with his duties, which require him to hunt down and brutally kill another female replicant, Zhora (Joanna Cassidy), who was located at an establishment featuring

exotic dancers, performing lewd acts by "taking the pleasures of the serpent" with artificial snakes.

There is a great deal of feminist subtext in the film, despite its initial misogynist appearance. Zhora was never shown performing her snake act on camera, which would have been tempting to do. Her act occurs off camera, as Deckard is shown watching, seeming unsure, and then pointedly turning away to his drink. We are led to believe that this reaction of his is of more importance. We do see her naked in the dressing room scene, but at this point she is shedding the accoutrements of her act, washing off the makeup and sequins. When Deckard begins to succumb to male tendency and tries to dry her with a towel, she strikes and attacks him with great viciousness.

Zhora's death scene is considered by some to be almost erotic, breaking through the glass panes in slow motion, her fetishistic see-through outfit glistening in the rain. However, what truly comes through seems to be shame. Deckard has shot her in the back. The fetishistic see-through outfit only serves to show even more clearly that she has been shot repeatedly in the back, and her boots, designed to appeal to males, only hobble her, making it difficult to run. Her face is shown in pain as she crashes through the windows.

Interestingly enough, at the first shot she falls to the ground, and we can see the feet of a man wearing black pants standing by casually watching the scene, neither afraid for his own safety nor attempting to help the injured woman. She gets up and still tries to stagger away through the glass corridor, which is, incidentally, a shop with mannequins lined up behind the glass—replicas of women wearing sexy boots and outfits almost exactly like the one Zhora is wearing.

The camera pans back at the final portion of the scene, and we see the mysterious man in the black suit again, wearing a matching hat pulled down to cover most of this face. Still he stands casually watching Zhora's horrible demise, hand in pocket. Who is this man? What does he represent? He may be the character Gaff, played by Edward James Olmos, whose importance wasn't defined until the director's cut was released.

The background music evokes sadness, and Deckard does not appear in the least bit happy that he has "retired" a dangerous

Opposite: Replicant Pris (Daryl Hannah) on the streets of downtown Los Angeles in *Blade Runner*.

A pensive shot of Rachel (Sean Young) from *Blade Runner*.

replicant. He is clearly distressed, as he is when he performs the Voight Kompf test on the replicants.

Deckard is also drawn to Rachel. Seeing her tears, he wants to comfort and protect her, in the standard male-savior model, despite his misgivings. When he takes time to do research and question the authorities, he begins to empathize with the replicants' plight. They are implanted with false memories, which could be read as socially conditioned, programmed. But this knowledge, this awakening of independent thought, appears to become overwhelming to Deckard. Later, during the love scene between Deckard and Rachel, he becomes forceful, angry. He shoves her around, pressing her up against a wall, as if desperate for an emotional response. He tries to kiss her but pulls back, perhaps repelled by the thought of kissing something that might be empty, artificial, without human emotion. In a sense, he fights displacing blame for any lack of arousal onto her. He doesn't want to accept her as inhuman. He wants her to be human, so that he can connect. He is desperate to penetrate her on an emotional level and not be made inadequate, impotent. This could partly explain why he turned away from Zhora during her erotic performance with the snake, mysteriously repelled. He feels inadequate with women, unable to connect emotionally.

In his apartment, we see old-fashioned photos of women lined up as if on an altar, one of which Rachel picks up while Deckard is sleeping. His mother? The photo resembles Rachel a great deal, right down to her style of dress. Rachel takes down her hair and looks at herself, comparing, blurring lines further. She plays his piano, on which a music book is already opened up to a song that we must assume is sentimental. Deckard awakens and is made vulnerable by the maternal connection. He sits down beside her at the piano and tells her she plays beautifully, leaning over and kissing her (not confrontationally on the lips, but more worshipfully, on the neck.) But her response is cold, detached. Not only that, she gets up to leave. He cannot bear it. He grabs her forcefully and commands her to kiss him, commands her to say out loud that she wants him. She must initiate it.

However violent Deckard appears pushing her around, he is actually so emotionally vulnerable at that moment that he is like a child. He cannot bear the thought of an empty shell of a

186

woman. And that perhaps goes even deeper, as his fantasy of a mother figure is so integral to his world. Rachel had shown him a picture of her mother before as evidence that she was human. If there is no mother figure, then he may be no different than the replicant Leon, for instance, who couldn't pass the Voight Kompf test in the beginning of the movie. Leon even shoots the interviewer when asked to talk about his mother.

Another model of replicant woman/surrogate mother resides, at least temporarily, in the Bradbury Building. She is Pris (Daryl Hannah), described by the commander of the Blade Runner unit as "a basic pleasure model, the standard item for military clubs in the outer colonies." Her incept (birth) date is February 14, 2016—Valentine's Day. Thus far all of the replicants were designed as slaves in some form or other. The female replicants were often intended for use as prostitutes, but sometimes as a different sort of slave—in Rachel's case, secretary to Tyrell. They have a male leader in Roy Batty (Rutger Hauer), though he is also a slave, albeit programmed for leadership. Their true father is Tyrell.

Pris takes to dressing herself in punk anarchist style, painting her face and eyes like a dark clown, perhaps symbolic of her feelings about her position as a "pleasure model," created for the entertainment and use of men. All the replicants are immature in a sense, mere teenagers in their short life spans. To disarm men, Pris even speaks with adorable innocence as a young girl. Her power is in her youthful sexual allure, which she uses as effectively as combat. She is like a living doll, and even pretends to be a doll amongst the many toys at the home she is hiding out in when Deckard breaks in. In her final scenes she is memorable for nearly killing Deckard by attempting to snap his neck between her powerful thighs. She appears almost grotesque at that point, like a crazed clown. She executes a number of acrobatic moves before being dispatched by a bullet to the stomach, a move that symbolically disarms her of her sexuality by blasting away the female uterus.

In the director's cut, *Blade Runner* ends differently than in the first release, without the "uplifting finale." The emotional impact is stronger, in a subtle but shocking ending reminiscent of *The Sixth Sense*. The incorporation of the unicorn vision in the director's cut further suggests that Deckard himself is a replicant.

Rachel (Sean Young), more wide-eyed and innocent here.

Dizzy (Dina Meyer) sparring in
Starship Troopers.

Starship Troopers, "You Can't Step On These Ones"

Director Paul Verhoeven purposely designed his campy *Starship Troopers* (1997) to resemble the science fiction serials of the forties, filled with overstated patriotism, corny emotions, and cliffhangers that defy reason. In this story of human versus alien bugs, there are two significant warrior women who are on opposite ends of the Amazon spectrum. Carmen Ibanez (Denise Richards) is a studious, intellectual, no-nonsense female who excels in school and eventually becomes a starship pilot. Carmen exemplifies the intellectual warrior woman who uses her intelligence and reason, rather than her physical skills, to fight the enemy. Dizzy Flores (Dina Meyer), on other hand, is more a palpable presence,

Bai Ling as the acrobatic cyborg villain in *Sky Captain and the World of Tomorrow.*

sexually as well as combatively. She trains alongside the men, even showering with them. She glories in physical battle, and so she is on the front line in the invasion of the alien fortresses. Both women are rivals for the love of the *pro forma* cardboard serial hero—Johnny (Casper Van Dien). Dizzy is, of course, much more direct in her pursuit of her sexual prey, while Carmen demands time and persuasion in order to submit.

Sky Captain and the World of Tomorrow

The filmmakers of *Sky Captain and the World of Tomorrow* (2004) have created a unique science fiction movie that seems to be made in the thirties or forties, looking forward to a future that never came about, similar in many ways to William

Cameron Menzies's *Things to Come* (1936). The two main warrior women in the film are the cyborg villain played by Bai Ling, and Franky Cook (Angelina Jolie), the fighter pilot who helps the ostensible hero (Jude Law) invade the island fortress of the evil Dr. Totenkopf. She dresses in a military uniform of the period and wears a patch over one eye to make her appear even more daring, as well as to connect her to daredevil characters in the comics and serials of the thirties and forties.

In *Sky Captain and the World of Tomorrow*, Ling returns to the type of villainous role that established her career in America (most notably in *The Crow*). Dressed again in the height of fetish style (hood, goggles, and catsuit), she throws the hero, Sky Captain, across the room, leads an army of robots who respond to her control, and defends her island fortress against discovery. It is only during her kendo-style battle with the Sky Captain that we discover that she is in fact a cyborg created by a mad doctor. Ling's character (called the Mysterious Woman) even battles Franky Cook, who leads a squadron of planes to aid the Sky Captain in his plan to destroy the island laboratory of the evil mastermind bent on world destruction.

Alien, Ripley Faces the Archaic Mother

The image of Ripley (Sigourney Weaver) from the *Alien* (1979–1997) series will haunt warrior women films for the next two decades. Her strength, her cool reason, her ferocious maternal instincts—all have informed the creations of numerous warrior women to follow.

In *Alien* (1979*)*, the first film in the series, director Ridley Scott does for Sigourney Weaver what he will do for Demi Moore in *G.I. Jane* eighteen years later. He strips his character of most of the trappings of cultural femininity in order to make her an equal and often superior soldier in a group of tough military men. She wears no makeup and sports cropped hair. She has tight control of her emotions, maintains a fit, muscular body, and interacts with the men on the spaceship with almost no reference to her gender. In order to further emphasize Ripley's equality/superiority, Ridley inserts the character of Lambert (Veronica Cartwright), a crew member who displays the more traditional markers of

Above: Sigourney Weaver as Ripley, transformed with shaved head in a male penile colony, in *Alien³*.

Opposite: A maternal image of Ripley (Sigourney Weaver) from James Cameron's *Aliens*.

femininity—indecision, emotionalism (she cries in several scenes), softer features, and a more mellifluous voice.

Ripley is, of course, the hero of this dramatic piece. When the spaceship is invaded by the alien, she is the one who keeps her composure and becomes the leader of the attack against the creature. She is also, to use Irene Karras's term, "the final girl." After the alien has destroyed the rest of the crew, she survives and launches a shuttle to escape the predator. Even when she discovers that the alien has hidden in the shuttle, she maintains her calm in the face of battle and ejects the alien into space.

In the sequel to *Alien*, *Aliens* (1986), director James Cameron simultaneously works at two purposes: "re-feminizing" Ripley and enhancing her prowess as a warrior. Ripley reluctantly returns to space to help rescue a group of colonists who may have been attacked by aliens similar to the one she defeated. Again her toughness, her composure in the face of danger, and keen intelligence serve her well as she becomes the ostensible leader of the group of Marines sent to "extract" the colonists.

Private Vasquez (Jenette Goldstein) plays another memorable character as a muscular, combative Latina grunt who doesn't back down from anything. When a macho cohort asks her if she has ever been mistaken for a man, she replies pointedly, "No. Have you?" When she first encounters Ripley, she mutters, "Who's Snow White?" She acts as a counterweight to the more mellow Ripley.

While on the colony, the party finds a young girl—Newt (Carrie Henn)—who has survived the massacre of her family by the aliens. She forms an attachment to Ripley, and Ripley responds by taking on the role of her surrogate mother. Ripley's mixed feelings about motherhood are relentlessly explored in a symbolic sense throughout all the *Alien* films.

Probably the most telling scene is Ripley's confrontation with the alien mother in her nest, based, like the entire series, on the designs of H. R. Giger. The two "mothers" confront each other in a chamber that resembles a primal womb more than a space station. It is wet, dark, and oozes fluid. During the scene Cameron often frames the mother alien and Ripley in two-shots, as Ripley defends her "adopted" child, Newt, as fiercely as the alien defends her brood. "Get away from her, you bitch" is one of the famous catch phrases of the movie.

Opposite: Jenette Goldstein as the tough-as-nails Private Vasquez in *Aliens*.

Alien³ becomes darker, as the ship carrying Ripley ends up on a remote planet inhabited only by male prisoners of a penal colony. She finds out the worst horror has happened: her own body contains one of the embryonic aliens, which will eventually grow and burst out and end her existence (a sort of ultimate pregnancy fear). Her femininity is stripped away yet again in response, and her head is memorably shaved before she ends up making the ultimate sacrifice.

Dark Angel, "Engineered to Raise Hell"

Max (Jessica Alba) astride her signature bike in *Dark Angel.*

James Cameron, of *Aliens* and *Terminator* fame, brought to the screen another haunted "third-wave" teen warrior in the form of Jessica Alba in *Dark Angel* (2000–2002). Alba plays Max Guevara (a not too subtle homage to revolutionary Che Guevara), a genetically enhanced human prototype who has escaped, along with a number of her fellow "transgenics," from the government facility Manticore, where they were scientifically engineered and trained. Max, like her "brothers and sisters," possesses superhuman powers designed to make her an ideal warrior. The world Max inhabits is nightmarish, filled with dark city spaces and *1984*-style government repression.

The audience first sees Max dressed in black in a series of shots as she speeds on her sleek motorcycle through the streets of a wet and dark Seattle. In the next scene she is shown on top of the Space Needle, where she crouches like a feline, wary and alert. Max, like so many female warriors of the last decade, draws her look from the Goth/fetish world, with a little bit of Catwoman thrown in for good measure. Her outfits are tight fitting and most often black. She favors leather, latex, and vinyl, emphasizing her speed and power, as well as her feline dimensions.

Max is a child of the streets, of the hip-hop generation. She alternates between a standard English dialect and a ghettoese, depending on to whom she is speaking. She expresses only disdain for the power structure (symbolized by the deeply flawed Lydecker—John Savage—and the brutal White—Martin Cummins) that created her and her "siblings" and so feels no qualms in using violence to defeat them. Her loyalties are to her "freak" outsider friends (the final episode where Max, her friends, and the transgenics defend their Terminal City from the government is in fact called "Freak Nation").

Max's best friend, Original Cindy (Valarie Rae Miller), is a lesbian; her "siblings" transgenics; and her "lover" a crippled, virus-ridden intellectual (Logan—Michael Weatherly) who runs a pirate, anti-government transmitting station. Max, like any typical Goth heroine, has her own demons. She has a difficult time controlling both her anger and her sexuality. Because of her altered DNA, she has intense emotions and hormonal shifts. She even goes into heat like a cat because of her "feline DNA." This makes it difficult for her to remain faithful to her off again/ on again boyfriend Logan. She fears overwhelming the fragile Logan with her sexuality, but, in addition, she feels guilt for having been indirectly responsible for both his physical handicap (he was paralyzed while defending a friend of Max's) and the virus he contracted, which was enhanced by his contact with Max's explosive DNA.

The lead males in *Dark Angel*, much like those in *Buffy*, fall into two categories: vulnerable, sensitive men who are never enough for the powerful warrior women of the series (Logan in *Dark Angel* and Riley in *Buffy*), or unreliable "bad boys" who will ultimately cause the heroine more grief than satisfaction (Angel and Spike in *Buffy*; Alec in *Dark Angel*). In this way the writers of the shows make very definite third-wave feminist statements about men. Be wary of them, but do not shun them as your feminist mothers might have done. They are a legitimate mode of sexual expression when they can be tamed, as well as companions when they can be trusted. Alec (Jensen Ackles), designed as Max's mate by Manticore and named by Max because she considers him a "smart aleck," alternates between destructive and supportive behavior. He relieves her sexual tension on several occasions, but he also infects her with a virus on orders from the government. He eventually joins her rebellion, but continues to "hit on" attractive women, even in her presence.

In the last episode of the series, Alec joins Max in her rebellion in Terminal City. There the transgenics and friends hold off the army of extermination led by White. In the final scenes Max joins hands with Logan, choosing, at least for the moment, the sensitive man as her companion in battle.

Trinity of *The Matrix* Series

One cannot underestimate the influence of *The Matrix* series (which premiered in 1999) on action movies in both style and philosophy. Admittedly, the films draw heavily on *Blade Runner*, as well as German expressionistic classics like *Metropolis*, for their visual style and assimilate Hong Kong action films for their superhuman fighting sequences. But all that said, the Wachowski Brothers have managed to blend these elements brilliantly while, at the same time, adding a few of their own to create a unique eclectic trilogy. Biblical allusions abound (Zion, Trinity, Nebuchadnezzar, Neo as messiah, the Oracle), as do historical references to African-American history, reinforced by the significant number of Black actors in the movie.

In addition, the Wachowski Brothers pepper their dialogue with zen-like koans as they lead their viewers through a complex discussion of the meaning of love, choice, and existence. And, finally, although the style of the movies owes much to expressionist films of the past, the Wachowskis have infused the films with their own predilection for the world of fetish, seen most obviously in the outfits of the characters—with an emphasis on leather and vinyl, black boots, high heels, flowing trench coats, and narrow shades—but also evident in the ritualistic orgy scene in *The Matrix Reloaded* (2003) and in the bondage club in *The Matrix Revolutions* (2003).

Trinity (Carrie-Anne Moss) is, of course, the key woman warrior in this trilogy, although in parts two and three Captain Niobe (Jada Pinkett) also comes into her own. Trinity, along with the "chosen one" Neo (Keanu Reeves) and the prophet/warrior Morpheus (Laurence Fishburne), acts as point person in the battle against the virtual world of the Matrix, which has managed to gain control of the minds of the majority of humans. Her skill as a martial arts fighter, as well as a weapons expert, is demonstrated over and over again in the numerous battle sequences against the machines and "agents" of the Matrix. She is intense in her devotion to the cause, as well as in her love of Neo. When Persephone (Monica Bellucci), the dominatrix wife of Merovingian, demands a kiss of Neo in order to guide him to the Keymaker, Trinity responds with anger. When Neo's life is at risk in both *Reloaded*

Opposite: Black-latex-covered Trinity (Carrie-Anne Moss) takes a shot in *The Matrix* series.

Trinity with Neo in *The Matrix Revolutions.*

and *Revolutions*, she does not pause, even in facing death, to save him and in fact gives her life twice for her love, the first time resurrected by the healing powers of Neo.

If the final message of *The Matrix* is, as many believe, that love and sacrifice, not violence, is the ultimate power against evil, then Trinity is the emotional core of the trilogy. She never wavers in her support of Neo. He tells her repeatedly that he needs her and that she is his center. Her final sacrifice in *Revolutions* facilitates the destruction of the Matrix itself and the concomitant liberation of humanity.

Star Wars' Two Female Protagonists: Mother, Sister, Princess, Queen, Senator, and Warrior Too

The universe George Lucas has manufactured with his six-part *Star Wars* epic is for the most part aimed at young males. Its emphasis on video-game-style action sequences, its almost complete lack of mature sexuality, its stiff dialogue, and, of course, its two young protagonists—Anakin (Hayden Christensen) in the first three episodes and Luke Skywalker (Mark Hamill) in the second three make it a world in which women are either figuratively or literally mothers or, at best, sisters, even when they are romantic interests. Though Jedi warrior women are said to exist, they are rarely ever shown. The only two significant warrior women in the *Star Wars* series are Padme Amidala (Natalie Portman—of Luc Besson's *The Professional*) and her daughter Leia Organa (Carrie Fisher).

Padme Amidala was elected queen of the planet Naboo at fourteen. She defended her home against the invading Neimoidians, leading the attack against her own palace where the Neimoidian viceroy had taken up residence. After serving her term as queen, she became a senator in the Republic, the federation of planets that governed the galaxy. Although she tried to preach compromise and reason, the disarray within the federation, prompted by dark forces intent on establishing a dictatorship, led her to doubt the senate's effectiveness.

Natalie Portman as Queen/Senator Padme from George Lucas's *Star Wars* epic.

Padme acted as a mother figure to the boy Anakin, who was discovered by the Jedi knights and touted as "the chosen one." Ten years later Anakin became Padme's bodyguard as the dark forces made several attempts on her life. Although she resisted, Anakin pressed his displaced Oedipal love upon her. Eventually she relented after witnessing his torment over her rejection of him, as well as his grief and anger after the murder of his mother. She voyaged to Geonosis with Anakin to rescue the Jedi Obi-Wan from the Separatists. They were captured, but bravely defeated a series of beasts set upon them in an arena. Padme ultimately gave birth to twins: Leia and Luke. However, she lost her lover to the dark side as Anakin became the feared Darth Vader.

Leia Organa was the daughter of Padme and Anakin and the sister of Luke Skywalker. She was raised in the royal house of Alderaan, unaware of the identity of her father or her brother. Trained as a princess, she entered the Imperial Senate, but was secretly aligned with the rebels who were fighting the forces of the Emperor. Captured by the imperial forces, Leia endured torture, supervised by her father Darth Vader, but refused to give up the

location of the rebels or their plans to destroy the empire's secret weapon—the Death Star.

Like her mother, Leia was a determined, forthright, and somewhat sassy woman who refused to yield to any man, even when in love. She had a brief flirtation with Luke Skywalker, again reinforcing the quasi-incestuous themes that run through the series. But in the end she married the cynical, although loyal, Han Solo. She later rescued her love from the hands of Jabba the Hutt, whom she strangled with the chain he had used to bind her as a slave. Leia continued her struggle against the empire and eventually discovered the true identity of her brother, father, and mother.

The Terminator Series

James Cameron made yet another foray into the universe of the warrior woman with *The Terminator* (1984) and *Terminator 2: Judgment Day* (1991). In both these films Cameron and his co writer Gale Hurd trace the character arc of their heroine, Sarah Cooper (Linda Hamilton), from timid single woman to intimidating fighter, eventually even a match for the cyborg terminators sent from the future to destroy her.

Our first glimpses of Sarah in *The Terminator* type her as victim. She exudes insecurity and fragile femininity in her appearance and in her choice of jobs, working as a waitress, a service position traditionally associated with females. When pursued at night by the Terminator (Arnold Schwarzenegger), she panics, unable to come up with a means to defend herself. Eventually she is rescued by a freedom fighter—Kyle (Michael Biehn), also sent from the past to defend her. When he is wounded in the struggle, she is even terrified of bandaging him, admitting to her fear of blood. In total, Sarah is the classic weak-willed female of the eighties in need of a strong male figure to rely on and to love. She makes stupid moves like calling her mother at a crucial time, therefore giving away their location.

But as the film progresses and her defender, Kyle, dies, Sarah begins to unearth the warrior within. Discovering that she is carrying a child who will defend the Earth against the machines that will rule it in a post-apocalyptic future, she gathers up her

Above: Linda Hamilton as Sarah, transformed into a hardened warrior in *Terminator 2: Judgment Day.*

Opposite: Princess Leia (Carrie Fisher) in her renowned slave girl outfit from *Return of the Jedi.*

Terminatrix (Kristanna Loken) dominates the obsolete male version of the Terminator (Arnold Schwarzenegger) in *Terminator 3: Rise of the Machines*.

strength and faces the seemingly invincible Terminator, crushing him in a hydraulic press and then heading for Mexico to give birth to the savior of humanity.

By *Terminator 2*, Sarah has evolved into a full-fledged fighter. While training with guerrillas in Latin America, she has developed a formidably muscular body, as well as an impressive skill with an arsenal of weapons. Housed in a mental institution because of her belief that a nuclear war, precipitated by the machines, is about to occur, she escapes from the institution, "taking down" several of the guards, as well as her psychiatrist, without a backward glance.

Meeting up again with her young son John (Edward Furlong), who is now protected by a reprogrammed terminator (Arnold Schwarzenegger again) against other, newer terminators, Sarah has become a fighting machine not unlike the cyborgs she battles. In developing this warrior persona, however, Sarah has lost her emotional connection to her son. By the end of the film she regains it only after she is able to cry, and so, in the minds of the audience, recapture a quality traditionally associated with females on-screen.

By *Terminator 3: Rise of the Machines*, Sarah has died, and her son has grown up a haunted, alienated man with visions of a post-apocalyptic world. The primary female warrior in this sequel is the Terminatrix (read: dominatrix), played by model-actress Kristanna Loken. The Terminatrix is the most advanced cyborg yet, far superior to the older model (Schwarzenegger), a fact that works ironically both within and without the movie as aging action hero Schwarzenegger seems less energetic and macho in this second sequel.

As soon as the Terminatrix transports herself into the world of the past, she immediately adopts the symbols of aggressive female sexuality: a red leather outfit, black boots, a sports car, and even larger breasts. She then proceeds to cause mayhem wherever she goes. The Terminator is no match for her, as he himself admits, and ends up decapitated by a blow from her boot heel. Even her final destruction, predictable in a genre movie of this kind, can only be accomplished by detonating a nuclear device that destroys not only her, but the original Terminator as well.

Chapter 8
Hell Hath No Fury

Probably the most effective motive for society to accept otherwise "nice" women breaking out of their traditional gender roles and committing very bad deeds is vengeance. Revenge is an action often more easily attributed to women than men, considering deep cultural fears about the duality of women and suppression. The revenge film displays what brutality might be lurking right beneath the surface, ready to be triggered off.

The old cliché applies here in spades: "Hell hath no fury like a woman scorned." In this chapter the reader confronts a series of women warriors who have taken the law into their own hands to right a wrong, restore justice and balance, or just because they get pleasure out of it.

The Deadly Viper Assassination Squad (DiVAS) of *Kill Bill*

"Bill's last bullet put me in a coma—a coma I was to lie in for four years. When I woke up, I went on what the movie advertisements refer to as a 'roaring rampage of revenge.' I roared. And I rampaged. And I got bloody satisfaction. I've killed a hell of a lot of people to get to this point, but I have only one more. The last one. The one I'm driving to right now. The only one left. And when I arrive at my destination, I am gonna KILL BILL."

—The Bride, *Kill Bill*

Opposite: Uma Thurman with veil and samurai sword in a publicity still for *Kill Bill*.

Beatrix (aka the Bride) faces off against the Crazy 88.

Kill Bill follows the classic female revenge format. The Bride suffers being severely beaten while pregnant, having her fiancé and entire wedding party killed, and being shot in the head. Upon waking from a four-year coma, she finds that her baby is gone and a corrupt nurse has arranged for her repeated rape by pimping out her body while she was unconscious. This is a case where motive has definitely been sufficiently established for an epic bloodbath of female revenge to take place.

Watching *Kill Bill Volume 1* (2003) and *Kill Bill Volume 2* (2004), or almost any Quentin Tarantino movie for that matter, one cannot help but feel that the film was ultimately made primarily for Tarantino's own viewing pleasure, with the audience of secondary concern. Yet it is easy to be drawn into it. Tarantino's universe is a frenetically paced world with all the trappings of a fourteen-year-old boy's adventure fantasy, a psychological counseling session, and a manic pop culture/multimedia experiment

put together. It's a bit of a surreal, bizarro world, where airplane seats are equipped with slots designed to hold passengers' samurai swords and women are in positions of power equal to or greater than men.

Tarantino's obsessive, almost fetishistic inclination toward homage is ever present. Dialogue references, choice of background music, custom name-branded props, Uma Thurman wearing the same yellow-and-black suit that Bruce Lee wore in *Game of Death*, the Crazy 88 wearing Kato masks like Bruce Lee in the old *Green Hornet* TV series, are only the tip of the iceberg. Each scene is packed with so many nostalgic or symbolic details that you can barely keep up. Some say he has "copied" films like *La Mariée était en noir* (1968), aka *The Bride Wore Black*, where the widowed bride character pulls out a notebook on an airplane with a "kill list" of five scribbled names, which she proceeds to cross out.

Left: Bruce Lee as Kato in *The Green Hornet* television series of the sixties.

Right: The famous yellow suit of the late Bruce Lee from his final film *Game of Death*.

207

Movie poster for the Francois Truffaut film *La Mariée était en noir.*

It is obvious that he takes bits and pieces of dozens of old films and TV shows, mixing and fusing old grindhouse cinema with his own material. *Lady Snowblood* (1973) was an influence, as well as *Shogun Assassin* (1972), *Hannie Caulder* (1971), *Black Sunday* (1977), *Master Killer (1978),* and so many more. Steve Rose of *The Guardian* says, "It is almost easier to list the films that haven't influenced Quentin Tarantino than those that have." It is also interesting to note the constant recycling and revitalizing of scenes and material. In a candid interview with Tomohiro Machiyama in the e-zine *JapAttack*, Tarantino remarks

> I went out to dinner with Kinji Fuaksaku and Kenta (Kinji's son), and I was going, "Man, I love this movie [*Battle Royale,* Kinji Fukasaku]! It is just so fantastic!" And I said, "I love the scene where the girls are shooting each other." And then Kenta starts laughing. So I ask, "Why are you laughing?" He goes, "The author of the original *Battle Royale* novel would be very happy to hear that you liked that scene." And I go, "Why?" And he says, "Well, because it's from *Reservoir Dogs*!" Even when I was watching it I was thinking, "God, these 14-year-old girls are shooting each other just like in *Reservoir Dogs*!" And Kenta said, "He took that from *Reservoir Dogs*, so he'll be very proud that you like that!"

One thing that is unique about the *Kill Bill* films in comparison with many other action films with female leads is its lack of consciousness about women being so powerful and accomplished. It doesn't go where other stories do in terms of challenging the gender role. It comes off completely natural that women are as powerful as men, if not more. Many films tend to spotlight the fact that the woman is breaking traditional gender roles, presenting it more as an anomaly than the norm. Or they do so as if patting themselves on the back for being so progressive, like TV shows that feature token gay or lesbian characters. Instead of presenting these characters naturally, they place such emphasis on their differences that many of them simply become caricatures. Not that the women of *Kill Bill* aren't way over-the-top in relation to the norm. It's just the fact that they are women is not brought so prominently to our attention. Note that even in the scene where O-Ren decapitates Boss Tanaka for challenging her leadership, she only mentions the fact that her heritage was brought up as a negative, not her gender, when he called her a "half-breed bitch."

The women of *Kill Bill* are anomalies as human beings for their incredible skills, not for gender. The male gaze cannot easily exploit them either, as their "female gaze" stares directly back in aggressive confrontation. They dress to please themselves, in attire that matches their position and personality, not the standard and often vulgar spandex. Even in the scene where Budd (Michael Madsen) is at the strip joint where he works, no opportunity is taken to momentarily display women dancing in the background or changing in a dressing room over his shoulder. Female characters wear sleek business suits, formal kimonos, casual jeans. There is a general lack of cleavage throughout the film, compared with most (if we don't count toe cleavage, that is). Tarantino does not hold back on his trademark foot-fetish shots. Interestingly enough, in one scene during the moments before the bloody battle at the House of Blue Leaves, the Bride walks across the glass floor as the public runs away in panic. The camera angle is shot upward, looking through the glass floor. The people running away are barefoot, while the Bride wears shoes. However, for a quick moment you can read the words FUCK U on the bottoms of her soles.

The Bride strides across the floor of the House of Blue Leaves.

The characters of *Kill Bill*, while not delved into very deeply, do not come off as one-sided. Nothing is really black-and-white, strictly good or evil, in most cases. Our brief glimpses of the characters' pasts make us appreciate their motives on some level. Uma Thurman, in an interview with *W* magazine (May, 2004), comments

> Quentin's not a moralist. He's freed himself from that traditional blanket distinction where there's a good guy and bad guy and each must behave according to his role. I think it's exciting to see something that's morally unpredictable, and in this twisted way you can feel the humanity inside a caricature-ish kind of storytelling.

Beatrix in training.

Beatrix Kiddo, aka the Bride, aka Black Mamba, aka Mommy (Uma Thurman)

Beatrix was Bill's lover and protégé. However, upon finding out she is pregnant one day, she makes a choice between his will and her own, for the first time defying him. She deserts him in order to provide a better life for her child, away from his corrupting influence. One on hand, this seems like a bit of a standard patriarchal theme. The female protagonist woman *must* be portrayed as maternally inclined above all else to be acceptable and likable. Her life *must* revolve around her child first and foremost in order to be a figure of sympathy and understanding for the audience. Breaking this rule of maternal love makes her into monster. She should be ready to throw herself in front of a truck for her child, otherwise risk alienation.

However, the Bride's actions may also be considered in other, less conventional ways. It could be read that the "child" also

Beatrix and her trainer Pai Mei
(Gordon Liu) in *Kill Bill Volume 2*.

represents a part of herself. It is made clear to us in the first film that her child is a girl, not a boy. We are not introduced to the girl beyond that until the very end. Before the pregnancy, she explains to Bill later, she would have "jumped a motorcycle onto a speeding train" for him. What spurred her to grow this independent streak? We do find out later that the Bride was nearly assassinated right at the moment of discovering her pregnancy, by her fellow female assassin Karen (Helen Kim). But when Karen realizes that the Bride is pregnant and her true intentions, strangely enough she spares her in a moment of sisterhood, even congratulating her.

Bill (David Carradine) himself is clearly a daddy-figure. Like the infamous Charlie and his Angels, Bill controls his female minions from a remote place. In the first film, we do not even see his face. Just as with Charlie, we only hear his voice. We also see his hand, stroking the handle of his sword, which is positioned close to his lap. He repeatedly pulls it partially out, then sheathes it again, appearing ominous and threatening. He names himself Snake Charmer, while all the rest of the DiVAS are given snake names. His brother Budd has been assigned a snake name also, as one of Bill's subordinates. However, his code name is never emphasized (with a title card or in a voice-over) to the extent that the women's are.

The Bride's real name is Beatrix Kiddo—a little girl's name, and one that increases the patronizing father-figure image when Bill speaks it to her. None of the other characters call her Kiddo. Just Bill. Her name is even bleeped out during early instances when others speak it. It is first heard out loud only from Bill's lips when he greets her outside the chapel. Soon after he requests to meet her fiancé. He makes his ownership of Beatrix quite clear when he says, "I happen to be very particular about who my gal marries." He is even introduced to her unsuspecting fiancé as her "father."

The growing child within her could represent her growing independence and rebellion against the patriarchal authority in her life. She makes a choice between his will and her own. In choosing her own will, Beatrix is punished severely. She is beaten down, and her child, the sign of her independent identity taking shape within her, becoming more developed every day, is forcibly taken from her and put back into the possession of the father.

Beatrix stalking her prey with gun and sword.

When she wakes up from her long coma and becomes aware that she was robbed of a part of herself, she cries out in gut-wrenching grief. We find out soon after, when the two men arrive at the hospital room, that she has been repeatedly raped on top of everything else, by dirty, greasy men. Her own will is removed, literally and symbolically. Her female parts penetrated and dirtied by these unsavory men. She even involuntarily spits during the act, we are told (note: *spit*, as opposed to *swallow*). The little girl that has been taken from her is a part of herself (look at her earlier scenes with Bill before the massacres—she is far more childlike in demeanor). Her previous innocence and naïveté have been surgically removed. "Now her plumbing down there don't work no more . . ." the nurse/pimp advises. She has lost touch with her feminine self. She steals the Pussy Wagon and takes up the phallic sword in order to hunt down the "cunts" who did that to her and the "dick who is responsible."

Enter: Vernita Green, aka Copperhead
(Vivica A. Fox)

Vernita: So when do we do this?

The Bride: It all depends. When do you want to die? Tomorrow? The day after tomorrow?

Vernita: How about tonight, bitch?

The Bride: Splendid, where?

Living in a green, doll-like house in Pasadena, complete with a lawn full of brightly colored kid's toys, Vernita Green has given up "the life," with Bill's consent, to settle down with her husband and raise her daughter. The fact that the interior of this house will be destroyed during the fight between Vernita and the Bride, all the accessories of the traditional family setting broken to pieces

Vernita (Vivica A. Fox) in *Kill Bill* faces off with the Bride in Vernita's Pasadena home.

and the "housewife" left dead on the kitchen floor (littered with multicolored kids' cereal), stabbed in the heart, sets the scene for the rest of the movie. There's no going back. Beatrix has not only abandoned her gender's customary place in society, she has blown it to pieces, including her implied maternal responsibilities.

Many people criticized Tarantino for his treatment of the scene between Beatrix and the little girl Nikki, saying that if he had children he would have made the scene with a more sympathetic tone, and that Beatrix would not have spoken to the girl as if she were an adult. But here we see evidence that perhaps Beatrix is not as maternally centered as we might have assumed. Certainly she held off from killing Vernita in front of her daughter. But she still fully planned to kill Vernita, even though her death would traumatize the girl. She doesn't talk down to the girl.

In an interesting touch, the cereal box with the hidden gun inside, used by Vernita in the death scene, is from an old favorite cereal of Tarantino's called Kaboom (General Mills). The box in this instance advertises a SURPRISE INSIDE.

O-Ren Ishii, aka Cottonmouth (Lucy Liu)

O-Ren (Lucy Liu) establishes order in her meeting through the power of the sword in *Kill Bill*.

"As your leader, I encourage you from time to time, and always in a respectful manner, to question my logic. If you're unconvinced that a particular plan of action I've decided is the wisest, tell me so, but allow me to convince you, and I promise you right here and now, no subject will ever be taboo. Except, of course, the subject that was just under discussion. The price you pay for bringing up either my Chinese or American heritage as a negative is . . . I collect your fucking head. Just like this fucker here. Now, if any of you sons of bitches got anything else to say, now's the fucking time! [*pause*] I didn't think so."

O-Ren's story is told partially in animated form, much like Lady Snowblood's. O-Ren, like Beatrix, is a survivor. Half-Chinese and half-Caucasian, she witnesses, as a small child, the murder of

Gogo (Chiaki Kuriyama), the deadly teenager in *Kill Bill.*

her mother and father by a yakuza boss. O-Ren, at the tender age of eleven, seduces and then murders the man she believes to have killed her family, as well as his companions. Under Bill's tutelage, she becomes one of the highest-paid assassins in the Viper Squad and ultimately the "Queen of the Tokyo Underworld."

After the bloody carnage of the fight between the Bride and the Crazy 88, the final scenes between O-Ren and the Bride are set in a beautiful, pristine snowy setting. The mood is wistful. They were once close, sisters under the father figure of Bill. But now he has caused a fracture in the sisterhood of all of the DiVAS.

Gogo Yubari (Chiaki Kuriyama)

Japanese Businessman: Do you like Ferraris?

GoGo Yubari: Ferraris . . . Italian trash.

[*Japanese Businessman giggles.*]

GoGo Yubari: Do you want to screw me?

[*Japanese Businessman giggles again.*]

GoGo Yubari: Don't laugh. Do you want to screw me, yes or no?

Japanese Businessman: Yes.

[*She stabs him in the stomach with a samurai short sword.*]

GoGo Yubari: How about now, big boy? Do you still wish to penetrate me? . . . Or is it I who has penetrated you?

Gogo is the youngest warrior in this movie, only seventeen and already O-Ren's chief bodyguard. She is, however, one of the most violent and memorable. She is the embodiment of Freud's theory of virgin anger. Dressed in a schoolgirl's outfit and giggling behind her hand, she is the incarnation of the ethos the Japanese call "lolicom," a term drawn from Vladimir Nabakov's novel *Lolita* that refers to the male obsession with and worship of young girls. Her character is established early when at a bar an older man tries to pick her up for a tryst, to which she responds by "penetrating" *him,* with her knife. When Beatrix attacks

O-Ren's retinue at a nightclub, of all those she encounters, Gogo is her most formidable opponent, one of the very few who is able to disarm her of her weapon.

Elle Driver, aka California Mountain Snake (Daryl Hannah)

> "The venom of a black mamba can kill a human in four hours, if, say, bitten on the ankle or the thumb. However, a bite to the face or torso can bring death from paralysis within twenty minutes. Now, you should listen to this, 'cause this concerns you. The amount of venom that can be delivered from a single bite can be *gargantuan*. You know, I've always liked that word . . . 'gargantuan' . . . so rarely have an opportunity to use it in a sentence."

Elle is the most closely associated with snakes in the movie, a sure sign of evil for any woman. Her preferred method of killing is through poisons and venom. Her sadistic killing of Budd left him helpless on his kitchen floor in excruciating pain, dying in the midst of a pile of old porn magazines.

She is also Beatrix's evil doppelgänger. They are both tall and blond; both trained under Pai-Mei (Gordon Liu); both were in relationships with Bill; both serve as mother to B.B.; and both were insulted by Budd for being blond. Elle is depicted as a *monstrous femme* also because of her deformity—she is missing one eye. She is an evil version of Beatrix. She is what Beatrix could become, her dark side. Beatrix is fighting a representation of herself. Their epic fight, designed by Tarantino as a "War of the Blond Garantuas" takes place in the abject mess of a trailer, complete with a toilet-dunking and an entire spittoon being dumped on Elle's face. Beatrix is covered in dirt and blood. One of the most abject/erotic foot scenes occurs when Beatrix crushes Elle's freshly plucked eyeball with her bare foot and we see the mess squish out from between her toes. The removal of the eyeball is significant in a rather biblical sense, considering their fight as a conflict of two natures. "If your right eye causes you to sin, pluck it out and cast it from you; for it is more profitable for you that one of your members perish, than for your whole body to be cast into hell." (Matthew 5:29)

Elle Driver (Daryl Hannah) standing in the trailer of the defeated Budd in *Kill Bill Volume 2*.

It is very interesting that Elle is not shown dying, only writhing about wildly, almost inhumanly screaming (much like Daryl Hannah's other famous character, Pris from *Blade Runner*). In the end credits her name is not crossed off the "kill list" like the rest, but rather a question mark is placed over it. Beatrix has not perhaps entirely retired her darker side.

The Bride's Death and Rebirth

Beatrix, determined and reborn.

Up until being shot full of rock salt by Budd, humiliated and buried alive in a pine box, Beatrix had relied on the phallic sword as an extension of herself. In multiple scenes swords are slowly and sensually unsheathed and threatened. In multiple scenes Beatrix literally cuts men's swords down to size with her superior blade. She has incorporated the male symbol as a part of herself. However, once again the male instrument has failed her. Budd, the least capable of all of them, was able to dispatch her with little trouble and send her back, deep into the shadowy realms of the Earth, into a womblike environment of darkness, the greatest of all fears, being buried alive and engulfed.

It is here that Beatrix reconnects with the feminine side of herself. Of all things, the male master Pai-Mei contributed to her independence from Bill by teaching her superior skills that didn't require a sword. Though Pai-Mei made out to despise women and taunted her for her gender, he showed her great respect in not treating her less harshly because of it. His unrelenting training was a sign of gender equality, and she earned her way to more power by her own merit.

Drawing upon Pai-Mei's lessons, she finds it within her to use her own two hands to free herself, without the help of the phallic instrument. She bursts out of her grave reborn, more confident than ever, finally in touch with herself. She must do battle with her nature through Elle before going on to "kill Bill." But she no longer needs the sword. She dispatches Elle by plucking out her other eye, now making her more monstrous by the deformity, which will likely be an issue to come up later.

The final journey to Bill brings her to the most difficult battle of all. Mommy against Daddy. Upon finding Bill, she discovers that her daughter is still alive (her feelings for him?). She is as-

Beatrix faces "Daddy" Bill (David Carradine) to reclaim her dignity and her daughter.

tounded. Her daughter B.B. (Is her daughter's name a combination of "Bill & Beatrix"? Like "Q & U" in the credits later, for the two who gave birth to the Bride?), played by Perla Haney Jardine, presents her with a warm and inviting family atmosphere, in essence an invitation and temptation to rejoin the patriarchal order and her assigned gender role as the "Mommy." Beatrix watches as Bill takes care of the little girl, tucking her in bed, looking after her (she too could be taken care of by "Daddy" again). She is allowed to commune with B.B. alone for a while, and for the first time she is happy, rejoined to her little girl (and herself). They watch a video together, and we hear the words from *Shogun Assassin*, "My father was famous; he was the greatest samurai in the empire . . ." It goes on to say, "When he would see her, he would forget the killings."

The final showdown with Bill is emotional for both of them. He holds a part of her. But it's a part she has begun to regain control of on her own, as evidenced by her more feminine appearance in this scene. She has come for an all-out battle to the death wearing a long skirt and pretty top. She looks freshly scrubbed and wears little makeup. Their true battle is in their conversations about why they parted ways and what went wrong. The actual killing is swift. They don't even get up from their chairs. The sword fight takes place sitting down. Bill strikes, she blocks and dodges. He is expert with his sword and disarms her quickly. The phallic symbol is taken from her. However, she still holds the

scabbard. In a swift movement she directs his oncoming blade back into its sheath, which is highly symbolic, of course, and as he is rendered powerless for a moment without his blade, she strikes him in the heart with the five-point-palm, exploding-heart technique, taught her by her former master Pai-Mei. Bill confirms her return to femininity by affectionately calling her a "real cunt" soon after. She is tender with him, and he dies five steps later, of an exploded (broken) heart.

In the final scenes Beatrice takes her daughter B.B. back to a hotel. We see that she has reclaimed the "little girl" part of herself that she had lost, as she is portrayed lying on the bathroom floor in girly pajamas, crying and laughing, clutching a stuffed animal. The warrior has won the most difficult battle of getting back in touch with her own kidnapped identity.

Pam Grier, Black Avenging Angel

Discovered while working as an office assistant at American International Pictures, Pam Grier within two years (1973–1975) and three films—*Coffy, Foxy Brown, and Sheba, Baby*—became a cult figure, recently deified again in Quentin Tarantino's *Jackie Brown*. There are several reasons for this elevated status. She was among the first African-American women to play a warrior woman within the genre of the action movie. (Although Tamara Dobson had made her mark with her *Cleopatra Jones* role, it is Grier's films that have stayed the course.) Before this decade the cinema had largely relegated Black women to two typical roles: the obedient servant/nanny, epitomized by Hattie McDaniel in a long series of movies and TV shows, and the savage temptress, as played by Dorothy Dandridge in *Carmen Jones* and *Porgy and Bess*. Grier satisfied male audiences' prurient desires with nude scenes displaying her Amazonish body and strong personality. Or as one of the characters in Grier's films says, after being beaten up by her, "She's a whole lot of woman."

The first film in the series starring Grier, *Coffy* (1973), is the most *noir* of the trio. The film opens with Coffy pretending to be a junkie in order to trap two drug dealers. When she finds them with their stash, she blasts the head off one with a shotgun and then shoots up the other with heroin so that he overdoses.

Opposite: Pam Grier as Black Avenging Angel.

Although this shocking level of violence is typical of Grier's movies, the filmmakers (including director Jack Hill, who also helmed the sequel *Foxy Brown*) take pains to justify, at least partially, Coffy's violent actions. The film shows her visiting her catatonic teenage sister in an institution where she has been hospitalized after overdosing. After the visit Coffy breaks down emotionally, showing the audience her vulnerable side. The scene reveals the source of the psychological burden Coffy carries and shows the most obvious reason for her intense anger at the criminal world.

The filmmakers also portray the social context for Coffy's actions. The city she lives in (clearly Los Angeles, judging from the numerous location shots in Hollywood and Malibu) is rife with corruption. Her lover, Brunswick (Booker Bradshaw), is a councilman running for Congress who talks Black power but also, unbeknownst to her, takes money from the mob. In addition, the commissioner of police, as well as a clique of L.A. cops, work with the mob in their activities, which include drugs and prostitution. When Coffy's ex-boyfriend, Officer Carter (William Elliott), tries to defy this corrupt cartel of cops, he is beaten senseless by two thugs. All this corruption around her drives Coffy to seek revenge and justice.

In all Grier's movies she uses her sexual allure, as well as her physical strength and acute intelligence, to defeat her enemies. Grier gains the trust of male characters in her films by using the sexual stereotypes they project on her, and then reverses the stereotype, to the consternation of the unwitting character. In *Coffy*, she becomes part of the stable of prostitutes run by King George (Robert DoQui) and seduces her way into the home of Vitroni (Allan Arbus), the mob boss and the main source of drugs in the city. Knowing he has a fetish for dark women that he can abuse, she pretends to be a submissive "nigger bitch," as he calls her. But as he attempts to fulfill his fantasy, she pulls a gun from her stuffed animal and brings him to his knees, telling him, "I'm going to piss on your grave."

Before Coffy can make good on her promise to Vitroni, she has to undergo several more arduous tests of her courage and ingenuity. She escapes her captors in the Los Angeles River, where they are trying to drug her up and murder her. She then steals a car and drives it into the home of Vitroni, killing everyone inside. Coffy, now weary of her battles and feeling like she is "in a dream," goes after her corrupt lover Brunswick. She finds him at his beach home with a young white girl. Outraged, she shoots off his genitals. Dropping the weapon, she wanders out onto the beach, no more fulfilled than she was at the beginning of the movie and maybe even a little more soiled by all the violence around her.

With *Foxy Brown* (1974) the filmmakers elevate the tone of the triad of movies. This shift in mood occurs with the titles of the film. Pam Grier, in silhouette, dances and performs martial arts moves in various costumes against multicolored backgrounds while her theme song blasts on the soundtrack. The sequence is a rather unsubtle takeoff on the James Bond movie title sequences. While the Bond movies usually featured beautiful female sex objects cavorting across the titles with a very masculine Bond appearing sporadically, Grier, in her usual transgressive manner, upsets the normal expectations of the audience (especially the males) by combining in herself the qualities of the sexy object and the hero. She is both Bond and a Bond "girl" simultaneously.

In *Foxy Brown*, our avenging angel has become more comfortable with her role and less prone to depression and guilt. She has accepted that the city is a *noir* jungle in which she must right wrongs when she sees them. "Vigilante justice? It's as American as apple pie," she ironically tells her lover, government agent Dalton Ford (Terry Carter). When her drug-dealing brother Link (Antonio Fargas) calls her in the middle of the night to protect him from two thugs, she tucks her gun into her bra, gets in her "muscle car," and speeds off to the rescue, taking a few "bad guys" with her as she knocks them off the road with her vehicle. Foxy's sense of justice even overrides her family ties. Later in the film when Link deceives her and continues to deal drugs, she destroys his apartment and shoots his ear off.

As in the earlier movie, Foxy uses her dominant sexual persona, which carries through all three movies, as a weapon as effectively as any piece of armament. After her lover is shot down by the mob, on the order of Katherine Wall (Kathryn Loder)—their gangster chieftain, she ramps up the action and infiltrates their inner circle by posing as a prostitute. Not only is Katherine

immediately taken with her charms, as is her lover Steve (Peter Brown), but so are her clients, particularly a prestigious judge whom Foxy humiliates by ridiculing the size of his penis and then pushing him out nude into the hallway of his swank hotel.

Foxy's plans to disrupt the mob's operations come to a temporary halt when she is exposed and sent to a drug lab in the desert. There she is raped and beaten. Using her innate ingenuity, she cuts her ropes and douses the desert lab with gasoline, immolating both the shack and its inhabitants. Foxy then approaches a Black power committee to help her destroy the rest of the mob. Once again shifting into her "sexpot" role, she convinces a pilot delivering drugs to take her to his desert rendezvous where she and her Black-power allies will seize the shipment and eliminate the mobsters. When the plane arrives, Foxy assumes the pilot's position and crashes it into the meeting place. She confronts Steve and has him castrated by the "brothers," then delivers his genitals to Katherine as a warning.

It is worth noting here that in both *Coffy* and *Foxy Brown* the Grier character castrates one of the chief male villains. In films filled with transgressive movements, this single act ranks among the most revolutionary. Very few films or even works of literature before or after have dared to deal with such a subject and violate this unofficial taboo. For this act not only directly attacks the patriarchal system by seizing the most potent symbol of male power, but it also evokes ancient cults based on self-castration in honor of such goddesses as Cybele and Astarte. In this way, in a semi-conscious manner, these films not only threaten male power, but also raise their heroine to the level of a goddess.

In the final film in the series, *Sheba, Baby* (1975), Pam Grier's character has finally entered the official world of detection and crime fighting by becoming a private investigator. This time she is operating out of a different *noir* jungle, Chicago. She has a successful business in the city, but finds herself embroiled again in family problems when her father calls her home to Kentucky to fight loan sharks who are threatening to eliminate him. By the third film, however, the formula is beginning to wear out, and much of the plot and action seems but a rehash of Grier's earlier avenger films.

Opposite: Pam Grier, ready for action in Tarantino's *Jackie Brown*.

The Long Kiss Goodnight, Film Noir and the Warrior Woman

Film noir has produced its share of deadly femme fatales, stretching all the way back to Barbara Stanwyck in the classic *Double Indemnity*. *The Long Kiss Goodnight* (1996) stands firmly in that tradition. Geena Davis plays Samantha—a heroine recovering from amnesia who wakes up to find her middle-class life as a single mom shattered by memories of her other self, a CIA hit woman named, appropriately, Charly Baltimore.

As the film develops, the viewer comes to understand that the deadly Charly is this woman's "true" persona and that Samantha's amnesia (a staple of *film noir*) was simply a coping mechanism manufactured by her psyche to deal with a series of traumatic events, including her pregnancy and a brutal attack by a cadre of terrorist operatives. When Charly is unleashed, Samantha finds herself in possession of fighting skills and a predilection toward violence.

By the end of the film, Charly/Samantha has fully unraveled her past, exacted her revenge on her abusers, as well as recovered her warrior woman side, with the aid of a supportive fellow agent (Samuel L. Jackson). In the uplifting resolution Charly gains the ability to reintegrate both personalities with the help of her daughter. And so she becomes both single mom and warrior woman in one stroke.

Foxfire, "It Took Them Seventeen Years to Learn the Rules, and One Week to Break Them"

Based on Joyce Carol Oates's novel of the same name, *Foxfire* tells the story of a gang of five girls who come together to dish out some punishment to a science teacher who has been sexually harassing teenage girls. This act forms a bond between the girls, and they become avengers on a small scale, forcing an abusive father to support his junkie daughter, punishing Neanderthal jocks for their sexist attitudes, and tattooing themselves with a sign of their solidarity.

Charly/Samantha (Geena Davis) reintegrates her two personalities in *The Long Kiss Goodnight*.

The leader of the girls is Legs (Angelina Jolie), a powerful personality who dominates the screen as soon as we first see her enter the classroom in the early moments of the movie. She is the glue that keeps them together, the electrical charge that initiates their acts of rebellion and rage. The relationship between Legs and Maddy (Hedy Burress) is particularly powerful, as Maddy is the only one who is able to penetrate the tough-girl façade of Legs.

The Naked Kiss, the Prostitute As Warrior

Samuel Fuller's *The Naked Kiss* (1964), much like Sartre's play *The Respectable Prostitute*, upset the expectations of the sixties audiences by presenting a call girl as the symbol of justice, rather than a pathetic victim or evil temptress, the two stereotypes most often seen in Hollywood. The film opens with a shockingly violent scene, at least for the period. A tall, angry, and intimidating woman (Kelly, played by Constance Towers), partially undressed, attacks the camera. This use of the subjective camera puts the viewer in the position of the man she is pummeling, her pimp, we later learn. She beats the man to the ground with her purse, and as she does, her wig falls off, revealing her shaved head, adding to the shock of the scene. As she continues to beat him bloody, she takes the money she is owed from his wallet and kicks him with her stiletto heel. Standing there over this supine man, Kelly is a visual foremother of Ripley in the *Alien* series, eerily resembling her, shaved head and all.

Mady (Hedy Burress), above, and Legs (Angelina Jolie) talk on the bridge in *Foxfire*.

In order to avoid the mobsters who want to punish her act of rebellion, Kelly loses herself in Middle America, a small town called Grantville, where everyone knows one another, where children play in the streets in safety, and where the sun always seems to shine. Fuller's re-creation of small-town America is purposely ironic, exaggerating all the clichés. As Kelly walks through the town, the music is peaceful and lilting. She passes children at play. Quaint houses beckon her. Immaculate yards and streets contrast with the dark, dank streets of the urban jungle from which she came.

Overwhelmed by the surface innocence and purity of the place, she takes a room with Josephine (Betty Bronson), the town seamstress and spinster, and gives up her profession, at least for

Poster for the Samuel Fuller movie
The Naked Kiss.

the time being. She finds a job as a nurse's aide working with crippled children. Even in this hospital environment, Kelly carries her city toughness with her. As the head nurse points out, she runs her ward like "Captain Bligh." And according to another nurse, who wants to quit because of the stress of working with "damaged children," Kelly has "iron in her veins."

The film also underlines Kelly's keen sense of justice and her willingness to act on it in two key scenes. In the first she advises an unwed pregnant nurse and then gives her money to have her baby. In the second Kelly learns that another nurse has been approached by the madam of a bordello and given money as an advance to work there. Kelly lectures the girl, slaps her into common sense, and then takes the advance from her. She marches over to the bordello and wrestles the madam down, stuffing the money in her mouth.

Kelly's strength of character, grown out of her arduous life experiences, which allows her to discipline the children in therapy and thereby achieve "miracles" in their progress, is not without its vulnerabilities. In one tender scene she cries over a small baby whose legs are in casts, revealing the motherly side of this warrior. But Kelly's most vulnerable characteristic is her romanticism. She loves Beethoven's "Moonlight Sonata" and dreams of traveling to Venice, a dream the audience sees come alive in a fantasy sequence.

This romanticism leads Kelly to fall in love with the "benefactor" and war hero of the town, Grant (Michael Dante). He promises her a life of ease, world travel, and does not judge her for her past. Like so much of this "ideal" town he seems perfect, too perfect—for throughout the movie Fuller has been setting up a revelation that will shake Kelly, as well as this complacent microcosm of Middle America.

Kelly makes an unexpected visit to her fiancé's house, her new wedding dress proudly in hand. There she finds him molesting a young child. Grant falls to his knees before the shocked Kelly and asks her to understand, explaining that he picked her as a wife because he knew she would understand being "abnormal." In a rage Kelly picks up the phone receiver and splits his skull with one blow as her wedding veil falls on his face, symbolizing the gender shift implied in the scene.

The town, of course, refuses to believe her, especially when it is revealed that she is a prostitute. They turn against her and are reconciled only when the little girl is found and confesses that she was sexually abused by Grant. The final scene of the movie drives home the irony and the theme as Kelly leaves the jail and faces the townspeople who, as the local detective tells her, now have her "on a pedestal." She embraces the few loyal friends she made there and proudly walks through the crowd, refusing to acknowledge its presence. She is the victor, the warrior, the whore who has proved more "respectable" than any of these "good American citizens."

Attack of the 50 Foot Woman (1958 and 1993)

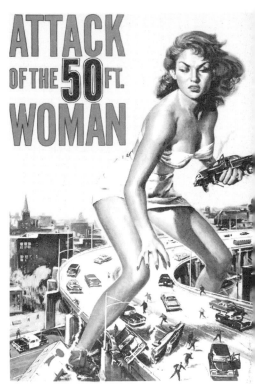

"See a female colossus . . . her mountainous torso, skyscraper limbs, giant desires!"

Nancy Archer (Allison Hayes) is a woman wronged. In the 1958 original film the audience first sees her driving erratically through the desert in the midst of an emotional breakdown. As she veers on and off the road, a huge, luminous ball appears in the desert before her, and a gargantuan hand emerges from the spaceship, reaching toward her.

The sheriff (George Douglas) and his deputy (Frank Chase) find Nancy wandering in the desert. They immediately assume she is drunk and proceed to humor her as she tells them her alien-visitation story. As becomes clear from the dialogue, they only agree to go look for the spaceship because she is the richest woman in town.

The film then cuts back to the small town itself and a scene between Harry (William Hudson), Nancy's philandering husband, and his newest mistress, Honey (Yvette Vickers). Honey has wearied of waiting around for Harry to find the courage to break with his wife. She is the archetypal femme fatale of the piece, a strong woman in her own right, intent on achieving her ends at any cost. She finally seduces/coerces Harry into agreeing to take some kind of action to get rid of his wife and, at the same time, get hold of some of Nancy's money for them to run away together.

Nancy Archer is a particularly fascinating character because she represents both the dominant and submissive side of women

The giantess Nancy awakens and wreaks havoc on the town in *Attack of the 50 Foot Woman* (1958).

as portrayed in Hollywood movies. On one side she is a wealthy woman used to getting her way. She orders men about, whether it is her servile and devoted servant Jesse (Ken Terrell) or the local sheriff and his bumbling deputy, whom she purposely almost runs down with her car when they refuse to believe her story. She calls her husband a "parasite" and a "gigolo," both of which roles the audience knows he fulfills from earlier scenes in the movie. No matter the insults, however, Nancy still feeds off his slavish attention, which includes carrying her to bed and sensually taking off her clothes.

It becomes obvious to the audience, however, that no matter her strengths, Nancy is far too romantic and obsessive. She knows about her husband's affairs, yet takes him back when he comes crawling. When the doctors come to study her, after she has begun to grow into a giantess due to the exposure to radiation at the site of the spaceship, she submits willingly to their extreme measures, which include chaining her to her room, pumping her full of sedatives, and pronouncing judgments that attribute her fear of growing old as the cause of her psychological problems. Like the real-life feminist writer Virigina Woolf, Nancy is surrounded by male doctors, servants, police, and a husband, all of whom want to manipulate her to fit their vision of what a female should be: submissive, obedient, and eternally forgiving. By constantly reinforcing the idea that she is irrational, they isolate her further, which prevents her from defending herself properly.

But this giantess does finally awaken and tap into her immense power. She breaks free of her literal and figurative chains and proceeds to cause havoc in this small desert town. Her im-

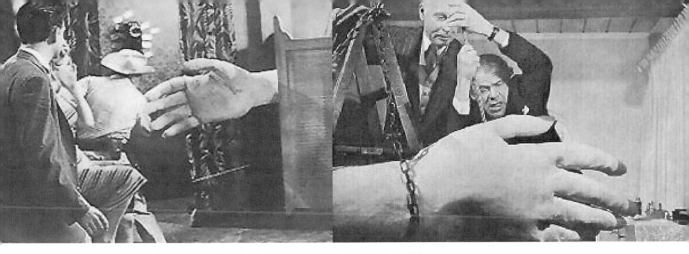

mense figure, dressed provocatively in a makeshift bikini, strides through the desert, shaking power lines and ripping up buildings, in search for her faithless husband and his seductive girlfriend. When she finds them at the their perpetual hangout, a nightclub, she rips the roof off of the establishment and crushes Honey with a beam. She then grabs on to her husband, this modern-day Gulliver, and struts back into the desert impervious to the bullets the sheriff and his deputy unload into her. As she reaches the power lines, however, one of the shotgun blasts causes a short circuit in the lines, and she is electrified, falling to her death, with the crushed body of Harry in her huge hand.

> "Do you ever get angry? What do you do when you get angry?"
> — The Psychiatrist, *Attack of the 50 Foot Woman*

In 1993 television remade *Attack of the 50 Foot Woman* for a postmodern, feminist time. Daryl Hannah played Nancy Archer and co-produced the movie. The director was Christopher Guest of *This Is Spinal Tap* and *A Mighty Wind* fame, known for his ironic tone and subtle satire. The adaptation of Mark Hanna's original screenplay for the 1958 film takes a similar approach.

In the beginning of the movie the character of Nancy Archer is much more submissive than her predecessor. Whereas the heroine of the 1958 movie constantly expressed her anger at the male world around her, this Nancy represses it. She is unable to even throw a rock at her cheating husband Harry's (Daniel Baldwin) sleek sports car when she finds him cavorting with Honey (Cristi

Conaway) at the local motel. And when dealing with her overbearing father (William Windom), she submits like a little girl. Her fate is foreshadowed when she toys with a little man in a dollhouse in her bedroom as her father and husband argue in the next room.

She also suffers from being constantly invalidated, made to feel she is irrational, hysterical, and otherwise mentally unstable (like her mother used to be). She, like many other female characters seeking the love and approval of their fathers, is often compared to her missing mother, blamed for her mother's sins or for resembling her. In this case, Nancy's mother is later revealed to have committed suicide. And it is when the husband and father disrespect her mother's memory that she loses control of her emotions and becomes tough and assertive with them. Even though they are being yelled at, they seem to be impressed by her take-charge attitude. But then the first surprising growth spurt occurs, as a result of the power of her outburst, causing Nancy to smash her head right through a ceiling, and suddenly she towers over the two men.

Consequently, this Nancy's encounter with the alien spaceship has, if possible, even more of a thematic impact than the original Nancy's encounter. The filmmakers of this new version transform the heroine's astronomical growth spurt into a blatant metaphor for female empowerment. It is brought up that Nancy's hormones are somehow to blame for her enormous growth spurt, a tongue-in-cheek allusion to classic abject-fear themes surrounding women's reproductive organs and cycles. Later several semi-trucks pass through town while Honey looks on from the beauty parlor where she works. One of the largest trucks has a SUMMER'S EVE douche advertisement painted across it.

As soon as Nancy recovers from the shock of waking up as a giantess, she begins to adjust with amazing rapidity as she feels empowered to express her emotions more freely because of her new size. Her voice takes on a deeper, almost ominous tone, and she chooses to change her style by putting together sexy dresses to wear, losing her frumpy ponytail, and wearing deep-red lipstick and vampish makeup.

This born-again feminist refuses treatment from her male medical doctor (Paul Benedict), who, like her husband and father, wants her institutionalized. "I have the authority of her husband and her father," the doctor proclaims. Instead of obeying, she seizes the phallic symbol of his profession, an oversized syringe full of fluid, and threatens him with it. She takes control of her dead mother's fortune by forcing her father to enlarge all documents so that she can read them and not just sign them. "I'm not a *little* girl," she tells him, now both figuratively and literally true.

But her Achilles' heel is still her husband, for whom she carries a torch even after discovering his infidelities, as well as his schemes to cheat her out of her fortune. Even after she has grown to her full height, she prepares a moonlight dinner for him and conjectures about ways a tiny man like him might love and pleasure a giantess like her. "There are pleasures waiting for you that you have never dreamed of," she happily informs him.

However, he harshly rejects her, calling her "unnatural," and says the idea of being intimate with her in that state (a symbolic state of rebellion) is sick and freakish. This is the final trigger for Nancy. After recovering, like her predecessor, she too goes on a rampage to express her anger over her husband's betrayal, heading across the desert to the town to confront him and his lover Honey. But there the similarity between the resolutions of the two films ends. This far more evolved Nancy does not kill her "sister" Honey. Instead she lectures her about her self-worth and lets her go. She does, however, roughly grab her husband. As helicopters attack, Nancy falls back on the power lines and is suddenly beamed up by the returning spaceship.

In the next scene the audience sees Harry in a group-therapy session with several other men who are discussing their feelings, as well as their retro attitudes toward women. Above them stand not one giantess, but three, staring into the little box in which they have placed the men. Nancy and her two sister goddesses observe the recalcitrant Harry, who is as stubborn and chauvinistic as ever. "You have to change to catch up with us," a disapproving Nancy tells him. In a comic and telling thematic reversal of the original movie, the alien giants who visit this planet and travel in space are not male, but female. And tiny men like Harry are put in re-education camps until they can accept this new feminist universe.

JAMES BOND 007

FOR YOUR EYES ONLY

The Little Man—Macrophilia in Media

In times when Nature, filled with fervor limitless,
Conceived and brought to birth many a monstrous child,
I fain had dwelt anigh to some young giantess,
Even as lies a cat, voluptuous and mild,

At a queen's feet. Full happily I would have seen
Her soul and body burgeoning in dreadful games;
Divining if her heart behind the matutine
Mists of her eyes concealed a sun of somber flames.

I would have roamed her mighty rondures at mine ease;
Crawled on the thighward slope of her enormous knees;
Or when at whiles, by summer-swollen suns oppressed,

She laid along the field her weary hugeness down,
I would have slumbered in the shadow of one breast
As at a mountain's foot a still and peaceful town.

—Baudelaire, "The Giantess"

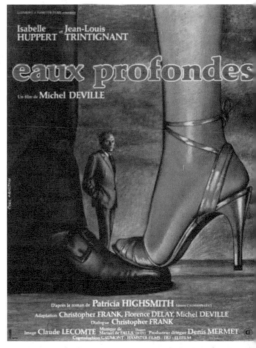

One can trace the image of the giantess deep into myth. Ancient goddesses of prehistoric times often appeared in stories as larger than life. In his eighteenth-century satirical novel *Gulliver's Travels*, Jonathan Swift took comic delight in setting his hero Gulliver in a land of giants, where he spent hours wandering over the naked body of his captor Mistress Glumdaclitch. Alice

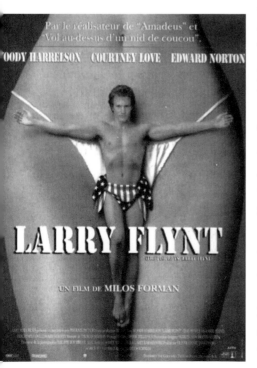

in Lewis Carroll's *Alice in Wonderland* too grew beyond her normal size after eating a forbidden mushroom, causing havoc in her world.

Today the erotic worship of giant women has taken on a life of its own. The powerful combination of fear and fascination of female power expressed in this dramatic physical form is the subject of countless message boards, Web sites, computer-generated art, and forums on the Internet. Technically the erotic obsession with such large women is labeled "macrophilia," but it is more commonly referred to as simply "GTS," short for *giantess*, by those who share the interest.

The giantess motif has long been interwoven with Amazon mythos, as Amazon women were rumored to be taller than average, not to mention strong and commanding. Comics such as *Femforce,* with its superheroine Garganta, a blond beauty with the power to increase her size, is just one popular-culture sample that links the giantess to Amazon origins. In *Femforce 43,* we see a standard twist of the lost-civilization theme when the Gammazons are introduced as an alien race of tall women from Galaxy G.

In film there are a few examples of giantess themes, such as the classic *Attack of the 50 Foot Woman* (1958 and 1993) and the campy *Village of the Giants* (1965), which featured a tiny male character desperately holding onto the bra straps of his gigantic, buxom captor while she convulsively danced about. In 1995 there was even a shameless parody titled *Attack of the 60 Foot Centerfold* that dealt with the side effects of a beauty-enhancing formula on two ambitious young models. The lesson in most cases is that when women become big (symbolically given power), they undoubtedly fail to use it in any rational way. They are motivated to seek revenge; they are petty and have little regard for human life. They revel in their newfound female power by toying with the little men or crushing them like ants. But this rather dark fantasy of female abuse is precisely what seems to appeal to the audience as yet another female vengeance theme.

The characters' drastic mutations are often attributed to a potion or chemical exposure of some sort. The woman is trying to make a change, maybe increase her powers of attraction or develop a diet drug or some form of vanity that will go awry and for which she will eventually be punished. In Corman's horror film *The Wasp Woman* (1960), a cosmetics maker develops an anti-aging formula from a jelly taken from queen wasps to regain her youth and beauty. From there on, it all goes wrong, of course, and she is punished for her vanity by becoming "a beautiful woman by day—a lusting queen wasp by night!" She kills all the men who lust after her new youthful face. In the original movie poster she is shown towering over a smaller, helpless man, ready to impale him with her stinger.

Most film mutations of women, whether they turn into a panther, a vampire, or another half-breed creature, are triggered by repressed passion and some type of hormonal response. The woman's anger (over a man's sins against her) becomes gargantuan and no longer manageable. Her wrath turns her into a vengeful giantess. She literally bursts out of her housewife clothing and becomes a fierce Amazon, forced to wear a makeshift loincloth and wrapping her breasts with a scant piece of cloth.

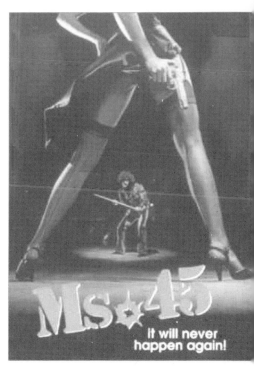

The other side of the coin is the shrinking man in movies like 1957's *The Incredible Shrinking Man*. (A modern version of this film is currently anticipated for release in 2006.) Even the shrinking theme gives the viewer the perspective of being at the mercy of a whole world of giants. The original *Attack of the 50 Foot Woman* of 1958, the *The Incredible Shrinking Man* of 1957, and even *The Wasp Woman* of 1960 may be indicative of postwar domestic tensions. Many changes caused by World War II and popular culture disrupted the traditional patriarchal family unit. Women were working, often in jobs previously exclusive to men, blurring the boundaries between masculine and feminine. Many films released during the time, particularly in the science fiction and horror genres, made the lines of sexual identity clear, even with a "he" or "she" specifically in the title. It was the *She Freak* (1966) or **Women** *of Devil's Island (1962)*. Hyperbolic imagery made gender crystal clear and unambiguous.

In Barry Keith Grant's book *The Dread of Difference*, he speaks about the threat to masculinity made graphically clear in the aforementioned films. He goes on to say

It is hardly surprising that in the 1970's the shrinking person is reinterpreted as a female who, instead of fighting a

A BEAUTIFUL WOMAN BY DAY—
A LUSTING QUEEN WASP BY NIGHT
The WASP WOMAN

spider over territory, is caught in the kitchen drain along with the garbage that swamps her domestic existence, or that in the 1990's the fifty-foot woman returns, into our very living rooms in a made-for-TV version, in the statuesque form of Daryl Hannah.

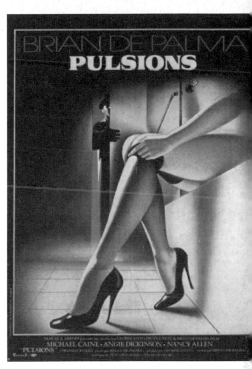

He also brings up Woody Allen's parody *Everything You Always Wanted to Know About Sex* (1973), which features a spoof segment on old B-movies with John Carradine. His "monster" is a giant breast bouncing around the countryside, squashing people or squirting them with milk.

It is interesting to note that even in cases where the films are not particularly about giant women, it is not uncommon to see movie poster art portraying men as tiny, next to a very large woman, evoking the theme of being under the control of the female sex or overwhelmed and engulfed by a situation, as evidenced by the examples on pages 234–239. Perhaps this imagery is about challenges to patriarchy, as has been mentioned. It may also be a form of fetishization of the female body, as women are depicted as larger-than-life body parts from whatever perspective is used, rather than as whole human beings. From the male's perspective, just her foot, or her breasts, are so large that they take up his entire vision, figuratively placing that body part on a pedestal.

Chapter 9
Enter the Dragons

"You are a child of the netherworlds. You are not a being of this earthly realm. You are a devil that abides by netherworldly principles, a beast . . . one whose disguise is human . . . one so evil that even Buddha cannot save you now."

—The priest to Yuki, *Lady Snowblood*

No other genre has placed as many women in hard-core action roles as martial arts cinema. The female warriors of Hong Kong and Japanese cinema have shaped many of the roles created today in mainstream film. Extremely prolific in their careers, some of these action stars have made more than fifty films, as well as being world-champion fighters off-screen. You may not always see their faces, but they also serve as the stunt doubles for many Hollywood actors who are untrained or too high a liability for such work.

Asian culture, although known for suppressing women throughout history, has highlighted strong female warriors on-screen since as early as the twenties in films like *Red Heroine* and *Swordswoman of Huangjiang*, which exemplify the operatic roots of wuxia pien tradition. Wuxia films, often identified by their mythical fantasy themes (not to mention wire-fighting sequences), have been a realm where women have flourished. They are consistently portrayed as being as capable as men in battle skills, if not more so. Government bans against female performances in early Chinese opera were also troublesome to early Chinese cinema, but the bans were eventually lifted as the popularity of female leads grew so remarkably.

Female warriors were highlighted in early films like *Red Heroine*.

It is interesting to note that in spite of allowing women to break gender barriers in battle, these films still quite strongly uphold other elements of classic femininity. Filmmakers often posit female action heroes as role models, emphasizing issues of loyalty to husband, elders, and family, as well as suppressing intentional sensuality (at least in most early films). We see many brother-and-sister fighting teams in Hong Kong films, such as the main two characters of *Swordswoman of Huangjiang*.

The master/disciple relationship is a sacred theme in the genre on many levels. The stance a character takes in preparing for a fight, often accentuated or exaggerated, is important not only in identifying the character's form, but also in many cases in signifying who her master is. In *Crouching Tiger, Hidden Dragon* (2000), Michelle Yeoh's character Shu Lien asks within moments of fighting Jen (Zhang Ziyi), "You've been trained at Wudan?" Jen's moves were light and esoteric, sucking in and redirecting the energy rather than exhibiting the more overtly aggressive Shaolin style, a trademark of Wudan. This is an important distinction because that small piece of information tells us so much more about the character.

Female characters also tend to pine away for dead husbands, fathers, or masters, ritually lighting incense to dead loved ones and killing off the perpetrators of heinous crimes against their house. Revenge is a generally considered honorable, even though it may be extremely vicious and bloody. In *Lady Snowblood* (1973), the mother of the main character Yuki (Meiko Kaji) commands her newborn child to seek revenge for her family. "Yuki . . . you were born for vengeance," she utters, just before dying from the difficult childbirth.

Angela Mao's role as Bruce Lee's sister in *Enter the Dragon* (1973) even touched upon the practice of female suicide in late Imperial China. Young Chinese women of that period were held up as icons for committing suicide if their husbands died at war or if they were sexually assaulted, or in some cases even if they were sullied by verbal harassment. Angela Mao's character Su Lin commits suicide in *Enter the Dragon* when cornered by a group of men. Rather than be raped, she chooses the higher calling of being chaste. This gives Bruce Lee's character even more reason to avenge his household, as he utters his famous pre-fight lines: "You have offended me, you have offended my family, and you have offended the Shaolin Temple."

Martial arts cinema includes a variety of styles and sub-genres, from the acrobatic classic Chinese kung fu to jidai-geki period films, a genre so vast that thousands of films have never been seen outside of Asia. Cultural differences make many of the films difficult for American audiences to fully appreciate. What may appear silly and over-the-top to Americans are often celebrated clichés in martial arts cinema— the impassioned vows of vengeance, the spurting blood (received with mixed audience reactions in Tarantino's *Kill Bill Volume 1)*, the dramatic stances. The many languages and dialects do not always translate properly, and besides that, Asian culture does not express everything as directly as Americans do, especially in period films heavy with tradition. Intent may be veiled within subtle poetry or references, not outwardly stated. Even colors have meaning. It is easy to label some films like *Hero* (2002) that use color in unusual ways as simply "art house," but the fact is filmmakers may use certain colors in a film not merely for aesthetic reasons, but to evoke meaningful political or spiritual associations.

Emotion also may be more private and repressed in the martial arts genre. We see emotion and romance featured far more prominently in crossover films like Ang Lee's *Crouching Tiger, Hidden Dragon* and Zhang Yimou's *House of Flying Daggers*. Their large budgets allow for not only spectacular visual components, but also actors with more than just athletic ability. Some, like Michelle Yeoh, are given the chance to express sides of themselves that have rarely been seen before, since many talented action stars become stuck in films that concentrate solely on the action.

Many American children of the seventies have grown up with some exposure to martial arts through the portals of TV shows like *Kung Fu* with David Carradine or the Bruce Lee films. Though Bruce Lee and Jackie Chan became internationally recognized, few women broke through the mainstream barriers. Angela Mao was recognized most often as "the girl who played Bruce Lee's sister." A few Caucasian male actors like karate world champion Chuck Norris continued to bring awareness of martial arts to mainstream American audiences. His students included personalities

such as Steve McQueen, Bob Barker, Priscilla Presley, and Donnie and Marie Osmond. But for decades, we rarely saw any real martial arts brought to screen besides the standard "Judo-kick!" that Mike Meyers makes fun of in his Austin Powers films.

Bruce Lee's son, Brandon Lee, began to break the barrier in one of his first films, *Rapid Fire* (1992), where he executed a number of exciting stunts reminiscent of Jackie Chan, using lots of props. He had more mainstream American looks than the typical martial arts hero, which probably helped his case. He was just about to break out on a large scale as the lead in *The Crow* (1994) when he died in a tragic accident on the set. Not long after that we would see Jackie Chan finally start to achieve some well-overdue popularity with American audiences when fan Quentin Tarantino presented him with a Lifetime Achievement Award at the 1995 MTV Movie Awards. His amazing skills were showcased in American theaters in *Rumble in the Bronx* (1996). Before that he had brought one of Asia's top female action stars, Michelle Yeoh, to the screen in *Supercop* (1992). Yeoh was also given a part in the 1997 James Bond film *Tomorrow Never Dies*, which made her internationally recognizable and opened many doors for her.

In recent years we have seen mainstream female action change dramatically, with martial arts becoming an essential skill for any action lead. Modern movies such as *Charlie's Angels*, which came out in the same year *Crouching Tiger, Hidden Dragon* was released (2000), employ wire harness work, but it is taken out of the mythical context of wuxia pien tradition. The result is many slick *Matrix*-style action shots with heavy film editing. The overuse of wirework and computer-generated effects these days borders on the absurd, resulting in comic-book-style characters and action. It is likely that comic book movies have recently become so abundant in part because of the availability of such technology.

Unfortunately the breadth of this book doesn't allow us to give proper coverage to the fascinating martial arts genre and the vast number of films and actors that have shaped its development over the years. The amazing work of the famous Shaw Brothers Studios alone couldn't be done justice in one book. So for the purpose of this study we will feature an overview of a few of the popular martial arts films of recent years and some of the well-known actors of the past and present who have influenced action cinema.

Crouching Tiger, Hidden Dragon

Jen Yu (Zhang Ziyi) and Shu Lien (Michelle Yeoh) in *Crouching Tiger, Hidden Dragon.*

———

"Master . . . I started learning from you in secret when I was ten. You enchanted me with your world of giang hu. But once I realized I could surpass you . . . I became so frightened!"

—Jen Yu to Jade Fox, *Crouching Tiger, Hidden Dragon*

———

Nominated for ten Academy Awards and grossing over $150 million in American theaters alone, Ang Lee's *Crouching Tiger, Hidden Dragon* appealed to mainstream Western audiences on a large scale by combining dramatic elements with spectacular action sequences, haunting music, and visual imagery. Though the film may have drawn some criticism from hardcore martial arts fans for attempting to appeal to Western sensibilities, director

Ang Lee simply brought his inner fantasy to reality. *Crouching Tiger, Hidden Dragon* is a like a dream translated to screen, obviously incorporating elements of other films such as *A Touch of Zen* (1969), which has many very similar scenes. Ang Lee's success has allowed other renowned directors like Zhang Yimou to make more expensive martial arts films with wider distribution in the West.

Crouching Tiger's stunning wirework was choreographed by veteran Woo-ping Yuen, who also worked on *The Matrix* series. The first major fight scene featuring Jen Yu (Zhang Ziyi) and Yu Shu Lien (Michelle Yeoh) running across rooftops is reminiscent of Trinity's (Carrie-Anne Moss) memorable rooftop run in the first *Matrix* movie. Hong Kong martial arts stars like Michelle Yeoh and Pei-pei Cheng as Jade Fox are prominently featured in these crucial roles, and Zhang Ziyi performs wonderfully also. All actors went through grueling training on many levels. Director Ang Lee made Zhang Ziyi sit for hours on end working on classical calligraphy in order to understand more of what being a aristocrat meant to a young woman—hours of sitting still, upholding traditions and social protocol, the high decorum that was always present. Michelle Yeoh also spent much of her time on the set learning from Lee, even when she was not required to be there. Actor Chow Yun-Fat showed amazing discipline and talent in training to learn martial arts for his role as Master Li Mu Bai, which he did to an impressive level. Difficult for all of them was correctly mastering the language. With four different intonations in Chinese, there is no room for mistakes, because changing intonation means changing the word.

Director Ang Lee freely admits a fascination with female repression. The very name of the film, *Crouching Tiger, Hidden Dragon*, speaks of an impression of female power—a tiger, silent and hidden, yet of great strength, ready to spring and tear its prey apart. At the time the film was released, it was not common to see women cast so prominently in action parts. One expected the movie to be focused on Chow Yun-Fat's character, especially since he was already such a famous and established actor. However, the fight scenes are predominantly between all of the women, each of whom in a sense represent different parts of a woman's nature. Jen is the young and spirited teenager, wishing to rebel against

Opposite: Zhang Ziyi as the petulant Jen Yu in the film that opened the eyes of mainstream audiences to martial arts.

247

Jen Yu battles Dark Cloud's soldiers.

authority. Shu Lien is more mature and traditional, a combination of physical strength and sensibility, a balancing force. "I am not an aristocrat as you are," she says to Jen, "but I must still respect a woman's duties." Cheng Pei-pei is a middle-aged woman, portrayed in a witch-like manner, her beauty faded and bitterness apparent. All of them are justified in their attitudes, even Cheng's character Jade Fox. "Your master underestimated us women," she says to Li Mu Bai. "Sure he'd sleep with me, but he would never teach me. He deserved to die by a woman's hand!" It is not surprising that her character uses poisoned needles as a weapon, poison almost inevitably symbolizing the evil of women.

The fight scenes are like a beautiful form of Chinese dance to a percussion background. The fantastic work of Yo-Yo Ma on cello is a haunting voice threading the scenes together. Ang Lee was enchanted with the idea of music that sounded like a woman's wailing voice. The "flying" scenes, standard in many wuxia films, denote a form of "enlightened" kung fu that is not necessarily a form a flying, as much as a form of floating. It is the

Michelle Yeoh as Shu Lien.

result of using mind over matter to alter the body's density and therefore resist gravity. The softness of the moves, walking on water and such, is another trademark of those trained at Wudan Mountain. It is all about mastering the internal, and therefore altering the external.

The film concentrates most often on Jen's internal struggles. She is another example of the dual personality so often attributed to women, in comics, science fiction, and even horror films. On one hand, she appears in full decorum as an aristocrat, and in one tea scene she and Shu Lien speak to each other on that courtly level. In veiled terms Shu Lien makes clear that she knows Jen is the thief of Li Mu Bai's sword and disciple of Jade Fox and what the consequences of such actions are. Jen is exposed in a memorable moment when Shu Lien purposely drops her teacup and Jen's sharp reflexes automatically cause her to reach out and smoothly catch it. (This scene was also blatantly borrowed in the Brad Pitt and Angelina Jolie movie *Mr. and Mrs. Smith*, where Brad Pitt's character drops a wine bottle during dinner and his wife smartly

Jen makes off with Li Mu Bai's sword.

catches it, giving herself away.) But behind the aristocratic façade, when Jen later runs away and takes on the disguise of a boy, she is a different person. She becomes rude to others, eats like an animal, and revels in the life of freedom.

Jade Fox encourages her disciple's rebellion against patriarchal structure. "You don't want to waste your life as the wife of some bureaucrat, denied your talent." As Jade Fox walks toward her, a shadow falls across Jen's face, splitting it down the middle, making one half dark, one light. Jade Fox invites her to come be free and even eliminate her own father if he stands in the way: "It's the giang hu fighter lifestyle . . . kill or be killed. Exciting, isn't it?"

The master-disciple relationships in this film are unique. Usually the disciple strives to be trained by a great master. Yet in this film Jen has already surpassed one master (Jade Fox), and the great master Li Mu Bai desperately desires to teach her. Rarely do you see the master chasing the student. But there is an underly-

One of the "flying" scenes in *Crouching Tiger, Hidden Dragon.*

ing sexual tension in it all. Jen has stolen Li Mu Bai's sword. We observe him later adoring his sword when he retrieves it, running his fingers across the length of it in ecstacy, training in the early morning with great pleasure, executing many thrusting moves as Shu Lien quietly watches from a dark corner. "The sword is back. Are you happy?" she asks. She herself doesn't seem happy about the matter.

"I must admit, having it back makes me realize how much I'd missed it," he replies. The sword seems to represent his essence. When Jen possesses his sword in such a way, having stolen it right out from under him, he is enchanted with her (supposedly only on a master–student level). Yet Jen resists his wish to be her master still, in spite of the fact that he seems to have good intentions. She does not want to be subject to a man. She refuses when he commands her to kneel, saying, "Never!" Her rebellion ends up costing his life, and burdening her with guilt for separating him from Shu Lien.

Flying Snow (Maggie Cheung) in a standoff with Broken Sword (Tony Leung) in Zhang Yimou's *Hero*.

House of Flying Daggers and *Hero*

With two back-to-back films, *Hero* (2002) and *House of Flying Daggers* (2004), renowned Chinese director Zhang Yimou exposed viewers to bold visual statements and a sensual cinematic journey, bringing more breathtaking female fight sequences to the screen. *Hero's* warrior women (Moon—Zhang Ziyi and Flying Snow—Maggie Cheung) form two sides of an isosceles love triangle with Broken Sword (Tony Leung). Moon is the junior partner in the relationship—the petulant teen who wants the affection of her mentor Broken Sword at any cost. But the real complexity lies in each character's inner battle. Broken Sword and Flying Snow, ostensibly both assassins, are bent on bringing down the emperor (depending, of course, on which point of view the story is told from in this *Rashomon*-like tale). They are equals

in their depth of feeling, as well as in their skills as fighters.

One of the most beautiful fight scenes takes place between wushu experts Moon and Flying Snow in a sea of autumn leaves. Wushu is an appropriate form for this sequence, derived from *shaolin,* which means "young forest." It is very much a dance, taking on elements of nature, from animal stances to the disposition of tree branches, bending back and rebounding with natural force.

House of Flying Daggers, on the other hand, is centered on Zhang Ziyi's character Mei, a member of the rebellious Flying Daggers, a female-led organization of assassins fighting a corrupt government during the Tang Dynasty. As in *Crouching Tiger, Hidden Dragon,* we see scenes that could be taken right out of 1969's *A Touch of Zen,* with fantastic fights that take place in a bamboo forest.

Maggie Cheung in *Hero* strikes an artful pose.

Mei (Zhang Ziyi) about to perform in a game of "echoes" in *House of Flying Daggers*.

Placed undercover in the Peony Pavilion as a blind performer, a decoy of the Flying Dagger leader's daughter, Mei dances while singing a traditional song:

> "A rare beauty in the North. She's the finest lady on Earth. A glance from her, the whole city goes down. A second glance leaves the nation in ruins. There exists no city or nation that has been more cherished than a beauty like this."

The following complex sequence, called the "echo dance," is also performed in the sumptuous pavilion setting, ending in a staged fight with the police officer Leo (prolific Hong Kong actor Andy Lau). The echo dance is a sensory feast that took a full twenty days to shoot and required Zhang Ziyi to perform in classical long dance sleeves. She later uses these sleeves as a

weapon to fling a sword at the police official Leo (who is later revealed to be part of the Flying Daggers and deeply in love with Mei).

It is quite interesting how the entire dance scene is turned around later in the film when Leo is blindfolded in the forest and made to perform the echo dance for Mei. He is subjugated by his love for her. The giggling "Madam" of the Peony Pavilion is later exposed to be one of the commanders of the Flying Daggers, right hand to its leader Nia. When Leo subsequently tries to rape Mei in the forest out of jealousy of her new love Jin (Takeshi Kaneshiro), Nia materializes out of nowhere and throws a dagger into his back. "You can't force a woman against her will," she says, and then commands him not to take the dagger out, but to leave it embedded in his back.

"I've sacrificed three years for you," Leo tells Mei as he departs. "How could you love Jin after just three days?"

Zhang Ziyi in *House of Flying Daggers*.

The Landlady from *Kung Fu Hustle*.

Kung Fu Hustle

———

"You may know kung fu, but you're still a fairy."

—The Landlady to the Tailor, *Kung Fu Hustle*

———

One of the most unique martial arts characters to be brought to the screen in the recent past is the Landlady from *Kung Fu Hustle* (2004), Stephen Chow's cartoonish martial arts parody. In spite of its comedy status, *Kung Fu Hustle* has a strong cast of established Hong Kong veterans. The Landlady is played by Qiu Yuen, a well-known stuntwoman and actor who attended (and took her last name from) the same school that produced stars Jackie Chan and Sammo Hung.

Perpetually stomping around in a housedress and slippers with curlers in her hair and a cigarette in her mouth, the Landlady rules her slum tenement and all its residents (including her husband) with an iron fist. When angry, she takes off her slipper and slaps the offender in the face with it. Her warrior strengths are later revealed. One of her amazing abilities is to scream, "Shut up!" at eardrum-blasting levels. Her husband the Landlord, actor Wa Yuen, also from the same school and famous for doubling for Bruce Lee in *Fist of Fury* and *Enter the Dragon*, performs brilliantly in comedic fashion, fighting in "Drunken Master" form. The film is chock-full of funny, unique characters such as the effeminate Tailor (Chiu Chi-ling) and the silly Barber, who walks around with his pants barely hanging on.

Yuen Wo-Ping again puts his considerable choreography skills to work for high visual impact. Each of the warrior characters in the tenement fights with tools of his trade—the Tailor with his rings, the baker with his rolling pins. One of the funnier moments occurs when the character Sing (played by Stephen Chow himself) tries to blackmail the barber and threatens the residents:

Sing: Whoever wants to die step forward!

[*The whole crowd steps forward.*]

Sing: That old woman with the onion! You look real tough. Want to try me? I'll let you hit me first.

[*The old woman walks up and punches Sing in the stomach so hard that he doubles over and blood runs from his mouth.*]

Sing: What do you do?

Old Woman: I'm a farmer.

A woman of the netherworlds.

Lady Snowblood

"I've come to take you away . . . to take you where you truly belong. Come now . . . it's time to start the journey of death."

—Lady Snowblood to her victim

Lady Snowblood (1973) is about a woman conceived, born, and raised for one purpose in life: to exact revenge for her family's brutal deaths and the rape and torture of her mother. Trained under the harshest circumstances from a young age, underneath her striking beauty Lady Snowblood is an accomplished killer, carrying her samurai sword in the handle of her parasol.

This Japanese film of the jidai-geki genre carries all the classic elements of samurai films, with the extreme bloodletting and violence that so directly influenced Quentin Tarantino's *Kill Bill*

Volume 1. Lady Snowblood is expressed in Tarantino's O-Ren character, who also wears a white kimono, as well as in aspects of the Bride, in her vicious quest for revenge. Besides using the same music ("The Flower of Carnage") and similar cut-in manga/anime moments, one scene in particular has Tarantino's character O-Ren speaking (in animation) almost precisely the same lines Lady Snowblood utters before killing a man:

> *Lady Snowblood:* Look closely at my face. Does this face remind you of somebody? Somebody that you raped?

> *O-Ren* (in *Kill Bill Volume 1*): Look at me, Matsumoto. Take a good look at my face. Look at my eyes. Look at my mouth. Do I look familiar? Do I look like someone you murdered?

Angela Mao.

In contrast to all the extreme bloodletting, Lady Snowblood is elegant and mesmerizing, with her snow-white skin and eyes that convey an unrelenting intensity. She wields her sword in a unique underhand hold and low guard that stand out among the rest. Her sword skills are deadly, and she has no trouble slicing off limbs without a second thought. In one scene she is so upset when her enemy hangs herself before she can kill her that she cuts the woman's entire lower body off in frustration. The film is memorable and uncompromising in its dark vision of female power.

Other "Dragons" of Martial Arts Cinema

Angela Mao   To many she is the queen of Hong Kong action films. One of the main reasons may be that she was one of the first women to break the patriarchal barrier that kept females from performing martial arts in movies. She began her career as a star in the Chinese opera, the training ground for so many of the martial arts stars. But she later specialized in kung fu and the Korean art of hapkido, which she used extensively in her films. In fact one of her most memorable films is called *Hapkido* (1972).

In a period when Hong Kong action films were dominated by the likes of Bruce Lee and Sammo Hung, she persevered, making

Cheng Pei-pei in *Come Drink with Me*.

scores of films for companies like Golden Harvest and, of course, playing Lee's sister in the international production of *Enter the Dragon* (1973). During the seventies and eighties she worked with the best directors of martial arts films, including Huang Feng and Luo Wei.

In one notable movie, *Invincible Eight* (1971), she continues the tradition of cross-dressing by warrior women. In the film she unites with her brothers to seek out the murderers of her parents. She plays the role with great subtlety, yet is able to project force and will, particularly in the battle scenes. Her revenge is complete, if somewhat bitter.

Cheng Pei-pei Western audiences are now familiar with Cheng Pei-pei because of her role as the devious Jade Fox in Ang Lee's *Crouching Tiger, Hidden Dragon*. But before Ang Lee revived her career in the West, Cheng was a star of the highest magnitude in Hong Kong, as well as a groundbreaker.

Cheng's fighting style was always heavily drawn from dance, particularly ballet, which was the basis for her training as a child. In fact when she married and came to the United States in the seventies, she continued her career as a choreographer for several dance companies, putting her film career on the back burner.

Cheng's two most memorable early films are *Come Drink with Me* (1966) and *Golden Swallow* (1968). She was one of the first females to be given a lead role in a martial arts movie and so opened the way for the flood of woman warriors to follow.

Cynthia Khan.

Cynthia Khan Cynthia Khan was born Yeung Lai Ching, but D & B studios changed her name in order to capitalize on the success of Cynthia Rothrock and Michelle Khan. Like many of the female martial arts stars, her background was in dance, which gave her the agility she needed for the parts she played. She took over from Michelle Khan in the successful *In the Line of Duty* series in 1988.

Playing Officer Yeung, who is itching for action but is held back by an overprotective uncle, she finally gets her chance to bring down a cartel of thieves. The action is violent and often gritty, and Khan demonstrates high levels of skill in the fight scenes. The following year she made another episode in the series. This time she played opposite martial arts star Donnie Yen, which added even more to her luster. She reunited with Yen in *Tiger Cage 2* in 1988. It too was a success.

Cynthia Rothrock A five-time undefeated World Karate Champion in Forms and Weapons, Cynthia Rothrock is an extraordinary athlete, holding multiple black belts in Korean and Chinese martial arts. She was one of the first women to appear on the covers of martial arts magazines. She appealed to Hong Kong producers with her all-American looks combined with hard-core action talent and appeared in dozens of Asian films.

Cynthia Rothrock.

Although Rothrock's films were of uneven quality, often poorly dubbed and cheaply made, she did exhibit dynamic fighting skills, including her trademark "scorpion kick." She is most remembered today for titles like *Blonde Fury* and *Millionaire's Express* and her China O'Brien films. She even made a guest appearance on *Hercules: The Legendary Journeys* in the episode "Not Fade Away."

Moon Lee Moon Lee was born Lee Choi Fong and entered the Hong Kong cinema in 1981 while still a teen. She received favorable notice for her role as Gigi in the popular *Mr. Vampire* series in 1986. But she did not become an action star until her watershed film *Angel* (1987) and its sequels.

In the *Angel* films, she played a character named after herself: Moon, one of the members of a band of crime fighters modeled after *Charlie's Angels*. Although Moon's character looked deceptively innocent, she could be tough and vicious in a fight, even utilizing the traditional male weapon of nunchakus. Her confrontation with Yukari Oshima remains the high point of the film.

Moon retired from movies in 1997 and opened a dance school. She has appeared in several documentaries about martial arts films, where she has expressed her negative feelings about the male-dominated martial arts film industry.

Kathy Long Kathy Long is probably most famous in this country for her stunt work on such big-budget films as *Batman Returns*, where she did Michelle Pfeiffer's more dangerous fighting scenes,

but she has also appeared as a kickboxing instructor in *Romy and Michelle's High School Reunion* (1997), as Fros-T in *Rage and Honor* (1992), and in episodic television shows like *Street Justice*.

"There's nothing more real and honest than getting hit in the face," Long says, regarding her work. She was kickboxing world champion off and on throughout the eighties and retired with an 18–1 record. She took up professional boxing and then entered the film industry as a stunt double. She continues to write for martial arts periodicals like *Blackbelt*.

Judy Lee, aka Ling Chia Like many of the Hong Kong stars, Judy Lee (Ling Chia) was educated for the Chinese opera. She took up a rigorous schedule in which she trained as many as sixteen hours a day. It paid off ultimately for Lee, as she became a famous stage star who was known for her acrobatic movements and high kicks.

In her movies Lee does not have the power that many of the other Hong Kong stars have, but she makes up for it in her stylized movements. She always held back in her performances for fear of harming the other actors, but her dancing and athletic background lend her a real grace on-screen.

Lee entered into the world arena of martial arts cinema with the low-budget movie *Queen Boxer* (1972), in which she went through two floors of villains in a teahouse scene that will resonate in later films like *Kill Bill*. She worked until the late eighties, starring in movies like *Iron Monkey Strikes Back* (1977) and *Imperial Sword* (1977).

Feng Hsu Feng Hsu's career stretches back into the early days of the Hong Kong martial arts cinema. She is in fact the star of probably one of the most influential genre films of the last forty years—*A Touch of Zen* (1969), in which she plays the part of the beautiful and mysterious heroine Yang who is being pursued by assassins. She enlists the aid of a smitten artist in her battle to defeat the forces arrayed against her. The film was originally shown in the United States in expurgated versions (the original is over three hours long) that turned it into a routine "chop-socky" film. But it has now been restored on DVD, and the more philosophical sections that illuminate the spiritual basis of martial arts are now intact.

Michiko Nishiwaki in *Avenging Quartet*.

Michiko Nishiwaki Virtually unknown to mainstream audiences, but a star in the world of martial arts, Michiko Nishiwaki was Japan's first female bodybuilding and weightlifting champion. In a society bound by rules and protocols, Nishiwaki defied many conventions and became a role model for women in Japan. She opened several gyms, became a personal trainer and a television celebrity.

She simultaneously developed her acting and martial arts skills on-screen. First in a series of movies for the Hong Kong cinema, including *In the Line of Duty 3* (1988), with Cynthia Khan, *Avenging Quartet* (1992) with Moon Lee, and *Magic Cop* (1990). She also was in great demand as a stunt artist for actresses like Lucy Liu (*Kill Bill*, *Charlie's Angels*) and in prestige films like *Blade*, *Rush Hour 2*, and *Collateral*.

Yukari Oshima Born of a Japanese father and Chinese mother in Japan, Oshima studied karate as a child and eventually found her way to the Hong Kong cinema via Japanese television. She also worked with action star Sonny Chiba and eventually was granted a role in *Millionaire's Express* (1987). The film featured an array of Hong Kong stars, including Sammo Hung.

Oshima is known for her androgynous appearance and extraordinary athleticism. She gained even more favorable notice when she appeared opposite Moon Lee in *Angel* (1987), playing the vicious villain of the piece and shocking audiences with her cruelty.

Eventually Oshima became dissatisfied with the small parts she was given in Hong Kong and began working in the Philippines cinema. There she was well received, already a star, based on her Hong Kong films. She adopted the name Cynthia Luster and has continued to work steadily.

Yukari Oshima.

Chapter 10
Float Like a Butterfly, Sting Like a Bee

An important subset of the warrior woman genre is women's sports films. Admittedly, the examples of this subgenre have been few and far between. But they do exist. In *Kansas City Bomber* (1972), Raquel Welch played a single mother, trying to make ends meet, who becomes a roller derby skater under the mentorship of the team's owner. In Robert Aldrich's . . . *All the Marbles* (1981), the female protagonists are tag team wrestlers whose battles outside the ring are as brutal as the ones inside, as the two fend off exploitative men, drugs, poverty, and sexism in their tawdry journey to recognition and fame. In *Girlfight* (2000), director-writer Karyn Kusama (*Aeon Flux*) paints the portrait of a barrio girl (Michelle Rodriguez) whose anger is channeled into boxing, through which she gains some control over her life. And most recently director Clint Eastwood resurrected the formula for his *Million Dollar Baby* (2004), which drew enough attention to win four Oscars.

The common theme in all these movies is professional sports as an avenue out of poverty, a violent method for women to break the bonds society has placed on them economically and socially in order to become self-actuated individuals. But in examining the films closer, we also see the theme of mentorship. In every one of the movies mentioned above, the women are trained by older men who adopt them as surrogate daughters, which often overlaps into a romantic/sexual relationship, implied or actual, replacing the missing or dysfunctional father figure. And more than most any other genre, this one almost requires that women bridge gender gaps. As female athletes in a traditionally male field in most cases, their battle is not only in the ring. They must overcome the great pressure of gender stereotypes, often participating in a series of harsh initiations to prove themselves.

girlfight

un film de **KARYN KUSA**

Girlfight, "Prove Them Wrong"

Diana (to Adrian): I love you. I really do.

[*Punches Adrian in the face*]

Girlfight follows the rise of an eighteen-year-old Latina girl out of the doldrums of despair and anger. Diana (Michelle Rodriguez) is still rocked by the tragic death of her mother and the cold distance of her emotionally abusive father (Paul Calderon), who cannot bear how much she resembles her deceased mother. At school she is on the verge of expulsion for numerous fights. At home she argues with her old-fashioned father, who favors her brother Tiny (Ray Santiago) and relegates her to the "womanly" duties of cooking and cleaning for the men of the house.

What is fascinating about the character is how extremely confrontational she is. She has no trouble making split-second decisions and acting upon them. When a stuck-up, popular girl from school hurts her best friend's feelings by sleeping with the guy she likes and then lying about it, Diana immediately demands that she apologize to her friend. When the apology is not forthcoming, she attacks her, even though her friend is disinterested in Diana's strong sense of loyalty. One more fight will mean Diana is kicked out of school.

In another situation, while stopping by her brother's gym during his boxing lessons, she notices that his sparring opponent plays dirty. He hits her inept brother in the face after the bell. Her brother, who would rather be an artist than a boxer, just shrugs off the insult, too passive to do anything about it. But when the other male boxer gets out of the ring, Diana immediately walks over and punches him in the face. "That's for my brother," she says.

The atmosphere at the gym fascinates her, and she soon realizes it is the outlet she needs. She convinces the trainer Hector (Jaime Tirelli) to take her on, after much reluctance on his part. Although the film follows the traditional formula for a boxing film—underprivilged tough kid finds success and self-worth through boxing—director-writer Kusama does not give in to all the standard clichés. There is no reconciliation between Diana and her father. In fact she has to deceive him in order to get money to

Opposite: Poster for the movie *Girlfight* with Michelle Rodriguez.

pay for her training. She is realistic and practical, and does what is necessary to look after herself. And although she is successful in the ring, there is no indication at the end as to whether this will be her chosen profession. The film does not paint a romantic picture of boxing. Hector warns her repeatedly of the dangers of this "dead-end" profession: "Most of these guys, they're going to lose . . . But it's all they know."

What is also refreshing about the film is that even though there is a male love interest, she is not made weak by it. If anything, she is far more balanced and professional than the boy is and ends up being a role model for him. She opens up to him and tells him about her mother, and shows emotional reaction when she runs into him with another girl at a party. But her reaction is decisive and swift. She knows her boundaries and won't let him walk over them. Their relationship is rocky at first, but it is clear that they are working things out and growing, whereas so many other films tend to indicate that strong women simply can't have functional relationships with the opposite sex and are destined to be constantly lonely as punishment for breaking traditional gender roles.

The Blood of Heroes, "The Time Will Come When Winning Is Everything"

The Blood of Heroes (1989), directed and written by David Webb Peoples, the co-writer of the cult classic *Blade Runner*, is an unusual mélange of science fiction and combat sports set in a vague post-apocalyptic future. Joan Chen (*Temptation of a Monk*, where she plays the assassin Violet and the princess Scarlet) incarnates the role of Kidda, an agile, athletic peasant girl who forces herself onto a ragged but determined team of "juggers" (contestants in a brutal game resembling football). She proves herself to them by taking the punishment they deliver in training and in helping them win several local games.

Kidda, however, has her own agenda. She tells the leader of the team (Rutger Hauer), who eventually becomes her lover as well as trainer, that she desires to travel to one of the remaining cities of the continent, where she believes she will gain the attention of the more professional jugger teams and become rich and famous. Although he initially tries to discourage her, he eventually submits to her will. In the final scenes of the movie, Kidda leads the team to victory, walking proudly to place the dog skull on the spike to mark their point as the other team lies bleeding in the arena. As the crowds of the wealthy fawn over Kidda, her mentor looks on wistfully in a resolution filled with ambiguity.

Million Dollar Baby

Maggie (Hilary Swank) relentlessly training in *Million Dollar Baby*.

———

"I'm thirty-two, Mr. Dunn, and I'm here celebrating the fact that I spent another year scraping dishes and waitressing, which is what I've been doing since thirteen, and according to you I'll be thirty-seven before I can even throw a decent punch, which I have to admit, after working on this speed bag for a month, may be the God's simple truth. Other truth is, my brother's in prison, my sister cheats on welfare by pretending one of her babies is still alive, my daddy's dead, and my momma weighs three hundred and twelve pounds. If I was thinking straight I'd go back home, find a used trailer, buy a deep fryer and some Oreos. Problem is, this the only thing I ever felt good doing. If I'm too old for this, then I got nothing. That enough truth to suit you?"

— Maggie Fitzgerald, *Million Dollar Baby*

———

Like *The Blood of Heroes, Million Dollar Baby* exhibits a bitter sense of irony about its characters, as well as the sport they have chosen. Maggie Fitzgerald (Hilary Swank) is "white trailer trash," according to her own description. She works in a low-paying waitressing job while desperately seeking an alternative to the roles modeled by her family. While training at a local gym, she latches onto Frankie (Clint Eastwood), an embittered older trainer who initially refuses to train "a girl." Undaunted, Maggie continues to hammer away at the seemingly impenetrable Frankie until he caves in.

Frankie (Clint Eastwood) watches with concern as Maggie (Hilary Swank) enters the fray in *Million Dollar Baby*.

Although Frankie tries to enforce his rules and train this determined "girlie" in the "backward" art of boxing, as described by ex-fighter and narrator Eddie (Morgan Freeman), it is Maggie who does most of the training as she chips away at the man she calls "boss" with more than a touch of humor. Eventually his hardened paternalistic façade, rooted in deep grief and loss, begins to crack, and he opens up to her and expresses long buried emotions. She becomes a replacement not only for the daughter he is estranged from, but also for the wife he never mentions. He gives Maggie a Gaelic fighting name, *moi cuishle* ("my darling, my blood"), and learns to follow her lead, accepting her choices both in the ring and in her dealings with her selfish, grasping family, even when he doubts the wisdom of those decisions. In the end he almost always takes a backseat and spoils this fighter who has become the emotional center of his universe.

Of course, the central and most harrowing irony of this movie

Maggie faces off against the intimidating Billie (Lucia Rijker) in *Million Dollar Baby*.

is that the final demand Maggie makes on Frankie destroys both of them. Against all his instincts, he agrees to let Maggie fight the vicious and unscrupulous Billie "the Blue Bear" (played by real-life welterweight boxing champion and adviser to the movie Lucia Rijker). Rijker, as Billie, is an extremely powerful and intimidating athlete, next to the more slight Maggie. After being hit after the bell, Maggie falls, receiving a blow to the neck and spinal column, and as a result she becomes a quadriplegic.

Unable to bear this life of immobility, Maggie asks Frankie to end her life. He initially refuses, but Maggie continues to fight to die, intent on going out as she has lived. She bites off her own tongue in order to bleed to death and refuses any sustenance. Frankie cannot resist her will or ignore his devotion to his *cuishle*, and so the film makes a political statement when he helps with her death. Maggie has won her release, and Frankie disappears into the night, having fulfilled his purpose.

G.I. Jane, "Failure Is Not an Option"

I never saw a wild thing sorry for itself.
A small bird will drop frozen dead from a bough
Without ever having felt sorry for itself

—D. H. Lawrence

When Lieutenant Jordan O'Neil (Demi Moore) is offered a special assignment to undergo the notoriously brutal Navy SEAL training as the first female test subject, she doesn't accept it for the glory or for the good of women everywhere. She accepts it because it will earn her the opportunity for promotion to a higher career position. In addition, she is interested in the personal challenge.

Jordan's boyfriend (Jason Beghe), however, objects to her enrolling in the Navy SEAL unit, concerned about her well-being. She reasons with him that the training will look good on her record and open doors for her. Senator DeHaven (Anne Bancroft), a political warrior in her own way, encourages her admission to the training to prove a political point that women should be allowed entrance into all areas the military. Later it is revealed that she deceitfully used Jordan as a "fall girl" to secure her own political career.

Many people who saw this film assumed that it was about whether or not a woman had what it took to serve in previously banned positions in the military, and that the film's political message might be to prove that women should be allowed equal opportunity in all military professions. However, the movie really demonstrated a different theme in the end—that it's not about women's ability to be up to the task; it's about *men* not being able to function as a cohesive team in combat with a woman in their midst.

In the spirit of the classic boot camp scenes of *Full Metal Jacket*, Jordan's drill instructor, Master Chief Urgayle (Viggo Mortensen), abuses the recruits violently and repeatedly, putting them through some of the most rigorous training the military offers. Jordan is no exception, and he gives her the respect of treating her just as harshly as the rest of the recruits, all men. As

Jordan (Demi Moore) determined to succeed in *G.I. Jane.*

sadistic as he comes off, he is an interesting character. The fact is he is the only one who shows Jordan true support throughout the film. He is not sexist and seems to have faith in her abilities, in opposition to her own boyfriend, who only wants her to quit and come home. Everyone else higher up in command either resents her or wants to take advantage of the situation for their own political motives.

Urgayle watches through a scope as she tosses aside the handicap benches and other cheats she is supposed to use as a woman on the training course. Instead she helps her team climb hurdles by allowing them to step on her back. But, regardless, the recruits continually try to sabotage her progress. Urgayle punishes the men who try to hinder her in the field, attempting to teach them that working as a team will be essential to their survival in real-life missions. He is not a stereotypical drill instructor; his methods don't always include yelling and abuse, which he leaves to others. His quiet reciting of D. H. Lawrence's poetry gives him an almost psychopathic aura, mixed as it is with relentless harsh discipline, as he and the other instructors taunt the recruits to come "ring the bell" signaling their resignation. Actor Viggo Mortensen talks about his role in a 1997 interview in *Detour* magazine.

> [The master chief is] a pretty isolated kind of character. He can't afford to let the people he's training know him very well or know what he's thinking. There's always a distance—you have to earn their respect, and also keep it by mentally being careful of how you deal with people.

Jordan (Demi Moore) before shaved head in *G.I. Jane*.

Jordan quickly realizes that she can never be a part of the team while she looks like a woman. She stands out, with her ponytail and segregated sleeping quarters. Her recognizable gender makes the men ostracize her. On her own accord, she skips sleeping during the short break they are allotted, instead stopping at the barber. Grabbing the instrument, she shaves off her long hair in a memorable scene (which was not staged, but done in one take on camera). Determined to succeed, despite the many obstacles against her, she moves her items into the men's barracks, much to their dismay. The men initially raise an uproar. One even loudly complains about the possibility of tampons being present, trying to humiliate her. But her drill instructor understands what she is doing and supports her move, immediately commanding the men to arrange a rotation schedule for using the showers and toilet. The only chance she has of succeeding is to blend in with the team and not allow the men to be distracted by her gender, which now gradually starts to take place.

Everything comes to a head when they undergo a special training mission that simulates enemy capture. Her drill instructor has been in enough combat situations to know the liability she could be as a woman. The entire point is not only how much she can handle, it is about how the men will react under duress. If she were captured, would the men be more inclined to attempt to

Master Chief Urgayle (Viggo Mortensen) abuses his first female trainee (Demi Moore) in a POW training exercise in *G.I. Jane.*

save her (perhaps to their own detriment), as opposed to a male? Or would they be more likely to break down and give up valuable "intel" because she is a woman? Would her gender interfere with their operation, because they might hesitate in certain circumstances? Master Chief Urgayle knows this is the true testing ground for all of them, and he beats her harder than all the rest, to the point that even his hardened fellow instructor Pyro questions his judgment and leaves the room in disgust. Everyone is led to believe that Urgayle is simply being sadistic and abusive, because he wants to break her down, he enjoys it.

Urgayle takes her outside, puts her on display to the other recruits, and continues to beat her mercilessly, suggesting rape by bending her over a table and cutting her belt off with a knife. The scenes are extremely brutal as the other recruits watch blood dripping from her mouth. The men who previously sabotaged her now resent their drill instructor's abuse. Clearly it is distressing to all to see a woman abused so badly. It appears that her teammates will break and give over valuable "intel" sooner than she will, even though she is the one suffering the abuse. They turn away from Urgayle. But aggression rises up within her when the drill instructor cuts off her belt. In spite of the fact that her hands are bound behind her back, she manages to strike back, violently turning the tables on her captor and bloodying him with her kicks. She overcomes the situation. Standing over Urgayle and kicking him, she yells, "Suck my dick!" invoking cheers from the recruits. At this point, the men recognize that she has earned her place with them.

After the simulated POW interrogation, Urgayle and Instructor Pyro debrief while Urgayle straightens his broken nose. Pyro apologizes for doubting Urgayle's judgment. Urgayle concludes, "She's not the problem. We are." And this is made clear by the very fact that even a seasoned professional like Pyro would break from orders under the pressure of seeing a woman beaten.

Regardless of her victory, Jordan is still sabotaged, this time by a woman. The senator who got her into the program in the first place sets up a dismissal by offering false evidence that she is a lesbian (touching upon another major issue—gays in the military). But when the senator tries to force Jordan to accept the dismissal on the trumped-up charges, Jordan confronts her right there in the halls of Congress and threatens to go to press. The senator has no choice but to agree to reinstate her.

Probably one of the most powerful scenes in the film, wonderfully executed by Viggo Mortensen, is when Urgayle approaches Jordan while she is taking a shower. She resists the natural inclination to cover herself, knowing that this too is a test. She must shed years of female social conditioning to work in this atmosphere. The scene suggests sexual harassment. Will he make a move on her? Is he taking advantage of his position? Once again Urgayle treats her like a man. He doesn't turn away or avert his eyes while she is naked, but at the same time he does not ogle her. He only advises her of some news, then leaves.

In the paradoxical ending, in spite of all of Urgayle's abuse and gender-blind treatment of Jordan, on a real-life mission he is the one who endangers the entire operation and nearly dies trying to protect her. During a sudden, unexpected mission, the SEAL team is split up to cover multiple targets. Through his scope, Urgayle notices an enemy soldier approaching Jordan's position, a large man who is unaware that Jordan is hiding there. She cannot use firearms because the sound will reveal their presence and jeopardize all of them. If she can take the target out quietly, they would still have a chance of success. Jordan pulls out her combat knife and readies herself. She communicates to Urgayle that she will make the kill. But seeing the large man nearly upon Jordan, Urgayle can't take it. He takes a shot and kills the man before he gets to Jordan, sounding off a full alert to the enemy. As a result, they must abort the mission, and Urgayle is repeatedly shot. He comes away with his life only because of Jordan's quick thinking and courage as she runs out and drags him to safety.

On the helicopter, as they pump morphine into him, Urgayle laments, "I'll never live this one down."

Chapter 11
Girl Power

In these days when Japanese anime (animation) is such a popular culture staple for both children and adults, it is hard to imagine that not so long ago Warner Bros. was airing racist cartoons against Japan such as *Bugs Bunny*'s "Tokio Jokio." Most people of color have not escaped some sort of negative racial caricature in early cartoons, and women still haven't entirely escaped sexism in that medium. Young women are constantly inundated with sexualized imagery of females in comics, cartoons, and popular video games. In the midst of all this, some creators have recognized the need to provide more empowering role models for girls and have attempted to fill the niche, each in their own way. This section covers a few of the younger female action characters (including some animated series) of past and recent influence.

The Powerpuff Girls, "Saving the World Before Bedtime"

The Powerpuff Girls was created in 1998 by one of the most unlikely show runners (writer/producers) in the business, Craig McCracken. Originally calling it "The Whoopass Girls," he animated the characters for a short he produced as a California Institute of the Arts student. While working for the Cartoon Network, he pitched *The Whoopass Girls*, which the network bought and put into production with McCracken as the show runner. He designed the three main characters (the titular Powerpuff Girls) in his version of the super-deformed Japanese anime style.

The super-deformed anime style of *The Powerpuff Girls*.

The best well-known example of a super-deformed character would have to be Hello Kitty. Super-deformed (also known as SD in both the American and Japanese animation industries) are characters that have unusually small bodies and very large heads. The best SD characters have heads that are the same size as their bodies (and the Powerpuffs are no exception). The rest of the characters in the original series and most of the design elements (especially the city of Townsville) were retro-American. Simplicity of design made the mesh possible and pleasing.

The three elementary-school-age girls (Blossom, Bubbles, and Buttercup) were superheroes who fought supercriminals, supervillains, and supermonsters (which were highly inspired by Godzilla). Each of the girls represented a different personality for audience members to identify with. Blossom, the redhead, was the leader, and on the two sides of her were Bubbles (the blonde, very much a cute little girl) and Blossom (the black-haired, always angry tomboy).

They were never warrior women; they were warrior girls. What made the show interesting was how they mostly remained little girls and yet forced the rest of their world to conform to their needs and view. Those who didn't conform were the hapless (like the Mayor of Townsville, who never flinched at calling for help on their special toy phone) or the deeply frustrated (Mojo Jojo, their number-one nemesis).

With very few exceptions, the criminals, villains, and monsters were always attacking Townsville (civilization), and it was up to these three little girls to ditch elementary school and fight these enemies of humanity. The girls were oblivious to the depth of violence around them. They had to be, for if they did have that consciousness, they would either have to stop fighting and have no confrontations, no drama, or lose our sympathy for knowingly causing so much mayhem and destruction. So as the powers of their enemies were raised, the violence heightened, with their lack of awareness becoming ever more comical and ironic.

These girls were lethal fighting machines who liked to have cookies and milk before going to bed. At first mothers would flock to the show, thinking that it would finally be a program that they could watch with their daughters, only to be surprised by the level of violence. The Cartoon Network received more complaints about *The Powerpuff Girls* than any other program. But with the show so successful (and still attracting advertisers), the network wasn't about to change the formula.

What the network lost in middle-aged female viewers it gained in other demographics. Besides slumming adults, the show attracted mostly boys (ages nine to fourteen) and was the number-one series for all kids, boys and girls, ages two to eleven. Even in weekday repeats, the program could easily attract more than a million viewers. The property was very successful, spawning a horde of merchandise spin-offs and a feature film.

The trio of *Harry Potter* all grown up in *Harry Potter and the Prisoner of Azkaban.*

Harry Potter's Intrepid Girl Detective/ Sorceress

The clever Hermione Granger (played by Emma Watson) of the *Harry Potter* movies (2001, 2002, 2004, and 2006) has provided girls with a dynamic and interesting character to relate to. She starts out the series filled with doubts and insecurities and then gradually evolves into the most inventive of the trio of friends (Harry, Ron, and Hermione).

Hermione's evolution into a powerful magician is challenging. She is portrayed as extremely driven, which one might attribute to the fact that, unlike the main character Harry (Daniel Radcliffe), Hermione was born to more common parents. She studies extra hard and seems to consider all the consequences of her actions far more than any other character. She seems to wish to transcend any perceived flaw based upon her heritage.

In the first two films of the series (*Harry Potter and the Sorcerer's Stone* and *Harry Potter and the Chamber of Secrets*),

Hermione (Emma Watson) becomes more confrontational in *Harry Potter and the Prisoner of Azkaban*.

Hermione is the classic "good girl," intent on pleasing those in power, especially her teachers. When the three friends investigate areas of the Hogwarts School mansion that are forbidden, Hermione worries more about being "expelled" from school than "[getting] killed." Her obedience to authority is more difficult to shed than it is for the boys.

What she lacks in self-esteem, at least in the first two movies, Hermione makes up for in intelligence, perseverance, and magical abilities. As the *Potter* movies are as much detective films (in the tradition of *Nancy Drew*) as they are forays into sorcery, Hermione is always crucial to discovering the mystery of the story. For example, in the second film, it is her plan and potion that allow the protagonists to infiltrate the Slytherin house and to discover the secret of the chamber. She is also the only one able to disperse the menacing pixies that the pompous Professor Lockhart (Kenneth Branagh) accidentally unleashes.

By the third film (*Harry Potter and the Prisoner of Azkaban*), Hermione has matured significantly. She also has shed many of her insecurities. Toward her enemies she is uncompromising. When the sorcerer Draco (Tom Felton) threatens her, she does not hesitate to respond in a confrontational manner. Toward her friends she is protective and even offers her own life to defend Harry. Toward innocents she takes on the burden of defender and uses her powers to "turn time" at several key points to save wronged characters like Sirius Black (Gary Oldman). There is a bit of a maternal/martyrdom complex in her actions, which is so commonly placed upon women, but it is obvious that she is a loyal friend. Overall, her qualities of intelligence and independence are inspiring.

Pippi Longstocking

Inger Nilsson plays the irrepressible *Pippi Longstocking*.

Pippi Longstocking was born from the mind of Swedish writer Astrid Lindgren. Lindgren developed the character over a fifteen-year period from 1944 to 1960 in a series of extremely successful novels for children. Swedish television bought the rights in the late sixties and churned out several movies that featured Inger Nilsson, the original and most unforgettable Pippi Longstocking.

Pippi could easily be a younger version of the punk hero *Tank Girl*. She has anarchist tendencies, a unique sense of style that is internally dictated (crazy orange pigtails and unmatched stockings), she has no fear of authority (no fear of anything, as a matter of fact), and makes no effort to conform. She lives in a house of her own without adults, which she has painted in whimsical colors of her choice. She laughs at those who try to capture her and easily escapes because of her super-strength.

In keeping with the Amazon archetype, she rides a horse (which she will occasionally pick up and carry also, if it seems tired), and she has a sense of sisterhood and kinship with her peers (boy and girls, in her case). She constantly challenges traditional rules of gender. For instance, in one episode at a carnival the children come across a strongman who is challenging the audience for an opponent. The promoter yells, "What man will fight the strongest man on Earth?" Pippi replies, "Why do they ask what *man*? Why not, what woman?" She proceeds to wrestle the strongman and beats him, of course. But generously she hands him the prize money, informing him he should use it to buy some iron medicine to make himself stronger.

Princess Mononoke, "The Fate of the World Rests on the Courage of One Warrior"

Princess Mononoke with her beloved wolf.

Hayao Miyazaki, the Walt Disney of Japanese anime, has had a long love affair with strong female characters. One of the most fierce has been San, the title character of *Princess Mononoke* (1997).

She defends the forest and its animal inhabitants against the encroaching humans and their mining operation. San literally runs with the wolves, was raised by them, and shows no empathy toward humans.

But as in all good dramas, she (and we) will learn otherwise. And so because of this, San actually becomes less of a warrior woman by the end of the story. (Some might find Princess Nausicaa, from the director's film of the same name, more of a warrior.)

By having an ecological warrior at the forefront, Miyazaki can comment on the selfishness of such movements but still side with preserving the wilderness. His problem is not with preservation but with groups who alienate others for a just and necessary cause.

Fierce Mononoke defending nature and the animals she loves.

Fans of foreign films may actually want to see this one in dubbed English. It's one of the best translations and casts for an anime. The translation was in fact written by Neil Gaiman of graphic novel fame. There are some changes from the original Japanese feature, but they are minor.

Miramax released the English-language version in the United States to terrible results. The film grossed less than $3 million in its initial release but has been slowly recouping its costs in VHS and DVD. In Japan it was (and still is) one of the highest-grossing films in history.

Mulan, China's Teen Warrior

Disney's animated feature *Mulan* (1998) tells the folkloric Chinese story of a young woman who, posing as a man, joined the army and helped defeat the invading Huns. Stories abound in all cultures of women posing as men to defend their people, leading researchers to believe that the incidence of cross-dressing by women in order to take on male roles in both work and war far exceeded the rare instances of it recorded in historical documents.

Princess Mononoke with Ashitaka.

Mulan is a teenage girl living in a small village who, like Joan in a far distant continent, bridles at the strictures imposed by family and culture. The Confucian precepts that rule her life are burdensome and restrictive, especially for women. Although her family lovingly tries to mold her into a demure, genteel "China doll," Mulan prefers riding horses and working on the farm. In an early song she bemoans her dilemma: "I'm not meant to play this part . . . Who am I inside?"

Her opportunity to release her "true spirit" comes with the invasion of the Huns and the Emperor's call to the *men* of the nation to take arms. In order to save her ailing father from recruitment, she poses as his son "Ping," enlists in the army, and is sent to a boot camp. The filmmakers use Mulan's training camp experience to satirize males and their antics. To deceive her cohorts, she must indulge her "manly instincts" and listen to their captain (Shang), who thinks he knows what it is to be "a man," illustrated musically in Shang's training aria. In other words, much like her live-action sister in *G.I. Jane*, Mulan must internalize the behavior of her fellow recruits in order to fit in.

Mulan, of course, far exceeds the standards set for "manly" bravura. She not only excels in boot camp, but saves her troop

Above: Artwork for Disney's retelling of a Chinese legend: Mulan.

from extinction by shooting a cannon and causing an avalanche that buries the Hun army. However, in the process of healing from a wound she suffers during the battle, her gender is revealed, and she is cast out by the captain of her troop. Bravery is no longer of value when performed by someone of the wrong gender.

The irony of the movie, as well as its political point, is driven home in the climax when Mulan returns to the Imperial City to warn the Emperor that the general of the Hun army has entered the city and is bent on killing him. However, because she is now dressed as a woman no one will listen to her. Ultimately the clever Mulan uses her female "invisibility" to save the Emperor. She convinces a few of her more loyal male fellow recruits to dress as concubines and with her access the Emporer's inner chambers, where he is being held prisoner by the Hun general. This culturally subversive maneuver works, and the Emperor is rescued. In a shocking gesture for the period the film is set in, the Emperor bows in thanks before this young girl. As the camera tracks back, the audience sees thousands bowing before her in response. Mulan has found the "spirit" within her and "outed" her true self.

Welcome to Japan, Round Eye! Now Die!

Sailor Moon, a Warrior Woman?

By David Koenigsberg

On the surface, Sailor Moon, the Japanese anime character, would hardly seem a likely choice for canonization in the warrior women hall of fame. Almost any of the leading ladies in a Hayao Miyazaki feature would be better (like San, the warrior princess of *Princess Mononoke*).

Sailor Moon is a coward most of the time, is obsessed with romance, eats constantly (especially sweets), and hates studying (including anything that would help her win battles). She's a screw-up, the comedy relief in a drama centered around her life. In short, she's like most 'tweens. And who wouldn't identify with that? Boys and men like her too—seeing in her the neighborhood girl they want, as opposed to the supermodel they will never meet. When an anime series has these sorts of demographics, I refer to it as an eight and eighty. (A show that will appeal to eight-year-old girls and eighty-year-old men.)

There's plenty of action for these two groups. As an example, one of the leaders of the Web site to save *Sailormoon* in the United States once remarked

> They can't go for a single episode without some young girl accidentally revealing her white panties. I know that if they ever show Sailor Moon's wedding, somehow, for some reason, those panties are going end up on-screen in full view.

This phenomenon confounds Western audiences—that some Japanese kids' shows have so much sexual titillation. Another bothersome aspect is the violence. Fred Ladd, the father

Sailor Moon holding her magic scepter.

of the American anime business and one of the adapters of this series, once confided to the author

> I could never get over the cruelty of some of the episodes. There were some characters that were so cruel to one another. I had to take that out.

Some of the fans objected to such cuts, but it was fascinating to watch the initial disconnect between them and the business. When the series premiered in English (in the fall of 1995), the only other recent anime import (which premiered that same year) was *Dragonball*. Both were heavily censored by companies and syndicators for independent TV stations and station groups. Within five years the entire business had changed. Anime was everywhere; the syndication business had evaporated; and censorship had loosened up significantly. *Sailormoon*, *Dragonball*, and then *Pokemon* changed everything in quick succession.

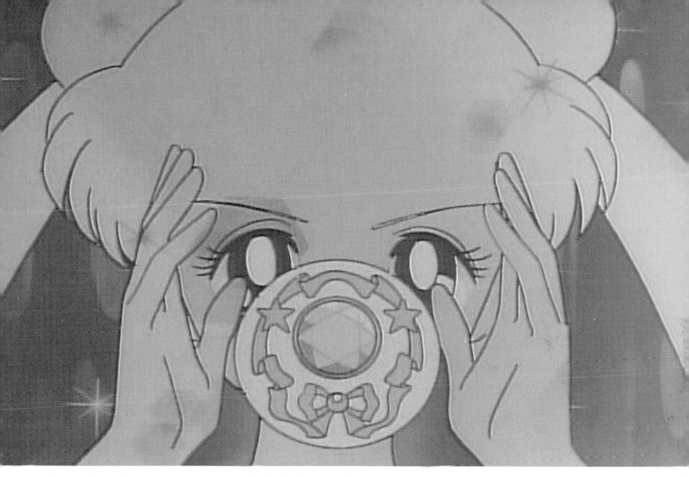

Sailor Moon's transformation.

Some fans have the mistaken belief that *Sailormoon* (and some other shows) provide a sort of window into Japan. What they don't realize is that *Sailormoon* is first and foremost a fantasy for Japanese girls and is sometimes an escape from their regimented world. No, in Japan, panties do not suddenly pop up in full view every day. No, people do not go around calling one another "Baka!" which means "fool" and is highly insulting.

But do Japanese girls dream of being able to have different-colored hair? Of having long, thin, shapely legs? Of being the savior and not feigning helplessness? Yes, you bet.

And so this is why Naoko Takeuchi created *Sailormoon*. She wanted to create a character that young girls could identify with (Usagi, the klutzy screw-up) and then have her transform herself into Sailor Moon (in the English dub she announces, "The warrior of love and justice").

It's also about puberty. Usagi is a fourteen-year-old girl with no breasts. She changes into Sailor Moon by yelling (in most in-

Sailor Mercury.

stances), "Moon Prism Power Makeup!" And then during her transformation, makeup appears via lipstick on her lips and/or nail polish on her nails. And breasts appear. Usagi is a girl. Sailor Moon is a woman.

Usagi/Sailor Moon is based on Naoko Takeuchi's experience of growing up. Ms. Takeuchi has said on many occasions that she was like Usagi but wished that she were like Sailor Moon. Western audiences catch on to most of this, but often jump to the conclusion that Usagi transforms into a superhero. To Japanese girls, she transforms into a woman who (eventually) is in control. That alone is enough. This is why it isn't necessary for Sailor Moon to have a lot of superpowers. She can't fly, isn't strong, and certainly would never want to be invisible. Many women already feel that way in Japan. (Sailor Moon always has at least one power, and we'll discuss this later.)

Sailor Moon's girlfriends: Sailor Mercury, Sailor Mars, Sailor Jupiter, Sailor Venus (each one a different archetype), all have some sort of superpower, but it is usually singular. Most of the time they need to work together as a team, and in almost every story they need Sailor Moon to win. Further, Sailor Moon's enemies always come from outer space or other dimensions but never from Japan itself. She is not at war against Japan's male-dominated society (in Japan that would be unacceptable). She struggles to restore order, often without Japan ever realizing what she has done. This series instructs little girls that achieving power does not have to come at the expense of fighting men.

In fact in the original comic book, or manga, Sailor Moon fights nothing but men (who are from a "black kingdom"), only to discover that their leader is a woman, Queen Beryl. And she in turn reports to another woman, the amorphous Queen Metallia. The lesson? You can fight all the men you want, but the real power is held by women.

Naoko also wanted to let girls know of all the choices they have in life. Each story was about a different aspect of being a woman. Episodes concerned idolizing rock stars, being a singer, shopping, singles' cruises, being a tennis pro, choosing your wedding gown, being a model, designing dolls, working in anime, going to balls, cooking, helping your friends with their love lives, being a painter, getting your hair done, attending finishing school, skiing, ice skating, and that was just in the first season!

Girls' options didn't stop there. More adult themes were introduced in later seasons, including the introduction of Sailor Saturn (a Goth girl) and Sailors Neptune and Uranus (a lesbian couple who are older than the other sailors). The English dub added a huge amount of sexual confusion by casting the actor who did the voice of Usagi's mother to also do the voice of Sailor Neptune. After that, anytime you heard Usagi's mom, all you could think was "You're a lesbian."

And yes, as in most warrior women stories, the men in Sailor Moon's universe are ineffectual.

The main man in her life, Mamoru, can also transform (into a character called Tuxedo Kamen, known as Tuxedo Mask in the English version). But alas, he has no real superpowers. He seems to be able to levitate, twirl his cane, and throw roses like spears, but his main job is to show up at the last minute and encourage Sailor Moon to fight on. Which she does, of course, and wins.

Perhaps the subversive lesson that *Sailormoon* teaches is actually for boys and not for girls at all. It's as if the series were constantly whispering to boys, "This is a girl's world. Your only job is to encourage us."

Sailor Moon's one superpower is the ability to destroy a monster or get rid of a monster that has taken over a human. Over the course of the stories and series she has a tiara, a scepter, or some sort of feminine object that helps her destroy the monster. But toward the end of the run Sailor Moon is given a two-foot-long pink rod (with some sort of ornamentation) that unmistakably resembles a penis (if not a deluxe vibrator). All sorts of effects come shooting out of it, laying waste to any monster in the way. Soon thereafter, in the final season, Mamoru leaves Japan to study abroad. And who could blame him?

Unlike some (but not all) woman warriors, Usagi has no problem with her parents. Her mom's a housewife, and her dad is a typical salaryman. He's not dead, missing, alcoholic, abusive; he barely matters. In fact he's almost never a pawn in a story. (That job would belong to a girlfriend of Usagi.)

Her father's being so unimportant might explain her infatuation with Mamoru. In the original manga, Usagi is only fourteen, and Mamoru is eighteen. In the West they call this child moles-

Sailor Venus.

295

Sailor Jupiter.

tation. But to be fair, it's Usagi who is constantly chasing after Mamoru. He is waiting for when she is old enough, though they do start to kiss pretty early.

But what is this teaching young girls? Well, in Japan you had better be ready for all sorts of encounters with older men. Most Asian societies demand that you respect your elders. Perhaps this is why everyone turns a blind eye to the practice of Japanese schoolgirls selling their panties to old men on the street. (Visiting Japan with your fourteen-year-old girl? Don't let her wear loose white socks. It's the calling card that you're in the market to sell.)

But what to do if an old man wants a sexual encounter? This is explicitly addressed in one story where Sailor Mars's grandfather is revealed to be a dirty old man. So which would you rather have? A children's entertainment that addresses molestation or one that avoids the problem altogether? I don't know if Japanese girls are better prepared for this situation or not, but I have noticed that in their supposedly male-dominated society, the women, privately, hold tremendous sway.

There seems to be a rage within the Japanese woman that is different from other women's. It is part of her eternal search for perfection. She really wants a world where we never grow old. Where eternal peace and happiness is found. Where you're King and Queen of the Earth and lead the solar system with your friends. And where childbirth isn't necessary.

Yes, all of the above really does happen in *Sailormoon*; but that last aspect is so wonderfully insane. It's never shown, but Usagi eventually gives birth to a daughter, Chibi-usa. What we do see is Chibi-usa, at around five years old, go back in time to be with her mother, Usagi, when Usagi is about fifteen. So the net effect is mother and daughter fighting together, but mother hasn't needed to go through all that childbirth-labor thing. One thing you have to say about Naoko: she strips away everything she doesn't like about the universe and goes directly for what she wants.

For some fans, *Sailormoon* became a religion of sorts. Like other modern mythologies (*Star Trek, Star Wars, Lord of the Rings*), *Sailormoon*, with its legends, characters, and rules, addressed contemporary issues that religion could never attempt to deal with. *Sailormoon* invites obsessive behavior. One famous incident occurred when the second to the last episode of the original anime aired in Japan in which Sailors Mercury, Mars, Jupiter, and Venus sacrifice themselves and die so that Sailor Moon can triumph over Queen Beryl. The television stations were instantly besieged with phone calls from crying schoolgirls and their upset parents that continued long into the night and lasted for several days. Needless to say, the other Sailors turned out to be not so dead, after all, and the anime went on for four more seasons and three features.

No such incident took place in the West. Instead endless nit-picking flooded the Internet—a never-ending game of one-upmanship in which fans claimed that they knew this new religion better than you. Was Chibi-usa really Usagi's and Mamoru's daughter? Was Sailor Uranus really a prince in a former life? And was the series spelled "Sailormoon" or "Sailor Moon" or "Pretty Soldier Sailor Moon" or "The Beautifully Suited Soldier Sailor Moon"?

Sailor Mars.

This type of response would never happen with an American creation. American media companies would not allow a *Kim Possible* or *The Powerpuff Girls* to have so much meaning or be truly inspiring. There is no cult surrounding them.

But when you spell out your own universe, you'd better be prepared to back it up (especially when it's successful). Filled with contradictions and ambiguity, *Sailormoon* (like all man-made things) was not perfect. But there was a worldwide audience, with fistfuls of dollars craving more, more, more!

And Naoko was clearly not ready. Suddenly she had to add on and on to the story until it lost its originality. And the animators on the show felt the same way. The woman in charge of the animation model sheets, Kazuko Tadano, had to take up residency in a hotel across the street from the studio just to meet her deadlines. She felt that she had temporarily surrendered her life. And then, on the other end, fans would stay up all night to create Web pages to help keep the show on the air in the West.

At one point, Naoko, Kazuko, and some of the fans had the same realization. They had all, willingly, become slaves to Sailor Moon. Now that's a warrior woman!

David Koenigsberg works in the movie and television business in Hollywood. He was an adviser to the "Save Our Sailors" Internet campaign to keep Sailormoon *on television in the United States.*

Chapter 12
Super-Sleuths, Spies, and Assassins

"Hi, I'm Dixie. Dixie Normous. I may be just a small-town FBI agent slash single mother, but I'm still tough . . . and sexy."

—Austin Powers, *Goldmember*

In this chapter we explore yet another variety of female warrior that has made a distinct mark in popular culture: sleuths, spies, and assassins. Though they may depend more on their deductive skills than their physical prowess, they fulfill the warrior archetype in a number of ways. They are competent in the use of weapons and in hand-to-hand combat techniques, and over time we have seen in the films increased physical action that includes far more sophisticated martial arts and elaborately choreographed fight scenes.

The tradition of women as sleuths and secret agents in movies goes back as far as the thirties with a series of Warner Bros. low-budget movies based on the *Nancy Drew* young-adult books and starring Bonita Granville. But as with most of the fictional women warriors, it was not until the sixties and seventies that this genre really found its home, though for the most part it was a very patriarchal home, often with a father figure on hand (or at least the voice of one through a speaker box) to run the show.

The Avengers

British television's *The Avengers* (1961–1969) became influential on many levels within a very short time. The series's ironic, very English sense of humor and its outlandish plots, centering around a pair of secret agents working to thwart the enemies of the British government, would influence many movies and television shows of the decade, including the James Bond movies, *The Prisoner*, *The Man from Uncle*, *The Girl from Uncle*, and so on.

Originally Steed (Patrick Macnee), the male lead, had no female partner, and the show stumbled along in the ratings. But in season two with the introduction of Honor Blackman as Catherine Gale, an anthropologist who was also an expert in martial arts and an aficionado of motorcycles, the series took off. Honor Blackman left the show to play the infamous character Pussy Galore in the James Bond movie *Goldfinger*. In an episode during the fourth season, Emma receives a Christmas card from her predecessor Cathy Gale (Honor Blackman) postmarked FORT KNOX in reference to Blackman's appearance in *Goldfinger*.

It took the presence of Diana Rigg in 1965 as the statuesque, smoky-voiced Emma Peel to raise the show to cult status. Emma Peel's name was actually a play on words taken from the British film industry's slang expression "M-Appeal" or "man-appeal." Her fighting outfits were sometimes referred to as "Emmapeelers." Like her predecessor Catherine Gale, Emma was proficient in martial arts, but also partial to catsuits and mod fashion. She was more likely than her partner Steed to resort to violence and verbal abuse to accomplish her ends. While Steed drove a traditional Bentley, she sped through the English countryside in a sports car. While the champagne-drinking Steed felt undressed without his umbrella and bowler hat, Emma changed her costume on a whim, depending on the mood and the situation.

However, despite Steed's seeming stuffiness and preference for tradition, their rather May-December relationship was very modern for its time. Unlike other male characters on similar shows, Steed had a true respect for Mrs. Peel and even acknowledged her intellectual superiority over him without reserve in many telling and good-humored ways. During "The Forget Me Knot" episode he asks, "What's that '–pology' you're interested in?" She informs him it is "Anthro."

Opposite: Diana Rigg, the original Emma Peel from *The Avengers* television show.

In "The See Through Man," Steed leaves his calling card on one of her microscope slides to catch her attention. He never displayed any shame or reluctance when acknowledging her in such ways. And he had enough faith in her abilities to use her for dangerous missions.

Despite all this, Mrs. Peel still repeatedly suffered being tied to chairs and played the sex-appeal card in sticky situations. The producers vetoed her using kung fu for fighting. Rigg learned it privately anyway, but was made to use traditional judo on the show and was later encouraged to soften her fighting skills by adding dance movements to "confuse" her adversaries.

On a sexual level, Mrs. Peel was extremely appealing to viewers in her trademark catsuits and leather. In the introductory scenes of each show the camera slowly pans over her trademark boots in a fetishizing manner. The show's fetish appeal went scandalously further in the 1966 episode "A Touch of Brimstone," which was banned in the United States because of Mrs. Peel's "Queen of Sin" outfit, consisting of a corset, a spiked dog collar, and thigh-high boots designed by Rigg herself.

In spite of all this, Emma was fantastically unique, independent, intellectual, stylish, and unafraid to assert herself. Her apartment was full of funky, memorable decorations. She seemed perfectly happy on her own, enjoying the study of thermodynamics or literature in her spare time.

In 1968 Diana Rigg left the series, and Linda Thorson replaced her, playing Steed's new partner Tara King. On the DVD, actor Patrick Macnee remarks

> Tara's innocence put ME in the position of being the hero . . . her knight in shining armor, which I'd never been before. I had always been slightly subservient to women.

The show was never a big success in America. It just didn't hold much appeal for an American audience that didn't share the British sense of humor.

In 1998 Uma Thurman resurrected Emma Peel in *The Avengers* movie. This was a painful remake, as it was an unfair task to match the unforgettable presence of Diana Rigg and the easy charm of Patrick Macnee. Big-budget special effects were

Opposite: Uma Thurman re-creates the role of Emma Peel in *The Avengers* movie.

used, big-name actors involved, but the movie held none of the appeal or unique surreal atmosphere of the original series. Most British people hated the movie because its American director portrayed the British characters as silly stereotypes. Uma Thurman's British accent was not very convincing. One viewer remarked that someone should pay back America by having a British director do a remake of *The A-Team* or *The Dukes of Hazzard*.

Modesty Blaise

In 1966 noted director Joseph Losey adapted a comic strip character named Modesty Blaise to film. Losey intended the movie to be a feminist/political answer to the male-centered, politically reactionary James Bond movies. Modesty (Monica Vitti) has the same prowess, both physical and mental, as her male English counterpart. She too has an array of high- and low-tech weapons, including hidden explosive devices, as well as her trademark bow and arrow and her powerful scorpion-tattooed thighs. She too boasts a string of lovers, some of which—as in the Bond films—are duplicitous like the government agent Paul (Michael Craig). And she too has a classy wardrobe. In fact her wardrobe is far more extensive than that of her male counterpart, with his traditional tuxedo and tie. Modesty changes into a new mod sixties outfit at the literal blink of an eye.

Modesty also works at times for the British government, when she is not out freelancing as a thief. But Modesty never trusts her bureaucratic employers. The Minister (Alexander Knox) is a stuttering half-wit who has a difficult time understanding even the simplest of concepts. Her immediate superior Tarrant (Harry Andrews) spends his time trying to cover for the Minister's mistakes while attempting to "play" Modesty for the greater glory of Britannia.

Modesty's loyalties are to herself and to those who have proved themselves friends, like Sheik Abu Tahir (Clive Revill), who raised her as his "son," and her working-class assistant Willie (Terence Stamp), who services her both sexually and professionally. When the British government tries to betray her in order to steal a cache of jewels, she turns the tables on them by taking the jewels from under their upper-class noses and return-

Opposite: The glamorous Monica Vitti as comic book heroine Modesty Blaise.

ing them to Abu Tahir, the third-world leader the imperialistic British ministers despise.

In addition, *Modesty Blaise* features its own archvillains, as do the Bond films. Gabriel (Dirk Bogarde) is an effete, hypocritical master criminal who weeps when he orders the death of two pilots but delights when his partner in crime, Mrs. Fothergill (Rossella Falk), tortures and kills men in the guise of training. In the final scene Modesty outwits Gabriel, who also wants the jewels, and defeats the murderous Mrs. Fothergill, who has more than a professional interest in the fetching Modesty.

Charlie's Angels

"Once upon a time there were three little girls who went to the police academy . . . "

The television series *Charlie's Angels* (1976–1981), like *Wonder Woman* and *The Bionic Woman*, remains a landmark in the emergence of the warrior woman in the seventies. It was one of the highest-rated shows in its time slot. It spawned merchandising for young girls from lunch boxes to action figures. One of its stars, Farrah Fawcett, single-handedly cornered the market on posters, producing an image of herself that became an icon of the period.

Like its sister shows of the decade, *Charlie's Angels* walks a fine line between feminism and patriarchy. Although all three private agents (who included at various times Farrah Fawcett, Kate Jackson, Jacklyn Smith, Cheryl Ladd, Tanya Roberts, and Shelley Hack) were intelligent, physically adept detectives who outsmarted the "bad guys" on a regular basis, they were ultimately controlled by an unseen male whose fatherly voice emanated from a speaker box. This surrogate father, Charles Townsend ("Charlie" of the title), spoke in a kindly but firm baritone while "his girls" sat quietly, for the most part, before his disembodied presence like the ideal feisty yet ultimately obedient daughters. Even the advertising for the show carefully combined the feminist emphasis on the women in action, of which there was a great deal in the

Opposite: The three Angels. From left to right: Jaclyn Smith, Kate Jackson, and Farrah Fawcett from the television series *Charlie's Angels*.

Charlie's Angels for a new millennium. From left to right, Lucy Liu, Cameron Diaz, and Drew Barrymore.

series, with cheesecake photos very much like Fawcett's astoundingly successful poster.

In her book *Tough Girls*, Sherrie A. Inness expresses this contradiction as she recalls her own reaction to the series as a child:

> My experience as a viewer of *Charlie's Angels* points out the paradoxical role this show played in the seventies. Even though they joined the police academy, pursued criminals, and excelled as super-sleuths, the way the Angels looked in bikinis was more important than their intelligence.

Inness goes on to discuss how the Angels dressed in designer fashions of the period and were perfectly coiffed and manicured even after the most arduous chase scene.

However, Inness does not denigrate the series's importance as an image of empowerment for young girls of the period. Even

The modern trio has fun even among the ruins and rubble.

though the Angels kept their positions as obedient, sexy daughters of their disembodied father (an interesting although unconscious reference to the emerging phenomenon of the estranged father in a society with a rising divorce rate), they still exhibited their expertise and physical prowess on a weekly basis as they outsmarted and defeated a long line of chiefly male antagonists.

It is appropriate and fitting that this significant show was revived for a third-wave feminist twenty-first century. By the time the movies *Charlie's Angels* (2000) and *Charlie's Angels: Full Throttle* (2003) came to fruition, the warrior woman was a mainstay of the media. The producers of the movies, particularly star Drew Barrymore, saw an opportunity to pay homage to a show that, even with its overlay of patriarchal sexism, had influenced them in a positive way. At the same time they were intent on updating the myth for a modern and youthful "girl power" audience.

The twenty-first century's *Charlie's Angels* combines a little

The trio demonstrates martial arts moves with a touch of humor.

of the old with a large dollop of the new. The three female stars (Drew Barrymore, Lucy Liu, and Cameron Diaz) are a multiethnic, postmodern feminist trio who perfectly encapsulate the third wave's aversion to what they interpret as the sexual puritanism of their feminist "mothers." They embrace the economic and social equality won for them by the second-wave feminists but disdain their views on sexuality. The women in this movie revel in their sensual natures while using sex as a powerful tool against a universe still dominated by men, including the fatherly Charlie.

The trio, like their television predecessors, dress seductively when the mood strikes them, or more practically when racing cars, motorbikes, helicopters, or just battling an array of villains. They dance not only for themselves when inspired by the music around them, but also for the men in the film when they believe that technique is required to gain an advantage in whatever "sleuthing game" they are involved in at the moment.

The exuberance and camaraderie off and on the set of the *Charlie's Angels* movies radiates in this photo.

The trio wave their rears at the camera or snap their whips (literally, in the case of Lucy Liu in her dance sequences before male audiences in each film) to get the attention of the males around them. Also like their older sisters, they rely on their fighting skills to defeat the villains, although in this post–*Crouching Tiger, Hidden Dragon* age, these modern Angels perform feats their technically limited sisters would not have dared attempt, including flying through the air. Set to fast-paced and popular music, the fight scenes resemble music videos, taking full advantage of the excitement generated by the choice of music itself.

There are, however, a few more significant differences between the new and old Angels. The new-millennium trio express a far more aggressive and cavalier attitude toward men, reflecting the third wave's internalization of certain traditionally male views toward sexuality. The Angels' primary commitment is to one another. Alex (Lucy Liu) initially lies to both her lover

Ex-Angel Madison (Demi Moore) injects seriousness into the otherwise frothy sequel *Charlie's Angels: Full Throttle*.

and her father about her career to protect the sisterhood. Dylan (Drew Barrymore) ultimately defeats her maniacal ex-boyfriend and even, at one point, considers leaving the Angels in order to take them out of harm's way. Lovers, male associates like the buffoon Bosley, and even biological fathers are extraneous and clearly expendable, as exemplified by Alex's on-and-off relationship with empty-headed "boy toy" Jason (Matt Le Blanc) and her tendency to physically manhandle him, albeit "accidentally."

The only exception to this rule is, of course, Charlie, the fatherly voice in the speaker box. Both films emphasize Charlie's caring attitude toward his female agents and downplay the "playboy" aspects of the original Charlie, who was represented onscreen as just a hand, usually holding a cocktail as a sexy woman stepped into a Jacuzzi in front of him. He would often use quips like "Sorry, Angels, can't talk anymore right now. Got my hands full," as a buxom woman leaned over to hand him a drink. Like

The trio rejects Madison's arguments and decides to support their surrogate father Charlie.

their older siblings, these new Angels speak of Charlie lovingly and react to his voice in a positive and affectionate manner. They even save his life at the end of the first movie.

To demonstrate, however, that they are aware of the power relationship between the Angels and Charlie, the filmmakers concocted a modern, ironic twist for the sequel. In *Charlie's Angels: Full Throttle*, they introduce the character of Madison (Demi Moore) as an older ex-Angel out for revenge. Madison comes back on the scene to defy the paternalistic Charlie. She chides the modern Angels for their devotion to this "speaker box," which she blows away with her oversized, gold-plated gun: "I don't take orders from a speaker box anymore." Madison preaches radical rebellion and makes a strong case for leaving Charlie and becoming independent like her. But ultimately the Angels cannot part with their "surrogate father" and defeat Madison before she can harm Charlie or his operations.

Alias

Jennifer Garner's successful television series *Alias* (2001–2006) resonates with themes present in both *Daredevil* and *Elektra*. In the show she plays Sydney Bristow, a double agent who is not only adept at disguise, but also an impressive fighter. Recruited out of college by an agency (SD-6) that purported to be the CIA, Sydney found herself duped by her employers and bereft of her fiancé, who is murdered by agents of SD-6.

In revenge Sydney turns to the real CIA and utilizes her skills as a double agent on their behalf. It is at this agency that Sydney encounters both her estranged father (Victor Garber) and her mysterious mother (Lena Olin). As with Garner's Elektra, Sydney is enmeshed in an Oedipal net. She is unable to trust either her mother or her father, both of whom manipulate her for their own purposes, as well as use her as a weapon against the other. In several episodes Sydney's father even tries to eliminate her mother, who is now working for one of the numerous secret organizations in the series. Needless to say, this bit of deception shatters whatever trust Sydney had left in her father.

Although Sydney continues to work with her father and even at times with her mother, most notably in the two-part episode "Passage," she struggles with her feelings of betrayal and abandonment throughout the series. These feelings are heightened in season three when she loses her memory and is captured by the NSC, which attempts to recover the valuable information she has stored in that memory. This world of double agents and deception takes its toll on Sydney as she changes from innocent college girl to hardened agent.

In season four, the series creators introduced another wrinkle into the Oedipal complex by bringing onto the scene Sydney's half-sister Nadia (Mia Maestro). As Nadia too begins to work for the "black ops" organization her sister has joined with her father, Sydney takes on the role of protective mother, defending her against the machinations of the various father figures in the show, as well as keeping her safe during operations. Ultimately their grief over the loss of their mother unites them as much as any shared mission with the government.

Sydney's love life is also fraught with loss and betrayal.

Opposite: Jennifer Garner from the television series *Alias* in one of many disguises.

Vaughn (Michael Vartan), a fellow spy and Sydney's love interest, marries another woman. After that woman's death he returns to a suspicious Sydney. As mentioned earlier, SD-6 murdered Sydney's first love and forced her into the arms of the CIA.

What Sydney ultimately learns through all these twists and turns of the plot—the convoluted fight against terrorism, the search for the Rambaldi (a medieval prophet and alchemist) artifacts that may or may not explain occult mysteries—is, simply, to trust no one.

La Femme Nikita, the Creation of an Assassin

Luc Besson's *La Femme Nikita* (1990) set the standard for female assassins for that decade and the next. Echoes of the film can be seen not only in the remakes it spawned on the American screen and on television, but also in such disparate works as Tarantino's *Kill Bill* films, Hong Kong movies like *Naked Killer,* and the popular Jennifer Garner series *Alias.*

Nikita (Anne Parillaud) starts the film as a punk drug addict who, while robbing a pharmacy, shoots a policeman. The French court sentences her to prison, but before she can be transported, a secret government operations unit fakes her death and imprisons her instead in a "re-education" facility where she is trained to be a compliant assassin.

Nikita is initially rebellious, attacking her trainers, painting her room with anarchistic symbols, while maintaining her defiant attitude. Gradually, however, as the years pass, the conditioning begins to have an effect. Nikita learns computers, martial arts, weapon use, and the fine art of being a seductive woman. For as her only female trainer (Jeanne Moreau) tells her somewhat cynically, there are "no limits to femininity . . . and the means of taking advantage of it."

However, no matter how attractive and professional Nikita becomes, "her world" remains a world controlled by men. The patriarchal special ops unit, symbolized by the fatherly and obviously smitten Bob (Tcheky Karyo), molds her into the image it desires, a sexually attractive and skilled killing machine who is

Peta Wilson as TV's Femme Nikita.

Anne Parillaud in the influential *La Femme Nikita.*

adept at disguise and subterfuge. She complies largely because if she does not they threaten to "terminate" her, but also because she has accepted, through conditioning, their dominance and power over her.

The unit's hold on Nikita begins to crack only when she is released into the world at large to do its bidding. Once free, she begins to discover her own personality and desires, formerly buried by her addiction and then later by the repression of the conditioning unit. She meets a sensitive man, Marco (Jean-Hughes Anglade), who pampers her and caters to her needs, supporting her even though he knows she is a government assassin. The Nikita who emerges in this loving relationship is spontaneous

Above: Nikita (Anne Parillaud) dutifully doing her job in Luc Besson's *La Femme Nikita*.

Opposite: Bridget Fonda in the American remake of *La Femme Nikita*, called *Point of No Return*.

and joyful, almost childlike in her enthusiasm for life, sex, food, and love.

Nikita's final break with the ops unit is a painful but necessary one. This woman warrior must have her freedom, and so she betrays her handlers to gain it. With the aid of her self-sacrificing boyfriend Marco, she disappears without a trace, cutting her ties to him. In the final scene her two "lovers"—Marco and Bob—face each other across a table, grief stricken by their loss but relieved that Nikita has achieved the freedom she so richly deserves.

The American remake of *La Femme Nikita*, *Point of No Return* (1993), features Bridget Fonda in the lead role. It follows the plot of the original almost slavishly, but has little of the anarchic energy and humor Besson brings to all his films.

The Canadian television series *La Femme Nikita* (1997–2001) is a different case. Its star Peta Wilson (who also played a warrior vampire in *The League of Extraordinary Gentlemen*) does recapture some of the toughness and sensual appeal of Anne Parillaud in the original movie. The series, however, pulls its punches at several key points, due to the demands of television censorship. Nikita was never a murderer in this series, as the charges were false, and she expresses moral objections to her handlers far more frequently than did either of her predecessors.

The Silence of the Lambs, the Legacy of Clarice

With *The Silence of the Lambs* (1991) Jodie Foster created for the screen a detective/sleuth who would have impact throughout the nineties and into the next decade. Her intelligence and courage, coupled with deep vulnerabilities, set the tone for many female detectives to follow, including Julianne Moore in the sequel *Hannibal* (2001), as well as Agent Scully in the series *The X-Files.*

Foster's performance is an impressively subtle one as she balances more traditionally "feminine" qualities with tougher sensibilities. When the audience first sees Clarice, she is running through the woods, looking very young and delicate, her ponytail bobbing behind her. Later at the FBI headquarters she is dwarfed by her fellow agents, who surround her and eye her somewhat suspiciously, a scene that is repeated later when she confronts a group of police officers in the funeral home where a victim's body is being examined.

Besides her diminutive physical stature, Clarice exhibits vulnerability in her interviews with serial killer Dr. Hannibal Lecter (Anthony Hopkins), when she exchanges personal information for clues to the identity of a second serial killer named "Buffalo Bill." It is through these series of interviews that the audience learns of her trauma over the murder of her law-enforcement father and of her angst over her inability to save one symbolic lamb from slaughter on a ranch she was sent away to after her father's demise.

Countering these softer qualities are the perseverance and intelligence she demonstrates even while exhibiting symptoms of fear and anguish. She holds her own against the several father figures in the film who attempt to exert their authority over her. She wins the confidence of the crafty Lecter, who supplies her with the tools to track down Buffalo Bill and save a "human lamb" from the slaughterhouse. She stands up to her boss (Scott Glenn) when he humiliates her in front of a group of officers. And she is the one who ultimately "takes down" Buffalo Bill (Ted Levine) in a harrowing climax and chase through his labyrinthine hideout.

Opposite: Clarice (Jodie Foster) confronts demons, both human and psychological, in *The Silence of the Lambs.*

Keira Knightley in *Domino,* a story loosely based on the life of bounty hunter/model Domino Harvey.

Domino

"Heads you live, tails you die!"

Keira Knightley's most recent return to warrior woman territory is the movie *Domino* (2005), which garnered a good deal of its press attention from the controversy surrounding the film. It is based on the true story of Domino Harvey, daughter of famed actor Laurence Harvey and model Sophie Wynn, who gave up her own modeling career to eventually become a bounty hunter. Sadly, the real Domino Harvey died on June 27, 2005, due to a drug overdose, just prior to the movie's original release date.

The film is partially narrated by Domino (Knightley) herself, whose tone is fractured and not always coherent. Director Tony Scott and writer Richard Kelly, of *Donnie Darko* fame, allow the

Domino (Keira Knightley) sports handcuffs and badge in the bio-pic *Domino*.

film to express this distorted sense of reality through the use of repeated scenes, rapid-fire editing, and throwaway pieces of action and dialogue. The dizzying effect is reminiscent of *Natural Born Killers* and not particularly to the liking of many viewers, who found it distracting.

Domino rebels against convention and the "jet set." Her mother tried to tame her after her father passed away by putting her in boarding school, but nothing could repress her strong-willed nature and desire for adventure. Domino's cultured British accent and beauty pose a stark contrast to the stereotypical image of the thrill-seeking bounty hunter. Director Tony Scott portrays her life in his own nonlinear vision, with no-holds-barred action, violence, and nudity. He takes artistic license with fact, adds a reality TV show, and assigns a male love interest, overall portraying what is perhaps his personal view of the rebel Domino.

Chapter 13
Sharpshooters of the West

An armed woman on a horse is certainly a very Amazonian motif. However, the western movie from its inception around the turn of the century by filmmakers like "Bronco" Billy Anderson, Thomas Ince, and W. S. Hart was an art form predominantly confined to male lead characters, such as those written by novelist Zane Grey, who helped create the western genre. The themes were traditional issues of loyalty, male camaraderie, revenge, self-sacrifice, and, of course, violence.

Despite the fact that cowgirls have been historically recognized and documented, they have rarely been immortalized on film the way men have in westerns. However, historically, in the days of the Old West women really did have to overcome traditional gender roles to survive. Pioneer women in the American West were a different breed. They worked on ranches, famously performed in Wild West shows and competed in rodeos, often in addition to customary gender duties such as taking care of home and family. In film, though, women of the West are generally portrayed in two categories: the morally loose "saloon girl" (read: prostitute) and the virginal "good girl," more often than not a "schoomarm" or the minister's daughter. This chapter explores some of the women who took on the great West of the cinema in lead action roles.

Hannie Caulder, Raquel Welch Takes On the Old West

—

"You're a hard woman, Hannie Caulder."

"Like the man said, there aren't any hard women, only soft men."

—

Opposite: Raquel Welch as Hannie Caulder makes an inviting advertisement for the film of the same name.

Since she first burst on the screen in *One Million Years B.C.* back in 1966, Welch continued playing dominant warrior-like women in a series of movies and television shows, including *Fathom, The Magic Christian, Kansas City Bomber,* and "Mork vs. the Necrotons"—*Mork and Mindy.* But it was not until 1971 that she returned to the role of a classic woman warrior. This time Welch took on the challenge of entering into the traditional male stronghold of genre convention: the American western.

Hannie Caulder begins with the robbery of a Mexican bank and follows three bumbling yet vicious thieves, the Clemens brothers (played by Ernest Borgnine, Strother Martin, and Jack Elam—all familiar faces to western audiences), as they flee across the border. At a stagecoach station they brutally murder the agent and repeatedly rape his young wife—Hannie (Raquel Welch). They then burn down her house and leave her to die inside.

A traumatized Hannie wanders out into the desert clothed only in a poncho and shoes. A bounty hunter—Price (Robert Culp)—discovers her there and gives her a hat and some water but refuses to help her beyond that. She begs him to train her to be a gunfighter, to be her mentor so she can take revenge on the Clemens brothers, even offering him her "ass," which he had admired. He still refuses, and finally agrees only when he is impressed with her courage as she follows him on foot in the hot desert. Their relationship ultimately begins to soften, particularly when he witnesses her anguish after suffering a series of flashbacks in which she relives her sexual assault.

Slowly falling in love with Hannie, Price takes her into town to collect his bounty on a dead criminal he is hauling in and to buy her "more appropriate" clothes. Slowly Hannie, with Price's help, transforms herself into the image of a gunfighter. She dresses in leather pants, cowboy boots and hat, poncho, and straps a six-gun around her waist. By the time she has completed her costume, Hannie has co-opted all the basic attire of the male western protagonist.

In a beach hideaway, Price begins to train Hannie in a method resembling the techniques of martial arts. As Hannie becomes proficient, Price begins to warn her about the life she is about to embark on, a life he knows too well: "You will not be the same person." And at first she does hesitate. When they are attacked

Studio portrait of the remarkable Barbara Stanwyck.

on the beach by a group of banditos, she fights back, downing one of them, but then is unable to make the "killing shot." Price does it instead.

All this changes once the Clemens brothers murder her lover Price. As she watches Price die on the bed of their hotel room, she becomes even more hardened. She heads over to the local saloon/whorehouse, kicks down Frank Clemens's (Elam) door, and dispatches the disbelieving outlaw who had laughed off the thought of a woman outdrawing him. She finds the next brother (Martin) and kills him after he calls her a "bitch." When she turns in his body to the sheriff for a reward, he calls her a "hard woman." Again she reverses the sexist insult: "There aren't any hard women. Just soft men."

The film ends in an abandoned prison where Hannie outdraws and kills the final brother (Borgnine). The final shot is of Hannie leading a horse carrying the last brother's body back to town to collect her reward. The transformation is complete. Hannie, devoted wife and lover to a station agent, has become Hannie Caulder, bounty hunter.

Barbara Stanwyck, "High Ridin' Warrior Woman"

Throughout her long career in films and television, Barbara Stanwyck battled on the front lines of Hollywood's on-going gender wars by portraying a diversity of "warrior women."

—Torey King, "Spiritual Ancestors to Xena"

As indicated in Torey King's thought-provoking article "Spiritual Ancestors to Xena: Barbara Stanwyck—Warrior Woman in Hollywood's Gender Wars," Stanwyck was part of a generation of female actors who came into their own in the thirties and forties. They were sharpshooters, reporters, bosses, aviatrixes, and femme fatales. Women like Katharine Hepburn, Rosalind Russell, Bette Davis, Joan Crawford, and, of course, Barbara Stanwyck marked the period as their own. But with the return of conservative values and uniformity in the fifties, these women were replaced by blonde bombshells like Marilyn Monroe and Jayne Mansfield and girl-next-door comediennes like Doris Day. But a few women, like Stanwyck, refused to be boxed in by the system and continued to make films about strong women even in the repressive fifties.

Whether Stanwyck was playing the role of a stripper (as in *Ball of Fire*) or a murdering femme fatale (as in *Double Indemnity*), she was always confrontational, making her male leads a little unsure, a little insecure. But her most important roles for the purposes of this study are her western characterizations. Beginning with George Stevens's *Annie Oakley* (1935), Stanwyck created a series of "high ridin' women" (the term comes from her film *Forty Guns*) who would stand out in a genre dominated by men.

Annie Oakley is based on the true story of the sharpshooter for the famed Buffalo Bill Wild West Show, which toured the world in the early part of the twentieth century. Like her true-life counterpart, Annie (Stanwyck) outshot every man she went up against, including her eventual husband. The movie remains true to these facts, as early in the film we see Annie "throwing a contest" for her future lover Toby (Preston Foster), so he will be able to pay his debts. Her skill is so impressive that Sitting Bull, the Sioux Chief, consents to join Buffalo Bill's troupe only after he witnesses Annie's expertise with firearms. The film even includes the historically accurate scene where Annie shoots a cigarette from the mouth of the crown prince of Germany.

In Samuel Fuller's *Forty Guns* (1957), the audience's first glimpse of Stanwyck is a powerful one. She comes riding at the head of a herd of gunmen as they shake the ground around them. As Jessica Drummond, Stanwyck projects strength and quiet power, as well as deftness with a whip. She is surrounded by her army of men, even at dinner, and they respond to her with slavish obedience. And although the filmmakers tacked on an ending in which she pursues the Wyatt Earp character who has saved her life, the audience, as Torey King points out, still identifies her as a strong character, a position she has earned through 98 per cent of the film, no matter the finale.

Undaunted by Hollywood's prejudice against aging actresses, Stanwyck took on television next, embracing the role of Victoria

Barbara Stanwyck as sharpshooter Annie Oakley in the film of the same name.

Barkley in the series *The Big Valley* (1965–1969). Like Jessica Drummond, Victoria ruled a vast empire of land, wielding power as well as acting as matriarch of her family of three sons and one daughter. Throughout the series she demonstrated her power through wisdom and physical prowess when necessary (she could still fight and shoot a gun as well as she did in 1935). Stanwyck ended up winning several Emmys for her portrayal of Victoria and the devotion of a new generation of audiences.

The Quick and the Dead

———

The Lady seeks revenge.

———

With director Sam Raimi's *The Quick and the Dead* (1995), producer-star Sharon Stone revisits the domain carved out by Raquel Welch in *Hannie Caulder*. Coming off the success of her role in *Basic Instinct* three years earlier, Stone exhibited sterling credentials to play this gunfighter/warrior. In the earlier film she had shocked and delighted audiences with her daring and frank portrayal of a femme fatale who challenged men not only with her kinky sexual practices, but also with her audacious writings and defiance of societal norms.

In *The Quick and the Dead*, Stone portrays a haunted and conflicted woman, known as the Lady, who returns to her hometown of Redemption to take revenge on the ruthless tyrant, appropriately named Herod (Gene Hackman), who caused the death of her father when she was a child. As in so many warrior woman plots, the trauma of a missing father is implied as the motivation for unconventional choices.

Like Hannie Caulder before her, as a woman who has taken on the traditional role of a man, she is derided and shunned for that decision. In the opening sequence a degenerate robber shoots at her and calls her a "bitch." She handily brings him down and handcuffs him to a wagon wheel. In town when she asks for a room, the saloon owner tells her "whores" belong in the building next door. She then kicks the stool from under the surprised barkeep. When she walks out to face her first opponent in the deadly

Opposite: Sharon Stone as the Lady in Sam Raimi's modernist western *The Quick and the Dead*.

331

The Lady (Sharon Stone), a crack shot with a six-gun, has an old score to settle in the western *The Quick and the Dead*.

fast-draw contest Herod has set up in the town, the townspeople vilify her.

Also like Hannie, the Lady initially has serious qualms about killing another person, even though she denies it to the reformed gunslinger Cort (Russell Crowe). In this way the filmmakers reinforce the theory that women are hardwired by nature to be nurturing and to preserve life rather than take it. The Lady has several opportunities to kill Herod but hesitates each time. Even when in a rage, after a gunfighter has raped the young daughter of the saloon owner, she can only manage to wound him until he attempts to shoot her in the back. It is only after Herod has killed his own son the Kid (Leonardo DiCaprio), echoing for her the moment the tyrant forced the young Lady to kill her father in an attempt to split the noose he was hanging by, that she finds the will to rid the town of this tyrant forever.

Stone also manages to play with gender roles in the film, par-

The Lady takes aim with her gun.

ticularly in the scene when she goes to dinner at Herod's mansion. She dresses in a traditional nineteenth-century dress and takes on the role of a more genteel lady to subvert Herod's natural defenses. As Herod sweet-talks her across the dinner table, Lady fondles the derringer strapped to her black-stockinged thigh. But when the opportunity to shoot presents itself, she fumbles with the gun, still too wracked by her moral concerns, coupled with a genuine fear of this imposing father figure.

In the final scene the Lady overcomes her scruples as she blows up half of the corrupt town with dynamite, referencing such classic westerns as W. S. Hart's *Hell's Hinges* (1916), and emerges from the flames reborn as an avenging angel. She dispatches the now frightened Herod, holsters her gun in what could be taken as a rather Freudian moment, and leaves the town without a backward glance, evoking the finale of so many traditional westerns.

Advertising artwork for the Roger Corman film *Gunslinger,* starring Beverly Garland.

Gunslinger, "Forced To Be a Man"

I have identified most of my life with the underdog, with the blacks, with "half- breeds," and with women to a degree, with any victim of society's prejudice. In an exploitation picture, if you had a strong woman protagonist, the story could be advertised from that angle, and it could be sold better.

—Roger Corman

Gunslinger (1956) was a positive feminist film at a time when examples of this kind were few and far between. The film opens in a marshal's office in a small and desolate western town (Oracle, Texas). Two killers arrive on horseback. Inside are the marshal (William Schallert) and his wife Rose (Beverly Garland). They are discussing the saloon owner Erica (Allison Hayes of *Attack of the 50 Foot Woman* fame) and his problems with her. Rose, sitting on the desk as her husband sits below her in a chair, dominates the frame physically as she proclaims her ability to stand up to Erica. Her husband puts her off with a traditionally patriarchal piece of advice: "You stick to making coffee, Rose." At that moment a double-barreled shotgun appears in the window, which was established in an earlier close-up, and blasts apart the man, who in most westerns would be the hero. In rapid-fire response, Rose grabs a rifle, chases and kills one of the murderers.

At the funeral that follows, Rose shows very little traditional female hysteria. Instead she recognizes the other killer near the grave, kicks dirt in his face, and shoots him. He falls into the grave, disrupting the funeral. Corman, through these two shocking scenes, establishes Rose as the protagonist, who acts with force, decisiveness, and precision, all qualities usually associated with male heroes.

The role reversal is a positive one. Rose takes upon herself the job of cleaning up the corrupt town ("Put it [the badge] on. I've got a pot roast in the oven"), which includes a cowardly mayor (Martin Kingsley) and a land-grabbing saloon owner. As soon as she pins on the badge of office, Rose is transformed mentally, as well as physically, as the camera dissolves to find her wearing shirt and pants with phallic guns strapped to her waist, rather than her customary "feminine" dress.

The gender reversal of this film carries over to the villain of the piece, Erica Paige, as well. Although she dresses more seductively, she remains as strong a character as Rose, her equal in determination and cunning. She is an acute businesswoman, buying up all the land in town to sell it to the railroad, whose tracks are slated to cross through Oracle. In addition, she dominates the men around her, particularly the servile Jake (Jonathan Haze), whom she demeaningly calls "little man." Erica and Rose are both women in control of their destinies, taking on traditional male functions, even brawling in the saloon like a conventional western hero and villain.

Sexually the females are aggressive as well. When Erica hires Cane (John Ireland) to kill Rose, she has no qualms about mixing business with pleasure as she leads the hesitant hit man up the stairs to her bedroom: "We have to talk shop . . . Come into my bedroom." Rose, too, can hold her own in a sexual/romantic encounter. Although Cane is hired to kill Rose, he finds himself falling in love with her. Their frustrations stretch throughout the film, acting as romantic relief from the violence. Double entendres (*Cane:* "Tell me, am I wanted around here?") and thinly veiled sexual references (*Cane:* "What do you do with your nights, Miss Marshal?") pepper their repartee, along with the standard gunplay. During their first flirtation in the marshal's office, Cane caresses a rifle while speaking until Rose takes it back, thereby regaining control of the phallus.

As their affair becomes more serious, so does the gunplay. Although Cane has no reservations about killing other inhabitants of the town, he cannot pull the trigger on Rose and instead saves her life by shooting Erica, who was about to finish his job for him. The end of the affair takes a page right out of David O. Selznick's *Duel in the Sun*. Rose pursues her lover Cane, who is now responsible for several deaths, including the mayor of the town, whom Cane had promised not to touch. Placing her emotions second to the demands of duty, she chases Cane on horseback and then by foot up a mountainside. As Cane asks, "Is it a two-way thing?" and Rose whispers her assent, they shoot at each other. Wounded physically, as well as emotionally, Cane

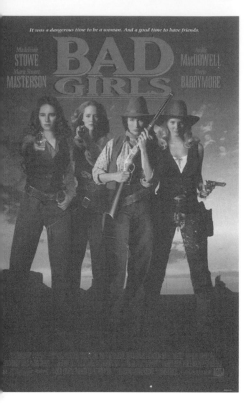

Poster for the movie *Bad Girls*.

calls out Rose's name, allowing her to pinpoint his location and fire the fatal shot. At the end, Rose rides out of town like a long line of western heroes before her, having fulfilled her duty, in this case at the price of love.

Bad Girls

————◆————

"It was a dangerous time to be a woman. And a good time to have friends."

————◆————

Bad Girls (1994) follows the standard cinematic tradition of delivering strong, independent female characters packaged in a completely unrealistic way for the time period and setting in order to achieve maximum commercial appeal. An amazingly clean, coiffed (and cute), white-toothed band of prostitutes in the Old West are forced to quit their way of life when their leader Cody (Madeleine Stowe) kills a customer who is abusing her friend Anita (Mary Stuart Masterson) and is sentenced to hang.

Anita and her two other former sex-worker friends (Drew Barrymore and Andie MacDowell) break her out of jail and head for the Southwest to pursue a new life. On the road they are pursued by Pinkerton agents and harassed by stereotypical "bad men" as the film slowly becomes a sort of *Thelma and Louise* out West.

The theme of female solidarity and sisterhood plays a major part in the film. Men are incidental to this sisterhood of four. They are either cardboard villains in pursuit of this quartet of fugitives or incidental sexual/romantic flings. Interestingly enough, this film was begun with director Tamra Davis and a script written by Yolande Finch and Becky Johnston, but a few weeks into filming the production company replaced Davis with a male director, Jonathan Kaplan, and had the entire script rewritten. Nothing remains of the original project.

Chapter 14
The Good, the Bad, and the Ugly

"Ladies and gentlemen, welcome to violence . . ."

—*Faster, Pussycat! Kill! Kill!*

Absurd, highly sexual, or shockingly violent, exploitation films are usually defined as moviemaking that tosses aside artist merit for more carnal and gratuitous displays of nudity, sex, and violence. However, many of the popular exploitation films of the past are not considered to be devoid of artistic merit—to some they are masterpieces in their own right. "Grindhouse cinema" has been reclaimed by many fans and filmmakers to become a major influence to modern-day directors like Quentin Tarantino. From the "nudie cutie" to the traditional "roughie," we also note many pop-culture Amazonian motifs. This chapter gives an overview of a few of these infamous films.

"Barbarella, Psychedella"

"Decrucify the angel . . . or I'll melt your face!"

Barbarella (1968) is one of the first science fiction movies (other than oddities like Maria in Fritz Lang's *Metropolis* or Allison Hayes in *Attack of the 50 Foot Woman*) to feature a woman warrior lead. Unfortunately the film is also notable for the significant loss of brain cells of any viewer watching it in its entirety. Based on a comic book and written by Roger Vadim (*And God Created*

Opposite: Jane Fonda as the outer-space sexpot Barbarella.

Barbarella (Jane Fonda) seductive with handy missile gun.

Woman, Pretty Maids All in a Row) and Terry Southern (*Candy, The Magic Christian*), both infamous for the objectification of women in their films, the character Barbarella, as played by Jane Fonda, is as much blond bimbo as "intergalactic astronautrix." There is also probably the oddest theme song ever used, with lyrics like, "Barbarella, psychedella, there's a kind of cockleshell about you . . ."

The tone of *Barbarella* is set in the opening sequence as the title character performs a striptease in outer space and then greets her commander. (This will be just one of many ways she will shed her clothing throughout the film.) She stands totally wide-eyed and naked before her elderly commander, very much like the "good girl" he patronizingly calls her. Although there are moments when Barbarella demonstrates her bravery, as when she shoots down the spaceships of the Black Queen (Anita Pallenberg) with her mini missile gun or destroys the doomsday weapon developed by Durand-Durand (Milo O'Shea), for much of the film she depends on men for aid as well as for sexual self-discovery. She is very much a sexy innocent in space, a live-action version of *Playboy*'s popular comic character of the period—Little Annie Fannie.

Although her devotion to the futuristic world of love and peace is never in doubt, she lacks the resourcefulness and intelligence to become a role model for future generations of cinematic warrior women. But she does survive being attacked by some very slow-walking plastic vampire dolls, being pecked by a flock of pet-store parakeets, smoking the "essence of man" from a large bong, and wearing a custom-made outfit of skunk fur, complete with a tail that gets easily caught in spaceship doors.

Barbarian Queen, "No Man Can Touch Her Naked Steel"

Gifted with the ability to smell out a trend, producer-director Roger Corman, no stranger to the universe of warrior women (most notably with the western *Gunslinger* and *Saga of the Viking Women)*, jumped onto the *Conan/Dungeons and Dragons/Heavy Metal* cart and in 1985 put into production a film called *Barbarian Queen.* For this film and its tongue-in-cheek sequel *Barbarian Queen II: The Empress Strikes Back* (1989), Corman cast Lana Clarkson, a six-foot-tall, athletic California blonde who in 1983 appeared in the *Deathstalker* fantasy epic and in 1987 in the spoof film *Amazon Women on the Moon.*

The movie opens with a scene that could double for a feminine douche commercial, as a virginal young girl sits alone by a lake sniffing a pink flower. But within less than a minute the peaceful scene is shattered, and the real action begins, as two stereotypical swarthy male soldiers show up and violently force her to the ground. Ripping her top off, they laugh while feverishly fondling her breasts. Titillating assault scenes like this are replayed over and over throughout the movie, putting the viewer in the position of viewing the rapes and molestations with an inevitably lustful eye, as from a male viewpoint the camera zooms in on one bodice after another being ripped away and breasts bursting forth.

The young girl of the first scene is the sister of Clarkson's character Amethea, the Queen, who is preparing for her wedding to a blond Ken-doll-like prince. Roman soldiers proceed to raid their village, killing and abducting the remaining inhabitants, save for three women who escape. Following the standard rape-revenge, pseudo-feminine-empowerment storyline, Amethea and her sister warriors make their way into the city with their swords to liberate the villagers and punish their captors.

In the course of the quest, however, Amethea is caught, stripped down to a pair of thong panties, and bound to a torture device for an unusually long portion of the movie. She shows nerves of steel during the long, cruel torture, which consists of unique sadistic methods such as dripping water onto her bare breasts and her captor verbally taunting her throughout while wearing a pair of absurd glasses. Fans complain that the R-rated DVD release edited out the best portions of the bondage scene, when the actress wraps her long legs around her captor, which was shown on the unrated VHS release. Either way, she still dispatches him and his silly glasses into a boiling vat of acid in the end.

I Spit on Your Grave, Radical Feminism Meets the Exploitation Movie

The 1978 cult film *I Spit on Your Grave* (aka *Day of the Woman*) draws heavily on the ethos of the Pam Grier films that preceded it—but with a major difference: the director-writer Meier Zarchi decided on a more minimalist and severe approach to the subject of female revenge. First of all, rather than casting a voluptuous, sensual actress like Grier (which is common for exploitation movies like those of director Russ Meyer), he chose Camille Keaton, a wispy, lanky woman who resembles, not accidentally we assume, that television role model of liberated seventies women—Mary Tyler Moore. And even though Keaton is nude in several scenes, the titillation quotient is low, as she is not portrayed, as opposed to Grier, as a sexually charged female who takes delight in aggressive sexuality. In addition, the director has adopted an almost documentary style for his film: eschewing all music except source music, utilizing practical locations (mostly Upper New York State), and allowing the actors' performances to develop in an almost improvisational style, reminiscent of Martin Scorsese's early movies.

The film tells the story of a modern liberated female writer—Jennifer Hill—who leaves New York City for the isolation of the country to work on a book. She radiates confidence, as well as a sense of self-esteem, in both her body language and speech. When she meets Matthew (Richard Pace), the mentally challenged delivery boy, she is kind to him and unembarrassed. When he asks if she has a "boyfriend," she answers forthrightly that she has "many."

It is, of course, this honesty about her love life, as well as her "audacity" in wearing "revealing" outfits like a bikini or a peignoir, that the villain Johnny (Eron Tabor) claims as his justification for leading a posse of friends to rape and beat her repeatedly, a defense still used by rapists in that decade, as well as in the decades before it. Zarchi's direction of Jennifer's serial rape and assault leaves nothing to the imagination. It is graphic and difficult for audiences to watch even today, as Jennifer is hunted like an animal, violated in all orifices, and left for dead.

When Jennifer finally heals and sets out on her mission of revenge, the director refuses to pull punches here either. Like Joan of Arc, she dons a costume (a black one in this case, making her seem like a dark avenging angel), says her prayers to her god, and methodically proceeds to eliminate the four offenders. Although her methods are brutal (she castrates one, hangs another, axes a third to death, and tears up the body of a fourth with an outboard motor), the audience maintains a level of sympathy for Jennifer because of the horrific crimes against her and the fact that the men are returning to kill her, so she will not give evidence to the police.

It is clear, though, that she is no longer quite right in the head. The underlying viciousness, the way she toys with the men before killing them in some cases causes an unsettling feeling of wonder about what women are capable of. The quiet revenge, devoid of outward emotion, makes it seem that she is no longer quite human. In the final scene of the movie Jennifer steers the motorboat away from the scene of her final extra-legal execution, and the camera lingers on her face as she smiles ever so slightly with a sense of accomplishment and victory.

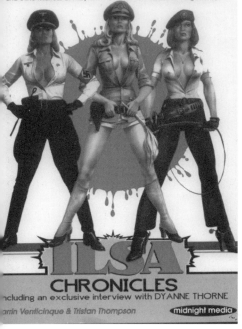

The *Ilsa* Collection

"You call yourselves men? I see no manhood between your legs!"

Ilsa, She Wolf of the SS opens with the following warning:

The film you are about to see is based upon documented fact. The atrocities shown were conducted as "medical experiments" in special concentration camps throughout Hitler's Third Reich. Although these crimes against humanity are historically accurate, the characters depicted are composites of notorious Nazi personalities; and the events portrayed have been condensed into one locality for dramatic purposes. Because of its shocking subject matter, this film is restricted to adult audiences only. We dedicate this film with the hope that these heinous crimes will never occur again.

In the opening sex scene Ilsa is introduced to us with the sound of her moaning as the camera pans over her bedroom. From there on, it is an uncompromising journey into scenes displaying her brutality as the commandant of a Nazi prison camp, subjecting prisoners to shocking medical experiments, using them as tools for her sadistic pleasures and sexual passions. No man seems to satisfy her rapacious lust adequately.

In the genre of exploitation, where extreme violence, torture, sex, and gore are commonplace, Ilsa stands out to this day as a pariah, too perverse even for infamous exploitation filmmaker David Friedman to keep his name in the credits and yet far too popular to fade away into obscurity. Why would the man who defined the "roughie" exploitation films of the sixties and produced such splatter classics as *Blood Feast* (1963), *2000 Maniacs* (1964), and *Color Me Blood Red* (1965) wish to have his name removed from the credits?

The four films in the *Ilsa* collection (aka *The Ilsa Chronicles*)—*Ilsa, She Wolf of the SS* (1975); *Ilsa, Harem Keeper of the Oil Sheiks* (1976); *Ilsa, the Tigress of Siberia* (1977); and

Ilsa, the Wicked Warden (1977)—have probably inspired more controversy than any of the films in this study. The series of loosely connected films, made in Europe with limited distribution and minuscule budgets, inspires outrage in some circles and devotion in others. Anchor Bay Entertainment's recent release of the fully restored DVD collection is marketed much the same as box sets of Bette Davis movies from Warner Bros. or film noir collections from Fox. Yet, despite the obvious cultural significance of the *Ilsa* films, universities that have included such films as *I Spit On Your Grave* (1978) in their curriculum will hardly touch *Ilsa*.

Ilsa, She Wolf of the SS is a prime example of Holocaust imagery sexualized and even gendered. But beyond the taboo elements of the Nazi content, Ilsa touches upon deeper elements of sadomasochism that elicit confusion in many viewers who otherwise experience secret titillation and pleasure in the heinous acts portrayed. As Rikke Schubart, director of the Center for Media Studies, University of Southern Denmark, points out in her article "A Perfect Dominatrix,"

> By making a phenomenon "cult" we frame it as "safe."
> It is a game, not reality. It belongs to modern-day male
> initiation rites, where transgression is part of youthful
> experimentation. To enjoy the "sickening" pleasures of
> Ilsa does not make one "sick." It teaches you about "sick"
> pleasures. Afterwards, the audience returns to normal.

Ilsa is never given an acceptable motive for her sadistic behavior. We are not aware of anything that has been done to her that would allow her the excuse of seeking revenge, which is so often the key factor in excusing brutal feminine violence in films. Usually if a woman castrates a man, it is because the man is a rapist or has committed some act of assault. However, Ilsa castrates out of pure sadistic pleasure, angry that the man has failed to fulfill her properly. She is aroused by the power of the castration, balancing out her earlier moments of vulnerability when she was a slave to her pleasure of being penetrated.

However, in the end of each of the *Ilsa* films, she is punished harshly for her lustful transgressions and for breaking with gender stereotype. She is even literally ripped to pieces by the pris-

oners at the end of *Ilsa, the Wicked Warden*. And so despite the roller coaster of violence and gore, order is restored when Ilsa is depowered and the male hero prevails. The male hero has, of course, taken pleasure with Ilsa already, as part of his job to save the others. He is nearly always an undercover agent of some sort, deceiving her and using his male endowments to manipulate. Ilsa also must bow down to at least one man who has given her power, who is also evil, but higher up on the chain than her. Order is reestablished when the masculine hero breaks off his sexual connection with Ilsa, destroys her, and saves the "good girl" of the film, usually an innocent victim who keeps her needs under tight control—the complete opposite of Ilsa. The hero has denied the sin of lust (after happily partaking in it and being sated) and assists in uplifting the model of the virtuous woman once again.

The primary attribute of these films, which suffer from cheap effects and amateurish acting, is the presence of star Dyanne Thorne. The part was originally offered to Phyllis Davis, who had made a name for herself in exploitation films like *Sweet Sugar* and *Terminal Island*, both in 1973, where she played sexually aggressive and often violent prison inmates. When Davis read the script, however, and realized she would have to perform a urination scene, she withdrew. To replace her, the producers cast a relatively unknown actress whose most memorable role to this point was in the horror film *Blood Sabbath* (1972), where she played the witch queen Alotta.

Whereas her co-stars might seem unsure in their performances, Thorne's amazing physical presence, as well as her commanding voice, are absolutely convincing. In later years Thorne, unlike so many exploitation stars, has remained proud of her performances, and in the DVD commentaries for the series she proudly claims the Ilsa character for the feminist movement:

> This is the first film where they had a female villain, and also this is the first one where she was the leader of the feminists, if you will, which many of the magazines had said. This was the first feminist.

Pamela Anderson in *Barb Wire*

Barb (Pamela Anderson) defends her club from the fascists of the future in *Barb Wire*.

"Don't call me babe"

Barb Wire opens with an elaborate dance/striptease by the hero-ine (played by *Baywatch* star Pamela Anderson, who would do the voice for a similar character in the MTV series *Stripperella*—2003). Barb (who could be a modern-day *Barbarella*) is squirted continuously with water from a long phallic hose as she writhes in and out of her tight-fitting gown. Intercut with her dance are shots of the male audience members raucously egging her on, asking for more. As the dance finishes, Barb's gaze changes from sexual abandon to anger as one of the patrons calls her "babe." She then slowly and provocatively unstraps one of her stiletto heels and without warning throws it like a dagger into the frontal lobe of the offending patron. As she walks offstage, she utters her signature line: "Don't call me babe."

While trying to raise money for her club, Barb poses as a dominatrix and lures a submissive man into a hotel where a fugitive with a bounty on his head is hiding. After dispatching him with the paddle he has given her to spank him, she blows open the wall to the next room and captures the fugitive. In later sequences she tramples the genitals of offenders who have taken her for granted, and in one scene empties her gun into the body of yet another hood who has foolishly called her "babe."

Amazons and Supermen, the Mix of the Century

Amazons and Supermen (the British title for this film) is the most coherent of all the many titles this film has been known as throughout the world, including most insanely *Three Stooges vs. the Wonder Woman*. This 1975 film is one of those multinational productions (in this case, Mexico, Hong Kong, and Italy) that attempt to appeal to all nations but in the end appeal to few. It is a campy mess of a movie that features European "sex star" Magda Konopka as another blond Amazon queen who conquers three musclemen who demonstrate more strength than common sense.

Queen of Outer Space

———

"Man's first fantastic flight to Venus—the female planet."

———

Amazons in outer space is the theme of the low-budget camp classic *Queen of Outer Space* (1958). Astronauts from Earth land on

Two fifties-style Amazons in *Queen of Outer Space*.

Poster for *Queen of Outer Space*.

Venus to find it is, as indicated by its name, ruled by women. All of the men have been eliminated in an ill-fated rebellion, and a disfigured Queen (Laurie Mitchell) has displaced all her hatred and bitterness onto the offending gender. Typical of the period (the Eisenhower fifties), the Amazons wear short skirts and high heels and seem more concerned with perfecting their makeup and hair than their fighting skills. The film is also notable for the presence of Zsa Zsa Gabor, the Paris Hilton of her generation.

The Films of Russ Meyer

"Ladies and gentleman, welcome to violence.

"While violence cloaks itself in a plethora of disguises, its favorite mantle still remains—sex. Violence devours all it touches, its voracious appetite rarely fulfilled. Yet violence doesn't only destroy, it creates and molds as well.

"Let's examine closely, then, this dangerous and evil creation, this new breed, encased and contained within the supple skin of woman. The softness is there, the unmistakable smell of female, the surface shiny and silky, and the body yielding yet wanton—but a word of caution—handle with care and don't drop your guard. This rapacious new breed prowls both alone and in packs, operating at any level, anytime, anywhere, and with any body.

"But who are they? One might be your secretary, your doctor's receptionist, or . . . a dancer in a go-go club."

—*Faster, Pussycat! Kill! Kill!*

Russ Meyer's name is synonymous with soft-core sex films. Of all the exploitation filmmakers in the field, Meyer has had the widest exposure, partially due to a brief but disastrous stint as a mainstream director at 20th Century Fox (*Beyond the Valley of the Dolls* [1970] and *The Seven Minutes* [1971]). But Meyer's fling with the majors does not entirely account for his cult status today, particularly among younger generations that have reclaimed his work. His *Faster, Pussycat! Kill! Kill!* shares part of

Left: The iconic Tura Satana.

Right: Miss Eva Von Slut, modern-day burlesque performer.
Photo courtesy of hypnox.com.

its name ("Faster Pussycat") with a well-known band, as well as a song by the Cramps. San Francisco's Miss Eva Von Slut, psychobilly singer and burlesque performer, cites the unforgettable Tura Satana, who played the character Varla in *Faster, Pussycat! Kill! Kill!*, as a major influence on her art and style. In a conversation with the author Miss Eva commented

> Meeting Tura was really an experience. She's lovely, sweet, and sexy still, but you can tell from talking to her for five minutes that she's no one to fuck with.

Meyer's larger-than-life heroines dominate his films with their exuberant, voracious sexuality and aggressive attitudes toward men. Beginning with *Lorna* in 1964 and ending with *Beneath the Valley of the Ultravixens* in 1980, Meyer made a string of low-budget erotic films that showcased aggressive women who violated one taboo after another, including incest.

Among the most enduring of Meyer's films, *Faster, Pussycat! Kill! Kill!* (1965) features a trio of go-go dancers who take great pleasure in using men alternately as punching bags and living sex toys. Meyer's often rapid-fire montages, coupled with his predilection for shooting his bosomy stars from a low angle (evoking images of Allison Hayes from *Attack of the 50 Foot Woman*), result in an almost surreal experience of violence and sex as perpetrated by his infamous bad-girl gang.

Tura Satana does what she does best in this scene from Russ Meyer's *Faster, Pussycat! Kill! Kill!*

City of Women, the Plight of Marcello Mastroianni

Federico Fellini spent his career in the worship of Amazon-like women. This worship has been very personal, often infantile and fraught with anxiety, and, as many feminists have pointed out, not always fair to the complexity of the individual character. But even accepting these criticisms, one cannot doubt his devo-

tion. Whether the character is played by the Nordic beauty Anita Ekberg in *La Dolce Vita* or *The Temptation of Dr. Anthony* or the earthy Mediterranean Sandra Milo in *8½* or *Juliet of the Spirits*, Fellini in his most autobiographical films paints a series of portraits of larger-than-life women who engulf Fellini at all stages of his life: childhood, adulthood, and middle age.

The 1980 release *City of Women* (the title comes from the proto-feminist fifteenth-century book by Christine de Pisan) is Fellini's most comprehensive and anxiety-ridden statement on the confounding mystery of women and fear of aging, all seen from the viewpoint of a middle-aged worshipper played by Fellini's alter ego Marcello Mastroianni.

The film posits a world in which women rule in one form or another. In the opening scene the aging Lothario (here given the ludicrous name Snaporaz) attempts to pick up a young, voluptuous woman he meets on a train. He does not succeed, and for his indiscretion is lead on a dreamlike, surreal adventure (typical of Fellini) through a world where women are in control and men are marginalized.

At a feminist conference where the women sport husband-slaves and heap abuse on men, they condemn Snaporaz for his sexist attitudes toward women, subtly referencing for the astute film buff Fellini's harem scenes in *The White Sheik* and *8½*. His sentence is castration. Escaping, he continues his journey through this new "city of women," where teenage girls taunt him, where his long-suffering wife records his infidelities, and where he attempts to return to the womb-like world of his childhood surrounded by women caring for him. In the final analysis, Fellini's film is a remarkable work of figurative self-flagellation. Fellini does not hesitate to show the pettiness and immaturity of Snaporaz even as he yearns to return to a world where he is engulfed by feminine flesh and love.

The final scenes show Snaporaz happily flying away in a hot-air balloon shaped like his "perfect woman," ready to drift off in the womb-like basket he is being carried in. His bubble is literally burst, though, when a masked "femi-nazi" comes out, aims her gun, and shoots down his balloon.

Filmography

Aeon Flux (TV series, 1995)
MTV/Colossal
Created by Peter Chung
Cast: Denise Poirier (Æon Flux (voice))

Aeon Flux (2005)
MTV/Lakeshore/Paramount/
Colossal
Directed by Karyn Kusama
Writing Credits: Phil Hay, Matt
Manfredi
Based on the characters of Peter Chung
Cast: Charlize Theron (Aeon Flux),
Marton Csokas (Chairman Trevor
Goodchild), Jonny Lee Miller
(Oren Goodchild), Sophie Okonedo
(Sithandra), Amelia Warner (Una Flux),
Caroline Chikezie (Freya), Frances
McDormand (The Handler)

Alias (TV series, 2001)
Touchstone
Created by J. J. Abrams
Cast: Jennifer Garner (Sydney Bristow),
Ron Rifkin (Arvin Sloane), Michael
Vartan (Michael Vaughn), Bradley
Cooper (William "Will" Tippin
(2001–2003)), Carl Lumbly (Marcus
Dixon), Merrin Dungey (Francine
"Francie" Calfo/Allison Doren (2001–
2003)), Kevin Weisman (Marshall
Flinkman), David Anders (Julian Sark

(2002–2004)), Melissa George (Lauren
Reed (2003–2004)), Mía Maestro
(Nadia Santos (2005–)), Greg Grunberg
(Eric Weiss (2001–)), Lena Olin (Irina
Derevko (2002–2003)), Victor Garber
(Jack Bristow)

Alien (1979)
20th Century Fox/Brandywine
Directed by Ridley Scott
Writing Credits: Dan O'Bannon,
Ronald Shusett
Cast: Tom Skerritt (Dallas), Sigourney
Weaver (Ripley), Veronica Cartwright
(Lambert), Harry Dean Stanton (Brett),
John Hurt (Kane), Ian Holm (Ash),
Yaphet Kotto (Parker), Bolaji Badejo
(Alien), Helen Horton (Mother (voice))

Alien: Resurrection (1997)
20th Century Fox/Brandywine
Directed by Jean-Pierre Jeunet
Writing Credits: Joss Whedon
Based on story by Dan O'Bannon and
Ronald Shusett
Cast: Sigourney Weaver (Lt. Ellen Ripley
Clone #8), Winona Ryder (Annalee
Call), Dominique Pinon (Vriess), Ron
Perlman (Johner), Gary Dourdan
(Christie), Michael Wincott (Elgyn), Kim
Flowers (Hillard), Dan Hedaya (General
Perez), J. E. Freeman (Dr. Wren), Brad
Dourif (Dr. Gediman), Raymond Cruz
(DiStephano), Leland Orser (Purvis)

Aliens (1986)
20th Century Fox/Brandywine
Directed by James Cameron
Writing Credits: James Cameron
Story by Cameron, Walter Hill, David
Giler, Ronald Shusett, Dan O'Bannon
Cast: Sigourney Weaver (Ellen Ripley),
Carrie Henn (Rebecca "Newt" Jorden),
Michael Biehn (Cpl. Dwayne Hicks),
Lance Henriksen (Bishop), Paul Reiser
(Carter Burke), Bill Paxton (Private
Hudson), William Hope (Lieutenant
Gorman), Jenette Goldstein (Private
Vasquez), Al Matthews (Sergeant
Apone), Mark Rolston (Private Drake),
Ricco Ross (Private Frost), Colette
Hiller (Corporal Ferro), Daniel Kash
(Private Spunkmeyer), Cynthia Dale
Scott (Corporal Dietrich), Tip Tipping
(Private Crowe), Trevor Steedman

(Private Wierzbowski), Paul Maxwell
(Van Leuwen), Valerie Colgan (ECA
Representative), Alan Polonsky
(Insurance Man), Alibe Parsons (Med
Tech), Blain Fairman (Doctor)

Alien³ (1992)
20th Century Fox/Brandywine
Directed by David Fincher
Writing Credits: David Giler, Walter
Hill, Larry Ferguson
Based on a story by Vincent Ward, Dan
O'Bannon, and Ronald Shusett
Cast: Sigourney Weaver (Ellen Ripley),
Charles Dutton (Dillon), Charles Dance
(Clemens), Paul McGann (Golic),
Brian Glover (Andrews), Ralph Brown
(Aaron), Daniel Webb (Morse),
Christopher John Fields (Rains), Holt
McCallany (Junior), Lance Henriksen
(Bishop II), Christopher Fairbank
(Murphy), Carl Chase (Frank), Leon
Herbert (Boggs), Vincenzo Nicoli (Jude),
Pete Postlethwaite (David)

. . . All the Marbles (1981)
Aldrich/MGM
Directed by Robert Aldrich
Writing Credits: Rich Eustis, Mel
Frohman
Cast: Peter Falk (Harry Sears), Vicki
Frederick (Iris), Laurene Landon
(Molly), Burt Young (Eddie Cisco),
Tracy Reed (Diane, Toledo Tiger),

Ursaline Bryant (June, Toledo Tiger), Claudette Nevins (Solly, Woman Promoter), Richard Jaeckel (Bill Dudley, Reno Referee), John Hancock ("Big John" Stanley, TT's Promoter), Lenny Montana (Jerome, Eddie's Bodyguard), Charlie Dell (Merle LeFevre, Open-Air-Fair Promoter), Chick Hearn (Himself: TV Reporter), Cliff "Fatty" Emmich (Obese Promoter), Clyde Kusatsu (Clyde Yamashito, Japanese Promoter), Joe Greene (Himself: Football Player)

Amazon Women on the Moon (1987)
Universal/Westward
Directed by Joe Dante, Carl Gottlieb, Peter Horton, John Landis, Robert K. Weiss
Writing Credits: Michael Barrie, Jim Mulholland
Cast: Monique Gabrielle (Taryn Steele), Steve Forrest (Captain Nelson), Robert Colbert (Blackie), Joey Travolta (Butch), Forrest J. Ackerman (U.S. President), Sybil Danning (Queen Lara), Lana Clarkson (Alpha Beta)

Amazons Against Supermen (1975)
Directed by Alfonso Brescia (aka Al Bradley)
Writing Credits: Alfonso Brescia, Aldo Crudo
Cast: Aldo Canti (Aru (as Nick

Jordan)), Marc Hannibal (Mug), Hua Yueh (Chang), Malisa Longo (Akela), Magda Konopka (Amazon Queen)

Andromeda (TV series, 2000–2005)
Tribune/Fireworks
Created by Gene Roddenberry
Cast: Kevin Sorbo (Capt. Dylan Hunt (2000–2005)), Lisa Ryder (Beka Valentine (2000–2005)), Keith Hamilton Cobb (Tyr Anasazi (2000–2003)), Lexa Doig (Andromeda Ascendant ("Rommie") (2000–2005)), Laura Bertram (Trance Gemini (2000–2005))

Angel (1987)
Columbia
Directed by Raymond Leung, Teresa Woo
Writing Credits: Teresa Woo
Cast: Hideki Saijo (Saijo), Moon Lee (Moon, Angel #2), Alex Fong (Alex, Angel #1), Elaine Lui (Elaine, Angel #3), Kwan Yeung (Drug Lord), Yukari Ôshima (Madame Yeoung)

Angel (TV series, 1999–2004)
20th Century Fox/Kuzui/Sandollar
Created by Joss Whedon, David Greenwalt
Cast: David Boreanaz (Angel (1999–2004)), Glenn Quinn (Doyle (Francis) (1999)), Charisma Carpenter (Cordelia Chase (1999–2003)), Alexis Denisof (Wesley Wyndham Pryce (1999–2004)), J. August Richards (Charles Gunn (2000–2004)), Andy Hallett (Lorne, The Host (2000–2004)), James Marsters (Spike (2003–2004)), Amy Acker (Winifred "Fred" Burkle (2001–2004)), Mercedes McNab (Harmony Kendall (2003–2004)), Vincent Kartheiser (Connor (2002–2003))

Anne of the Indies (1951)
20th Century-Fox
Directed by Jacques Tourneur
Writing Credits: Arthur Caesar, Philip Dunne, Herbert Ravenel Sass
Cast: Jean Peters (Capt. Anne Providence), Louis Jourdan (Capt. Pierre François LaRochelle), Debra Paget (Molly LaRochelle), Herbert Marshall (Dr. Jameson), Thomas Gomez (Blackbeard), James Robertson Justice (Red Dougal), Francis

Pierlot (Herkimer), Sean McClory (Hackett)

The Arena (1974)
New World
Directed by Steve Carver, Joe D'Amato
Writing Credits: John William Corrington, Joyce Hooper Corrington
Cast: Margaret Markov (Bodicia), Pam Grier (Mamawi), Lucretia Love (Deirdre), Paul Muller (Lucilius), Daniele Vargas (Timarchus), Marie Louise (Livia), Mary Count (Lucinia), Rosalba Neri (Cornelia (as Sara Bay)), Vassili Karis (Marcus), Sid Lawrence (Priscium), Mimmo Palmara (Rufinius)

Armitage III: Poly Matrix (1997)
AIC
Directed by Takuya Sato
Writing Credits: Chiaki Konaka
Cast: Elizabeth Berkley (Naomi Armitage (voice)), Kiefer Sutherland (Ross Sylibus (voice)), Dan Woren (D'Anclaude (voice)), Wanda Nowicki (Julian Moore (voice)), Mike Reynolds (Lieutenant Randolph (voice)), Bryan Cranston (Eddie (voice)), Stephen Apostolina (Chris (voice)), Barry Stigler (Dr. Asakura (voice)), Doug Stone (Coroner (voice))

Attack of the 50 Foot Woman (1958)
Woolner Brothers
Directed by Nathan Juran (as Nathan Hertz)
Writing Credits: Mark Hanna
Cast: Allison Hayes (Nancy Fowler Archer), William Hudson (Harry Archer), Yvette Vickers (Honey Parker), Roy Gordon (Dr. Isaac Cushing), George Douglas (Sheriff Dubbitt), Ken Terrell (Jess Stout), Otto Waldis (Dr. Heinrich Von Loeb), Eileen Stevens (Nurse Attending Nancy), Michael Ross (Tony, The Bartender/Space Giant), Frank Chase (Deputy Charlie)

Attack of the 50 Foot Woman (1993)
HBO/Warner Bros./Bartleby
Directed by Christopher Guest
Writing Credits: Mark Hanna, Joseph Dougherty
Cast: Daryl Hannah (Nancy Archer), Daniel Baldwin (Harry Archer), William

Windom (Hamilton Cobb), Frances Fisher (Dr. Theodora Cushing), Cristi Conaway (Louise "Honey" Parker), Paul Benedict (Dr. Victor Loeb), O'Neal Compton (Sheriff Denby), Victoria Haas (Deputy Charlotte "Charlie" Spooner), Lewis Arquette (Mr. Ingersol)

Audition (1999)
Omega/AFDF
Directed by Takashi Miike
Writing Credits: Daisuke Tengan
Based on the novel by Ryu Murakami
Cast: Ryo Ishibashi (Shigeharu Aoyama), Eihi Shiina (Asami Yamazaki), Tetsu Sawaki (Shigehiko Aoyama), Jun Kunimura (Yasuhisa Yoshikawa), Renji Ishibashi (Old Man in Wheelchair), Miyuki Matsuda (Ryoko Aoyama), Toshie Negishi (Rie), Ren Osugi (Shibata), Shigeru Saiki (Toastmaster), Ken Mitsuishi (Director)

The Avengers (TV series, 1961–1969)
Associated British Corp.
Created by Sydney Newman
Cast: Patrick Macnee (John Wickham Gascone Berresford Steed), Honor Blackman (Dr. Catherine "Cathy" Gale (1962–1964)), Ingrid Hafner (Carol Wilson (1961–1962)), Ian Hendry (Dr. David Keel (1961–1962)), Douglas Muir (One-Ten (1961–1962)), Rhonda Parker (Rhonda (1968–1969)), Diana Rigg (Emma Peel (1965–1967)), Jon Rollason

(Dr. Martin King (1962)), Julie Stevens (Venus Smith (1962–1963)), Linda Thorson (Tara King (1968–1969))

The Avengers (1998)
Warner Bros.
Directed by Jeremiah S. Chechik
Writing Credits: Don MacPherson
Based on Sydney Newman's television series
Cast: Ralph Fiennes (John Steed), Uma Thurman (Emma Peel), Sean Connery (Sir August de Wynter), Patrick Macnee (Invisible Jones (voice)), Jim Broadbent (Mother), Fiona Shaw (Father), Eddie Izzard (Bailey), Eileen Atkins (Alice), John Wood (Trubshaw), Carmen Ejogo (Brenda), Keeley Hawes (Tamara), Shaun Ryder (Donavan), Nicholas Woodeson (Dr. Darling), Michael Godley (Butler), Richard Lumsden (Boodle's Porter), Daniel Crowder (Messenger), Nadim Sawalha (World Council of Ministers), Christopher Godwin (World Council of Ministers), David Webber (World Council of Ministers)

Azumi (2003)
Toho
Directed by Ryuhei Kitamura
Writing Credits: Isao Kiriyama, Yu Koyama, Rikiya Mizushima
Based on the comic
Cast: Aya Ueto (Azumi), Shun Oguri (Nachi), Hiroki Narimiya (Ukiha), Kenji

Kohashi (Hyuga), Takatoshi Kaneko (Amagi), Yuma Ishigaki (Nagara), Yasuomi Sano (Yura), Shinji Suzuki (Awa), Eita (Hiei), Shogo Yamaguchi (Komoru), Kazuki Kitamura (Inoue, Kanbe'e), Kenichi Endo (Sajiki Isshin), Kazuya Shimizu (Sajiki Nisai)

Bad Girls (1994)
Ruddy Morgan/20th Century Fox
Directed by Jonathan Kaplan
Writing Credits: Ken Friedman, Yolande Turner
Based on a story by Albert Ruddy, Charles Finch, and Gray Frederickson
Cast: Madeleine Stowe (Cody Zamora), Mary Stuart Masterson (Anita Crown), Andie MacDowell (Eileen Spenser), Drew Barrymore (Lilly Laronette), James Russo (Kid Jarrett), James LeGros (William Tucker), Robert Loggia (Frank Jarrett), Dermot Mulroney (Josh McCoy), Jim Beaver (Pinkerton Detective Graves), Nick Chinlund (Pinkerton Detective O'Brady), Neil Summers (Ned, Jarrett Gang)

Barb Wire (1996)
Dark Horse/Polygram/Propaganda
Directed by David Hogan
Writing Credits: Chris Warner, Ilene Chaiken, Chuck Pfarrer
Based on the comic characters of Chris Warner
Cast: Pamela Anderson (Barb Wire), Temuera Morrison (Axel Hood), Victoria Rowell (Cora D/Corrina

Devonshire), Jack Noseworthy (Charlie Kopetski), Xander Berkeley (Alexander Willis), Udo Kier (Curly), Andre Rosey Brown (Big Fatso), Clint Howard (Schmitz), Jennifer Banko (Spike), Steve Railsback (Colonel Pryzer), Amir Aboulela (Patron), Adriana Alexander (Redhead), David Andriole (Goon), Vanessa Lee Asher (Emily), Ron Balicki (Customs Agent #1), Candace Kita (Dancer), Tony Bill (Foster), Alex Bookston (Man in White Suit)

Barbarella (1968)
De Laurentiis Productions
Directed by Roger Vadim
Writing Credits: Terry Southern, Roger Vadim, Claude Brule, Vittorio Bonicelli, Clement Biddle Wood, Brian Degas, Tudor Gates
Based on the comic by Jean Claude Forest
Cast: Jane Fonda (Barbarella), John Phillip Law (Pygar), Anita Pallenberg (The Great Tyrant), Milo O'Shea (Concierge/Durand Durand), Marcel Marceau (Professor Ping), Claude Dauphin (President of Earth), Véronique Vendell (Captain Moon), Serge Marquand (Captain Sun), Catherine Chevallier (Stomoxys), Marie Therese Chevallier (Glossina), David Hemmings (Dildano), Ugo Tognazzi (Mark Hand)

Barbarian Queen (1985)
Concorde/Rodeo/ACA
Directed by Héctor Olivera
Writing Credits: Howard R. Cohen
Cast: Lana Clarkson (Amethea), Katt Shea (Estrild), Frank Zagarino (Argan), Dawn Dunlap (Taramis), Susana Traverso (Tiniara), Victor Bo (Strymon), Arman Chapman (Arrakur), Andrea Barbieri (Zoraida), Tony Middleton (Zohar), Andrea Scriven (Dariac), Robert Carson (Shibdiz), Matilde Mur (Eunuco),
Eddie Little Sky (Vendedor), Patrick Duggan (Shaman), Alfred Alexander (Warrior), Arthur Neal (Warrior)

Barbarian Queen II: The Empress Strikes Back (1989)
Concorde/Triana
Directed by Joe Finley
Writing Credits: Howard R. Cohen, Lance Smith
Cast: Lana Clarkson (Princess Athalia), Greg Wrangler (Aurion), Rebecca Wood

(Zarla), Elizabeth A. Jaeger (Noki), Roger Cudney (Hofrax)

Basic Instinct (1992)
Carolco/Tristar
Directed by Paul Verhoeven
Writing Credits: Joe Eszterhas
Cast: Michael Douglas (Det. Nick Curran), Sharon Stone (Catherine Tramell), George Dzundza (Gus Moran), Jeanne Tripplehorn (Dr. Beth Garner), Denis Arndt (Lt. Philip Walker), Leilani Sarelle (Roxy), Bruce A. Young (Andrews), Chelcie Ross (Captain Talcott), Dorothy Malone (Hazel Dobkins), Wayne Knight (John Correli)

Batman (TV series, 1966–1968)
ABC
Writing Credits: Stanley Ralph Ross, Charles Hoffman, Lorenzo Semple Jr.
Cast: Adam West (Bruce Wayne/Batman), Burt Ward (Dick Grayson/Robin), Alan Napier (Alfred Pennyworth), Neil Hamilton (Police Commissioner James Gordon), Stafford Repp (Police Chief O'Har), Yvonne Craig (Barbara Gordon/Batgirl), Julie Newmar, Eartha Kitt, and Lee Meriwether (The Catwoman)

Batman & Robin (1997)
Warner Bros.
Directed by Joel Schumacher
Writing Credits: Akiva Goldsman

Based on the characters created by Bob Kane
Cast: Arnold Schwarzenegger (Mr. Freez), George Clooney (Bruce Wayne/Batman), Chris O'Donnell (Dick Grayson/Robin), Uma Thurman (Dr. Pamela Isley/Poison Ivy), Alicia Silverstone (Barbara Wilson/Batgirl), Michael Gough (Alfred Pennyworth), Pat Hingle (Commissioner Gordon), John Glover (Dr. Jason Woodrue), Elle Macpherson (Julie Madison), Vivica A. Fox (Ms. B. Haven), Vendela Kirsebom (Nora Fries), Elizabeth Sanders (Gossip Gerty), Jeep Swenson (Bane), John Fink (Aztec Museum Guard), Michael Reid MacKay (Antonio Diego), Eric Lloyd (Young Bruce Wayne), Jon Simmons (Young Alfred), Jim McMullan (Party Guest), Patrick Leahy (Himself), Jesse Ventura (Arkham Asylum Guard)

Batman Returns (1992)
Warner Bros.
Directed by Tim Burton
Writing Credits: Sam Hamm, Daniel Waters
Based on the characters created by Bob Kane
Cast: Michael Keaton (Bruce Wayne/Batman), Danny DeVito (Oswald Cobblepot/The Penguin), Michelle Pfeiffer (Selina Kyle/Catwoman), Christopher Walken (Max Shreck), Michael Gough (Alfred Pennyworth), Michael Murphy (Mayor), Cristi Conaway (Ice Princess), Andrew Bryniarski (Chip Shreck), Pat

Hingle (Commissioner Gordon), Vincent Schiavelli (Organ Grinder), Steve Witting (Josh, Shreck Image Consultant), Jan Hooks (Jen, Shreck Image Consultant), John Strong (Sword Swallower), Rick Zumwalt (Tattooed Strongman)

Battle Royale (2000)
Toei
Directed by Kinji Fukasaku
Writing Credits: Kenta Fukasaku
Based on the novel by Koushun Takami
Cast: Tatsuya Fujiwara (Shuya Nanahara, Boys #15), Aki Maeda (Noriko Nakagawa, Girls #15), Taro Yamamoto (Shougo Kawada, Boys #5), Masanobu Ando (Kazuo Kiriyama, Boys #6), Kou Shibasaki (Mitsuko Souma, Girls #11), Chiaki Kuriyama (Takako Chigusa, Girls #13), Osamu Ohnishi (Youji Kuramoto, Boys #8), Gou Ryugawa (Lieutenant Anjo), Takeshi Kitano (Beat Takeshi)

Battlestar Galactica (TV series, 2003–2005)
Sci-Fi Channel/USA Cable
Created by Ronald Moore, Glen A. Larson
Cast: Edward James Olmos (Comdr. William Adama "Husker"), Mary McDonnell (Pres. Laura Roslin), Katee Sackhoff (Lt. Kara Thrace "Starbuck"), Jamie Bamber (Capt. Lee Adama "Apollo"), James Callis (Dr./Vice Pres. Gaius Baltar), Tricia Helfer (Number Six), Grace Park (Lt. Sharon Valerii "Boomer")

The Big Valley (TV series, 1965–1969)
Four Star/Margate
Created by A. I. Bezzerides, Louis F. Edelman
Cast: Barbara Stanwyck (Victoria Barkley), Richard Long (Jarrod Barkley), Peter Breck (Nick Barkley), Lee Majors (Heath Barkley), Linda Evans (Audra Barkley), Napoleon Whiting (Silas)

The Bionic Woman (TV series, 1976–1978)
MCA
Directed by Gwen Arner, Jack Arnold
Writing Credits: Harve Bennett, Judy Burns
Cast: Lindsay Wagner (Jaime Sommers),

Richard Anderson (Oscar Goldman), Martin E. Brooks (Dr. Rudy Wells)

Birds of Prey (TV series, 2002–2003)
WB
Directed by David Carson, Shawn Levy
Cast: Ashley Scott (Helena Kyle/The Huntress), Dina Meyer (Barbara Gordon/The Oracle/Batgirl), Rachel Skarsten (Dinah Redmond Lance), Shemar Moore (Jesse Reese), Ian Abercrombie (Alfred Pennyworth)

Black Scorpion (TV series, 1995 and 2001)
Corman Productions
Cast: Joan Severance (Black Scorpion: 1995), Michelle Lintel (Black Scorpion: 2001)

Blade Runner (1982)
Warner Bros./Ladd Co.
Directed by Ridley Scott
Writing Credits: Hampton Fancher, David Webb Peoples, Roland Kibbee
Based on the novel *Do Androids Dream of Electric Sheep?* by Philip K. Dick
Cast: Harrison Ford (Rick Deckard), Rutger Hauer (Roy Batty), Sean Young (Rachael), Edward James Olmos (Gaff), M. Emmet Walsh (Bryant), Daryl Hannah (Pris), William Sanderson (J. F. Sebastian), Brion James (Leon), Joe Turkel (Tyrell), Joanna Cassidy (Zhora), James Hong (Hannibal Chew), Morgan

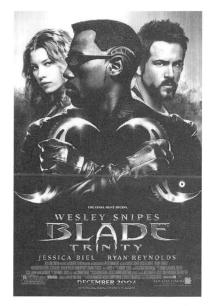

Paull (Holden), Kevin Thompson (Bear), John Edward Allen (Kaiser), Hy Pyke (Taffey Lewis), Kimiko Hiroshige (Cambodian Lady)

Blade: Trinity (2004)
New Line/Marvel/Imaginary Forces/Shawn Danielle
Directed by David S. Goyer
Writing Credits: David S. Goyer
Based on a story by Marv Wolfman and Gene Colan
Cast: Wesley Snipes (Blade), Kris Kristofferson (Abraham Whistler), Dominic Purcell (Drake), Jessica Biel (Abigail Whistler), Ryan Reynolds (Hannibal King), Parker Posey (Danica Talos), Mark Berry (Chief Martin Vreede), John Michael Higgins (Dr. Edgar Vance), Callum Keith Rennie (Asher Talos), Paul Michael Levesque (Jarko Grimwood), Paul Anthony (Wolfe), Françoise Yip (Virago), Michael Rawlins (Wilson Hale), James Remar (Ray Cumberland), Natasha Lyonne (Sommerfield), Haili Page (Zoe), Patton Oswalt (Hedges), Ron Selmour (Dex), Christopher Heyerdahl (Caulder), Eric Bogosian (Bentley Tittle), Scott Heindl (Gedge)

Blonde Fury (1989)
Golden Harvest
Directed by Hoi Mang, Corey Yuen
Cast: Cynthia Rothrock (Cindy), Siu-hou Chin (Undercover Officer), Billy

Chow (Billy Chow), Fat Chung (Break-and-Enter Thief), Jeffrey Falcon (Thug), Keith Kwan (Keith), Elizabeth Lee (Judy Yu), Vincent Lyn (Thug)

The Blood of Heroes (1989)
New Line/King's Road
Directed by David Webb Peoples
Writing Credits: David Webb Peoples
Cast: Rutger Hauer (Sallow), Delroy Lindo (Mbulu), Ana Alexander (Big Cimber), Vincent D'Onofrio (Young Gar), Gandhi MacIntyre (Gandhi), Justin Monjo (Dog Boy), Aaron Martin (Samchin Boy), Joan Chen (Kidda), Casey Huang (Kidda's Father), Quang Dinh (Samchin Head Elder)

The Bone Collector (1999)
Columbia/Universal
Directed by Phillip Noyce
Writing Credits: Jeremy Iacone
Based on the book by Jeffery Deaver
Cast: Denzel Washington (Lincoln "Linc" Rhyme), Angelina Jolie (Amelia Donaghy), Queen Latifah (Thelma), Michael Rooker (Capt. Howard Cheney), Mike McGlone (Detective Kenny Solomon), Luis Guzmán (Eddie Ortiz), Leland Orser (Richard Thompson), John Benjamin Hickey (Dr. Barry Lehman), Bobby Cannavale (Steve, Amelia's Boyfriend), Ed O'Neill (Detective Paulie Sellitto), Richard Zeman (Lt. Carl Hanson), Olivia Birkelund (Lindsay Rubin), Gary Swanson (Alan Rubin)

Boudica (2003)
Box TV
Directed by Bill Anderson
Writing Credits: Andrew Davies
Cast: Alex Kingston (Boudica), Steven Waddington (King Prasutagus), Emily Blunt (Isolda), Leanne Rowe (Siora), Ben Faulks (Connach), Hugo Speer (Dervalloc), Gary Lewis (Magior the Shaman), Alex Hassell (Roman Officer), James Clyde (Roman Sergeant), Angus Wright (Severus), Steve John Shepherd (Catus), Jack Shepherd (Claudius), Gideon Turner (Didius), Frances Barber (Agrippina), Andrew Lee Potts (Nero)

The Breed (2001)
Motion Picture Corp.
Directed by Michael Oblowitz
Writing Credits: Christos N. Gage, Ruth Fletcher
Cast: Adrian Paul (Aaron Gray), Bokeem Woodbine (Steve Grant), Ling Bai (Lucy Westenra), Péter Halász (Cross), James Booth (Fleming), Lo Ming (Seward), Paul Collins (Calmet), Debbie Javor (Section Chief), Reed Diamond (Phil), John Durbin (Boudreaux)

The Bride Wore Black (1968)
De Laurentiis Productions/Films du Carosse
Directed by François Truffaut
Writing Credits: Jean-Louis Richard, François Truffaut
From the novel by Cornell Woolrich (as William Irish)
Cast: Jeanne Moreau (Julie Kohler), Michel Bouquet (Coral), Jean-Claude Brialy (Corey), Charles Denner (Fergus), Claude Rich (Bliss), Michael Lonsdale (Rene Morane), Daniel Boulanger (Delvaux), Alexandra Stewart (Mlle Becker), Sylvine Delannoy (Mme Morane), Luce Fabiole (Julie's Mother), Michèle Montfort (Fergus's Model), Paul Pavel (Mechanic)

The Brothers Grimm (2005)
MGM
Directed by Terry Gilliam
Writing Credits: Ehren Kruger
Cast: Petr Ratimec (Young Will), Barbara Lukêsova (Mother Grimm), Anna Rust (Sister Grimm), Jeremy Robson (Young Jacob), Matt Damon (Wilhelm Grimm), Heath Ledger (Jacob

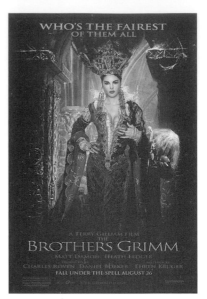

Grimm), Radim Kalvoda (Gendarme), Martin Hofmann (Gendarme), Josef Pepa Nos (German War Veteran), Harry Gilliam (Stable Boy), Miroslav Táborský (Old Miller), Roger Ashton-Griffiths (Mayor), Marika Sarah Procházková (Miller's Daughter), Mackenzie Crook (Hidlick), Richard Ridings (Bunst), Alena Jakobova (Red-Hooded Girl), Rudolf Pellar (Watchman), Dana Dohnalova (Twin Sister), Petra Dohnalova (Twin Sister), Hanus Bor (Twins' Father), Ota Filip (Tavern Owner), Audrey Hamm (Traveler), Annika Murjahn (Traveler), Lukás Bech (Barman), Karel Kohlicek (Bald French Soldier), Peter Stormare (Cavaldi), Julian Bleach (Letorc), Bruce MacEwen (Dax), Jonathan Pryce (Delatombe), Martin Kavan (Delatombe's Valet), Eva Reitererova (Serving Wench), Denisa Vokurkova (Greta), Martin Svetlik (Hans), Jan Unger (Gregor), Laura Greenwood (Sasha), Frantisek Velecký (Old Crone), Jakub Zindulka (Minister), Milan Gargula (Contemptuous Villager), Drahomira Fialkova (Grandmother), Ludek Elias (Grizzled Elder), Jana Radojcicová (Angry Woman), Lena Headey (Angelika), Tomás Hanák (Woodsman), Denisa Malinovska (Young Angelika), Monica Bellucci (Mirror Queen)

Bubblegum Crisis (1987)
Directed by Katsuhito Akiyama, Hiroaki Gôda, Hiroki Hayashi, Masami

Obari, Fumihiko Takayama
Writing Credits: Katsuhito Akiyama, Shinji Aramaki, Hideki Kakinuma, Kenichi Matsuzaki, Toshimichi Suzuki
Cast: Yoshiko Sakakibara (Sylia Stingray (voice)), Kinuko Ômori (Priscilla S. Asagiri "Priss" (voice)), Michie Tomizawa (Linna Yamazaki (voice)), Akiko Hiramatsu (Nene Romanova (voice)), Nozomu Sasaki (Mackie Stingray (voice)), Toshio Furukawa (Leon McNichol (voice)), Kenyû Horiuchi (Daley Wong (voice)), Shûichi Ikeda (Brian J. Mason (voice))

Buffy the Vampire Slayer

(1992)
20th Century Fox/Sandollar
Directed by Fran Rubel Kuzui
Writing Credits: Joss Whedon
Cast: Kristy Swanson (Buffy Summers), Donald Sutherland (Merrick Jamison-Smythe), Paul Reubens (Amilyn), Rutger Hauer (Lothos), Luke Perry (Oliver Pike), Michele Abrams (Jennifer Walkens), Hilary Swank (Kimberly Hannah), Paris Vaughan (Nicole Bobbittson), David Arquette (Benny Jacks), Randall Batinkoff (Jeffrey), Andrew Lowery (Andy), Sasha Jenson (Grueller), Stephen Root (Gary Murray), Natasha Gregson Wagner (Cassandra), Mark DeCarlo (Coach), Thomas Jane (Zeph), Candy Clark (Buffy's Mom), James Paradise (Buffy's Dad), David Sherrill (Knight), Liz Smith (Reporter)

Buffy the Vampire Slayer

(TV series, 1997–2003)
20th Century Fox
Created by Joss Whedon
Cast: Sarah Michelle Gellar (Buffy Summers), Nicholas Brendon (Xander Harris), Alyson Hannigan (Willow Rosenberg), Charisma Carpenter (Cordelia Chase (1997–1999)), Anthony Head (Rupert Giles (1997–2001)), David Boreanaz (Angel/Angelus (1997–1999)), Seth Green (Daniel "Oz" Osbourne (1997–1999)), James Marsters (Spike (1999–2003)), Marc Blucas (Riley Finn (1999–2000)), Emma Caulfield (Anya Jenkins/Anyanka (1999–2003)), Michelle Trachtenberg (Dawn Summers (2000–2003)), Amber Benson (Tara Maclay (2000–2002)), *Regular guests:* Danny Strong (Jonathan Levinson (29 episodes)), Thomas Lenk (Andrew Wells/Cyrus (27 episodes)),

Eliza Dushku (Faith Lehane (20 episodes)), Armin Shimerman (Principal Snyder (19 episodes)), Juliet Landau (Drusilla (17 episodes))

Catwoman (2004)

Warner Bros./Frantic/Maple Shade/DiNovi
Directed by Pitof
Writing Credits: John D. Brancato, Michael Ferris, John Rogers
Based on characters created by Bob Kane and a story by Theresa Rebeck
Cast: Halle Berry (Patience Phillips/Catwoman), Benjamin Bratt (Tom Lone), Sharon Stone (Laurel Hedare), Lambert Wilson (George Hedare), Frances Conroy (Ophelia), Alex Borstein (Sally), Michael Massee (Armando), Byron Mann (Wesley), Kim Smith (Drina), Christopher Heyerdahl (Rocker), Peter Wingfield (Dr. Ivan Slavicky), Berend McKenzie (Lance)

Cat-Women of the Moon

(1953)
Z-M Productions
Directed by Arthur Hilton
Writing Credits: Roy Hamilton
Cast: Sonny Tufts (Laird Grainger), Victor Jory (Kip Reissner), Marie Windsor (Helen Salinger), William Phipps (Douglas "Doug" Smith), Douglas Fowley (Walter "Walt" Walters), Carol Brewster (Alpha), Susan Morrow (Lambda), Suzanne Alexander (Beta), Bette Arlen (Cat-Woman), Roxann Delman (Cat-Woman), Ellye Marshall (Cat-Woman), Judy Walsh (Cat-Woman)

Charlie's Angels (TV series, 1976–1981)

ABC/Spelling-Goldberg
Created by Ivan Goff, Ben Roberts
Cast: Kate Jackson (Sabrina Duncan (1976–1979)), Farrah Fawcett (Jill Munroe (1976–1977)), Jaclyn Smith (Kelly Garrett), Cheryl Ladd (Kris Munroe (1977–1981)), Shelley Hack (Tiffany Welles (1979–1980)), Tanya Roberts (Julie Rogers (1980–1981)), David Doyle (John Bosley)

Charlie's Angels (2000)

Columbia/Flower/Tall Trees
Directed by McG
Writing Credits: Ryan Rowe, Ed Solomon, John August
Based on the TV series written by Ivan Goff and Ben Roberts
Cast: Cameron Diaz (Natalie Cook), Drew Barrymore (Dylan Sanders), Lucy Liu (Alex Munday), Bill Murray (John Bosley), Sam Rockwell (Eric Knox), Kelly Lynch (Vivian Wood), Tim Curry (Roger Corwin), Crispin Glover (Thin Man), Luke Wilson (Pete Komisky), John Forsythe (Charles Townsend (voice)), Matt LeBlanc (Jason Gibbons), Tom Green (Chad), LL Cool J (Mr. Jones), Sean Whalen (Pasqual)

Charlie's Angels: Full Throttle (2003)

Columbia/Flower/Tall Trees
Directed by McG
Writing Credits: John August, Cormac Wibberley, Marianne Wibberley
Based on characters created by Ivan

Goff and Ben Roberts
Cast: Cameron Diaz (Natalie Cook), Drew Barrymore (Dylan Sanders), Lucy Liu (Alex Munday), Bernie Mac (Jimmy Bosley), Crispin Glover (Thin Man), Justin Theroux (Seamus O'Grady), Robert Patrick (Ray Carter), Demi Moore (Madison Lee), Rodrigo Santoro (Randy Emmers), Shia LaBeouf (Max), Matt LeBlanc (Jason), Luke Wilson (Pete), John Cleese (Mr. Munday), Ja'net DuBois (Momma Bosley), Cheung-Yan Yuen (Deranged Mongol), Daxing Zhang (Demented Mongol), John Chow (Eager Mongol), Bruce Comtois (Large Mongol), Khin-Kyaw Maung (Crooked-Tooth), Russell Bobbitt (Madison's Minion), Charles Townsend (Madison's Minion), Al Kahn (Madison's Minion), Béla Károlyi (Himself), Tanoai Reed (Wrestler), Joshua Miller (Chess Kid), Clifford Happy (Fleeing Suspect), Mushond Lee (FBI Agent), Robert Forster (Roger Wixon)

Charmed (TV series, 1998–)
Spelling/Paramount
Created by Constance M. Burge
Cast: Shannen Doherty (Prue Halliwell (1998–2001)), Holly Marie Combs (Piper Halliwell), Alyssa Milano (Phoebe Halliwell), Rose McGowan (Paige Matthews)

Cherry 2000 (1987)
Orion
Directed by Steve De Jarnatt
Writing Credits: Michael Almereyda, Lloyd Fonvielle
Cast: David Andrews (Sam Treadwell), Jennifer Balgobin (Glory Hole Hotel Clerk), Marshall Bell (Bill), Harry Carey Jr. (Snappy Tom), Laurence Fishburne (Glu Glu Lawyer), Pamela Gidley (Cherry 2000), Melanie Griffith (Edith "E." Johnson, Tracker), Michael C. Gwynne (Slim, Robot Designer), Brion James (Stacy, Tracker), Ben Johnson (Six-Fingered Jake, Tracker), Jeff Levine (Marty)

China O'Brien (1990)
Golden Harvest
Directed by Robert Clouse
Writing Credits: Robert Clouse
Based on a story by Sandra Weintraub
Cast: Cynthia Rothrock (China O'Brien), Richard Norton (Matt Conroy), Keith Cooke (Dakota), Doug Wright (Termite),

Nijel (Jonsey), Arturo Rivera (Oscar), Scott McMillan (Police Captain)

The Chronicles of Riddick (2004)
Universal
Directed by David Twohy
Writing Credits: David Twohy
Based on characters by Jim Wheat and Ken Wheat
Cast: Vin Diesel (Riddick), Colm Feore (Lord Marshal), Thandie Newton (Dame Vaako), Judi Dench (Aereon), Karl Urban (Vaako), Alexa Davalos (Kyra), Linus Roache (Purifier), Yorick van Wageningen (The Guv), Nick Chinlund (Toombs), Keith David (Imam), Mark Gibbon (Irgun), Roger R. Cross (Toal), Terry Chen (Merc Pilot), Christina Cox (Eve Logan)

The City of Women (1980)
Gaumont
Directed by Federico Fellini
Writing Credits: Federico Fellini, Paula Mitchell, Brunello Rondi, Bernardino Zapponi
Cast: Marcello Mastroianni (Snàporaz), Anna Prucnal (Elena), Bernice Stegers (Woman on Train), Donatella Damiani (Donatella), Jole Silvani (Motorcyclist), Ettore Manni (Dr. Xavier Katzone), Fiammetta Baralla (Onlio), Hélène Calzarelli (Feminist), Catherine Carrel (Commandant), Stéphane Emilfork (Feminist), Marcello Di Falco (Slave),

Silvana Fusacchia (Skater), Gabriella Giorgelli (Fishwoman of San Leo)

Cleopatra Jones (1973)
Warner Bros.
Directed by Jack Starrett
Writing Credits: Max Julien, Sheldon Keller
Cast: Tamara Dobson (Cleopatra Jones), Bernie Casey (Reuben), Brenda Sykes (Tiffany), Antonio Fargas (Doodlebug Simkins), Dan Frazer (Crawford), Bill McKinney (Purdy), Stafford Morgan (Sergeant Kert), Michael Warren (Andy), Albert Popwell (Matthew Johnson), Caro Kenyatta (Melvin Johnson), Esther Rolle (Mrs. Johnson), Keith Hamilton (Maxwell Woodman), Jay Montgomery (Jimmy Beekers), Arnold Dover (Art), Angela Gibbs (Annie), John Alderman (Mommy's Assistant), Eugene Jackson (Henry), Lee Weaver (Friend)

Cleopatra 2525 (TV series, 2000–2001)
Renaissance
Directed by John Laing, Wayne Rose
Writing Credits: Chris Black, Melissa Blake
Cast: Jennifer Sky (Cleopatra), Gina Torres (Helen), Victoria Pratt (Sarge/ "Rose"), Patrick Kake (Mauser)

Coffy (1973)
AIP
Directed by Jack Hill
Writing Credits: Jack Hill
Cast: Pam Grier (Coffy), Booker Bradshaw (Howard Brunswick), Robert DoQui (King George), William Elliott (Carter), Allan Arbus (Arturo Vitroni), Sid Haig (Omar), Barry Cahill (McHenry), Lee de Broux (Nick), Ruben Moreno (Ramos), Lisa Farringer (Jeri), Carol Locatell (Priscilla), Linda Haynes (Meg), John Perak (Aleva), Mwako Cumbuka (Grover)

Colossus and the Amazon Queen (1960)
Galatea/Glomer
Directed by Vittorio Sala
Writing Credits: Ennio De Concini, Fulvio Fo, Augusto Frassinetti, Giorgio Mordini, Vittorio Nino Novarese, Vittorio Sala, Duccio Tessari
Cast: Rod Taylor (Pirro), Ed Fury (Glauco), Dorian Gray (Antiope),

Gianna Maria Canale (La Regina), Alberto Farnese (Il Pirata), Ignazio Leone (Sofo the Egyptian), Adriana Facchetti (High Priestess), Alfredo Varelli (Merchant)

Come Drink with Me (1966)
Shaw Bros.
Directed by King Hu (as Hu Chuan)
Writing Credits: King Hu (as King Chuan), Ye Yang
Cast: Pei-pei Cheng, Hua Yueh, Hei Chan, Hung Lieh Chen, Yang Chiang, Siu-Tung Ching, Alan Chui Chung San, Ngai Fung, Siu Tien Yuen, Jackie Chan

Conan the Barbarian (1982)
De Lauentiis/Universal
Directed by John Milius
Writing Credits: John Milius, Oliver Stone, Edward Summer
Based on the stories of Robert E. Howard
Cast: Arnold Schwarzenegger (Conan), James Earl Jones (Thulsa Doom), Max von Sydow (King Osric), Sandahl Bergman (Valeria), Ben Davidson (Rexor), Cassandra Gava (The Witch), Gerry Lopez (Subotai), Mako (The Wizard/Narrator), Valérie Quennessen (The Princess), William Smith (Conan's Father), Luis Barboo (Red Hair), Franco Columbu (Pictish Scout), Leslie Foldvary (Sacrificial Snake Girl), Gary Herman (Osric's Guard)

Conan the Destroyer (1984)
De Lauentiis/Universal
Directed by Richard Fleischer
Writing Credits: Stanley Mann
Based on the stories of Robert E. Howard and a story by Roy Thomas and Gerry Conway
Cast: Arnold Schwarzenegger (Conan), Grace Jones (Zula), Wilt Chamberlain (Bombaata), Mako (Akiro "The Wizard"), Tracey Walter (Malak), Sarah Douglas (Queen Taramis), Olivia d'Abo (Princess Jehnna), Pat Roach (Man Ape/Toth-Amon), Jeff Corey (Grand Vizier), Sven-Ole Thorsen (Togra), Bruce Fleischer (Village Heckler), Ferdy Mayne (The Leader)

Crimson Bat (1969)
Shochiku
Directed by Sadaji Matsuda
Writing Credits: Ikuro Suzuki, Teruo Tanashita
Cast: Yoko Matsuyama (Oichi), Isamu Nagato (Jubei), Akitake Kôno (Yasuke), Jun Tatara (Nihei), Bin Amatsu (Denzo), Chizuko Arai (Omon)

Crouching Tiger, Hidden Dragon (2000)
Sony/Columbia/United China/Good Machine/Asia Union Film
Directed by Ang Lee
Writing Credits: Hui-Ling Wang, James Schamus, Kuo Jung Tsai
Based on the book by Du Lu Wang
Cast: Yun-Fat Chow (Master Li Mu Bai), Michelle Yeoh (Yu Shu Lien), Ziyi Zhang (Jen Yu), Chen Chang (Lo "Dark Cloud"), Sihung Lung (Sir Te), Pei pei Cheng (Jade Fox), Fa Zeng Li (Governor Yu), Xian Gao (Bo, Sir Te's Head Servant), Yan Hai (Madame Yu), De Ming Wang (Police Inspector), Li-Li Li (May, Tsai's Daughter), Su Ying Huang (Auntie Wu), Jin Ting Zhang (De Lu), Rei Yang (Maid), Kai Li (Gou Jun Pei), Jian Hua Feng (Gou Jun Sinung)

The Crow (1994)
Miramax/Crowvision/Pressman/Jeff Most
Directed by Alex Proyas
Writing Credits: David J. Schow, John Shirley
Based on the comic books by James O'Barr
Cast: Brandon Lee (Eric Draven), Rochelle Davis (Sarah), Ernie Hudson (Sergeant Albrecht), Michael Wincott (Top Dollar), Ling Bai (Myca), Sofia Shinas (Shelly Webster), Anna Levine (Darla), David Patrick Kelly (T-Bird), Angel David (Skank), Laurence Mason (Tin Tin), Michael Massee (Funboy), Tony Todd (Grange)

Cyborg 2 (1993)
Trimark/Freedom Filmworks
Directed by Michael Schroeder
Writing Credits: Mark Geldman, Michael Schroeder, Ron Yanover
Cast: Elias Koteas (Colson "Colt" Ricks), Angelina Jolie (Casella "Cash" Reese), Jack Palance (Mercy), Billy Drago (Danny Bench), Karen Sheperd (Chen), Allen Garfield (Martin Dunn), Ric Young (Bobby Lin), Renee Griffin (Dreena), Sven-Ole Thorsen (Doorman), Tracey Walter (Wild Card), Alain Joel Silver (Surgeo)

Daredevil (2003)
20th Century Fox/Marvel/New Regency/Horseshoe Bay
Directed by Mark Steven Johnson
Writing Credits: Mark Steven Johnson
Cast: Ben Affleck (Matt Murdock/Daredevil), Jennifer Garner (Elektra Natchios), Colin Farrell (Bullseye), Michael Clarke Duncan (The Kingpin/Wilson Fisk), Jon Favreau (Franklin "Foggy" Nelson), Scott Terra (Young Matt), Ellen Pompeo (Karen Page), Joe Pantoliano (Ben Urich), Leland Orser (Wesley Owen Welch), Lennie Loftin (Nick Manolis), Erick Avari (Nikolas Natchios), Derrick O'Connor (Father Everett), Paul Ben-Victor (José Quesada), David Keith (Jack Murdock)

Dark Angel (TV series, 2000–2002)
20th Century Fox
Created by James Cameron, Charles H. Eglee
Cast: Jessica Alba (Max Guevera/X5-452), Michael Weatherly (Logan Cale/Eyes Only), Alimi Ballard (Herbal Thought (2000–2001)), Jennifer Blanc (Kendra Maibaum (2000–2001))

Deadly China Doll (1972)
Panasia
Directed by Feng Huang
Writing Credits: Ho Jen
Cast: Angela Mao (Hei Lu), Ke Hsiang-ting (Chin), Yen I-feng (Han Fei)

D.E.B.S. (2004)
Screen Gems/Destination/
Anonymous
Directed by Angela Robinson
Writing Credits: Angela Robinson
Cast: Sara Foster (Amy Bradshaw),
Jordana Brewster (Lucy Diamond),
Meagan Good (Max Brewer), Devon
Aoki (Dominique), Jill Ritchie (Janet),
Geoff Stults (Bobby Matthews), Jimmi
Simpson (Scud), Holland Taylor (Mrs.
Petrie), Michael Clarke Duncan (Mr.
Phipps), Jessica Cauffiel (Ninotchka
Kaprova), Christina Kirk (Madeline), J.
B. Ghuman Jr. (Dustin), Scoot McNairy
(Stoner), Jean St. James (Waitress)

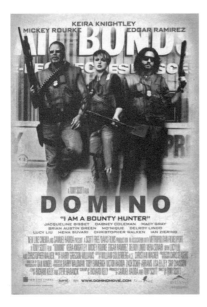

Domino (2005)
Domino/Scott Free
Directed by Tony Scott
Writing Credits: Richard Kelly
Based on a story by Steve Barancik
Cast: Keira Knightley (Domino Harvey),
Mena Suvari (Kimmie, Assistant TV
Producer), Shondrella Avery (Lashandra
Davis), Julian Berlin (Sorority Girl),
Jacqueline Bisset (Pauline Stone,
Domino's Mother), Tabitha Brownstone
(Young Domino), Mary Castro (Exotic
Dancer), Ash Christian (Keg President),
Adam Clark (FBI Agent Cosgrove),
Ashley Monique Clark (Kee Kee),
Matt Clifford (Wardrobe Production
Assistant)

Double Indemnity (1944)
Paramount
Directed by Billy Wilder
Writing Credits: Billy Wilder, Raymond
Chandler
Based on the novel by James M. Cain
Cast: Fred MacMurray (Walter Neff),
Barbara Stanwyck (Phyllis Dietrichson),
Edward G. Robinson (Barton Keyes),
Porter Hall (Mr. Jackson), Jean Heather
(Lola Dietrichson), Tom Powers
(Mr. Dietrichson), Byron Barr (Nino
Zachetti), Richard Gaines (Edward S.
Norton Jr.), Fortunio Bonanova (Sam
Garlopis), John Philliber (Joe Peters)

Dragon Gate Inn (1966)
Union Film
Directed by King Hu
Writing Credits: King Hu
Cast: Kuan Shang, Shih Chun, Bo Ying,
Tsao Jian, Xue Han

Dungeons & Dragons (2000)
Silver/Stillking/Sweetpea
Directed by Courtney Solomon
Writing Credits: Topper Lilien, Carroll
Cartwright
Based on the video game
Cast: Jeremy Irons (Profion), Bruce
Payne (Damodar), Justin Whalin (Ridley
Freeborn), Marlon Wayans (Snails),
Robert Miano (Azmath), Tomás Havrlik
(Mage), Thora Birch (Empress Savina),
Edward Jewesbury (Vildan Vildir),
Zoe McLellan (Marina Pretensa), Lee
Arenberg (Elwood Gutworthy), Kristen
Wilson (Norda), Martin Astles (Orc #1),
Matthew O'Toole (Orcs), David O'Kelly
(Three Eyes), Richard O'Brien (Xilus),
Kia Jam (Thief #1), Nicolas Rochette
(Thief #2), David Mandis (Thief #3)

Earth: Final Conflict (TV
series, 1997–2002)
Created by Gene Roddenberry
Cast: Kevin Kilner (William Boone
(1997–1998)), Robert Leeshock (Liam
Kincaid (1998–2001)), Lisa Howard
(Lili Marquette (1997–1999)), Jayne
Heitmeyer (Renee Palmer (1999–2002)),
Von Flores (Ronald Sandoval), Richard
Chevolleau (Marcus "Augur" Deveraux
(1997–2000)), David Hemblen
(Jonathan Doors (1997–2000)), Melinda
Deines (Juliet Street (2000–2002))

Elektra (2005)
20th Century Fox/Marvel/New
Regency/Horseshoe Bay
Directed by Rob Bowman
Writing Credits: Mark Steven Johnson,
Zak Penn, Stu Zicherman, Raven
Metzner
Based on characters by Frank Miller
Cast: Jennifer Garner (Elektra), Goran
Visnjic (Mark Miller), Kirsten Prout
(Abby Miller), Will Yun Lee (Kirigi),
Cary-Hiroyuki Tagawa (Roshi),
Terence Stamp (Stick), Natassia Malthe
(Typhoid), Bob Sapp (Stone), Chris
Ackerman (Tattoo), Edson T. Ribeiro
(Kinkou), Colin Cunningham (McCabe),
Hiro Kanagawa (Meizumi), Mark
Houghton (Bauer), Laura Ward (Young
Elektra), Kurt Max Runte (Nikolas
Natchios), Nathaniel Arcand (Hand
Ninja #1)

Enter the Dragon (1973)
Warner Bros./Concord/Sequoia
Directed by Robert Clouse
Writing Credits: Michael Allin
Cast: Bruce Lee (Lee), John Saxon
(Roper), Kien Shih (Han), Ahna Capri
(Tania), Angela Mao (Su Lin), Jim Kelly
(Williams), Robert Wall (Oharra), Bolo
Yeung (Bolo), Betty Chung (Mei Ling),
Geoffrey Weeks (Braithwaite), Peter
Archer (Parsons), Ho Lee Yan (Old
Man), Marlene Clark (Secretary), Allan
Kent (Golfer)

362

Enterprise (TV series, 2001–2005)
Paramount
Created by: Rick Berman, Brannon Braga
Cast: Scott Bakula (Capt. Jonathan Archer), John Billingsley (Dr. Phlox), Jolene Blalock (Subcommander/Commander T'Pol), Dominic Keating (Lt. Malcolm Reed), Anthony Montgomery (Ens. Travis Mayweather), Linda Park (Ens. Hoshi Sato), Connor Trinneer (Comdr. Charles "Trip" Tucker III)

Fantastic Four (2005)
20th Century Fox/Marvel
Directed by Tim Story
Writing Credits: Michael France, Mark Frost
Based on the comic books by Jack Kirby and Stan Lee
Cast: Ioan Gruffudd (Reed Richards/Mr. Fantastic), Michael Chiklis (Ben Grimm/The Thing), Jessica Alba (Susan Storm/The Invisible Woman), Chris Evans (Johnny Storm/The Human Torch), Julian McMahon (Victor Von Doom/Dr. Doom), Kerry Washington (Alicia Masters)

Faster, Pussycat! Kill! Kill! (1965)
Eve Productions
Directed by Russ Meyer
Writing Credits: Russ Meyer, Jack Moran
Cast: Tura Satana (Varla), Haji (Rosie), Lori Williams (Billie), Sue Bernard (Linda), Stuart Lancaster (The Old Man), Paul Trinka (Kirk), Dennis Busch (The Vegetable), Ray Barlow (Tommy)

Fathom (1967)
20th Century Fox
Directed by Leslie H. Martinson
Writing Credits: Lorenzo Semple Jr.
Based on the novel by Larry Forrester
Cast: Anthony Franciosa (Peter Merriweather), Raquel Welch (Fathom Harvill), Ronald Fraser (Col. Douglas Campbell, Chief of HADES), Richard Briers (Flight Lt. Timothy Webb), Greta Chi (Maj. Jo-May Soon (KGB)), Tom Adams (Mike, Owner of Casa Miguel), Elizabeth Ercy (Ulla), Ann LanCaster (Mrs. Trivers), Tutte Lemkow (Mehmed,

Serapkin's Servant), Reg Lye (Mr. Trivers), Clive Revill (Sergi Serapkin)

La Femme Nikita (1990)
Gaumont/Cecchi Gori/Films du Loup
Directed by Luc Besson
Writing Credits: Luc Besson
Cast: Anne Parillaud (Nikita), Marc Duret (Rico), Patrick Fontana (Coyote), Alain Lathière (Zap), Laura Chéron (La punk), Jacques Boudet (Le pharmacien), Helene Aligier (La pharmacienne), Pierre-Alain de Garrigues (Flic pharmacie), Patrick Pérez (Flic pharmacie), Bruno Randon (Flic pharmacie), Vincent Skimenti (Flic pharmacie), Roland Blanche (Flic interrogatoire), Joseph Teruel (Stagiaire flic), Jacques Disses (Avocat), Stéphane Fey (President tribunal), Philippe Dehesdin (1er magistrat), Michel Brunot (2ème magistrat), Rodolph Freytt (1er infirmier), Pavel Slaby (2ème infirmier), Tchéky Karyo (Bob), Jean-Luc Caron (Professeur d'informatique), Rénos Mandis (Professeur de tir), Jean-Marc Merchet (Professeur de judo), Jeanne Moreau (Amande)

La Femme Nikita (TV series, 1997–2001)
CTV/Fireworks
Directed by Reza Badiyi, George Bloomfield
Writing Credits: David Wolkove, Peter Bellwood
Cast: Peta Wilson (Nikita), Roy Dupuis (Michael Samuelle), Don Francks (Walter), Matthew Ferguson (Seymour Birkoff/Jason Crawford), Eugene Robert Glazer (Operations), Alberta Watson (Madeline)

The Fifth Element (1997)
Gaumont/Columbia
Directed by Luc Besson
Writing Credits: Luc Besson, Robert Mark Kamen
Cast: Bruce Willis (Maj. Korben Dallas), Gary Oldman (Jean-Baptiste Emanuel Zorg), Ian Holm (Fr. Vito Cornelius), Milla Jovovich (Leeloo), Chris Tucker (DJ Ruby Rhod), Luke Perry (Billy), Brion James (General Munro), Tom "Tiny" Lister Jr. (President Lindberg), Lee Evans (Fog), Charlie Creed-Miles

(David), Tricky (Right Arm), John Neville (General Staedert), John Bluthal (Professor Pacoli), Mathieu Kassovitz (Mugger), Christopher Fairbank (Mactilburgh), Kim Chan (Mr. Kim), Richard Leaf (Neighbor), Julie T. Wallace (Major Iceborg), Al Matthews (General Tudor)

Forty Guns (1957)
20th Century Fox/Globe
Directed by Samuel Fuller
Writing Credits: Samuel Fuller
Cast: Barbara Stanwyck (Jessica Drummond), Barry Sullivan (Griff Bonnell), Dean Jagger (Sheriff Ned Logan), John Ericson (Brockie Drummond), Gene Barry (Wes Bonnell), Robert Dix (Chico Bonnell), Jidge Carroll (Barney Cashman), Paul Dubov (Judge Macy), Gerald Milton (Shotgun Spanger), Ziva Rodann (Rio), Hank Worden (Marshal John Chisum), Neyle Morrow (Wiley), Chuck Roberson (Swain), Chuck Hayward (Charlie Savage)

Foxfire (1996)
Goldwyn/Rysher/Chestnut Hill
Directed by Annette Haywood-Carter
Writing Credits: Elizabeth White
Based on the novel by Joyce Carol Oates
Cast: Hedy Burress (Madeline "Maddy" Wirtz), Angelina Jolie (Margret "Legs" Sadovsky), Jenny Lewis (Rita Faldes),

Jenny Shimizu (Goldie Goldman), Sarah Rosenberg (Violet Kahn), Peter Facinelli (Ethan Bixby), Dash Mihok (Dana Taylor), Michelle Brookhurst (Cindy), Elden Henson (Bobby), Cathy Moriarty (Martha Wirtz), Richard Beymer (Mr. Parks), Fran Bennett (Judge Holifield), John Diehl (Mr. Buttinger), Chris Mulkey (Dan Goldman), Jay Acovone (Chuck), Arwen Carter (Leaflet Girl)

Foxy Brown (1974)
AIP
Directed by Jack Hill
Writing Credits: Jack Hill
Cast: Pam Grier (Foxy Brown), Antonio Fargas (Link Brown), Peter Brown (Steve Elias), Terry Carter (Michael Anderson/Dalton Ford), Kathryn Loder (Katherine Wall), Harry Holcombe (Judge Fenton), Sid Haig (Hays), Juanita Brown (Claudia), Sally Ann Stroud (Deb), Bob Minor (Oscar), Tony Giorgio (Eddie), Fred Lerner (Bunyon), Judith Cassmore (Vicki)

Ghost in the Shell (1995)
Bandai/Kodansha/Manga Entertainment
Directed by Mamoru Oshî
Writing Credits: Kazunori Itô
Based on the comic by Masamune Shirow
Cast: Atsuko Tanaka (Maj. Motoko Kusanagi (voice)), Akio Ôtsuka (Batô (voice)), Tamio Ôki (Section 9 Department Chief Aramaki (JPN) (voice)), Iemasa Kayumi (Project 2501

aka "The Puppet Master" (voice)), Kôichi Yamadera (Togusa (voice)), Tesshô Genda (Section 6 Department Chief Nakamura (voice))

G.I. Jane (1997)
Buena Vista/Caravan/Hollywood/Largo/Trap-Two-Zero/Moving Pictures
Directed by Ridley Scott
Writing Credits: David Twohy, Danielle Alexandra
Cast: Demi Moore (Lt. Jordan O'Neil), Viggo Mortensen (M. Chief John James "Jack" Urgayle), Anne Bancroft (Sen. Lillian DeHaven), Jason Beghe (Royce), Daniel von Bargen (Theodore Hayes), John Michael Higgins (Chief of Staff), Kevin Gage (Sgt. Max Pyro, Instructor), David Warshofsky (Sergeant Johns, Instructor), David Vadim (Sergeant Cortez), Morris Chestnut (McCool), Josh Hopkins (Ens. F. Lee "Flea" Montgomery), James Caviezel ("Slov" Slovnik), Boyd Kestner ("Wick" Wickwire), Angel David (Newberry), Stephen Ramsey (Stamm), Gregg Bello (Miller), Scott Wilson (C.O. Salem), Lucinda Jenney (Lieutenant Blondell)

The Girl from U.N.C.L.E. (TV series, 1966–1967)
MGM
Directed by Richard C. Bennett, John Brahm
Writing Credits: Joseph Calvelli, Boris Sobelman
Cast: Stefanie Powers (April Dancer), Noel Harrison (Mark Slate), Randy Kirby (Randy Kovacs), Leo G. Carroll (Alexander Waverly)

Girlfight (2000)
IFC/Green/Renzi
Directed by Karyn Kusama
Writing Credits: Karyn Kusama
Cast: Michelle Rodriguez (Diana Guzman), Jaime Tirelli (Hector), Paul Calderon (Sandro), Santiago Douglas (Adrian), Ray Santiago (Tiny), Víctor Sierra (Ray), Elisa Bocanegra (Marisol), Shannon Walker Williams (Veronica), Louis Guss (Don), Herb Lovelle (Cal), Thomas Barbour (Ira)

Golden Swallow (1968)
Shaw Bros.
Directed by Cheh Chang

Writing Credits: Cheh Chang
Cast: Pei-pei Cheng, Lieh Lo, Yu Wang, Hsin Yen Chao

Gunslinger (1956)
Corman Productions
Directed by Roger Corman
Writing Credits: Charles B. Griffith, Mark Hanna
Cast: Beverly Garland (Marshal Rose Hood), John Ireland (Cane Miro), Allison Hayes (Erica Page), Jonathan Haze (Jake Hayes), Martin Kingsley (Mayor Gideon Polk), Margaret Campbell (Felicity Polk), Chris Alcaide (Deputy Joshua Tate), Chris Miller (Tessie, a Dancer), Bruno VeSota (Zebelon Tabb), William Schallert (Marshal Scott Hood), Dick Miller (Pony Express Rider), Aaron Saxon (Nate Signo)

Hannibal (2001)
De Laurentiis/MGM/Universal
Directed by Ridley Scott
Writing Credits: David Mamet Steven Zaillian
Based on the novel by Thomas Harris
Cast: Anthony Hopkins (Dr. Hannibal Lecter), Julianne Moore (Agent Clarice Starling), Giancarlo Giannini (Inspector Rinaldo Pazzi), Gary Oldman (Mason Verger), Ray Liotta (Paul Krendler), Frankie Faison (Barney Matthews), Francesca Neri (Allegra Pazzi), Zeljko Ivanek (Dr. Cordell Doemling), Hazelle Goodman (Evelda Drumgo), David Andrews (FBI Agent Clint Pearsall), Francis Guinan (FBI Director Noonan), James Opher (DEA Agent Eldridge), Enrico Lo Verso (Gnocco), Ivano Marescotti (Carlo Deogracias), Fabrizio Gifuni (Matteo Deogracias), Alex Corrado (Piero), Marco Greco (Tommaso), Robert Rietty (Sogliato)

Hannie Caulder (1971)
Paramount/Curtwel
Directed by Burt Kennedy
Writing Credits: David Haft, Burt Kennedy
Based on a story by Peter Cooper
Cast: Raquel Welch (Hannie Caulder), Robert Culp (Thomas Luther Price), Ernest Borgnine (Emmett Clemens), Christopher Lee (Bailey), Jack Elam (Frank Clemens), Strother Martin (Rufus Clemens), Diana Dors (Madame)

Hapkido (1972)

Golden Harvest
Directed by Feng Huang
Cast: Angela Mao, Carter Wong, Hung Kam-Bo, Ing-Sik Whang, Pai Ying, Han Jae Ji, Ping-Ao Wei, Ching-Ying Lam, Billy Chan, Corey Yuen, Hsiao Liang, Biao Yuen, Jackie Chan

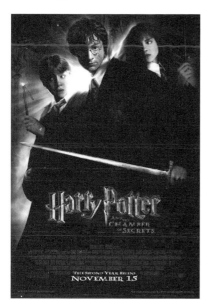

Harry Potter and the Chamber of Secrets (2002)

Warner Bros./1492/Heyday
Directed by Chris Columbus
Writing Credits: Steven Kloves
Based on the novel by J. K. Rowling
Cast: Daniel Radcliffe (Harry Potter), Rupert Grint (Ron Weasley), Emma Watson (Hermione Granger), Richard Griffiths (Uncle Vernon), Fiona Shaw (Aunt Petunia), Harry Melling (Dudley Dursley), Toby Jones (Dobby the House Elf (voice)), Jim Norton (Mr. Mason), Veronica Clifford (Mrs. Mason), James Phelps (Fred Weasley), Oliver Phelps (George Weasley), Julie Walters (Molly Weasley), Bonnie Wright (Ginny Weasley), Mark Williams (Arthur Weasley), Chris Rankin (Percy Weasley), Tom Felton (Draco Malfoy), Jason Isaacs (Lucius Malfoy), Edward Tudor-Pole (Mr. Borgin), Jenny Tarren (Aged Witch), Robbie Coltrane (Rubeus Hagrid), Tom Knight (Mr. Granger), Heather Bleasdale (Mrs. Granger), Isabella Columbus (Girl in Bookstore), Kenneth Branagh (Gilderoy Lockhart), Peter O'Farrell (Short Man - Daily Prophet), Ben Borowiecki (Angus (Diagon Boy)), Harry Taylor (Station Guard), Matthew Lewis (Neville Longbottom), Devon Murray (Seamus Finnigan), David Bradley (Argus Filch), Alan Rickman (Professor Snape), Richard Harris (Albus Dumbledore), Maggie Smith (Prof. Minerva McGonagall), Jamie Waylett (Vincent Crabbe), Joshua Herdman (Gregory Goyle), Miriam Margolyes (Professor Sprout), Gemma Padley (Penelope Clearwater), John Cleese (Nearly Headless Nick)

Harry Potter and the Goblet of Fire (2005)

Warner Bros.
Directed by Mike Newell
Writing Credits: Steven Kloves
Based on the novel by J. K. Rowling
Cast: Daniel Radcliffe (Harry Potter), Rupert Grint (Ron Weasley), Emma Watson (Hermione Granger), Robbie Coltrane (Rubeus Hagrid), Ralph Fiennes (Lord Voldemort), Michael Gambon (Albus Dumbledore), Brendan Gleeson (Prof. Alastor "Mad-Eye" Moody), Jason Isaacs (Lucius Malfoy), Gary Oldman (Sirius Black), Miranda Richardson (Rita Skeeter), Alan Rickman (Prof. Severus Snape), Maggie Smith (Prof. Minerva McGonagall), Timothy Spall (Peter Pettigrew), Adrian Rawlins (James Potter), Tolga Safer (Karkaroff's Aide), Phil Selway (Band Member), Charlotte Skeoch (Hannah Abbot), Geraldine Somerville (Lily Potter), David Tennant (Barty Crouch Jr.), Jamie Waylett (Vincent Crabbe), Robert Wilfort (The Photographer), Mark Williams (Arthur Weasley), Bonnie Wright (Ginny Weasley)

Harry Potter and the Prisoner of Azkaban (2004)

Warner Bros./1492/Heyday
Directed by Alfonso Cuarón
Writing Credits: Steven Kloves
Based on the novel by J. K. Rowling
Cast: Daniel Radcliffe (Harry Potter), Richard Griffiths (Uncle Vernon), Pam Ferris (Aunt Marge), Fiona Shaw (Aunt Petunia), Harry Melling (Dudley Dursley), Adrian Rawlins (James Potter), Geraldine Somerville (Lily Potter), Lee Ingleby (Stan Shunpike), Lenny Henry (Shrunken Head), Jimmy Gardner (Ernie the Bus Driver), Gary Oldman (Sirius Black), Jim Tavaré (Tom the Innkeeper), Robert Hardy (Cornelius Fudge), Abby Ford (Young Witch Maid), Rupert Grint (Ron Weasley), Emma Watson (Hermione Granger), Oliver Phelps (George Weasley), James Phelps (Fred Weasley), Chris Rankin (Percy Weasley), Julie Walters (Mrs. Molly Weasley), Bonnie Wright (Ginny Weasley), Mark Williams (Mr. Arthur Weasley), David Thewlis (Professor Lupin), Devon Murray (Seamus Finnegan), Warwick Davis (Wizard), David Bradley (Argus Filch), Michael Gambon (Albus Dumbledore), Alan Rickman (Prof. Severus Snape), Maggie Smith (Prof. Minerva McGonagall), Robbie Coltrane (Rubeus Hagrid), Matthew Lewis (Neville Longbottom), Sitara Shah (Parvati Patel), Jennifer Smith (Lavender Brown), Tom Felton (Draco Malfoy)

Harry Potter and the Sorcerer's Stone (2001)

Warner Bros./Heyday/1492 Pictures
Directed by Chris Columbus
Writing Credits: Steven Kloves
Based on the novel by J. K. Rowling
Cast: Richard Harris (Albus Dumbledore), Maggie Smith (Prof. Minerva McGonagall), Robbie Coltrane (Rubeus Hagrid), Saunders Triplets (Harry Potter (Age 1)), Daniel Radcliffe (Harry Potter), Fiona Shaw (Aunt Petunia), Harry Melling (Dudley Dursley), Richard Griffiths (Uncle Vernon), Derek Deadman (Tom), Ian Hart (Professor Quirrell), Ben Borowiecki (Diagon Alley Boy), Warwick Davis (Professor Flitwick/Goblin Bank Teller), Verne Troyer (Griphook the Goblin), John Hurt (Mr. Ollivander), Richard Bremmer (He Who Must Not Be Named (voice)), Geraldine Somerville (Mrs. Lily Potter), Harry Taylor (Station Guard), Julie Walters (Mrs. Molly Weasley), Bonnie Wright (Ginny Weasley), Chris Rankin (Percy Weasley), James Phelps (Fred Weasley), Oliver Phelps (George Weasley), Rupert Grint (Ron Weasley), Jean Southern (Dimpled Woman on Train), Emma Watson (Hermione Granger), Matthew Lewis (Neville Longbottom), Tom Felton (Draco Malfoy), Jamie Waylett (Vincent Crabbe), Joshua Herdman (Gregory Goyle), Devon Murray (Seamus Finnigan), Alfred Enoch (Dean Thomas), Leslie Phillips (The Sorting Hat (voice)),

Eleanor Columbus (Susan Bones), John Cleese (Nearly Headless Nick), Terence Bayler (The Bloody Baron), Simon Fisher-Becker (Fat Friar), Nina Young (The Grey Lady), David Bradley (Argus Filch), Alan Rickman (Prof. Severus Snape), Zoë Wanamaker (Madame Hooch), Luke Youngblood (Lee Jordan), Sean Biggerstaff (Oliver Wood)

Heavy Metal (1981)
CDC/Columbia/Famous Players/ Atkinson
Directed by Gerald Potterton, Jimmy T. Murakami
Writing Credits: Len Blum, Corny Cole
Cast: Harvey Atkin (Alien/Henchman (voice)), Thor Bishopric (Boy (voice)), Rodger Bumpass (Hanover Fiste/Dr. Anrak (voice)), Jackie Burroughs (Katherine (voice)), John Candy (Desk Sergeant/Dan/Den/Robot (voice)), Ned Conlon (Councilman (voice)), Len Doncheff (Barbarian (voice))

Hero (2002)
Beijing New Picture/Miramax
Directed by Yimou Zhang
Writing Credits: Feng Li, Bin Wang, Yimou Zhang
Cast: Jet Li (Nameless), Tony Leung Chiu Wai (Broken Sword), Maggie Cheung (Flying Snow), Ziyi Zhang (Moon), Daoming Chen (King of Qin), Donnie Yen (Sky), Liu Zhong Yuan (Scholar), Zheng Tia Yong (Old Servant), Yan Qin (Prime Minister), Chang Xiao Yang

(General), Zhang Ya Kun (Commander), Ma Wen Hua (Head Eunuch)

The Heroic Trio (1993)
China Entertainment/Paka
Directed by Johnny To
Writing Credits: Susanne Chan, Jack Maeby, Sandy Shaw
Cast: Michelle Yeoh (Ching/Invisible Woman/Number 3), Anita Mui (Tung/ Wonder Woman/Shadow Fox), Maggie Cheung (Chat/Thief Catcher/Mercy), Damian Lau (Inspector Lau), Anthony Wong Chau-Sang (Kau), Paul Chu (Chief of Police (as Pei Chun)), James Pak (Inventor), Yee Kwan Yan (Evil Master)

House of Flying Daggers (2004)
Beijing New Picture/EDKO Film
Directed by Yimou Zhang
Writing Credits: Feng Li, Bin Wang, Yimou Zhang
Cast: Takeshi Kaneshiro (Jin), Andy Lau (Leo), Ziyi Zhang (Mei), Dandan Song (Yee)

I Spit on Your Grave (Day of the Woman) (1978)
Cinemagic
Directed by Meir Zarchi
Writing Credits: Meir Zarchi
Cast: Camille Keaton (Jennifer Hill), Eron Tabor (Johnny), Richard Pace (Matthew), Anthony Nichols (Stanley),

Gunter Kleemann (Andy), Alexis Magnotti (Attendant's Wife), Tammy Zarchi (The Children), Terry Zarchi (The Children), Traci Ferrante (Waitress)

Ilsa, Harem Keeper of the Oil Sheiks (1976)
Mount Everest
Directed by Don Edmonds
Writing Credits: Langston Stafford
Cast: Dyanne Thorne (Ilsa), Max Thayer (Commander Adam, U.S. Navy), Uschi Digard (Inga Lindström), Sharon Kelly (Nora Edward), Haji (Alina Cordova), Tanya Boyd (Satin), Marilyn Joi (Velvet), Su Ling (Katsina), Richard Kennedy (Kaiser)

Ilsa, She Wolf of the SS (1975)
Aeteas
Directed by Don Edmonds
Writing Credits: Jonah Royston
Cast: Dyanne Thorne (Ilsa), Gregory Knoph (Wolfe), Tony Mumolo (Mario), Maria Marx (Anna), Nicolle Riddell (Kata), Jo Jo Deville (Ingrid), Sandy Richman (Maigret), George "Buck" Flower (Binz), Rodina Keeler (Gretchen), Richard Kennedy (General), Lance Marshall (Richter)

Ilsa, Tigress of Siberia (1977)
New World
Directed by Jean LaFleur
Writing Credits: Marven McGara
Cast: Dyanne Thorne, Michel-René Labelle, Gilbert Beaumont, Jean-Guy Latour, Ray Landry, Terry Haig

Ilsa, the Wicked Warden (Greta) (1977)
Elite Film
Directed by Jesus Franco
Writing Credits: Erwin C. Dietrich (aka Manfred Gregor), Jesus Franco
Cast: Dyanne Thorne (Greta), Tania Busselier (Abbie Phillips), Lina Romay (Juana)

In the Line of Duty IV (1989)
D&B Films
Directed by Woo-ping Yuen
Writing Credits: Anthony Wong Chau-Sang
Cast: Cynthia Khan (Madam Yeung), Donnie Yen (Donny), Michael Wong

(Michael Wong), Yat Chor Yuen (Luk Wan-Ting), Wing Cho (Triad/Bespectacled CIA Fighter)

Innocent Blood (1992)
Warner Bros.
Directed by John Landis
Writing Credits: Michael Wolk
Cast: Anne Parillaud (Marie), David Proval (Lenny), Rocco Sisto (Gilly), Chazz Palminteri (Tony), Anthony LaPaglia (Joe Gennaro), Robert Loggia (Sallie "The Shark" Macelli), Tony Sirico (Jacko), Tony Lip (Frank), Kim Coates (Ray), Marshall Bell (Marsh), Leo Burmester (Dave Flinton), Rohn Thomas (Coroner), Angela Bassett (U.S. Attorney Sinclair), Luis Guzmán (Morales), Don Rickles (Emmanuel "Manny" Bergman), Tom Savini (News Photographer), Gil Cates Jr. (Dog Boy), Charlie Gomorra (Gorilla)

Invincible Eight (1971)
Golden Harvest
Directed by Wei Lo
Cast: Yin-Chieh Han, Sammo Hung Kam-Bo, Quin Lee, Angela Mao, Nora Miao, James Tien, Yin Tse, Pai Ying

Isis (TV series, 1975)
CBS/Filmation
Directed by Earl Bellamy, Arnold Laven
Writing Credits: Kathleen Barnes, Russell Bates
Cast: JoAnna Cameron (Isis/Andrea Thomas), Brian Cutler (Rick Mason)

Jana of the Jungle (TV series, 1978–1979)
Hanna-Barbera
Cast: Ross Martin (voice), B. J. Ward (Jana (voice))

Jason and the Argonauts (2000)
Hallmark
Directed by Nick Willing
Writing Credits: Matthew Faulk, Mark Skeet
Cast: Jason London (Jason), Jolene Blalock (Medea), Dennis Hopper (Pelias), Frank Langella (Aertes), Natasha Henstridge (Hypsipyle), Derek Jacobi (Phineas), Brian Thompson (Hercules), Mark Lewis Jones (Mopsus), Diana Kent (Polymele), Tom Harper (Acastus)

GREATEST OF ALL SPECTACLES!

Joan of Arc (1948)
RKO/Sierra
Directed by Victor Fleming
Writing Credits: Maxwell Anderson, Andrew Solt
Based on the play *Joan of Lorraine* by Maxwell Anderson
Cast: Ingrid Bergman (Joan of Arc), Francis L. Sullivan (Pierre Cauchon, Count-Bishop of Beauvais), J. Carrol Naish (John, Count of Luxembourg, Joan's Captor), Ward Bond (La Hire), Shepperd Strudwick (Father Massieu, Joan's Bailiff), Gene Lockhart (Georges de la Trémouille, the King's Chief Counselor), John Emery (Jean, Duke d'Alencon, Cousin of Charles), Leif Erickson (Dunois, Bastard of Orleans), Cecil Kellaway (Jean le Maistre, Inquisitor of Rouen), José Ferrer (The Dauphin Charles VII, later King of France), Selena Royle (Isabelle d'Arc, Joan's Mother), Robert Barrat (Jacques d'Arc, Joan's Father), Jimmy Lydon (Pierre d'Arc, Joan's Younger Brother), Rand Brooks (Jean d'Arc, Joan's Older Brother), Roman Bohnen (Durand Laxart, Joan's Uncle), Irene Rich (Catherine de Royer, Joan's Friend), Nestor Paiva (Henri le Royer, Catherine's Husband), Richard Derr (Jean de Metz, a Knight), Ray Teal (Bertrand de Poulengy, a Squire), David Bond (Jean Fournier, Curé of Vaucouleurs), George Coulouris (Sir Robert de Baudricourt, Governor of Vaucoulers), George Zucco (Constable

of Clerveaux), Nicholas Joy (Reginault de Chartres, Archbishop of Rheims and Chancellor of France), Richard Ney (Charles de Bourbon, Duke de Clermont), Vincent Donahue (Alain Chartier, Court Poet), John Ireland (Capt. Jean de la Boussac, St. Severe), Henry Brandon (Capt. Giles de Rais)

Joan of Arc (1999)
CBC-TV
Directed by Christian Duguay
Writing Credits: Michael Alexander Miller, Ronald Parker
Cast: Leelee Sobieski (Joan D'Arc), Jacqueline Bisset (Isabelle D'Arc), Powers Boothe (Jacques D'Arc), Neil Patrick Harris (The Dauphin, later King Charles VII of France), Maury Chaykin (Sir Robert de Baudricourt), Olympia Dukakis (Mother Babette), Jonathan Hyde (Duke of Bedford), Robert Loggia (Father Monet), Shirley MacLaine (Madame de Beaurevoir), Peter O'Toole (Bishop Cauchon), Maximilian Schell (Brother John Le'Maitre), Peter Strauss (La Hire), Chad Willett (Jean de Metz), Ron White (Dunois), Jaimz Woolvett (Duke of Burgundy)

Joan of Arcadia (TV series, 2003–)
CBS/Sony
Created by Barbara Hall
Cast: Joe Mantegna (Will Girardi), Mary Steenburgen (Helen Girardi), Amber Tamblyn (Joan Girardi), Jason Ritter (Kevin Girardi), Michael Welch (Luke Girardi)

Judith of Bethulia (1914)
Biograph
Directed by D. W. Griffith
Writing Credits: Thomas Bailey Aldrich, D. W. Griffith, Grace Pierce, Frank E. Woods
Cast: Blanche Sweet (Judith), Henry B. Walthall (Holofernes), Mae Marsh (Naomi), Robert Harron (Nathan), Lillian Gish (The Young Mother), Dorothy Gish (The Crippled Beggar)

Jungle Girl (1941)
Republic
Directed by John English, William Witney
Writing Credits: Alfred Batson, Ronald Davidson, Norman S. Hall, William

Lively, Joseph O'Donnell, **Joseph F. Poland**
Based on the novel by Edgar Rice Burroughs
Cast: Frances Gifford (Nyoka Meredith), Tom Neal (Jack Stanton), Trevor Bardette (Dr. John Meredith/Bradley Meredith), Gerald Mohr (Slick Latimer), Eddie Acuff (Curly Rogers), Frank Lackteen (Shamba), Tommy Cook (Kimbu), Robert Barron (Bombo), Al Kikume (Chief Lutembi)

Kansas City Bomber (1972)
Welch/MGM/Levy-Gardner-Laven
Directed by Jerrold Freedman
Writing Credits: Calvin Clements Sr., Thomas Rickman
Based on a story by Barry Sandler
Cast: Raquel Welch (K. C. Carr), Kevin McCarthy (Burt Henry), Helena Kallianiotes (Jackie Burdette), Norman Alden ("Horrible Hank" Hopkins), Jeanne Cooper (Vivien, Trainer), Richard Lane (Jen, TV Spokesman), Jodie Foster (Rita)

Kill Bill Volume 1 (2003)
Miramax/A Band Apart/Super Cool Manchu
Directed by Quentin Tarantino
Writing Credits: Uma Thurman, Quentin Tarantino
Cast: Uma Thurman (The Bride), Lucy Liu (O-Ren Ishii), Vivica A.

Fox (Vernita Green), Daryl Hannah (Elle Driver), David Carradine (Bill), Michael Madsen (Budd), Julie Dreyfus (Sofie Fatale), Chiaki Kuriyama (Gogo Yubari), Sonny Chiba (Hattori Hanzo), Chia Hui Liu (Johnny Mo), Michael Parks (Earl McGraw), Michael Bowen (Buck), Jun Kunimura (Boss Tanaka), Kenji Ohba (Bald Guy (Sushi Shop)), Yuki Kazamatsuri (Proprietor), James Parks (Edgar McGraw), Sakichi Satô (Charlie Brown), Jonathan Loughran (Trucker), Yoshiyuki Morishita (Tokyo Businessman)

Kill Bill Volume 2 (2004)
Miramax/A Band Apart
Directed by Quentin Tarantino
Writing Credits: Quentin Tarantino, Uma Thurman
Cast: Uma Thurman (The Bride, Beatrix Kiddo, "Black Mamba"), David Carradine (Bill, "Snake Charmer"), Lucy Liu (O-Ren Ishii, "Cottonmouth"), Vivica A. Fox (Vernita Green, "Copperhead"), Chia Hui Liu (Pai Mei (as Gordon Liu)), Michael Madsen (Budd, "Sidewinder"), Daryl Hannah (Elle Driver, "California Mountain Snake"), Michael Parks (Esteban Vihaio), Bo Svenson (Reverend Harmony), Jeannie Epper (Mrs. Harmony), Stephanie L. Moore (Joleen), Shana Stein (Erica), Caitlin Keats (Janeen), Christopher Allen Nelson (Tommy Plympton), Samuel L.

Jackson (Rufus), Reda Beebe (Lucky), Sid Haig (Jay), Larry Bishop (Larry Gomez), Laura Cayouette (Rocket), Clark Middleton (Ernie), Claire Smithies (Clarita), Perla Haney-Jardine (B. B. Kiddo), Helen Kim (Karen Kim), Venessia Valentino (First-Grade Teacher), Thea Rose (Melanie Harrhouse)

Kilma, Queen of the Amazons (1975)
Profilmes SA
Directed by Miguel Iglesias (aka M. I. Bonns)
Writing Credits: Miguel Cussó, Miguel Iglesias
Cast: Blanca Estrada (Kilma (as Eva Miller)), Frank Braña (Dan Robinson), Claudia Gravy (Tiyu)

Kim Possible (TV series, 2002–)
Disney
Created by Mark McCorkle, Robert Schooley
Cast: Christy Carlson Romano (Kimberly Ann "Kim" Possible (voice)), Will Friedle (Ronald "Ron" Stoppable (voice)), Tahj Mowry (Wade Load (voice)), Nancy Cartwright (Rufus (voice)), Gary Cole (Dr. Possible (Dad) (voice)), Jean Smart (Dr. Possible (Mom) (voice))

King Arthur (2004)
Touchstone/Bruckheimer
Directed by Antoine Fuqua
Writing Credits: David Franzoni
Cast: Clive Owen (Arthur), Ioan

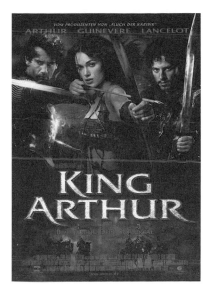

Gruffudd (Lancelot), Mads Mikkelsen (Tristan), Joel Edgerton (Gawain), Hugh Dancy (Galahad), Ray Winstone (Bors), Ray Stevenson (Dagonet), Keira Knightley (Guinevere), Stephen Dillane (Merlin), Stellan Skarsgård (Cerdic), Til Schweiger (Cynric), Sean Gilder (Jols), Pat Kinevane (Horton), Ivano Marescotti (Bishop Germanius), Ken Stott (Marius Honorius), Lorenzo De Angelis (Alecto), Stefania Orsola Garello (Fulcinia), Alan Devine (British Scout), Charlie Creed-Miles (Ganis), Johnny Brennan (Lucan)

Kung Fu Hustle (2004)
Columbia
Directed by Stephen Chow
Writing Credits: Tsang Kan Cheong, Stephen Chow, Xin Huo, Chan Man Keung
Cast: Stephen Chow (Sing), Xiaogang Feng (Crocodile Gang Boss (as Feng Xiao Gang)), Wah Yuen (Landlord), Zhi Hua Dong (Donut), Kwok Kuen Chan (Brother Sum (as Chan Kwok Kwan)), Chi Chung Lam (Bone (as Lam Tze Chung)), Qiu Yuen (Landlady)

Lady Snowblood (1973)
Toho
Directed by Toshiya Fujita
Writing Credits: Kazuo Uemura, Kazuo Koike
Cast: Meiko Kaji (Yuki Kashima), Toshio Kurosawa (Ryûrei Ashio), Masaaki Daimon (Gô Kashima), Miyoko Akaza (Sayo Kashima), Shinichi Uchida (Shirô Kashima), Takeo Chii

(Tokuichi Masakage), Noboru Nakaya (Banzô Takemura), Yoshiko Nakada (Kobue Takemura), Akemi Negishi (Tajire no Okiku), Kaoru Kusuda (Otora Mikazuki), Sanae Nakahara (Okono Kitahama), Hosei Komatsu (Genzô Shibayama), Makoto Matsuzaki (Daikashi), Hiroshi Hasegawa (Daihachi Kachime)

Lana, Queen of the Amazon (1964)
Transocean
Directed by Cyl Farney, Géza von Cziffra
Writing Credits: Richard Anden, Cyl Farney, Rita Niederer, Ernst von Hasselbach
Cast: Anton Diffring (Professor van Vries), Catherine Schell (Queen Lana), Christian Wolff (Peter van Vries), Michael Hinz (Mathias/Emmanuel)

Lara Croft: Tomb Raider (2001)
Paramount/Lawrence Gordon
Directed by Simon West
Writing Credits: Simon West, Patrick Massett, John Zinman
Based on the story by Sara B. Cooper, Mike Werb, and Michael Colleary
Cast: Angelina Jolie (Lara Croft), Jon Voight (Lord Richard Croft), Iain Glen (Manfred Powell), Noah Taylor (Bryce), Daniel Craig (Alex West), Richard Johnson (Distinguished Gentleman), Chris Barrie (Hillary), Julian Rhind-Tutt

(Mr. Pimms), Leslie Phillips (Wilson), Robert Phillips (Julius, Assault Team Leader), Rachel Appleton (Young Lara), Henry Wyndham (Boothby's Auctioneer), David Cheung (Head Laborer), David K. S. Tse (Head Laborer), Ozzie Yue (Aged Buddhist Monk), Wai-Keat Lau (Young Buddhist Monk)

Lara Croft Tomb Raider: The Cradle of Life (2003)
Paramount/Lawrence Gordon
Directed by Jan de Bont
Writing Credits: Dean Georgaris
Based on the story by Steven E. de Souza and James V. Hart
Cast: Angelina Jolie (Lara Croft), Gerard Butler (Terry Sheridan), Ciarán Hinds (Jonathan Reiss), Chris Barrie (Hillary), Noah Taylor (Bryce), Djimon Hounsou (Kosa), Til Schweiger (Sean), Simon Yam (Chen Lo), Terence Yin (Xien), Daniel Caltagirone (Nicholas Petraki), Fabiano Martell (Jimmy Petraki), Jonathan Coyne (Gus Petraki), Robert Cavanah (MI6 Agent Stevens), Ronan Vibert (MI6 Agent Calloway), Lenny Juma (Village Leader)

The League of Extraordinary Gentlemen (2003)
20th Century Fox/Angry/JD
Directed by Stephen Norrington
Writing Credits: James Robinson
Based on comic books by Alan Moore and Kevin O'Neill
Cast: Sean Connery (Allan Quatermain), Naseeruddin Shah (Captain Nemo), Peta Wilson (Mina Harker), Tony Curran (Rodney Skinner (The Invisible Man)), Stuart Townsend (Dorian Gray), Shane West (Tom Sawyer), Jason Flemyng (Dr. Henry Jekyll/Edward Hyde), Richard Roxburgh (M), Max Ryan (Dante), Tom Goodman-Hill (Sanderson Reed), David Hemmings (Nigel), Terry O'Neill (Ishmael), Rudolf Pellar (Draper), Robert Willox (Constable Dunning)

The Long Kiss Goodnight (1996)
New Line Cinema/Forge
Directed by Renny Harlin
Writing Credits: Shane Black
Cast: Geena Davis (Samantha Caine/Charly Baltimore), Samuel L. Jackson (Mitch Henessey), Yvonne Zima (Caitlin

Caine), Craig Bierko (Timothy), Tom Amandes (Hal), Brian Cox (Dr. Nathan Waldman), Patrick Malahide (Leland Perkins), David Morse (Luke/Daedalus), Joseph McKenna (One-Eyed Jack), Melina Kanakaredes (Trin), Dan Warry-Smith (Raymond), Kristen Bone (Girl #1), Jennifer Pisana (Girl #2), Rex Linn (Man in Bed), Alan North (Earl), Edwin Hodge (Todd Henessey), Bill MacDonald (Hostage Agent), Gladys O'Connor (Alice Waldman), Frank Moore (Surveillance Man), G. D. Spradlin (President), Graham McPherson (CIA Director)

The Lord of the Rings: The Fellowship of the Ring (2001)
Warner Bros./New Line/Wingnut
Directed by Peter Jackson
Writing Credits: Fran Walsh, Philippa Boyens, Peter Jackson
Based on the novel by J. R. R. Tolkien
Cast: Noel Appleby (Everard Proudfoot), Sean Astin (Sam Gamgee), Sala Baker (Sauron), Sean Bean (Boromir), Cate Blanchett (Galadriel), Orlando Bloom (Legolas Greenleaf), Billy Boyd (Pippin), Marton Csokas (Celeborn), Megan Edwards (Mrs. Proudfoot), Michael Elsworth (Gondorian Archivist), Mark Ferguson (Gil-Galad), Ian Holm (Bilbo Baggins), Ian McKellen (Gandalf), Christopher Lee (Saruman), Lawrence Makoare (Lurtz), Brent McIntyre (Witch-King), Peter McKenzie (Elendil), Sarah McLeod

(Rosie Cotton), Dominic Monaghan (Merry), Viggo Mortensen (Aragorn), Ian Mune (Bounder), Craig Parker (Haldir), Cameron Rhodes (Farmer Maggot), John Rhys-Davies (Gimli), Martyn Sanderson (Gate Keeper), Andy Serkis (Gollum), Harry Sinclair (Isildur), Liv Tyler (Arwen), David Weatherley (Barliman Butterbur), Hugo Weaving (Elrond), Elijah Wood (Frodo Baggins), Alan Howard (The Ring (voice))

The Lord of the Rings: The Return of the King (2003)
Warner Bros./Wingnut/New Line
Directed by Peter Jackson
Writing Credits: Fran Walsh, Philippa Boyens, Peter Jackson
Based on the book by J. R. R. Tolkien
Cast: Noel Appleby (Everard Proudfoot), Alexandra Astin (Elanor Gamgee), Sean Astin (Sam), David Aston (Gondorian Soldier #3), John Bach (Madril), Sean Bean (Boromir), Cate Blanchett (Galadriel), Orlando Bloom (Legolas), Billy Boyd (Pippin), Sadwyn Brophy (Eldarion), Alistair Browning (Damrod), Marton Csokas (Celeborn), Richard Edge (Gondorian Soldier #1), Jason Fitch (Uruk #2), Bernard Hill (Theoden), Ian Holm (Bilbo), Bruce Hopkins (Gamling), Ian Hughes (Irolas), Lawrence Makoare (Witch King/Gothmog), Ian McKellen (Gandalf), Bret McKenzie (Elf Escort), Sarah McLeod (Rosie Cotton), Maisie McLeod-Riera (Baby Gamgee), Dominic Monaghan (Merry), Viggo Mortensen (Aragorn), John Noble (Denethor), Paul Norell (King of the Dead), Miranda Otto (Eowyn), Bruce Phillips (Grimbold), Shane Rangi (Harad Leader #2), John Rhys-Davies (Gimli), Todd Rippon (Harad Leader #1), Thomas Robins (Deagol), Andy Serkis (Gollum/Smeagol), Harry Sinclair (Isildur), Peter Tait (Shagrat), Joel Tobeck (Orc Lieutenant #1), Liv Tyler (Arwen), Karl Urban (Eomer), Stephen Ure (Gorbag), Hugo Weaving (Elrond), David Wenham (Faramir), Elijah Wood (Frodo), Alan Howard (The Ring (voice)), Sala Baker (Orc/Sauron)

The Lord of the Rings: The Two Towers (2002)
Warner Bros./WingNut/New Line
Directed by Peter Jackson
Writing Credits: Fran Walsh, Philippa Boyens, Stephen Sinclair, Peter Jackson

Based on the novel by J. R. R. Tolkien
Cast: Elijah Wood (Frodo Baggins), Ian McKellen (Gandalf the Grey/Gandalf the White), Liv Tyler (Arwen), Viggo Mortensen (Aragorn), Sean Astin (Samwise "Sam" Gamgee), Cate Blanchett (Galadriel), John Rhys-Davies (Gimli/Voice of Treebeard), Bernard Hill (Theoden), Christopher Lee (Saruman the White), Billy Boyd (Peregrin "Pippin" Took), Dominic Monaghan (Meriadoc "Merry" Brandybuck), Orlando Bloom (Legolas Greenleaf), Hugo Weaving (Elrond), Miranda Otto (Eowyn), David Wenham (Faramir), Brad Dourif (Grima Wormtongue), Andy Serkis (Gollum/Sméagol), Karl Urban (Eomer), Craig Parker (Haldir), Bruce Allpress (Aldor), John Bach (Madril), Sala Baker (Man Flesh Uruk), Jed Brophy (Sharku/Snaga), Sam Comery (Éothain), Calum Gittins (Haleth, Son of Hámas), Bruce Hopkins (Gamling), Paris Howe Strewe (Théodred, Prince of Rohan), Nathaniel Lees (Uglúk), John Leigh (Háma), Robbie Magasiva (Mauhur), Robyn Malcolm (Morwen)

Love Slaves of the Amazons (1957)
Universal
Directed by Curt Siodmak
Writing Credits: Curt Siodmak
Cast: Don Taylor (Dr. Peter Masters), Gianna Segale (Gina Vanni), Eduardo Ciannelli (Dr. Crespi), Harvey Chalk (Aldamar Silver), Wilson Viana (Fernando, a Pirate), Eugenio Carlos (Carlos, His Brother), Tom Payne (Dr. Mario Dellaman), Gilda Nery (Amazon Guard), Ana Maria Nabuco (Amazon Queen)

The Matrix (1999)
Warner Bros./Silver Pictures/ Groucho II
Directed by Andy Wachowski, Larry Wachowski
Writing Credits: Andy Wachowski, Larry Wachowski
Cast: Keanu Reeves (Neo), Laurence Fishburne (Morpheus), Carrie-Anne Moss (Trinity), Hugo Weaving (Agent Smith), Gloria Foster (Oracle), Joe Pantoliano (Cypher), Marcus Chong (Tank), Julian Arahanga (Apoc), Matt Doran (Mouse), Belinda McClory (Switch), Anthony Ray Parker (Dozer), Paul Goddard (Agent Brown), Robert

Taylor (Agent Jones), David Aston (Rhineheart), Marc Gray (Choi), Ada Nicodemou (Dujour), Denni Gordon (Priestess), Rowan Witt (Spoon Boy), Elenor Witt (Potential)

The Matrix Reloaded (2003)

Warner Bros./Silver/NPV Entertainment
Directed by Andy Wachowski, Larry Wachowski
Writing Credits: Andy Wachowski, Larry Wachowski
Cast: Ray Anthony (Power Station Guard), Christine Anu (Kali), Andy Arness (Police #2), Alima Ashton-Sheibu (Link's Niece), Helmut Bakaitis (The Architect), Steve Bastoni (Soren), Don Battee (Vector), Monica Bellucci (Persephone), Daniel Bernhardt (Agent Johnson), Valerie Berry (Priestess), Ian Bliss (Bane), Liliana Bogatko (Old Woman at Zion), Michael Budd (Zion Controller), Stoney Burke (Bike Carrier Driver), Kelly Butler (Ice), Josephine Byrnes (Zion Virtual Control Operator), Noris Campos (Woman with Groceries), Sing Ngai (Seraph), Paul Cotter (Corrupt), Marlene Cummins (Another Old Woman at Zion), Attila Davidhazy (Young Thomas Anderson at 12), Essie Davis (Maggie), Terrell Dixon (Wurm), Nash Edgerton (Security Guard #5), Laurence Fishburne (Morpheus), Gloria Foster (The Oracle), David Franklin (Maitre D'), Austin Galuppo (Young Thomas Anderson at 4), Nona M. Gaye (Zee), Daryl Heath (A.P.U. Escort), Roy Jones Jr. (Ballard), Malcolm Kennard (Abel), David Kilde (Agent Jackson), Randall Duk Kim (The Keymaker), Christopher Kirby (Mauser), Peter Lamb (Colt), Nathaniel Lees (Mifune), Harry J. Lennix (Commander Lock), Tony Lynch (Computer Room Technician), Robert Mammone (AK), Joshua Mbakwe (Link's Nephew), Matt McColm (Agent Thompson), Scott McLean (Security Bunker Guard #2), Chris Mitchell (Power Station Guard), Steve Morris (Computer Room Guard), Carrie-Anne Moss (Trinity), Tory Mussett (Beautiful Woman at Le Vrai), Rene Naufahu (Zion Gate Operator), Robyn Nevin (Councillor Dillard), David No (Cain), Genevieve O'Reilly (Officer Wirtz), Socratis Otto (Operator), Harold Perrineau Jr. (Link), Jada Pinkett Smith (Niobe), Montaño Rain (Young Thomas Anderson at 8), Adrian Rayment (Twin #2), Neil Rayment (Twin #1), Rupert Reid (Lock's Lieutenant), Keanu Reeves (Neo), David Roberts (Roland), Shane C. Rodrigo (Ajax), Nick Scoggin (Gidim Truck Driver), Kevin Scott (18-Wheel Trucker), Tahei Simpson (Binary), Frankie Stevens (Tirant), Nicandro Thomas (Young Thomas Anderson at 2), Gina Torres (Cas), Andrew Valli (Police #1), Steve Vella (Malachi), John Walton (Security Bunker Guard), Clayton Watson (Kid), Hugo Weaving (Agent Smith), Cornel West (Councillor West), Leigh Whannell (Axel), Bernard White (Rama-Kandra), Lambert Wilson (Merovingian), Anthony Wong (Ghost), Anthony Zerbe (Councillor Hamann)

The Matrix Revolutions (2003)

Warner Bros./NPV/Silver
Directed by Andy Wachowski, Larry Wachowski
Writing Credits: Andy Wachowski, Larry Wachowski
Cast: Mary Alice (The Oracle), Tanveer K. Atwal (Sati), Helmut Bakaitis (The Architect), Kate Beahan (Coat-Check Girl), Francine Bell (Councillor Grace), Monica Bellucci (Persephone), Rachel Blackman (Charra), Henry Blasingame (Deus Ex Machina), Ian Bliss (Bane), David Bowers (Q-Ball Gang Member #), Zeke Castelli (Operations Officer Mattis), Sing Ngai (Seraph), Essie Davis (Maggie), Laurence Fishburne (Morpheus), Nona M. Gaye (Zee),
Dion Horstmans (Q-Ball Gang Member #2), Lachy Hulme (Sparks), Christopher Kirby (Mauser), Peter Lamb (Colt), Nathaniel Lees (Mifune), Harry J. Lennix (Lock), Robert Mammone (AK), Joe Manning (First Operator at Command), Maurice Morgan (Tower Soldier), Carrie-Anne Moss (Trinity), Tharini Mudaliar (Kamala), Rene Naufahu (Zion Gate Operator), Robyn Nevin (Councillor Dillard), Genevieve O'Reilly (Officer Wirtz), Harold Perrineau Jr. (Link), Jada Pinkett Smith (Niobe), Kittrick Redmond (Second Operator at Command), Keanu Reeves (Neo), Rupert Reid (Lock's Lieutenant), Kevin Michael Richardson (Deus Ex Machina (voice)), David Roberts (Roland), Bruce Spence (Trainman), Richard Sydenham (Dock Sergeant), Che Timmins (Radio Bunker Man), Gina Torres (Cas), Clayton Watson (Kid), Hugo Weaving (Agent Smith), Cornel West (Councillor West), Bernard White (Rama-Kandra), Lambert Wilson (Merovingian), Anthony Wong (Ghost), Anthony Zerbe (Councillor Hamann)

The Messenger: The Story of Joan of Arc (1999)

Columbia/Gaumont/Leeloo
Directed by Luc Besson
Writing Credits: Luc Besson, Andrew Birkin
Cast: Milla Jovovich (Joan of Arc), Dustin Hoffman (The Conscience), Faye Dunaway (Yolande D'Aragon),

John Malkovich (Charles VII), Tchéky Karyo (Dunois), Vincent Cassel (Gilles de Rais), Pascal Greggory (The Duke of Alençon), Richard Ridings (La Hire), Desmond Harrington (Aulon), Timothy West (Pierre Cauchon), Rab Affleck (Comrade), Stéphane Algoud (Look Out), Edwin Apps (Bishop), David Bailie (English Judge), David Barber (English Judge), Christian Barbier (Captain), Timothy Bateson (English Judge), David Begg (Nobleman at Rouen's Castle), Christian Bergner (Captain), Andrew Birkin (Talbot), Dominic Borrelli (English Judge), John Boswall (Old Priest), Matthew Bowyer (The

Bludgeoned French Soldier), Paul Brooke (Domremy's Priest), Bruce Byron (Joan's Father), Charles Cork (Vaucouleur's Priest), Patrice Cossoneau (Captain)

Metropolis (1927)
UFA
Directed by Fritz Lang
Writing Credits: Fritz Lang, Thea von Harbou
Cast: Alfred Abel (Johhan (Joh) Fredersen), Gustav Fröhlich (Freder Fredersen), Brigitte Helm (Maria/Der Maschinen-Mensch (The Robot)), Rudolf Klein-Rogge (C. A. Rotwang, der Erfinder), Fritz Rasp (Der Schmale/Slim), Theodor Loos (Josaphat)

Million Dollar Baby (2004)
Warner Bros./Malpaso/Lakeshore/Ruddy
Directed by Clint Eastwood
Writing Credits: Paul Haggis
Based on the stories of F. X. Toole
Cast: Clint Eastwood (Frankie Dunn), Hilary Swank (Maggie Fitzgerald), Morgan Freeman (Eddie Scrap-Iron Dupris), Jay Baruchel (Danger Barch), Mike Colter (Big Willie Little), Lucia Rijker (Billie "The Blue Bear"), Brian F. O'Byrne (Father Horvak), Anthony Mackie (Shawrelle Berry), Margo Martindale (Earline Fitzgerald), Riki Lindhome (Mardell Fitzgerald), Michael Pena (Omar), Benito Martinez (Billie's Manager), Bruce MacVittie (Mickey Mack), David Powledge (Counterman

at Diner), Joe D'Angerio (Cut Man), Marcus Chait (J. D. Fitzgerald), Tom McCleister (Lawyer)

Millionaire's Express (1986)
Directed by Sammo Hung Kam-Bo
Writing Credits: Sammo Hung Kam-Bo
Cast: Yasuaki Kurata (Samurai), Biao Yuen (Tsao Cheuk Kin), Sammo Hung Kam-Bo (Fong-Tin Ching), Rosamund Kwan (Chi), Kenny Bee (Fook Loi), Lung Chan (Firefighter/Security officer), Olivia Cheng (Siu-Hon), Kar Lok Chin (Firefighter/Security Officer), Emily Chu (Bo), Fat Chung (Bandit), Mui Sang Fan (Bandit (as Mei-Sheng Fan)), Hou Hsiao (Firefighter/Security Officer), Jang Lee Hwang (Yukio Fushiki), Sek Kin (Master Sek)

Modesty Blaise (1966)
20th Century Fox
Directed by Joseph Losey
Writing Credits: Evan Jones
Based on the story by Stanley Dubens and Peter O'Donnell and the comic strip by Jim Holdaway
Cast: Monica Vitti (Modesty Blaise), Terence Stamp (Willie Garvin), Dirk Bogarde (Gabriel), Harry Andrews (Tarrant), Michael Craig (Paul), Clive Revill (McWhirter/Sheik Abu Tahir), Alexander Knox (Minister), Rossella Falk (Mrs. Fothergill), Scilla Gabel (Melina), Michael Chow (Weng), Joe Melia (Crevier), Saro Urzì (Basilio), Tina Aumont (Nicole), Oliver MacGreevy (Tattooed Man), Jon Bluming (Hans), Lex Schoorel (Walter), Marcello Turilli (Strauss), Giuseppe Paganelli (Friar)

Mork & Mindy (TV
series, 1978–1982: "Mork vs. the Necrotons," Parts I and II [1979])
Paramount/ABC
Directed by Don Barnhart, Frank Buxton
Writing Credits: Cindy Begel, Gene Braunstein
Cast: Robin Williams (Mork (from Ork)), Pam Dawber (Mindy McConnell), Raquel Welch (Alien Amazon Queen)

Mortal Kombat (1995)
Columbia/New Line/Threshold
Directed by Paul W. S. Anderson
Writing Credits: Ed Boon, John Tobias,

Kevin Droney
Based on the video game
Cast: Christopher Lambert (Lord
Raiden), Robin Shou (Liu Kang), Linden
Ashby (Johnny Cage), Cary-Hiroyuki
Tagawa (Shang Tsung), Bridgette Wilson
(Sonya Blade), Talisa Soto (Princess
Kitana), Trevor Goddard (Kano), Chris
Casamassa (Scorpion), François Petit
(Sub-Zero), Keith Cooke (Reptile),
Hakim Alston (Fighting Monk),
Kenneth Edwards (Art Lean), John
Fujioka (Chief Priest), Daniel Haggard
(Assistant Director), Sandy Helberg
(Director), Steven Ho (Chan Kang),
Peter Jason (Master Boyd), Lloyd Kino
(Grandfather)

Mr. and Mrs. Smith (2005)
New Regency/Summit/20th
Century Fox
Directed by Doug Liman
Writing Credits: Simon Kinberg
Cast: Brad Pitt (John Smith), Angelina
Jolie (Jane Smith), Elijah Alexander
(Marco Racin), Theresa Barrera (Janet)

Ms. 45 (1981)
Navaron
Directed by Abel Ferrara
Writing Credits: Nicholas St. John
Cast: Zoë Lund (Thana (as Zoë
Tamerlis)), Albert Sinkys (Albert),
Darlene Stuto (Laurie), Helen McGara

(Carol), Nike Zachmanoglou (Pamela),
Abel Ferrara (First Rapist), Peter
Yellen (Burglar (Second Rapist)), Editta
Sherman (Mrs. Nasone (Landlady)),
Vincent Gruppi (Heckler on Corner), S.
Edward Singer (Photographer), Stanley
Timms (Pimp)

Mulan (1998)
Disney/Buena Vista
Directed by: Tony Bancroft, Barry Cook
Writing Credits: Rita Hsiao, Chris
Sanders, Philip LaZebnik, Raymond
Singer, Eugenia Bostwick-Singer, Dean
DeBlois, David Reynolds
Based on the story by Robert D. San
Souci
Cast: Ming-Na (Fa Mulan/Fa Ping
(voice)), B.D. Wong (Captain Li Shang
(voice)), Soon-Tek Oh (Fa Zhou (voice)),
Eddie Murphy (Mushu the Demoted
One (voice)), Harvey Fierstein (Yao
(voice)), Gedde Watanabe (Ling (voice)),
Miguel Ferrer (Shan-Yu (voice)), James
Hong (Chi Fu (voice)), Pat Morita (The
Emperor of China (voice)), June Foray
(Grandmother Fa (voice)), James Shigeta
(General Li (voice)), Lea Salonga (Fa
Mulan/Fa Ping (singing voice)), Freda
Foh Shen (Fa Li (voice))

Naked Killer (1992)
Golden Harvest
Directed by Clarence Fok Yiu-leung

Writing Credits: Wong Jing
Cast: Chingmy Yau (Kitty/Vivian
Shang), Simon Yam (Tinam), Carrie Ng
(Princess), Madoka Sugawara (Baby),
Wai Yiu (Sister Cindy), Ken Lo (Bee)

The Naked Kiss (1964)
Allied Artists/F&F
Directed by Samuel Fuller
Writing Credits: Samuel Fuller
Cast: Constance Towers (Kelly),
Anthony Eisley (Captain Griff),
Michael Dante (J. L. Grant), Virginia
Grey (Candy), Patsy Kelly (Mac, Head

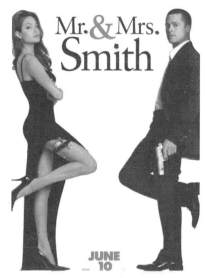

Nurse), Betty Bronson (Miss Josephine),
Marie Devereux (Buff), Karen Conrad
(Dusty), Linda Francis (Rembrandt),
Barbara Perry (Edna), Walter Mathews
(Mike), Betty Robinson (Bunny), Jean-
Michel Michenaud (Kip), Christopher
Barry (Peanuts), Georg H. Schnell (Tim),
Patty Robinson (Angel Face)

Naked Weapon (2002)
Jing/Media Asia
Directed by Siu-Tung Ching
Writing Credits: Wong Jing
Cast: Marit Thoresen (Fiona Birch),
Almen Wong Pui-Ha (Madam M),
Daniel Wu (Jack Chen), Kai Yan Kwok
(Little Katherine), Renee Nichole
Rommeswinkel (Young Charlene
Ching), Mo Ka Lai (Little Jing),
Augustin Aguerreberry (Drillmaster),
Maggie Q (Charlene Ching), Anya
(Katherine), Jewel Lee (Jing), Monica Lo

(Student Murdered in Cage), Benny Lai (Tattooed Yakuza Boss), Pei-pei Cheng (Faye Ching), Dennis Chan (Mr. Chan), Andrew Lin (Ryuichi)

Nancy Drew . . . Detective (1938)

Warner Bros.
Directed by William Clemens
Writing Credits: Kenneth Gamet
Based on a story by Mildred Wirt Benson (Carolyn Keene)
Cast: Bonita Granville (Nancy Drew), John Litel (Carson Drew), James Stephenson (Challon), Frankie Thomas (Theodore "Ted" Nickerson), Frank Orth (Captain Tweedy), Helena Phillips Evans (Mary Eldredge), Renie Riano (Effie Schneider, Drew's Maid), Charles Trowbridge (Hollister), Dick Purcell (Keiffer), Edward Keane (Adam Thorne), Mae Busch (Miss Tyson, the Nurse)

Nausicaa (1984)

Hakuhodo
Directed by Hayao Miyazaki
Writing Credits: Hayao Miyazaki
Cast: Sumi Shimamoto (Nausicaä (voice)), Mahito Tsujimura (Jihl (voice)), Hisako Kyôda (Oh-Baba (voice)), Gorô Naya (Yupa (voice)), Ichirô Nagai (Mito (voice)), Kôhei Miyauchi (Goru (voice)), Jôji Yanami (Gikkuri (voice)), Minoru Yada (Niga (voice))

One Million Years B.C. (1966)

Hammer Films
Directed by Don Chaffey
Writing Credits: George Baker, Michael Carreras, Joseph Frickert, Mickell Novack
Cast: Raquel Welch (Loana), John Richardson (Tumak), Percy Herbert (Sakana), Robert Brown (Akhoba), Martine Beswick (Nupondi), Jean Wladon (Ahot), Lisa Thomas (Sura), Malya Nappi (Tohana), Richard James (Young Rock Man)

La Passion de Jeanne d'Arc (1928)

Dreyer Films
Directed by Carl Theodor Dreyer
Writing Credits: Joseph Delteil, Carl Theodor Dreyer
Cast: Maria Falconetti (Jeanne d'Arc), Eugene Silvain (Évêque Pierre Cauchon), André Berley (Jean d'Estivet), Maurice

Schutz (Nicolas Loyseleur), Antonin Artaud (Jean Massieu), Michel Simon (Jean Lemaître), Jean d'Yd (Guillaume Evrard), Louis Ravet (Jean Beaupère), Armand Lurville (Juge), Jacques Arnna (Juge), Alexandre Mihalesco (Juge)

Pippi Longstocking (1969)

Svenks AB/KB Nord Art
Directed by Olle Hellbom
Writing Credits: Astrid Lindgren (based on the novels)
Cast: Inger Nilsson (Pippi Långstrump), Maria Persson (Annika), Pär Sundberg (Tommy), Margot Trooger (Fröken Prysselius)

Pirates of the Caribbean: The Curse of the Black Pearl (2003)

Disney/Bruckheimer
Directed by Gore Verbinski
Writing Credits: Ted Elliott, Terry Rossio
Based on the story by Jay Wolpert and Stuart Beattie
Cast: Johnny Depp (Jack Sparrow), Geoffrey Rush (Barbossa), Orlando Bloom (Will Turner), Keira Knightley (Elizabeth Swann), Jack Davenport (Norrington), Jonathan Pryce (Governor Weatherby Swann), Lee Arenberg (Pintel), Mackenzie Crook (Ragetti), Damian O'Hare (Lieutenant Gillette), Giles New (Murtogg), Angus Barnett (Mullroy), David Bailie (Cotton), Michael Berry Jr. (Twigg), Isaac C. Singleton Jr.

(Bo'sun), Kevin McNally (Joshamee Gibbs), Treva Etienne (Koehler)

Point of No Return (1993)

Warner Bros.
Directed by John Badham
Writing Credits: Luc Besson, Robert Getchell, Alexandra Seros
Cast: Bridget Fonda (Maggie Hayward/Claudia Anne Doran/Nina), Gabriel Byrne (Bob), Dermot Mulroney (J.P.), Miguel Ferrer (Kaufman), Anne Bancroft (Amanda), Olivia d'Abo (Angela), Richard Romanus (Fahd Bahktiar), Harvey Keitel (Victor the Cleaner), Lorraine Toussaint (Beth), Geoffrey Lewis (Drugstore Owner)

Police Woman (TV series, 1974–1978)

Columbia/Gerber
Created by Robert E. Collins
Cast: Angie Dickinson (Sgt. Suzanne "Pepper" Anderson (1974–1978)), Earl Holliman (Lt. Bill Crowley (1974–1978)), Ed Bernard (Det. Joe Styles (1974–1978)), Charles Dierkop (Det. Pete Royster (1974–1978)), Val Bisoglio (Lt. Paul Marsh (1974–1976))

The Powerpuff Girls (TV series, 1998–2004)

Hanna-Barbera
Created by Craig McCracken

Prehistoric Women (1967)

Hammer Films
Directed by Michael Carreras
Writing Credits: Michael Carreras (aka Henry Younger)
Cast: Martine Beswick (Kari), Edina Ronay (Saria), Michael Latimer (David), Stephanie Randall (Amyak), Carol White (Gido), Alexandra Stevenson (Luri), Yvonne Horner (First Amazon), Sydney Bromley (Ullo), Frank Hayden (Arja), Robert Raglan (Colonel Hammond), Mary Hignett (Mrs. Hammond), Louis Mahoney (Head Boy), Bari Jonson (High Priest), Danny Daniels (Jakara), Steven Berkoff (John)

Princess Mononoke (1997)

Nippon Television
Directed by Hayao Miyazaki
Writing Credits: Neil Gaiman (English adaptation), Hayao Miyazaki

Cast: Yôji Matsuda (Prince Ashitaka (voice)), Yuriko Ishida (San, The Princess Mononoke (voice)), Yûko Tanaka (Eboshi-gozen (voice)), Kaoru Kobayashi (Jiko-bô (voice)), Masahiko Nishimura (Kouroku (voice)), Tsunehiko Kamijô (Gonza (voice)), Sumi Shimamoto (Toki (voice)), Tetsu Watanabe (Yama-inu (voice)), Mitsuru Satô (Tatari-gami (voice)), Akira Nagoya (Usi-kai (voice))

Princess of Thieves (2001)

Granada/ABC-TV
Directed by Peter Hewitt
Writing Credits: Robin Lerner
Cast: David Barrass (Cardaggian), Malcolm McDowell (Sheriff of Nottingham), Hannah Cresswell (Marion (voice)), Keira Knightley (Gwyn), Del Synnott (Froderick), Stuart Wilson (Robin O'Locksley (Robin Hood)), Crispin Letts (Will Scarlett), Roger Ashton-Griffiths (Friar Tuck), Jonathan Hyde (Prince John), Adam Ryan (Conrad), Brendon Gregory (Coachman), Stephen Moyer (Prince Philip)

The Professional: Leon

(1994)
Gaumont/Dauphin
Directed by Luc Besson
Writing Credits: Luc Besson
Cast: Jean Reno (Leon), Gary Oldman (Stansfield), Natalie Portman (Mathilda), Danny Aiello (Tony), Peter Appel (Malky), Willi One Blood (First Stansfield man), Don Creech (Second Stansfield man), Keith A. Glascoe (Third Stansfield man), Randolph Scott (Fourth Stansfield man), Michael Badalucco (Mathilda's Father), Ellen Greene (Mathilda's Mother), Elizabeth Regen (Mathilda's Sister), Carl J. Matusovich (Mathilda's Brother), Frank Senger (Fatman)

Queen of Outer Space

(1958)
Allied Artists
Directed by Edward Bernds
Writing Credits: Charles Beaumont, Ben Hecht
Cast: Zsa Zsa Gabor (Talleah), Eric Fleming (Capt. Neal Patterson), Dave Willock (Lt. Mike Cruze), Laurie Mitchell (Queen Yllana), Lisa Davis (Motiya), Paul Birch (Professor Konrad), Patrick Waltz (Lt. Larry Turner), Barbara Darrow (Kaeel), Marilyn Buferd (Odeena)

Queen of the Amazons

(1947)
Screen Guild Productions
Directed by Edward Finney
Writing Credits: Roger Merton
Cast: Robert Lowery (Gary Lambert), Patricia Morison (Jean Preston), J. Edward Bromberg (Gabby), John Miljan (Narrator/Colonel Jones), Amira Moustafa (Zita, the Amazon Queen), Keith Richards (Wayne Monroe), Bruce Edwards (Greg Jones)

The Quick and the Dead

(1995)
Columbia/Tristar
Directed by Sam Raimi
Writing Credits: Simon Moore
Cast: Sharon Stone (The Lady/Ellen), Gene Hackman (John Herod), Russell Crowe (Cort), Leonardo DiCaprio (The Kid), Tobin Bell (Dog Kelly), Roberts Blossom (Doc Wallace), Kevin Conway (Eugene Dred), Keith David (Sgt. Clay Cantrell), Lance Henriksen (Ace Hanlon), Pat Hingle (Horace), Gary Sinise (The Marshal/Young Ellen's Father), Mark Boone Junior (Scars), Olivia Burnette (Katie), Fay Masterson (Mattie Silk), Raynor Scheine (Ratsy), Woody Strode (Charlie Moonlight)

Red Sonja (1985)

De Laurentiis/MGM/UA
Directed by Richard Fleischer
Writing Credits: Clive Exton, George MacDonald Fraser
Based on the stories of Robert E. Howard
Cast: Arnold Schwarzenegger (Kalidor), Brigitte Nielsen (Red Sonja), Sandahl Bergman (Queen Gedren), Paul L. Smith (Falkon), Ernie Reyes Jr. (Prince Tarn), Ronald Lacey (Ikol), Pat Roach (Brytag), Terry Richards (Djart), Janet Agren (Varna), Donna Osterbuhr (Kendra), Lara Naszinsky (Gedren's Handmaid)

Relic Hunter (TV series, 1999–2002)

Beta/Fireworks/Gaumont
Directed by Wade Eastwood, Jonathan Hackett
Writing Credits: Rob Gilmer, Bill Taub
Cast: Tia Carrere (Sydney Fox (1999–2002)), Christien Anholt (Nigel Bailey (1999–2002)), Lindy Booth (Claudia (1999–2001)), Tanja Reichert (Karen Petrusky (2001–2002))

Remington Steele (TV series, 1982–1987)

MTM
Created by: Robert Butler, Michael Gleason
Cast: Stephanie Zimbalist (Laura Holt), Pierce Brosnan (Remington Steele), James Read (Murphy Michaels (1982–1983)), Janet DeMay (Bernice Foxe (1982–1983)), Doris Roberts (Mildred Krebs (1983–1987))

Resident Evil (2002)

Sony/New Legacy/Impact/Constantin
Directed by Paul W. S. Anderson, Chris "Flimsy" Howes
Writing Credits: Paul W. S. Anderson
Cast: Milla Jovovich (Alice), Michelle Rodriguez (Rain Ocampo), Eric Mabius (Matt Addison), James Purefoy (Spence Parks), Martin Crewes (Chad Kaplan), Colin Salmon (One), Ryan McCluskey (Mr. Grey), Oscar Pearce (Mr. Red), Indra Ové (Ms. Black), Anna Bolt (Dr. Anna Bolt), Joseph May (Dr. Blue), Robert Tannion (Dr. Brown), Heike Makatsch (Dr. Lisa Addison), Jaymes Butler (Clarence, the Security Guard), Stephen Billington (Mr. White), Fiona Glascott (Ms. Gold), Pasquale Aleardi (J. D. Salinas), Liz May Brice (Medic)

Resident Evil: Apocalypse
(2004)
Sony/Impact/Constantin
Directed by Alexander Witt
Writing Credits: Paul W. S. Anderson
Cast: Milla Jovovich (Alice), Sienna Guillory (Jill Valentine), Oded Fehr (Carlos Olivera), Thomas Kretschmann (Major Cain), Sophie Vavasseur (Angie Ashford), Razaaq Adoti (Peyton Wells), Jared Harris (Dr. Ashford), Mike Epps (L.J.), Sandrine Holt (Terri Morales), Matthew G. Taylor (Nemesis), Zack Ward (Nicholai Sokolov), Iain Glen (Dr. Isaacs), Dave Nichols (Captain Henderson), Stefan Hayes (Yuri Loginova), Geoffrey Pounsett (Mackenzie), Shaun Austin-Olsen (Priest)

The Saga of the Viking Women and Their Voyage to the Waters of the Great Sea Serpent (1957)
AIP/Malibu
Directed by Roger Corman
Writing Credits: Irving Block, Lawrence L. Goldman
Cast: Abby Dalton (Desir), Susan Cabot (Enger), Bradford Jackson (Vedric), June Kenney (Asmild), Richard Devon (Stark, King of the Grimolts), Betsy Jones-Moreland (Thyra), Jonathan Haze (Ottar), Jay Sayer (Senya, Son of Stark), Lynette Bernay (Dagda), Sally Todd (Sanda)

Sailormoon (TV series, 1995–2000)
Dic Enterprises
Directed by Junichi Sato
Created by Naoko Takeuchi

Saint Joan (1957)
UA
Directed by Otto Preminger
Writing Credits: Graham Greene
Based on the play by George Bernard Shaw
Cast: Richard Widmark (The Dauphin Charles VII), Richard Todd (Dunois, Bastard of Orleans), Anton Walbrook (Cauchon), John Gielgud (Warwick), Felix Aylmer (Inquisitor), Archie Duncan (Robert de Baudricourt), Harry Andrews (John de Stogumber), Margot Grahame (Duchesse de la Tremouille), Barry Jones (De Courcelles), Francis De Wolff (La Tremouille), Finlay Currie (Archbishop of Rheims), Victor Maddern (English Soldier), Bernard Miles (Master Executioner), David Oxley (Gilles de Rais), Patrick Barr (Captain La Hire), Sydney Bromley (Baudricourt's Steward), Kenneth Haigh (Brother Martin Ladvenu), David Langton (Captain of Warwick's Guard), Jean Seberg (St. Joan of Arc)

Serenity (2005)
Universal
Directed by Joss Whedon
Writing Credits: Joss Whedon

Cast: Nathan Fillion (Mal), Gina Torres (Zoe), Alan Tudyk (Wash), Morena Baccarin (Inara), Adam Baldwin (Jayne), Jewel Staite (Kaylee), Sean Maher (Simon), Summer Glau (River), Ron Glass (Shepherd)

Sheba, Baby (1975)
AIP
Directed by William Girdler
Writing Credits: William Girdler
Based on a story by David Sheldon
Cast: Pam Grier (Sheba Shayne), Austin Stoker (Brick), D'Urville Martin (Pilot), Rudy Challenger (Andy), Dick Merrifield (Shark), Christopher Joy (Walker), Charles Kissinger (Phil), Charles Broaddus (Hammerhead), Maurice Downs (Killer), Ernest Cooley (Whale), Edward Reece Jr. (Rocker)

Sheena (1984)
Columbia
Directed by John Guillermin
Writing Credits: David Newman, Leslie Stevens, David Newman, Lorenzo Semple Jr.
Based on the comic strip characters created by S. M. Eiger and Will Eisner
Cast: Tanya Roberts (Sheena), Ted Wass (Vic Casey), Donovan Scott (Fletcher ("Fletch")), Elizabeth of Toro (Shaman), France Zobda (Countess Zanda), Trevor Thomas (Prince Otwani), Clifton Jones (King Jabalani), John Forgeham (Colonel Jorgensen), Errol John (Boto), Sylvester Williams (Juka), Bob Sherman (Grizzard), Michael Shannon (Phillip Ames)

Sheena: Queen of the Jungle (1955) (TV)
Nassour
Produced by Edward Nassour
Based on the comic strip characters created by Will Eisner and S. M. Eiger
Cast: Irish McCalla (Sheena), Chris Drake (Bob)

The Silence of the Lambs (1991)
Orion
Directed by Jonathan Demme
Writing Credits: Ted Tally
Based on the novel by Thomas Harris
Cast: Jodie Foster (Clarice Starling), Anthony Hopkins (Dr. Hannibal Lecter), Scott Glenn (Jack Crawford), Anthony Heald (Dr. Frederick Chilton), Ted

Levine (Jame "Buffalo Bill" Gumb), Frankie Faison (Barney Matthews), Kasi Lemmons (Ardelia Mapp), Brooke Smith (Catherine Martin), Paul Lazar (Pilcher), Dan Butler (Roden), Lawrence T. Wrentz (Agent Burroughs), Don Brockett (Friendly Psychopath in Cell), Frank Seals Jr. (Brooding Psychopath in Cell), Stuart Rudin (Miggs), Masha Skorobogatov (Young Clarice Starling), Jeffrie Lane (Clarice's Father), Leib Lensky (Mr. Lang, Storage Manager), George "Red" Schwartz (Mr. Lang's Driver), Jim Roche (TV Evangelist), James B. Howard (Boxing Instructor), Bill Miller (Mr. Brigham), Chuck Aber (Agent Terry), Gene Borkan (Oscar), Pat McNamara (Sheriff Perkins), Tracey Walter (Lamar), Kenneth Utt (Dr. Akin), Adelle Lutz (TV Anchorwoman), Obba Babatundé (TV Anchorman), George Michael (TV Sportscaster), Diane Baker (Sen. Ruth Martin (TN)), Roger Corman (FBI Director Hayden Burke), Ron Vawter (Paul Krendler), Charles Napier (Lieutenant Boyle), Jim Dratfield (Senator Martin's Aide)

Sin City (2005)
Miramax
Directed by Frank Miller, Robert Rodriguez
Writing Credits: Frank Miller, Robert Rodriguez
Cast: Jessica Alba (Nancy Callahan), Rosario Dawson (Gail), Elijah Wood (Kevin), Bruce Willis (John Hartigan), Benicio Del Toro (Jack Rafferty), Michael Clarke Duncan (Manute), Carla Gugino (Lucille), Josh Hartnett (The Salesman), Michael Madsen (Bob), Jaime King (Goldie/Wendy), Brittany Murphy (Shellie), Clive Owen (Dwight), Mickey Rourke (Marv), Nick Stahl (Junior/Yellow Bastard), Marley Shelton (The Customer), Arie Verveen (Murphy), Devon Aoki (Miho), Alexis Bledel (Becky), Chelsea Bulte (Waitress), Jude Ciccolella (Commissioner Liebowitz), Jason Douglas (Hit Man), Penny Drake (Old Town Girl), Lauren-Elaine Edleson (Old Town Girl), Rick Gomez (Mr. Shlubb), Rutger Hauer (Cardinal Roark), Natalie Hess (Old Town Girl), Chris Warner (Bozo #3), Katherine Willis (Nurse)

The Sisterhood (1988)
Image/Media
Directed by Cirio H. Santiago
Writing Credits: Thomas McKelvey Cleaver
Cast: Rebecca Holden (Alee), Chuck Wagner (Mikal), Lynn-Holly Johnson (Marya), Barbara Patrick (Vera (as Barbara Hooper)), Robert Dryer (Lord Barak), Henry Strzalkowski (Jon), David Light (Jev), Jim Moss (Alek)

Sky Captain and the World of Tomorrow (2004)
Paramount/Brooklyn/Riffraff/Natural Nylon/Blue Flower/Filmauro
Directed by Kerry Conran
Writing Credits: Kerry Conran
Cast: Gwyneth Paltrow (Polly Perkins), Jude Law (Sky Captain), Giovanni Ribisi (Dex), Michael Gambon (Editor Paley), Ling Bai (Mysterious Woman), Omid Djalili (Kaji), Laurence Olivier (Dr. Totenkopf), Angelina Jolie (Franky), Trevor Baxter (Dr. Jennings), Julian Curry (Dr. Vargas), Peter Law (Dr. Kessler), Jon Rumney (German Scientist), Khan Bonfils (Creepy), Samta Gyatso (Scary), Louis Hilyer (Executive Officer), Mark Wells (Communications Engineer), James Cash (Uniformed Officer), Tenzin Bhagen (Kalacakra Priest)

Slayers: The Motion Picture (1995)
ADV Films
Directed by Hiroshi Watanabe

Writing Credits: Kazuo Yamazaki
Cast: Megumi Hayashibara (Lina Inverse (voice)), Maria Kawamura (Naga (voice)), Brad Atwell (Additional Voices (voice)), David Bell (Young Rowdy (voice))

Species (1995)
MGM
Directed by Roger Donaldson
Writing Credits: Dennis Feldman
Cast: Ben Kingsley (Xavier Fitch), Michael Madsen (Preston Lennox), Alfred Molina (Dr. Stephen Arden), Forest Whitaker (Dan Smithson, Empath), Marg Helgenberger (Dr. Laura Baker), Natasha Henstridge (Sil), Michelle Williams (Young Sil), Jordan Lund (Aide), Don Fischer (Aide), Scott McKenna (Train Hobo), Virginia Morris (Mother), Jayne Luke (Snack Shop Clerk), David K. Schroeder (German Tourist), David Jensen (Conductor), Esther Scott (Female Conductor), Shirley Prestia (Dr. Victoria Roth, Ph.D.), William Utay (Colleague), David Selburg (Government Man), Herta Ware (Mrs. Morris), Melissa Bickerton (Fitch's Secretary), Lucy Rodriguez (Wedding Dress Saleswoman), Scott Sproule (Team Driver), Stogie Kenyatta (Cop)

Star Trek (TV series, 1966 1969)
Paramount
Created by Gene Roddenberry
Cast: William Shatner (Capt. James T. Kirk), Leonard Nimoy (Lieutenant Commander/Commander Spock), DeForest Kelley (Lt. Cmdr. Leonard H. "Bones" McCoy, M.D.), Grace Lee Whitney (Yeoman Janice Rand (1966–1967)), James Doohan (Lt. Cmdr. Montgomery "Scotty" Scott), George Takei (Lt. Hikaru Sulu), Nichelle Nichols (Lieutenant Uhura), Walter Koenig (Ens. Pavel Chekov (1967–1969)), Majel Barrett (Nurse Christine Chapel)

Star Trek: First Contact (1996)
Paramount
Directed by Jonathan Frakes
Writing Credits: Gene Roddenberry, Brannon Braga, Ronald D. Moore
Based on a story by Ronald D. Moore and Rick Berman
Cast: Patrick Stewart (Capt. Jean-Luc Picard), Jonathan Frakes (Cmdr.

William Riker), Brent Spiner (Lieutenant Commander Data), LeVar Burton (Lt. Cmdr. Geordi La Forge), Michael Dorn (Lieutenant Commander Worf), Gates McFadden (Dr. Beverly Crusher), Marina Sirtis (Counselor Deanna Troi), Alfre Woodard (Lily Sloane), James Cromwell (Dr. Zefram Cochrane), Alice Krige (Borg Queen), Michael Horton (Lieutenant Daniels), Neal McDonough (Lieutenant Hawk), Marnie McPhail (Lieutenant Eiger), Robert Picardo (Emergency Medical Hologram), Dwight Schultz (Lt. Reginald Barclay)

Star Trek V: The Final Frontier (1989)
Paramount
Directed by William Shatner
Writing Credits: Gene Roddenberry, David Loughery
Based on the story by William Shatner, Harve Bennett, and David Loughery
Cast: William Shatner (Capt. James T. Kirk), Leonard Nimoy (Captain Spock), DeForest Kelley (Dr. Leonard "Bones" McCoy), James Doohan (Capt. Montgomery "Scotty" Scott), Walter Koenig (Cmdr. Pavel Chekov), Nichelle Nichols (Commander Uhura), George Takei (Cmdr. Hikaru Sulu), David Warner (St. John Talbot), Laurence Luckinbill (Sybok)

Star Trek IV: The Voyage Home (1986)
Paramount
Directed by Leonard Nimoy
Writing Credits: Gene Roddenberry, Steve Meerson, Peter Krikes, Harve Bennett, Nicholas Meyer
Based on the story by Harve Bennett and Leonard Nimoy
Cast: William Shatner (Adm./Capt. James T. Kirk), Leonard Nimoy (Captain Spock), DeForest Kelley (Dr. Leonard "Bones" McCoy), James Doohan (Capt. Montgomery "Scotty" Scott), George Takei (Cmdr. Hikaru Sulu), Walter Koenig (Cmdr. Pavel Chekov), Nichelle Nichols (Commander Uhura), Jane Wyatt (Amanda), Catherine Hicks (Dr. Gillian Taylor), Mark Lenard (Ambassador Sarek), Robin Curtis (Lieutenant Saavik), Robert Ellenstein (Federation Council President), John Schuck (Klingon Ambassador), Brock Peters (Admiral Cartwright)

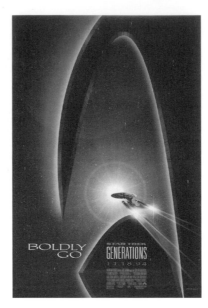

Star Trek: Generations (1994)
Paramount
Directed by David Carson
Writing Credits: Gene Roddenberry, Ronald D. Moore, Brannon Braga
Based on a story by Rick Berman, Ronald D. Moore, Bannon Braga
Cast: Patrick Stewart (Capt. Jean-Luc Picard), Jonathan Frakes (Cmdr. William T. Riker), Brent Spiner (Lieutenant Commander Data), LeVar Burton (Lt. Cmdr. Geordi La Forge), Michael Dorn (Lieutenant Commander Worf), Gates McFadden (Dr. Beverly Crusher), Marina Sirtis (Counselor Deanna Troi), Malcolm McDowell (Dr. Tolian Soran), James Doohan (Capt. Montgomery "Scotty" Scott), Walter Koenig (Pavel Chekov), William Shatner (James T. Kirk), Alan Ruck (Capt. John Harriman), Jacqueline Kim (Ens. Demora Sulu), Jenette Goldstein (Enterprise-B Science Officer), Thomas Kopache (Enterprise-B Communications Officer), Glenn Morshower (Enterprise-B Conn Officer), Tim Russ (Enterprise-B Tactical Lieutenant)

Star Trek: Insurrection (1998)
Paramount
Directed by Jonathan Frakes
Writing Credits: Gene Roddenberry, Michael Piller
Based on a story by Rick Berman and Michael Piller
Cast: Patrick Stewart (Capt. Jean-Luc

Picard), Jonathan Frakes (Cmdr. William T. Riker), Brent Spiner (Lieutenant Commander Data), LeVar Burton (Lt. Cmdr. Geordi La Forge), Michael Dorn (Lieutenant Commander Worf), Gates McFadden (Dr. Beverly Crusher), Marina Sirtis (Counselor Deanna Troi), F. Murray Abraham (Ru'afo), Donna Murphy (Anij), Anthony Zerbe (Vice-Admiral Dougherty), Gregg Henry (Gallatin), Daniel Hugh Kelly (Sojef), Michael Welch (Artim), Mark Deakins (Tournel), Stephanie Niznik (Perim), Michael Horton (Lieutenant Daniels)

Star Trek: The Motion Picture (1979)
Paramount
Directed by Robert Wise
Writing Credits: Harold Livingston, Gene Roddenberry, Leonard Nimoy, William Shatner
Based on a story by Alan Dean Foster
Cast: William Shatner (Adm./Capt. James T. Kirk), Leonard Nimoy (Commander Spock), DeForest Kelley (Dr. Leonard "Bones" McCoy), James Doohan (Cmdr. Montgomery "Scotty" Scott), George Takei (Lt. Cmdr. Hikaru Sulu), Majel Barrett (Dr. Christine Chapel), Walter Koenig (Lt. Pavel Chekov), Nichelle Nichols (Lieutenant Commander Uhura), Persis Khambatta (Lieutenant Ilia), Stephen Collins (Capt./Cmdr. Willard Decker), Grace Lee Whitney (CPO Janice Rand), Mark Lenard (Klingon Captain), Billy Van Zandt (Alien Boy), Roger Aaron Brown (Epsilon Technician), Gary Faga (Airlock Technician), David Gautreaux (Commander Branch)

Star Trek: Nemesis (2002)
Paramount
Directed by Stuart Baird
Writing Credits: Gene Roddenberry, John Logan
Based on a story by John Logan, Rick Berman, and Brent Spiner
Cast: Patrick Stewart (Capt. Jean-Luc Picard), Jonathan Frakes (Cmdr./Capt. William T. Riker), Brent Spiner (Lieutenant Commander Data/B-4), LeVar Burton (Lt. Cmdr. Geordi La Forge), Michael Dorn (Lieutenant Commander Worf), Marina Sirtis (Counselor Deanna Troi), Gates McFadden (Dr. Beverly Crusher), Tom Hardy (Praetor Shinzon), Ron

Perlman (The Reman Viceroy),
Shannon Cochran (Senator Tal'aura),
Dina Meyer (Commander Donatra),
Jude Ciccolella (Commander Suran),
Alan Dale (Praetor Hiren), John Berg
(Senator), Michael Owen (Helm Officer
Branson), Kate Mulgrew (Adm. Kathryn
Janeway), Robertson Dean (Reman
Officer), David Ralphe (Commander),
J. Patrick McCormack (Commander),
Wil Wheaton (Wesley Crusher), Majel
Barrett (Computer Voice (voice))

Star Trek: The Next Generation (TV series, 1987–1994)

Paramount
Created by Gene Roddenberry
Cast: Patrick Stewart (Capt. Jean-Luc
Picard), Jonathan Frakes (Cmdr. William
T. Riker), LeVar Burton (Lt./Lt. Cmdr.
Geordi La Forge), Denise Crosby (Lt.
Tasha Yar (1987–1988)), Michael Dorn
(Lieutenant Worf), Gates McFadden
(Dr. Beverly Crusher (1987–1988,
1989–1994)), Marina Sirtis (Counselor
Deanna Troi), Brent Spiner (Lieutenant
Commander Data/Dr. Noonian Soong/
Lore), Wil Wheaton (Ens. Wesley
Crusher (1987–1990))

Star Trek VI: The Undiscovered Country (1991)

Paramount
Directed by Nicholas Meyer

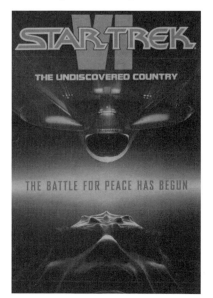

Writing Credits: Gene Roddenberry,
Nicholas Meyer, Denny Martin Flinn
Based on a story by Leonard Nimoy,
Lawrence Konner, and Mark Rosenthal
Cast: William Shatner (Capt. James
T. Kirk), Leonard Nimoy (Captain
Spock), DeForest Kelley (Dr. Leonard
"Bones" McCoy), James Doohan
(Capt. Montgomery "Scotty" Scott),
Walter Koenig (Cmdr. Pavel Chekov),
Nichelle Nichols (Commander Uhura),
George Takei (Capt. Hikaru Sulu), Kim
Cattrall (Lieutenant Valeris), Mark
Lenard (Ambassador Sarek), Grace Lee
Whitney (Cmdr. Janice Rand), Brock
Peters (Admiral Cartwright), Leon
Russom (Starfleet Commander in Chief),
Kurtwood Smith (Federation President),
Christopher Plummer (General Chang),
Rosanna DeSoto (Azetbur), David
Warner (Chancellor Gorkon), John
Schuck (Klingon Ambassador), Michael
Dorn (Colonel Worf), Paul Rossilli
(Brigadier General Kerla)

Star Trek III: The Search for Spock (1984)

Paramount
Directed by Leonard Nimoy
Writing Credits: Gene Roddenberry,
Harve Bennett, Leonard Nimoy
Cast: William Shatner (Adm. James
T. Kirk), Leonard Nimoy (Captain
Spock/Elevator Voice), DeForest Kelley
(Dr. Leonard "Bones" McCoy), James
Doohan (Cmdr./Capt. Montgomery
"Scotty" Scott), George Takei (Cmdr.
Hikaru Sulu), Walter Koenig (Cmdr.
Pavel Chekov), Nichelle Nichols
(Commander Uhura), Merritt Butrick
(Dr. David Marcus), Phil Morris
(Trainee Foster), Scott McGinnis (Mr.
Adventure), Robin Curtis (Lieutenant
Saavik), Robert Hooks (Admiral
Morrow), Carl Steven (Spock (Age 9)),
Vadia Potenza (Spock (Age 13)), Stephen
Manley (Spock (Age 17)), Joe W.
Davis (Spock (Age 25)), Paul Sorenson
(Captain), Cathie Shirriff (Valkris),
Christopher Lloyd (Commander Kruge),
Stephen Liska (Torg)

Star Trek: Voyager (TV series, 1995–2001)

Paramount
Created by Rick Berman, Michael Piller,
Jeri Taylor
Cast: Kate Mulgrew (Capt. Kathryn
Janeway), Robert Beltran (Commander

Chakotay), Roxann Dawson (B'Elanna
Torres), Jennifer Lien (Kes (1995–
1997)), Robert Duncan McNeill
(Thomas "Tom" Paris), Ethan Phillips
(Neelix), Robert Picardo (Emergency
Medical Holographic Program), Tim
Russ (Lieutenant Commander Tuvok),
Jeri Ryan (Seven of Nine (1997–2001)),
Garrett Wang (Ens. Harry Kim)

Star Trek: The Wrath of Khan (1982)

Paramount
Directed by Nicholas Meyer
Writing Credits: Gene Roddenberry,
Jack B. Sowards, Nicholas Meyer
Based on a story by Harve Bennett, Jack
B. Sowards, Samuel A. Peeples
Cast: William Shatner (Adm. James
T. Kirk), Leonard Nimoy (Captain
Spock), DeForest Kelley (Dr. Leonard
"Bones" McCoy), James Doohan
(Cmdr. Montgomery "Scotty" Scott),
Walter Koenig (Pavel Chekov), George
Takei (Hikaru Sulu), Nichelle Nichols
(Commander Uhura), Bibi Besch (Dr.
Carol Marcus), Merritt Butrick (Dr.
David Marcus), Paul Winfield (Capt.
Clark Terrell), Kirstie Alley (Lieutenant
Saavik), Ricardo Montalban (Khan
Noonian Singh), Ike Eisenmann
(Midshipman Peter Preston)

Star Wars: Episode I, The Phantom Menace (1999)

Lucasfilm/20th Century Fox
Directed by George Lucas
Writing Credits: George Lucas
Cast: Liam Neeson (Qui Gon Jinn),
Ewan McGregor (Obi-Wan Kenobi),
Natalie Portman (Queen Padmé
Naberrie Amidala), Jake Lloyd (Anakin
Skywalker), Pernilla August (Shmi
Skywalker), Frank Oz (Yoda (voice)),
Ian McDiarmid (Senator Palpatine/
Darth Sidious), Oliver Ford Davies
(Gov. Sio Bibble), Hugh Quarshie
(Captain Panaka), Ahmed Best (Jar Jar
Binks (voice)), Anthony Daniels (C-
3PO), Kenny Baker (R2-D2), Terence
Stamp (Chancellor Finis Valorum), Brian
Blessed (Boss Nass), Andrew Secombe
(Watto), Ray Park (Darth Maul), Lewis
Macleod (Sebulba (voice)), Steven Spiers
(Captain Tarpals), Silas Carson (Viceroy
Nute Gunray/Ki-Adi-Mundi/Lott Dodd/
Radiant VII Pilot), Ralph Brown (Ric
Olié), Celia Imrie (Fighter Pilot Bravo
5), Benedict Taylor (Fighter Pilot Bravo

2), Karol Cristina da Silva (Rabé), Clarence Smith (Fighter Pilot Bravo 3), Samuel L. Jackson (Mace Windu), Dominic West (Palace Guard), Liz Wilson (Eirtaé), Candice Orwell (Yané), Sofia Coppola (Saché), Keira Knightley (Sabé, Queen's Decoy), Bronagh Gallagher (Radiant VII Captain), John Fensom (TC-14), Greg Proops (Beed (voice)), Scott Capurro (Fode (voice))

Star Wars: Episode II, Attack of the Clones (2002)
Lucasfilm/20th Century Fox
Directed by George Lucas
Writing Credits: George Lucas, Jonathan Hales
Cast: Ewan McGregor (Obi-Wan Kenobi), Natalie Portman (Sen. Padmé Amidala), Hayden Christensen (Anakin Skywalker), Christopher Lee (Count Dooku/Darth Tyranus), Samuel L. Jackson (Mace Windu), Frank Oz (Yoda (voice)), Ian McDiarmid (Supreme Chancellor Palpatine/Darth Sidious), Pernilla August (Shmi Skywalker-Lars), Temuera Morrison (Jango Fett), Daniel Logan (Boba Fett), Jimmy Smits (Sen. Bail Organa), Jack Thompson (Cliegg Lars), Leeanna Walsman (Zam Wesell), Ahmed Best (Jar Jar Binks (voice)), Rose Byrne (Dormé), Oliver Ford Davies (Gov. Sio Bibble), Ron Falk (Dexter

Jettster (voice)), Jay Laga'aia (Captain Typho), Andrew Secombe (Watto (voice)), Anthony Daniels (C-3PO), Silas Carson (Ki-Adi-Mundi/Viceroy Nute Gunray), Ayesha Dharker (Queen Jamillia), Joel Edgerton (Owen Lars), Bonnie Piesse (Beru Whitesun)

Star Wars: Episode III, Revenge of the Sith (2005)
20th Century Fox/Lucasfilm
Directed by George Lucas
Writing Credits: George Lucas
Cast: Ewan McGregor (Obi-Wan/Ben Kenobi), Hayden Christensen (Anakin Skywalker/Lord Darth Vader), Natalie Portman (Senator Amidala/Padmé Naberrie-Skywalker), Ian McDiarmid (Supreme Chancellor/Emperor Palpatine/Darth Sidious), Samuel L. Jackson (Mace Windu), Christopher Lee (Count Dooku/Darth Tyranus), Anthony Daniels (C-3PO), Kenny Baker (R2-D2), Peter Mayhew (Chewbacca), Frank Oz (Yoda (voice)), Jimmy Smits (Sen. Bail Organa), Genevieve O'Reilly (Sen. Mon Mothma), Ahmed Best (Jar Jar Binks), Jay Laga'aia (Captain Typho), Joel Edgerton (Owen Lars), Bonnie Piesse (Beru Whitesun-Lars), Oliver Ford Davies (Gov. Sio Bibble), Temuera Morrison (Commander Cody/Commander Thire/Commander

Bly), Bodie Taylor (Clonetroopers/Stormtroopers), Keisha Castle-Hughes (Queen Apailana), Rebecca Jackson Mendoza (Queen of Alderaan), Bruce Spence (Tion Medon), Kee Chan (Senator Male-Dee), Ling Bai (Sen. Bana Breemu), Warren Owens (Sen. Fang Zar), Rena Owen (Sen. Nee Alavar), Christopher Kirby (Sen. Giddean Danu), Silas Carson (Viceroy Nute Gunray/Ki-Adi-Mundi), Matt Sloan (Plo Koon), Kenji Oates (Saesee Tiin), Ben Cooke (Kit Fisto), Mary Oyaya (Luminara Unduli), Nalini Krishan (Barriss Offee), Mimi Daraphet (Bultar Swan), Orli Shoshan (Shaak Ti), Lily Nyamwasa (Stass Allie), Tux Akindoyeni (Agen Kolar), David Bowers (Vice Chairman Mas Amedda)

Star Wars: Episode IV (1977)
Lucasfilm/20th Century Fox
Directed by George Lucas
Writing Credits: George Lucas
Cast: Mark Hamill (Luke Skywalker), Harrison Ford (Han Solo), Carrie Fisher (Princess Leia Organa), Peter Cushing (Grand Moff Tarkin), Alec Guinness (Ben Obi-Wan Kenobi), Anthony Daniels (C-3PO), Kenny Baker (R2-D2), Peter Mayhew (Chewbacca), David Prowse (Darth Vader), James Earl Jones (Darth Vader (voice)), Phil Brown

A JEDI SHALL NOT KNOW ANGER

NOR HATRED

NOR LOVE

(Uncle Owen), Shelagh Fraser (Aunt Beru), Jack Purvis (Chief Jawa), Alex McCrindle (General Dodonna), Eddie Byrne (General Willard), Drewe Henley (Red Leader)

Star Wars: Episode V, The Empire Strikes Back (1980)
Lucasfilm/20th Century Fox
Directed by Irvin Kershner
Writing Credits: George Lucas, Leigh Brackett, Lawrence Kasdan
Cast: Mark Hamill (Luke Skywalker/Echo Base Announcer), Harrison Ford (Han Solo), Carrie Fisher (Princess Leia Organa), Billy Dee Williams (Lando Calrissian), Anthony Daniels (C-3PO), David Prowse (Darth Vader), Peter Mayhew (Chewbacca), Kenny Baker (R2-D2), Frank Oz (Yoda (voice)), Alec Guinness (Obi-Wan Kenobi), Jeremy Bulloch (Boba Fett), John Hollis (Lobot, Lando's Aide), Jack Purvis (Chief Ugnaught), Des Webb (Wampa (Snow Creature)), Clive Revill (The Emperor (voice)), Kenneth Colley (Captain/Admiral Piett), Julian Glover (General Veers), Michael Sheard (Admiral Ozzel), Michael Culver (Captain Needa)

Star Wars: Episode VI, Return of the Jedi (1983)
Lucasfilm/20th Century Fox
Directed by Richard Marquand
Writing Credits: Lawrence Kasdan, George Lucas, David Webb Peoples
Cast: Mark Hamill (Luke Skywalker),

Harrison Ford (Han Solo), Carrie Fisher (Princess Leia Organa), Billy Dee Williams (Lando Calrissian), Anthony Daniels (C-3PO), Peter Mayhew (Chewbacca), Ian McDiarmid (The Emperor Palpatine), Sebastian Shaw (Anakin Skywalker/Darth Vader's Face), Frank Oz (Yoda (voice)), James Earl Jones (Darth Vader (voice)), David Prowse (Darth Vader), Alec Guinness (Obi-Wan Kenobi), Kenny Baker (R2-D2/Paploo), Michael Pennington (Moff Jerjerrod), Kenneth Colley (Admiral Piett), Michael Carter (Bib Fortuna), Denis Lawson (Wedge Antilles), Timothy M. Rose (Admiral Ackbar), Dermot Crowley (Gen. Crix Madine), Caroline Blakiston (Mon Mothma), Warwick Davis (Wicket), Jeremy Bulloch (Boba Fett)

Stargate: Atlantis (TV series, 2004–)
MGM
Created by Brad Wright, Robert C. Cooper
Cast: Joe Flanigan (Maj./Lt. Col. John Sheppard), Torri Higginson (Dr. Elizabeth Weir), Rachel Luttrell (Teyla Emmagan), Rainbow Francks (Lt. Aiden Ford (2004–2005)), Jason Momoa (Ronon Dex (2005–)), Paul McGillion (Dr. Carson Beckett (2005–)), David Hewlett (Dr. Rodney McKay)

Stargate SG-1 (TV series, 1997–)
MGM
Directed by Mario Azzopardi, Dennis Berry
Writing Credits: Brad Wright, Jonathan Glassner
Cast: Richard Dean Anderson (Gen. Jonathan "Jack" O'Neill), Michael Shanks (Dr. Daniel Jackson), Amanda Tapping (Samantha Carter), Christopher Judge (Teal'c)

Starship Troopers (1997)
Touchstone/Tristar/Big Bug
Directed by Paul Verhoeven
Writing Credits: Edward Neumeier
Based on the book by Robert A. Heinlein
Cast: Casper Van Dien (Johnny Rico), Dina Meyer (Dizzy Flores), Denise Richards (Carmen Ibanez), Jake Busey (Pvt. Ace Levy), Neil

Patrick Harris (Col. Carl Jenkins), Clancy Brown (Career Sergeant Zim), Seth Gilliam (Pvt. Sugar Watkins), Patrick Muldoon (Zander Barcalow), Michael Ironside (Lt. Jean Rasczak), Rue McClanahan (Biology Teacher), Marshall Bell (General Owen), Eric Bruskotter (Breckinridge), Matt Levin (Kitten Smith), Blake Lindsley (Katrina McIntire), Anthony Ruivivar (Shujumi)

Stealth (2005)
Columbia/Original/Phoenix/Ziskin/AGF Talons
Directed by Rob Cohen
Writing Credits: W. D. Richter
Cast: Josh Lucas (Lt. Ben Gannon), Jessica Biel (Kara Wade), Jamie Foxx (Henry Purcell), Sam Shepard (Capt. George Cummings), Richard Roxburgh (Keith Orbit), Joe Morton (Capt. Dick Marshfield), Ian Bliss (Lt. Aaron Shaftsbury), Ebon Moss-Bachrach (Josh Hudson), Michael Denkha (Naval Controller), Rocky Helton (Master at Arms), Clayton Adams (USS Abraham Lincoln Sailor), Maurice Morgan (USS Abraham Lincoln Sailor), Christopher Naismith (USS Abraham Lincoln Sailor), Charles Ndibe (USS Abraham Lincoln Sailor), Nicholas Hammond (Executive Officer)

Stripperella (TV series, 2003)
MTV
Writing Credits: Stan Lee, Kevin Kopelow, Heath Seifert, Steve Holland
Cast: Pamela Anderson (Stripperella (Erotica Jones) (voice)), Dee Bradley Baker (voice), Jon Cryer (voice), Sirena Irwin (Various (voice)), Tom Kenny (Various (voice)), Kid Rock (Stiffy Woods (voice)), Maurice LaMarche (Various (voice)), Vince McMahon (Dirk McMahon (voice))

Supergirl (1984)
Tristar
Directed by Jeannot Szwarc
Writing Credits: David Odell
Cast: Faye Dunaway (Selena), Helen Slater (Kara/Supergirl/Linda Lee), Peter O'Toole (Zaltar), Mia Farrow (Alura), Brenda Vaccaro (Bianca), Peter Cook (Nigel), Simon Ward (Zor-El), Marc McClure (Jimmy Olsen), Hart Bochner (Ethan)

Sweet Sugar (1973)
Dimension Films
Directed by Michel Levesque
Writing Credits: Stephanie Rothman, Don Spencer
Cast: Phyllis Davis, Juan Antillon Baker, Nicholas Baker, Timothy Brown, Antonio Casas Figueroa, Albert Cole, Pamela Collins, Ramón Coll, Laurencio Cordero, Angus Duncan, Ella Edwards

Tank Girl (1995)
MGM/UA/Trilogy
Directed by Rachel Talalay
Writing Credits: Tedi Sarafian
Based on the comic strip by Alan Martin and Jamie Hewlett
Cast: Lori Petty (Tank Girl), Ice-T (T-Saint), Naomi Watts (Jet Girl), Don Harvey (Sergeant Small), Jeff Kober (Booga), Reg E. Cathey (Deetee), Scott Coffey (Donner), Malcolm McDowell (Kesslee), Stacy Linn Ramsower (Sam), Ann Cusack (Sub Girl), Brian Wimmer (Richard), Iggy Pop (Rat Face), Dawn Robinson (Model), Billy L. Sullivan (Max), James Hong (Che'tsai)

Temptation of a Monk (1993)
Golden Harvest
Directed by Clara Law
Writing Credits: Eddie Ling-Ching Fong, Lillian Lee
Cast: Joan Chen (Princess Scarlet/Violet), Michael Lee (The Abbot), Lisa Lu (Shi's Mother), Hsing-kuo Wu (Gen. Shi Yan-sheng), Fengyi Zhang (Gen. Huo Da)

Terminal Island (1973)
Dimension
Directed by Stephanie Rothman
Writing Credits: James Barnett, Stephanie Rothman, Charles S. Swartz
Cast: Don Marshall (A.J.), Phyllis Davis (Joy), Ena Hartman (Carmen), Marta Kristen (Lee Phillips), Barbara Leigh (Bunny), Randy Boone (Easy), Sean Kenney (Bobby), Tom Selleck (Dr. Milford), Roger E. Mosley (Monk), Geoffrey Deuel (Chino), Ford Clay (Cornell), Jo Morrow (Newswoman), Clyde Ventura (Dylan), Frank Christi (Teale)

The Terminator (1984)
Orion/Hemdale/Euro
Directed by James Cameron
Writing Credits: James Cameron, Gale Anne Hurd, William Wisher Jr.
Based on the story by Harlan Ellison
Cast: Arnold Schwarzenegger (The Terminator), Michael Biehn (Kyle Reese), Linda Hamilton (Sarah Connor), Paul Winfield (Lt. Ed Traxler), Lance Henriksen (Detective Vukovich), Bess Motta (Ginger Ventura), Earl Boen (Dr. Peter Silberman), Rick Rossovich (Matt Buchanan), Dick Miller (Pawnshop Clerk), Shawn Schepps (Nancy), Bruce M. Kerner (Desk Sergeant), Franco Columbu (Future Terminator)

Terminator 2: Judgment Day (1991)
Carolco/Lightstorm/Pacific Western
Directed by James Cameron
Writing Credits: James Cameron, William Wisher Jr.
Based on stories by Harlan Ellison
Cast: Arnold Schwarzenegger (The Terminator (T-800 Model 101)), Linda Hamilton (Sarah Connor), Edward Furlong (John Connor), Robert Patrick (T-1000), Earl Boen (Dr. Peter Silberman), Joe Morton (Dr. Miles Bennett Dyson), S. Epatha Merkerson (Tarissa Dyson), Castulo Guerra (Enrique Salceda), Danny Cooksey (Tim), Jenette Goldstein (Janelle Voight), Xander Berkeley (Todd Voight), Leslie Hamilton Gearren (T-1000 Sarah), Ken Gibbel (Douglas), Robert Winley (Cigar-Smoking Biker), Peter Schrum (Lloyd), Shane Wilder (Trucker), Michael Edwards (Old John Connor)

Terminator 3: Rise of the Machines (2003)
Warner Bros./IMF/Mostow-Lieberman
Directed by Jonathan Mostow
Writing Credits: John D. Brancato, Michael Ferris
Based on a story by Tedi Sarafian, James Cameron, Gale Anne Hurd, Harlan Ellison
Cast: Arnold Schwarzenegger (The Terminator), Nick Stahl (John Connor), Claire Danes (Kate Brewster), Kristanna Loken (T-X), David Andrews (Robert Brewster), Mark Famiglietti (Scott Petersen), Earl Boen (Dr. Peter Silberman), Moira Harris (Betsy), Chopper Bernet (Chief Engineer), Christopher Lawford (Brewster's Aide), Carolyn Hennesy (Rich Woman)

Thelma & Louise (1991)
MGM/Pathe
Directed by Ridley Scott
Writing Credits: Callie Khouri
Cast: Susan Sarandon (Louise Elizabeth Sawyer), Geena Davis (Thelma Dickerson), Harvey Keitel (Hal), Michael Madsen (Jimmy), Christopher McDonald (Darryl Dickerson), Stephen Tobolowsky (Max), Brad Pitt (J.D.), Timothy Carhart (Harlan), Lucinda Jenney (Lena, Waitress), Jason Beghe (State Trooper), Marco St. John (Truck Driver), Sonny Carl Davis (Albert), Ken Swofford (Major)

KATE BECKINSALE   SCOTT SPEEDMAN

AN IMMORTAL BATTLE
FOR SUPREMACY.

UNDERWORLD

EnterTheUnderworld.com

A Touch of Zen (1969)

Union/Lian Bang
Directed by King Hu
Writing Credits: King Hu, Songling Pu
Cast: Billy Chan, Ping-Yu Chang, Roy Chiao, Shih Chun, Hsue Han, Yin-Chieh Han, Feng Hsu, Ching-Ying Lam, Tien Miao, Peng Tien, Cien Tsao, Pai Ying

Transporter 2 (2005)

20th Century Fox
Directed by Louis Leterrier
Writing Credits: Luc Besson, Robert

Mark Kamen
Cast: Jason Statham (Frank Martin), Alessandro Gassman (Gianni), Amber Valletta (Audrey Billings), Kate Nauta (Lola), Matthew Modine (Mr. Billings), Jason Flemyng (Dimitri), Keith David (Stappleton), Hunter Clary (Jack Billings), Shannon Briggs (Max), François Berléand (Tarconi), Raymond Tong (Rastaman), George Kapetan (Dr. Sonovitch), Jeff Chase (Vasily), Gregg Weiner (Tipov), Gregg Davis (Techie at Billings)

Tru Calling (TV series, 2003–2005)

20th Century Fox
Created by Jon Harmon Feldman
Credited Cast: Eliza Dushku (Tru Davies), Shawn Reaves (Harrison Davies), Zach Galifianakis (Davis), A. J. Cook (Lindsay Walker (2003–2004)), Jessica Collins (Meredith Davies (2003–2004)), Benjamín Benítez (Gardez (2003–2004)), Matthew Bomer (Luc (2003–2004)), Jason Priestley (Jack Harper (2004–2005))

2 Fast 2 Furious (2003)

Universal/Original/Moritz
Directed by John Singleton   *Writing Credits:* Michael Brandt, Derek Haas Based on a story by Gary Scott Thompson
Cast: Paul Walker (Brian O'Conner), Tyrese (Roman Pearce), Eva Mendes (Monica Fuentes), Cole Hauser (Carter Verone), Ludacris (Tej), Thom Barry (Agent Bilkins), James Remar (Agent Markham), Devon Aoki (Suki)

Underworld (2003)

Lakeshore/Subterranean
Directed by Len Wiseman
Writing Credits: Danny McBride Based on the story by Kevin Grevioux, Len Wiseman
Cast: Kate Beckinsale (Selene), Scott Speedman (Michael Corvin), Michael Sheen (Lucian), Shane Brolly (Kraven), Bill Nighy (Viktor), Erwin Leder (Singe), Sophia Myles (Erika), Robbie Gee (Kahn), Wentworth Miller (Dr. Adam Lockwood), Kevin Grevioux (Raze), Zita Görög (Amelia), Dennis J. Kozeluh (Dignitary), Scott McElroy (Soren), Todd Schneider (Trix)

Underworld Evolution (2006)

Lakeshore/Screen Gems
Directed by Len Wiseman
Writing Credits: Danny McBride Based on the story by Len Wiseman, Kevin Grevioux
Cast: Kate Beckinsale (Selene), Scott Speedman (Michael Corvin), Bill Nighy (Viktor), Shane Brolly (Kraven), Michael Sheen (Lucian), Kurt Carley (Lycan), Julius Chapple (Cleaner), Tony Curran (Marcus), Zita Görög (Amelia), Alexander Grant (Lead Police

Officer), Derek Jacobi (Alexander Corvinus), Steven Mackintosh (Tanis), Scott McElroy (Soren), James Melody (Pimp), Dany Papineau (Death Dealer #1), Sean Rogerson (Death Dealer #2), Brian Steele (William), Christopher R. Sumpton (Lycan), Georgianna Tarjan (Adr)

Van Helsing (2004)
Carpathian/Universal/Sommers
Directed by Stephen Sommers
Writing Credits: Stephen Sommers
Cast: Hugh Jackman (Van Helsing), Kate Beckinsale (Anna Valerious), Richard Roxburgh (Count Vladislaus Dracula), David Wenham (Carl), Shuler Hensley (Frankenstein's Monster), Elena Anaya (Aleera), Will Kemp (Velkan), Kevin J. O'Connor (Igor), Alun Armstrong (Cardinal Jinette), Silvia Colloca (Verona), Josie Maran (Marishka), Tom Fisher (Top Hat), Samuel West (Dr. Victor Frankenstein), Robbie Coltrane (Mr. Hyde), Stephen Fisher (Dr. Jekyll)

Veronica Mars (TV series, 2004–)
Warner Bros.
Created by Rob Thomas
Cast: Kristen Bell (Veronica Mars), Percy Daggs III (Wallace Fennel), Teddy Dunn (Duncan Kane), Jason Dohring (Logan Echolls)

The Viking Queen (1967)
Hammer Films
Directed by Don Chaffey
Writing Credits: Clarke Reynolds, John Temple-Smith
Cast: Don Murray (Justinian), Carita (Salina), Donald Houston (Maelgan), Andrew Keir (Octavian), Adrienne Corri (Beatrice), Niall MacGinnis (Tiberian), Wilfrid Lawson (King Priam), Nicola Pagett (Talia), Percy Herbert (Catus), Patrick Troughton (Tristram), Sean Caffrey (Fergus), Denis Shaw (Osiris)

The Warrior's Husband (1933)
Fox
Directed by Walter Lang
Writing Credits: Walter Lang, Sonya Levien, Ralph Spence
Based on the play by Julian Thompson
Cast: Elissa Landi (Antiope), David Manners (Theseus), Ernest Truex (Sapiens)

Witchblade (TV series, 2000–2002)
Warner Bros.
Directed by Ralph Hemecker
Writing Credits: J. D. Zeik
Based on the comic book by Marc Silvestri
Cast: Yancy Butler (Sara Pezzini), Anthony Cistaro (Kenneth Irons), Conrad Dunn (Gallo), David Chokachi (Jake McCartey), Kenneth Welsh (Joe Siri), Will Yun Lee (Danny Woo), Eric Etebari (Ian Nottingham)

Wonder Woman (1974)
WB/ABC
Directed by Vincent McEveety
Writing Credits: Margaret Armen, John D. F. Black, William M. Marston
Cast: Cathy Lee Crosby (Wonder Woman/Diana Prince), Kaz Garas (Steve Trevor), Ricardo Montalban (Abner Smith), Andrew Prine (George Calvin), Anitra Ford (Ahnjayla), Charlene Holt (Hippolyte), Robert Porter (Joe), Jordan Rhodes (Bob)

Wonder Woman (TV series, 1976–1979)
ABC/Warner
Created by William M. Marston
Cast: Lynda Carter (Wonder Woman

(Princess Diana aka Diana Prince)), Lyle Waggoner (Steve Trevor)

Xena: Warrior Princess (TV series, 1995–2001)
MCA/Universal
Created by John Schulian, Robert G. Tapert
Cast: Lucy Lawless (Xena), Renée O'Connor (Gabrielle), Ted Raimi (Joxer (1996–2001)), Adrienne Wilkinson (Livia/Eve (2000–2001)), Hudson Leick (Callisto (1996–2000))

The X-Files (TV series, 1993–2002)
20th Century Fox
Created by Chris Carter
Cast: David Duchovny (Fox Mulder (1993–2001, 2002)), Gillian Anderson (Dana Scully), Robert Patrick (John Doggett (2000–2002)), Annabeth Gish (Monica Reyes (2001–2002)), Mitch Pileggi (Walter Skinner (1994–2002)), William B. Davis (Cigarette-Smoking Man/C. G. B. Spender)

The X-Files (1998)
20th Century Fox
Directed by Rob Bowman
Writing Credits: Chris Carter
Based on a story by Frank Spotnitz
Cast: David Duchovny (Special Agent Fox Mulder), Gillian Anderson (Special Agent Dana Scully), John Neville (The Well-Manicured Man), William B. Davis (The Cigarette-Smoking Man/C. G. B. Spender), Martin Landau (Dr. Alvin Kurtzweil), Mitch Pileggi (Asst. Director Walter Skinner), Jeffrey DeMunn (Dr. Ben Bronschweig), Blythe Danner (Jana Cassidy), Terry O'Quinn (Darius Michaud), Armin Mueller-Stahl (Conrad Strughold), Lucas Black (Stevie)

X-Men (2000)
20th Century Fox/Bad Hat Harry/Marvel/Genetics/Springwood/Donner/Shuler
Directed by Bryan Singer
Writing Credits: David Hayter
Based on the story by Bryan Singer and Tom DeSanto
Cast: Hugh Jackman (Logan/Wolverine), Patrick Stewart (Professor Xavier), Ian McKellen (Magneto), Famke Janssen (Jean Grey), James Marsden (Cyclops), Halle Berry (Storm), Anna Paquin

(Rogue), Tyler Mane (Sabretooth), Ray Park (Toad), Rebecca Romijn-Stamos (Mystique), Bruce Davison (Senator Kelly), Matthew Sharp (Henry Gyrich), Brett Morris (Young Magneto), Rhona Shekter (Magneto's Mother), Kenneth McGregor (Magneto's Father), Shawn Roberts (Rogue's Boyfriend), Donna Goodhand (Rogue's Mother), John Nelles (Rogue's Father)

X-Men 3 (2006)

20th Century Fox
Directed by Brett Ratner
Writing Credits: Zak Penn
Cast: Shohreh Aghdashloo (Dr. Kavita Rao), Shawn Ashmore (Bobby Drake/ Iceman), Halle Berry (Ororo Munroe/ Storm), Cayden Boyd (Young Warren Worthington), Cameron Bright (Leech), Daniel Cudmore (Peter Rasputin/ Colossus), Bill Duke (Bolivar Trask), Ben Foster (Warren Worthington/Angel), Kelsey Grammer (Hank McCoy/Beast), Bryce Hodgson (Arite), Hugh Jackman (Logan/Wolverine), Famke Janssen (Jean Grey/Phoenix), Vinnie Jones (Cain Marko/Juggernaut), Shauna Kain (Theresa Rourke/Siryn), James Marsden (Scott Summers/Cyclops), Ian McKellen (Eric Lensherr/Magneto), Michael Murphy (Warren Worthington Sr.), Ellen Page (Kitty Pryde/Shadowcat), Anna Paquin (Rogue), Luke Pohl (X-Kid), Haley Ramm (Young Jean), Rebecca Romijn (Mystique), Aaron Stanford (John Allerdyce/Pyro), Patrick Stewart (Prof. Charles Xavier), Connor

Widdows (Jones), Olivia Williams (Dr. Moira MacTaggert)

X2: X-Men United (2003)

20th Century Fox/Bad Hat Harry/ Marvel/Donner/Shuler
Directed by Bryan Singer
Writing Credits: Michael Dougherty, Dan Harris, David Hayter
Based on the story by Bryan Singer and Zak Penn
Cast: Patrick Stewart (Prof. Charles Xavier), Hugh Jackman (Logan/ Wolverine), Ian McKellen (Eric Lensherr/Magneto), Halle Berry (Ororo Munroe/Storm), Famke Janssen (Jean Grey), James Marsden (Scott Summers/ Cyclops), Anna Paquin (Rogue), Rebecca Romijn-Stamos (Mystique), Brian Cox (William Stryker), Alan Cumming (Kurt Wagner/Nightcrawler), Bruce Davison (Senator Kelly), Aaron Stanford (John Allerdyce/Pyro), Shawn Ashmore (Bobby Drake/Iceman), Kelly Hu (Yuriko Oyama/Deathstrike), Katie Stuart (Kitty Pryde), Kea Wong (Jubilee), Cotter Smith (President McKenna), Chiara Zanni (White House Tour Guide), Jackie A. Greenbank (President's Secretary), Michael Soltis (White House Checkpoint Agent)

Timeline

1914 *Judith of Bethulia*
1927 *Metropolis*
1935 *Annie Oakley*
1938 *Nancy Drew*
1941 *Jungle Girl*
1942 *Cat People*
1944 *Double Indemnity*
1947 *Queen of the Amazons*
1948 *Joan of Arc*
1951 *Anne of the Indies*
1953 *Cat-Women of the Moon*
1955 *Sheena, Queen of the Jungle* (TV)
1956 *The Gunslinger*
1957 *Forty Guns*
1957 *Love Slaves of the Amazon*
1957 *Saga of the Viking Women*
1957 *Saint Joan*
1958 *Attack of the 50 Foot Woman*
1958 *Queen of Outer Space*
1960 *Colossus and the Amazon Queen*
1961 *The Avengers* (TV)
1964 *Lana, Queen of the Amazon*
1964 *The Naked Kiss*
1965 *The Big Valley* (TV)
1965 *Faster, Pussycat! Kill! Kill!*
1966 *Batman* (TV)
1966 *The Girl from U.N.C.L.E.*
1966 *Modesty Blaise*
1966 *One Million Years B.C.*
1966 *Prehistoric Women*
1966 *Star Trek* (TV)
1967 *Prehistoric Women*
1967 *The Viking Queen*
1968 *Barbarella*
1968 *The Bride Wore Black*
1969 *Crimson Bat*
1969 *Pippi Longstocking*

1969 *Touch of Zen*
1971 *Hannie Caulder*
1971 *Invincible Eight*
1972 *Hapkido*
1972 *Kansas City Bomber*
1973 *Cleopatra Jones*
1973 *Coffy*
1973 *Enter the Dragon*
1973 *Lady Snowblood*
1973 *Sweet Sugar*
1973 *Terminal Island*
1974 *The Arena*
1974 *Foxy Brown*
1974 *Police Woman* (TV)
1974 *Wonder Woman* (TV)
1975 *Amazons Against Supermen*
1975 *Isis* (TV)
1975 *Kilma, Queen of the Amazons*
1975 *Sheba, Baby*
1975–1977 *Ilsa* series
1976 *The Bionic Woman* (TV)
1976 *Charlie's Angels* (TV)
1977–1983 *Star Wars IV, V, VI*
1978 *I Spit on Your Grave*
1978 *Jana of the Jungle*
1979–1997 *Alien* series
1979–2002 *Star Trek* series
1980 *City of Women*
1981 *Ms. 45*
1982 *Blade Runner*
1982 *Conan the Barbarian*
1982 *Remington Steele* (TV)
1984 *Conan the Destroyer*
1984 *Sheena*
1984 *Supergirl*
1984, 1991 *The Terminator 1* and *2*
1985 Red Sonja

1986 *Millionaire's Express*

1987 *Amazon Women on the Moon*

1987 *Angel*

1987 *Star Trek: The Next Generation* (TV)

1988 *Sisterhood*

1988, 1989 *In the Line of Duty 3* and *4*

1989 *The Blood of Heroes*

1990 *La Femme Nikita*

1991 *The Silence of the Lambs*

1991 *Thelma and Louise*

1992 *Basic Instinct*

1992 *Batman Returns*

1992 *Buffy the Vampire Slayer*

1992 *Innocent Blood*

1992 *Naked Killer*

1993 *Attack of the 50 Foot Woman*

1993 *Cyborg 2*

1993 *Heroic Trio*

1993 *Point of No Return*

1993 *Temptation of a Monk*

1994 *Bad Girls*

1994 *The Crow*

1994 *The Professional: Leon*

1995 *Black Scorpion* (TV)

1995 *Ghost in the Shell*

1995 *Mortal Kombat*

1995 *The Quick and the Dead*

1995 *Sailormoon* (animated)

1995 *Species*

1995 *Tank Girl*

1995 *Voyager* (TV)

1995 *Xena* (TV)

1996 *Barb Wire*

1996 *Foxfire*

1996 *Long Kiss Goodnight*

1997 *Armitage III: Poly Matrix* (animated)

1997 *Batman and Robin*

1997 *Buffy the Vampire Slayer* (TV)

1997 *Earth: Final Conflict* (TV)

1997 *La Femme Nikita* (TV)

1997 *The Fifth Element*

1997 *G.I. Jane*

1997 *Princess Mononoke*

1997 *Stargate SG-1* (TV)

1997 *Starship Troopers*

1998 *The Avengers*

1998 *Charmed* (TV)

1998 *Mulan*

1998 *Powerpuff Girls* (TV)

1999 *Angel* (TV)

1999 *Audition*

1999 *The Bone Collector*

1999 *Joan of Arc*

1999 *The Messenger*

1999 *Relic Hunter* (TV)

1999–2003 *Matrix* series

1999–2005 *Star Wars 1, 2, 3*

2000 *Andromeda* (TV)

2000 *Battle Royale*

2000 *Cleopatra 2525*

2000 *Crouching Tiger, Hidden Dragon*

2000 *Dark Angel* (TV)

2000 *Dungeons and Dragons*

2000 *Girlfight*

2000 *Jason and the Argonauts*

2000 *Witchblade* (TV)

2000, 2003 *Charlie's Angels* series

2000, 2003, 2006   *X-Men* series

2001 *Alias* (TV)

2001 *Black Scorpion* (TV)

2001 *The Breed*

2001 *Enterprise* (TV)

2001 *Princess of Thieves*

2001, 2003 *Lara Croft* series

2001–2003 *Lord of the Rings*

2001–2005 *Harry Potter* series

2002 *Birds of Prey* (TV)

2002 *Hero*

2002 *The League of Extraordinary Gentlemen*

2002 *Naked Weapon*

2002, 2004 *Resident Evil* series

2003 *Azumi*

2003 *Battlestar Galactica* (TV)

2003 *Boudica*

2003 *Daredevil*

2003 *Joan of Arcadia* (TV)

2003 *Pirates of the Caribbean*

2003 *T3*

2003 *Tru Calling* (TV)

2003 *2 Fast 2 Furious*

2003, 2004 *Kill Bill 1* and *2*

2004 *Blade: Trinity*

2004 *Catwoman*

2004 *Chronicles of Riddick*

2004 *D.E.B.S.*

2004 *House of Flying Daggers*

2004 *King Arthur*

2004 *Kung Fu Hustle*

2004 *Million Dollar Baby*

2004 *Sky Captain and the World of Tomorrow*

2004 *Stargate Atlantis* (TV)

2004 *Veronica Mars* (TV)

2005 *Aeon Flux*

2005 *The Brothers Grimm*

2005 *Domino*

2005 *Elektra*

2005 *Fantastic Four*

2005 *Mr. and Mrs. Smith*

2005 *Serenity*

2005 *Sin City*

2005 *Stealth*

2005 *Transporter 2*

Major Warrior Woman Movies and Television Series

Aeon Flux   Charlize Theron

Alias   Jennifer Garner

Alien series   Sigourney Weaver

Amazon Women on the Moon   Lana Clarkson

Amazons Against Supermen   Magda Konopka

Andromeda (TV)   Lexa Doig

Angel (TV)   Charisma Carpenter, Amy Acker

Angel   Moon Lee

Anne of the Indies   Jean Peters

Annie Oakley   Barbara Stanwyck

Arena   Pam Grier, Margaret Markov

Attack of the 50 Foot Woman   Allison Hayes

Attack of the 50 Foot Woman   Daryl Hannah

Audition   Yamazaki Asami

Avengers (The) (TV)   Diana Rigg

Avengers (The)   Uma Thurman

Azumi   Aya Ueto

Bad Girls   Drew Barrymore, Andie MacDowell, Mary Stuart Masterson, Madeleine Stowe

Barb Wire   Pamela Anderson

Barbarella   Jane Fonda

Basic Instinct   Sharon Stone

Battle Royale   Chiaki Kuriyama

Battlestar Galactica (TV)   Grace Park, Katee Sackhoff

Batman (TV)   Julie Newmar, Eartha Kitt, Yvonne Craig, Lee Meriwether

Batman and Robin   Uma Thurman, Alicia Silverstone

Batman Returns   Michelle Pfeiffer

Big Valley (TV)   Barbara Stanwyck

Bionic Woman (TV)   Lindsay Wagner

Birds of Prey (TV)   Ashley Scott, Dina Meyer

Black Scorpion (TV)   Joan Severance, Michelle Lintel

Blade Runner   Daryl Hannah

Blade: Trinity   Jessica Biel

Blonde Fury   Cynthia Rothrock

Blood of the Heroes   Joan Chen

Bone Collector (The)   Angelina Jolie

Breed (The)   Bai Ling

Bride Wore Black (The)   Jeanne Moreau

Brothers Grimm (The)   Monica Bellucci, Lena Headey

Buffy the Vampire Slayer   Kristy Swanson

Buffy the Vampire Slayer (TV)   Sarah Michelle Gellar, Alyson Hannigan, Charisma Carpenter, Eliza Dushku

Cat People   Simone Simon

Catwoman   Halle Berry, Sharon Stone

Cat-Women of the Moon

Charlie's Angels series   Lucy Liu, Demi Moore, Cameron Diaz, Drew Barrymore

Charlie's Angels (TV)   Jaclyn Smith, Farrah Fawcett, Cheryl Ladd, Tanya Roberts, Kate Jackson

Charmed (TV)   Shannen Doherty, Alyssa Milano, Holly Marie Combs, Rose McGowan

Cherry 2000   Melanie Griffith

Chronicles of Riddick   Alexa Davalos

City of Women   Bernice Stegers

Cleopatra Jones   Tamara Dobson

Cleopatra 2525 (TV)   Gina Torres, Jennifer Sky, Victoria Pratt

Coffy   Pam Grier

Colossus and the Amazon Queen   Dorian
    Gray

Conan the Barbarian   Sandahl Bergman

Conan the Destroyer   Grace Jones

Crimson Bat   Yoki Matsuyama

Crouching Tiger   Zhang Ziyi, Michelle
    Yeoh, Cheng Pei-Pei

Crow   Bai Ling

Cyborg 2   Angelina Jolie

Daredevil   Jennifer Garner

Dark Angel   Jessica Alba, Ashley Scott

D.E.B.S.   Devon Aoki

Domino   Keira Knightley

Double Indemnity   Barbara Stanwyck

Dungeons and Dragons   Thora Birch

Elektra   Jennifer Garner

Enter the Dragon   Angela Mao

Enterprise (TV)   Jolene Blalock

Fantastic Four   Jessica Alba

Faster, Pussycat! Kill! Kill!   Tura Santana

Femme Nikita   Annie Parillaud

Femme Nikita (TV)   Peta Wilson

Fifth Element (The)   Milla Jovovich

Forty Guns   Barbara Stanwyck

Foxfire   Angelina Jolie

Foxy Brown   Pam Grier

Ghost in the Shell (animated)

G.I. Jane   Demi Moore

Girlfight   Michelle Rodriguez

Gunslinger   Beverly Garland, Allison Hayes

Hannibal   Julianne Moore

Hannie Caulder   Raquel Welch

Hapkido   Angela Mao

Harry Potter series   Emma Watson

Hero   Zhang Ziyi, Maggie Cheung

Heroic Trio   Maggie Cheung, Anita Mui,
    Michelle Yeoh

House of Flying Daggers   Zhang Ziyi

I Spit on Your Grave   Camille Keaton

Ilsa series   Dyanne Thorne

In the Line of Duty series   Cynthia Khan,
    Michiko Nishiwaki

Innocent Blood   Anne Parillaud

Invincible Eight   Angela Mao

Isis (TV)   Joanna Cameron

Jana of the Jungle (animated)

Jason and the Argonauts   Jolene Blalock

Joan of Arc   Ingrid Bergman

Joan of Arc   Lee Lee Sobieski

Joan of Arcadia (TV)   Amber Tamblyn

Judith of Bethulia   Blanche Sweet

Jungle Girl   Frances Gifford

Kansas City Bomber   Raquel Welch

Kill Bill   Uma Thurman, Lucy Liu, Daryl
    Hannah, Vivica A. Fox, Chiaki Kuriyama

Kilma, Queen of the Amazons   Blanca
    Estrada

King Arthur   Keira Knightley

Kung Fu Hustle   Qiu Yuen

Lady Snowblood   Kaji Meiko

Lana, Queen of the Amazon   Catherine
    Schell

Lara Croft series   Angelina Jolie

League of Extraordinary Gentlemen (The)
    Peta Wilson

Long Kiss Goodnight (The)   Geena Davis

Lord of the Rings (The)   Liv Tyler,
    Miranda Otto

Love Slaves of the Amazon

Matrix series   Carrie-Anne Moss, Jada
    Pinkett, Monica Bellucci
Messenger (The)   Milla Jovovich
Metropolis   Brigitte Helm
Million Dollar Baby   Hilary Swank
Millionaire's Express   Yukari Oshima
Modesty Blaise   Monica Vitti
Mork vs. the Necrotons (TV)   Raquel
    Welch
Mortal Kombat   Bridgette Wilson
Mr. and Mrs. Smith   Angelina Jolie
Ms. 45   Zoe Tamerlis-Lund
Mulan (animated)

Naked Killer   Chingmy Yau, Carrie Ng
Naked Kiss (The)   Constance Towers
Naked Weapon   Maggie Q
Nancy Drew series   Bonita Granville

One Million Years B.C.   Raquel Welch

Pippi Longstocking   Inger Nilsson
Pirates of the Caribbean   Kiera Knightley
Point of No Return   Bridget Fonda
Police Woman (TV)   Angie Dickinson
Prehistoric Women   Martine Beswick
Princess of Thieves   Kiera Knightley
Professional (The)   Natalie Portman

Queen of Outer Space   Laurie Mitchell
Queen of the Amazons   Amira Moustafa
Quick and the Dead (The)   Sharon Stone

Red Sonja   Brigitte Nielsen, Sandahl
    Bergman
Relic Hunter (TV)   Tia Carrere
Remington Steele (TV)   Stephanie Zimbalist

Resident Evil series   Milla Jovovich,
    Michelle Rodriguez

Saga of the Viking Women   Abby Dalton,
    Susan Cabot
Sailormoon (animated)
Saint Joan   Jean Seberg
Serenity   Gina Torres
Sheba, Baby   Pam Grier
Sheena   Tanya Roberts
Sheena (TV)   Irish McCalla
Silence of the Lambs (The)   Jodie Foster
Sin City   Rosario Dawson, Jessica Alba,
    Devon Aoki
Sisterhood (The)   Lynn-Holly Johnson
Sky Captain and the World of Tomorrow
    Bai Ling, Angelina Jolie
Species   Natasha Henstridge
Star Trek (TV and movies)   Nichelle
    Nichols
Star Trek: Next Generation (TV)   Denise
    Crosby
Star Wars series   Carrie Fisher, Natalie
    Portman
Stargate Atlantis (TV)   Rachel Luttrell
Stargate SG-1(TV)   Amanda Tapping
Starship Troopers   Dina Meyer, Denise
    Richards
Stealth   Jessica Biel
Supergirl   Helen Slater
Sweet Sugar   Phyllis Davis

Tank Girl   Lori Petty
Temptation of a Monk   Joan Chen
Terminal Island   Phyllis Davis
Terminator 1 and 2   Linda Hamilton
Thelma and Louise   Geena Davis and Susan
    Sarandon
Touch of Zen   Feng Hsu

Transporter 2   Kate Nauta
Tru Calling   Eliza Dushku
T3   Kristanna Loken
2 Fast 2 Furious   Devon Aoki

Underworld series   Kate Beckinsale

Van Helsing   Kate Beckinsale
Veronica Mars (TV)   Kristen Bell
Viking Queen (The)   Carita
Voyager (TV)   Jeri Ryan, Kate Mulgrew,
    Roxann Dawson
Witchblade (TV)   Yancy Butler
Wonder Woman   Cathy Lee Crosby
Wonder Woman (TV)   Lynda Carter

Xena (TV)   Lucy Lawless, Renee O'Connor,
    Hudson Leick
X-Files (TV and movie)   Gillian Anderson
X-Men series   Rebecca Romjin, Halle
    Berry, Anna Paquin, Famke Janssen, Kelly
    Hu

Selected Bibliography

Bader, Michael J. *Arousal: The Secret Logic of Sexual Fantasies*. New York: St. Martin's Press, 2002.

Baumgardner, Jennifer and Richards, Amy. *Manifesta: Young Women, Feminism, and the Future*. New York: Farrar, Straus, Giroux, 2000.

ComicBooks.com—The History of Comic Books. 2005. http://www.collectortimes.com/~comichistory/

Cooper, J. C. *Dictionary of Symbolic and Mythological Animals*. New York: Thorsons, 1995.

Creed, Barbara. *The Monstrous-Feminine: Film, Feminism, Psychoanalysis*. London: Routledge, 1993.

Davis-Kimball, Jeannine with Mona Behan. *Warrior Women: An Archaeologist's Search for History's Hidden Heroines*. New York: Warner Books, 2003.

Delinksi, Barbara. *Uplift: Secrets from the Sisterhood of Breast Cancer Survivors*. Rev. ed. New York: Washington Square Press, 2003.

Eby, Douglas. "Warrior Women on Screen." *Talent Development Resources*. http://www.talentdevelop.com/wwos.html

Eisner, Will and Miller, Frank. *Eisner/Miller*. New York: Dark Horse, 2005.

Faludi, Susan. *Backlash: The Undeclared War Against American Women*. New York: Doubleday, 1991.

Gilman, Charlotte Perkins. *Herland*. New York: Dover, 1998.

Grant, Barry K. *The Dread of Difference: Gender and the Horror Film*. Texas: University of Texas Press, 1996.

Greer, Germaine. *The Female Eunuch*. New York: Farrar, Straus, Giroux, 2002.

Haskell, Molly. *Holding My Own in No Man's Land: Women and Men and Film and Feminists*. Oxford: Oxford University Press, 1997.

Inness, Sherrie A. *Tough Girls: Women Warriors and Wonder Women in Popular Culture*. Philadelphia: University of Pennsylvania Press, 1999.

Isaacs, Susan. *Brave Dames and Wimpettes*. New York: Ballantine, 1999.

Johnson, Merri Lisa. *Jane Sexes It Up: True Confessions of Feminist Desire*. New York: Thunder's Mouth Press, 2002.

Jones, David. E. *Women Warriors: A History*. Virginia: Brassey's, 1997.

Karras, Irene. "The Third Wave's Final Girl: Buffy the Vampire Slayer." *Thirdspace*. March, 2002. http://www.thirdspace.ca/articles/karras.htm

Kilbourne, Jean. *Can't Buy My Love: How Advertising Changes the Way We Think and Feel*. New York: Touchstone, 1999.

Lawrence, D. H. *The Lost Girl*. New York: Modern Library, 2003.

Miller, Frank. *Sin City*. New York: Dark Horse, 2005.

Miller, Frank and Rodriguez, Robert. *Frank Miller's Sin City: The Making of the Movie*. New York: Troublemaker Publishing, 2005.

Nin, Anais. *D. H. Lawrence: An Unprofessional Study*. London: Swallow Press, 1964.

Paglia, Camille. *Vamps and Tramps*. New York: Vintage, 1994.

Prasso, Sheridan. *The Asian Mystique: Dragon Ladies, Geisha Girls, and Our Fantasies of the Exotic Orient*. New York: Public Affairs Press, 2005.

Raphael, Hillary. *I (Heart) Lord Buddha*. New York: Creation Books, 2004.

Richie, Donald and Anderson, Joseph L. *The Japanese Film*. Princeton: Princeton University Press, 1983.

Schubart, Rikke and Gjekvik, eds. *Femme Fatalities: Representations of Strong Women in the Media*. Gothenburg: Nordicom, 2004.

Silver, Alain and Ursini, James. *Film Noir Reader 4*. New York: Limelight Editions, 2004.

Silver, Alain and Ursini, James. *Horror Film Reader*. New York: Limelight Editions, 2001.

Superheroines' Demise. http://www.sooperheroes.com

Weinbaum, Batya. *Islands of Women and Amazons: Representations and Realities*. Texas: University of Texas Press, 2000.

Whoosh! Online Edition. 2005. http://www.whoosh.org

Wiegand, Chris. *Federico Fellini*. Germany: Taschen, 2003.

Wilde, Lyn Webster. *On the Trail of Women Warriors*. New York: St. Martin's Press, 1999.

Wolf, Naomi. *Fire with Fire*. New York: Ballantine Books, 1994.

Women in Refrigerators. http://www.the-pantheon.net/wir/

Wurtzel, Elizabeth. *Bitch: In Praise of Difficult Women*. New York: Anchor, 1999.

Actors Chapter Index

Moss, Carrie-Anne   *Matrix* series (Trinity), Chap. 7

Moustafa, Amira   *Queen of the Amazons* (Zita), Chap. 3

Mulan (animated)   *Mulan*, Chap. 11

Mulgrew, Kate   *Voyager* (TV) (Captain Janeway), Chap. 7

Nauta, Kate   *Transporter 2* (Lola), Chap. 5

Newmar, Julie   *Batman* (TV) (Catwoman), Chap. 6

Nichols, Nichelle   *Star Trek* (TV and series) (Uhura), Chap. 7

Nielsen, Brigitte   *Red Sonja* (Sonja), Chap. 4

Nilsson, Inger   *Pippi Longstocking* series (Pippi), Chap. 11

Nishiwaki, Michiko   *Avenging Quartet* (Sen); *In the Line of Duty 3* (Michiko), Chap. 9

O'Connor, Renee   *Xena* (TV) (Gabrielle), Chaps. 2, 4

Oshima, Yukari   *Millionaire's Express* (Samurai); *Avenging Quartet* (Oshima), Chap. 9

Otto, Miranda   *Lord of the Rings* (Eowyn), Chap. 4

Paquin, Anna   *X-Men* series (Rogue), Chap. 6

Parillaud, Annie   *La Femme Nikita* (Nikita); *Innocent Blood* (Marie), Chap. 12

Park, Grace   *Battlestar Galactica* (TV) (Boomer), Chap. 7

Park, Linda   *Enterprise* (TV) (Hoshi), Chap. 7

Pei-pei, Cheng   *Crouching Tiger* (Jade Fox), Chap. 9

Petty, Lori   *Tank Girl* (Tank Girl), Chaps. 1, 6

Pfeiffer, Michelle   *Batman Returns* (Selina/Catwoman), Chap. 6

Pinkett, Jada   *Matrix 2 and 3* (Captain Niobe), Chap. 7

Portman, Natalie   *The Professional* (Mathilda); *Star Wars* (Padme), Chap. 7

Powerpuff Girls (animated)   *Powerpuff Girls*, Chap. 11

Richards, Denise   *Starship Troopers* (Carmen), Chap. 7

Rigg, Diana   *Avengers* (TV) (Emma), Intro, Chap. 12

Rijker, Lucia   *Million Dollar Baby* (Billie), Chap. 10

Roberts, Tanya   *Sheena* (Sheena); *Charlie's Angels* (TV) (Julie), Chaps. 1, 3, 12

Rodriguez, Michelle   *Resident Evil* (Rain); *Girlfight* (Diana), Chaps. 5, 10

Romjin, Rebecca   *X-Men* series (Mystique), Chap. 6

Rothrock, Cynthia   *Blonde Fury* (Cindy), Chap. 9

Ryan, Jeri   *Voyager* (TV) (Seven of Nine), Chap. 7

Sackhoff, Katee   *Battlestar Galactica* (TV) (Starbuck), Chap. 7

Sailor Moon (animated)   *Sailormoon*, Chap. 11

Santana, Tura   *Faster, Pussycat! Kill! Kill!* (Varla), Chap. 14

Schell, Catherine   *Lana, Queen of the Amazon* (Lana), Chap. 3

Seberg, Jean   *Saint Joan* (Joan), Chaps. 1, 4

Silverstone, Alicia   *Batman and Robin* (Batgirl), Chap. 6

Slater, Helen   *Supergirl* (Supergirl), Chap. 6

Smith, Jaclyn   *Charlie's Angels* (TV) (Kelly), Chaps. 1, 12

Sobieski, Lee Lee   *Joan of Arc* (Joan), Chap. 4

Stanwyck, Barbara   *Annie Oakley* (Annie); *Double Indemnity* (Phyllis); *Forty Guns* (Jessica); *The Big Valley* (TV) (Victoria), Chap. 13

Stone, Sharon   *Catwoman* (Laurel); *The Quick and the Dead* (The Lady); *Basic Instinct* (Catherine), Chaps. 6, 13

Stowe, Madeleine   *Bad Girls* (Cody), Chap. 13

Swank, Hilary   *Million Dollar Baby* (Maggie), Chap. 10

Swanson, Kristy   *Buffy the Vampire Slaye* (Buffy), Chap. 5

Tamblyn, Amber   *Joan of Arcadia* (TV) (Joan), Chap. 4

Tamerlis-Lund, Zoe   *Ms. 45* (Tanya), Chap. 8

Theron, Charlize   *Aeon Flux* (Aeon), Chap. 6

Thorne, Dyanne   *Ilsa* series (Ilsa), Chap. 14

Thorson, Linda   *The Avengers* (TV) (Tara), Chap. 12

Thurman, Uma   *Batman and Robin* (Poison Ivy); *Kill Bill* (Beatrix); *The Avengers* (Mrs. Peel), Intro, Chaps. 2, 8, 12

Torres, Gina   *Cleopatra 2525* (Helen); *Serenity* (Zoe); *Angel* (TV) (Goddess), Chaps. 5, 7

About the Authors

DOMINIQUE MAINON is a writer/researcher, martial arts aficionado, guerilla artist, and producer for an independent film company. She is currently residing in Laguna Beach, California. For information on current projects, please visit: www.dominiquemainon.com

JAMES URSINI is the author, co-author, and co-editor of over twenty books on film history, including *The Vampire Film* and *The Film Noir Reader* series, both available from Limelight Editions, *Noir Style*, and *L.A. Noir*. He is also a noted DVD commentator, having done over a dozen commentaries for both Fox and Warner Bros. He has written for various magazines, as well as film journals. He has a doctorate from UCLA and teaches in Los Angeles. He is at present writing a noir novel.